Debtor–Creditor Law and Procedure

FIFTH EDITION

Laurence M. Olivo
DeeAnn Gonsalves

emond ▪ Toronto, Canada ▪ 2018

Emond Montgomery Publications Limited
60 Shaftesbury Avenue
Toronto ON M4T 1A3
http://www.emond.ca/highered

Printed in Canada.

We acknowledge the financial support of the Government of Canada. Canada

Vice president, publishing: Anthony Rezek
Publisher: Lindsay Sutherland
Director, development and production: Kelly Dickson
Developmental editor: Sarah Fulton
Production supervisor: Laura Bast
Copy editors: Janet MacMillan, Cindy Fujimoto
Permissions editor: Alison Lloyd-Baker
Typesetter: Christopher Hudson
Text designer: Tara Agnerian
Proofreader: Darryl Kamo
Indexer: Michael Bunn
Cover image: Naresuan261/Shutterstock

Library and Archives Canada Cataloguing in Publication

Olivo, Laurence M., 1946-, author
Debtor-creditor law and procedure / Laurence M. Olivo, DeeAnn Gonsalves. — Fifth edition.

Includes index.
ISBN 978-1-77255-131-0 (softcover)

1. Debtor and creditor—Ontario—Textbooks. I. Gonsalves, DeeAnn, 1965-, author II. Title.

KEO417.O44 2018   346.71307'7   C2017-904935-6   KF1536.ZB3O44 2018

To Joyce, as always, and with thanks to my students for their insights and feedback, and to my co-author for chasing the devils that were in the details.

To Brian, Kevin, and Lauren for their love and support, and to my co-author for providing ongoing patience and support.

Brief Contents

Detailed Contents

5 Commencement of Proceedings

6 Default Judgment

7 Summary Judgment

8 Defended Proceedings and Settlement

9 Enforcement of Superior Court Judgments

10 Small Claims Court Proceedings

PART III

DEBTORS' REMEDIES

15 Debtors' Remedies

List of Figures

Preface

The law in general continues to evolve and change, and debtor–creditor law is no exception. Since the publication of the previous edition of this text, the law governing collection agencies has been completely overhauled: the *Collection Agencies Act* was replaced by the *Collection and Debt Settlement Services Act*. Many of the changes in this legislation were designed to more tightly control and oversee collection agents, and the Act imposes limits on what paralegals may do, effectively preventing them from sending demand letters to debtors unless they have already started legal proceedings. The *Construction Act* (formerly the *Construction Lien Act)* has undergone a number of changes. These changes include the establishment of a prompt payment system and an adjudication process.

Another area to watch for change is civil enforcement of orders in Ontario. In 2016, the province launched a review of civil enforcement. The focus of the review is not on the tools of enforcement—the various writs that have been used since the late Middle Ages to enforce judgments and orders remains largely unaltered. Instead, changes will affect who is permitted to carry out enforcement. Currently, civil enforcement orders are enforced by public officials—primarily sheriffs and their officers—in the various counties and districts across Ontario. The province is looking to privatize enforcement and is considering two models within which to do this: the first, a private administrative body to carry out enforcement procedures and to oversee and licence those who carry out enforcement; the second, a local service provider under which private service providers would apply for licences to provide enforcement services across the province, with the province being responsible for regulating licensees. In both models, the enforcing orders would pay the full cost of having orders enforced. As of the date of publication, it is not entirely clear how civil enforcement of orders will change, but this issue bears watching.

In the Superior Court of Justice, the procedure used to dismiss slow-moving cases has been revised to dispense with notification from the court that cases will be dismissed when they are not set down for trial in the allotted time. The rules concerning the time given to set a matter down for trial and to have the trial heard have also been changed.

Court fees have increased, and future increases will be made in accordance with fluctuations in the cost of living, based on changes in the consumer price index.

There have also been changes to the amounts that determine whether a debtor's asset is exempt from seizure. Under the new regulations, the exemption amount will increase from time to time, based on inflation, which will require periodic checks of the regulations to determine the exemption limits.

The *Rules of the Small Claims Court* have been amended to permit the electronic filing of claims. In many cases, default judgment can now be obtained online.

The Small Claims Court monetary jurisdiction is likely to double from $25,000 to $50,000. Construction lien claims within the monetary amount can now be referred to the Small Claims Court rather than being heard in the Superior Court.

Increasingly, law firms and paralegal firms are expanding their use of and reliance on electronic documents. Many firms are transitioning to "the paperless office," where most client and file documentation is, or will be, in electronic format. In Chapter 2 we have provided information on how the "paperless office" may be created, with suggestions on how it will operate in practice. The court system now permits electronic issuance and registration of some documents, including claims and writs. In the near future, the online filing of court documents system will be expanding. Procedures for such e-filings have been added to this edition.

In addition to revising this text to incorporate updates to the law since the last edition, the text has been entirely rewritten using gender neutral language.

All court documents have been updated to the latest versions available at press time.

As with past editions, in creating this new edition we paid careful attention to suggestions from faculty and students who use this text. One of the key requests concerned providing better and clearer explanations of how judgment amounts and interest are calculated, so in this edition we provided clearer examples and clear walk-throughs of various calculations, and added further calculation practice questions. In particular, Chapter 4, Determining the Amount Owing on a Claim, has been substantially revised and rewritten, keeping in mind students who do not yet feel secure in carrying out calculations.

The number of students who become paralegals continues to increase each year. Because this text is used by students in both paralegal and law clerk programs, in this edition we have paid close attention to identifying procedures that are particular to either law clerks or paralegals, recognizing that it is important for readers in both programs to know where there may be limits on the kind of work they can carry out, and requirements that may be particular to either law clerks or paralegals.

We hope that our readers, both students and faculty, will continue to give us feedback on the text so that we can continue to provide them with relevant teaching and learning materials.

Acknowledgments

Nature abhors a vacuum, and whatever we as authors think of vacuums, we know that we did not write this edition in one. First, we are grateful to our families for allowing us the time to focus on writing this new edition. Second, the editorial support we received from our publisher, Emond Publishing, was, as always, of high quality; we are especially grateful to Sarah Fulton May, Cindy Fujimoto, and Laura Bast for keeping an eagle eye on the work as it took shape and progressed through to publication. We are also grateful to the reviewers: Stacey Pipicelli, Fanshawe College; Mary Aroukatos, Durham College; Michelle Arbour, Lambton College; and Kirk Rintoul, Humber College. Our colleagues from the School of Legal and Public Administration and the Faculty of Continuing Education, as well as the students of Seneca College were, as they have been in the past, supportive and helpful—free with their comments and advice, whether we asked them for it or not.

Laurence Olivo
DeeAnn Gonsalves
November 2017

About the Authors

DeeAnn Gonsalves, BA, JD, is a lawyer and full-time professor at Seneca College in the law clerk and paralegal diploma programs. She also sits as a Deputy Judge of the Ontario Small Claims Court in Richmond Hill. In addition to this book, she co-authored *Small Claims Court Practice and Procedure in Ontario*, and is a contributing author to *Introduction to Law in Canada*. DeeAnn has practised in the areas of civil and criminal litigation.

Laurence M. Olivo, BA, MA, JD, is a lawyer. He was a professor in the Faculty of Business at Seneca College for over 30 years, with experience in post-secondary teaching in a variety of college programs, and in the Law Society's Bar Admission program. His legal practice experience includes civil litigation and family law, as well as policy development work with the Ontario Ministry of the Attorney General. He is the author of more than 15 texts in various areas of law and has developed specialized online courses for use by post-secondary institutions. He currently sits as a Deputy Judge of the Ontario Small Claims Court in Richmond Hill.

PART I

The Debt Collection Process

In this part, we examine the process of collecting debts, first by attempting to obtain voluntary payment and, if that fails, by commencing proceedings in the Ontario Superior Court of Justice or in the Small Claims Court, depending on the amount of the claim. We then examine the steps and procedures that may be taken to enforce a judgment after one has been obtained.

1 Introduction

LEARNING OUTCOMES

After reading this chapter, students will:

- Have a general understanding and overview of the law and procedure for collecting unpaid debts, including how a debt collection procedure works, and strategy and techniques used by creditors to obtain payment prior to taking legal action.
- Have a general knowledge of the debt collection process from commencement of proceedings to the enforcement of judgments.
- Understand how a lawyer's practice and a paralegal's practice differ with respect to debt collection.
- Understand the role of collection agents and debt settlement providers and the requirements they must meet under the *Collection and Debt Settlement Services Act*.
- Understand what a paralegal needs to do to comply with the *Collection and Debt Settlement Services Act*.
- Understand the nature and role of a law clerk in the debt collection process.
- Know the effects of and protections available to creditors by registering notice of secured personal property transactions under the *Personal Property Security Act*.
- Know how a notice of a lien is registered under the *Personal Property Security Act* and how priorities are determined under the Act when several creditors have registered notices of liens against the same property owned by a debtor.
- Know how interests in property secured under the *Personal Property Security Act* are enforced.
- Understand the techniques and practices creditors use in the course of extending credit.

The Nature of a Debt Collection Practice

Debt collection litigation has some features that allow much of the work to be done by law clerks in law firms or by independent paralegals. This book focuses on doing the work of debt collection.

Most debt collection cases arise from the failure to pay what is owing on a contract for goods or services or for the loan of money, where the debt is based on a promise to pay and is **unsecured**. Cases fall into three categories:

unsecured credit a loan or extension of credit to a debtor where the creditor has no right to seize the debtor's property to satisfy an unpaid debt

assignment in bankruptcy when a debtor has insufficient income to pay debts when due, they can retain a trustee in bankruptcy and assign most of their assets to the trustee for distribution to creditors, then they emerge from bankruptcy with most of their debts wiped out; sometimes called voluntary bankruptcy, it is distinguished from a petition in bankruptcy, where a creditor forces the debtor into involuntary bankruptcy by filing a petition in bankruptcy

consumer proposal a debtor's plan submitted to their creditors, through a trustee in bankruptcy, suggesting a reduction of debt, interest, and/or a longer period to pay debt

1. *The debtor cannot pay.* This happens most often in consumer debt situations, where an individual's income is not enough to cover debts as they fall due. Many individuals do not know what to do in this situation. Although they may be entitled to make an **assignment in bankruptcy** or negotiate a **consumer proposal**, often out of ignorance they do nothing when sued. In this case, a creditor obtains a judgment by default and then proceeds to enforce it.

   A debtor who receives proper advice might make an assignment in bankruptcy or negotiate a consumer proposal, in which case an ordinary creditor's lawsuit will be stayed, and the debt will usually be wiped out in the bankruptcy process or reduced in the consumer proposal.
2. *The debtor will not pay.* In this instance, the debtor could perhaps pay but chooses not to and resorts to various delaying tactics to make it difficult for the creditor both to obtain a judgment and to enforce that judgment. This requires some skill and knowledge, which clever debtors can use to render themselves "judgment proof" or to make it so difficult for the creditor to collect that the creditor agrees to take less than what is owed. In this situation, a creditor may obtain a judgment and then find that the debtor's financial affairs have been arranged so that there are no assets in the debtor's name to seize and sell or income to pay the amount due to the creditor on the judgment.

   For example, the car that a debtor drives and the house that a debtor lives in may be in a spouse's name, in an adult child's name, or possibly in the name of a corporation. If so, it is no longer the debtor's legal property and therefore cannot be seized to pay the debtor's debt. Although some consumer debtors engage in these practices, commercial or business debtors are more likely to do so, particularly those who are in a business where cash flow is uneven. Here, the business may be sound but, because its income fluctuates, it sometimes cannot pay bills when they fall due. The debtor may try to stave off payment until funds become available. A commercial debtor may also delay matters, knowing that the creditor may be prepared to settle for less than the full amount owing rather than spend money on legal fees trying to obtain or enforce a judgment where the expense of doing so may be high when compared with the debt owing. For example, a creditor would probably think twice about paying a lawyer $5,000 in fees and expenses to collect an $8,000 debt. It may be more rational to accept payment of the principal amount and forgo the interest the creditor is entitled to than to spend thousands of dollars on a case where the creditor collects little or nothing.

3. *The debtor has a defence for nonpayment.* In this situation, the debtor is a dissatisfied customer for goods or services who has refused to pay because they allege that the creditor has sold them a defective product or that the creditor has been negligent in providing a service. If the debtor is aggressive, they may sue the creditor for breach of contract or for furnishing a defective product or service. In this case, the lawsuit is framed as an action for breach of contract or for negligence and not framed as an action in debt. However, often the debtor will just refuse to pay, and when the creditor sues for payment of the price, the debtor responds with a vigorous defence claiming that the money is not owing because the creditor is in breach of their duty or has breached a contract. In addition, if the creditor commences an action to collect the debt, the debtor may **counterclaim** for damages caused by the defective product or service or other wrong done by the creditor.

counterclaim
where A sues B and B defends A's claim and makes their own claim against A

Where there is no substantive defence to nonpayment, and the debtor is simply refusing or is unable to pay, cases need not be treated as if they require highly specialized legal services. Rather, these cases can be efficiently processed as routine matters by paralegals.[1] Trained support personnel, such as law clerks working under the supervision of a lawyer, can also process undefended cases.

Paralegals and the Debt Collection Process

Paralegals are individuals, licensed by the Law Society of Ontario (LSO),[2] who are authorized to provide some legal services directly to the public.[3] To qualify as a paralegal, an individual must complete an accredited paralegal education program and pass a licensing examination.[4] They must also demonstrate that they are of good character. In order to provide legal services to the public, a paralegal must carry errors and omissions insurance. Paralegals are not lawyers and are restricted in their practice to those areas authorized by the LSO. Included in these services is representation in courts and before tribunals where a statute permits agents or non-lawyers to appear. These courts and tribunals are as follows:

- the Ontario Court of Justice, Provincial Offences Court;
- the Ontario Court of Justice, Criminal Court on summary conviction offences where the maximum prison sentence does not exceed six months;

---

1 A paralegal on their own can handle cases where the debt is $25,000 or less. For cases above this amount, paralegals must be supervised by a lawyer.

2 In November 2017, the Law Society of Upper Canada changed its name to the Law Society of Ontario. The new name is being phased in over the course of 2018.

3 The jurisdiction of paralegals to appear in court is governed by the *Law Society Act*, RSO 1990, c L.8 and By-Law 4 of the LSO made under the authority of the *Law Society Act*.

4 A list of accredited paralegal education programs can be found at <http://www.lsuc.on.ca/For-Paralegals/About-Your-Licence/Paralegal-Education-Program-Accreditation/>.

- the Small Claims Court, where actions for damages or the return of property valued at $25,000 or less can be heard;[5] and
- tribunals where representation by an agent or non-lawyer is permitted.

Non-Paralegals and the Debt Collection Process

In addition to lawyers and paralegals, the LSO, under By-Law 4,[6] sets out a number of categories of non-licensed persons who, based on their occupation or relationship to their employer or a family member, may appear before some courts and tribunals, such as the Small Claims Court, without a licence. By-Law 4 exempts certain representatives from requiring a licence by deeming their work to not constitute practising law or providing legal services. Such workers include Aboriginal court workers. The second category of persons not requiring a licence to provide certain legal services includes legal aid clinic workers, parliamentary constituency assistants, in-house legal service providers, and those who occasionally represent friends or family. Also included are persons who provide legal services occasionally as an ancillary part of their job. These persons include some human resources professionals, appraisers, and those working for trade unions.

Paralegals and the Collection and Debt Settlement Services Act

Collection agents and debt settlement service providers are regulated under the *Collection and Debt Settlement Services Act* (CDSSA)[7] and Ontario Regulation 74, which was made under the CDSSA. The CDSSA replaced the *Collection Agencies Act*. In addition to the regulation of collection agents, the CDSSA also governs debt settlement service providers. **Collection agents** act on behalf of creditors to collect debts. **Debt settlement service providers** act on behalf of debtors to negotiate debt settlements with creditors.

collection agent
a person or a corporation, licensed and governed by the Ontario government to act on behalf of creditors to collect debts

debt settlement service provider
a person or a corporation authorized by the Ontario government to act on behalf of debtors to negotiate debt settlements with creditors

The statute and its regulation set out disclosure requirements, establish advertising restrictions, and impose a fee cap for debt settlement services. A unique aspect of the legislation is that it permits the licensing of agents to act on behalf of creditors in collecting on a debt while at the same time governing debt settlement service providers who work with debtors in negotiating with creditors to settle a debt, and does so without prohibiting agents from acting in both capacities at the same time. In other words, an agent may be actively pursuing a particular debtor to make payment to a creditor while at the same time attempting to broker a settlement with the creditor on behalf of that debtor. Conversely, in some provinces, such as Alberta, a

5 *Courts of Justice Act*, RSO 1990, c C.43, s 23(1) and O Reg 626/00, s 1(1).

6 By-Law 4 is made under the authority of the *Law Society Act*. The by-law can be found in its entirety at <http://www.lsuc.on.ca/by-laws/>.

7 RSO 1990, c C.14. You will find official copies of Ontario's statutes and regulations at the Ontario e-laws website: <ontario.ca/laws>.

choice must be made between acting as a collection agent or a debt settlements services agent; one is not permitted to do both. Note that in Ontario, if a paralegal wishes to act for creditors on a regular basis in debt collection cases, they will need to register their business as a collection agency. Employees of a paralegal practising in this area must also be registered.[8] Lawyers in a regular practice and their employees are not governed by the CDSSA and are not required to register under the Act. It had been hoped by those in the paralegal profession that, when the CDSSA came into effect, paralegals would no longer have to register as collection agents. Paralegals, as licensed members of the same governing body as lawyers (the LSO), are required to maintain trust accounts and submit to financial audits of their books and records, as lawyers do. The LSO's control over paralegals is intended to prevent paralegals from defrauding creditor-clients, making the bonding and oversight controls in the Act unnecessary. The CDSSA did bring in one change that recognized paralegals as equal to lawyers in collection and debt settlement. Written notice can now be given to a collection agency by either a lawyer or a paralegal to stop the debt collector from dealing directly with the debtor and requiring them to direct future communications on the matter to the lawyer or paralegal.

The CDSSA prevents abuse of debtors by those who engage in collection work and ensures that creditors who use a collection agency are paid what they are entitled to out of the collection proceeds. The CDSSA also offers debtors using debt settlement services some protection by requiring disclosure of the conditions of debt settlement offers, allowing them to compare differing proposals. The Act also mandates a 10-day "cooling-off period," during which time a debtor may cancel a services agreement.[9] Additionally, there are restrictions on how debt settlement services can be advertised. A collection agency is prohibited from the following:[10]

- attempting to collect payment without having sent a notice to the debtor that sets out the name of the creditor to whom the debt is owed and the balance owing on the debt, and advising the debtor that the agency is acting on behalf of the creditor to collect the debt. This notice may be included in a demand for payment sent to the debtor;
- phoning the debtor before the sixth day after mailing the above mentioned notice;
- commencing proceedings without first giving notice to the debtor of its intention to sue on behalf of the creditor;
- threatening or commencing proceedings or other collection activity without authorization in writing by the creditor;
- continuing to contact a debtor when the debtor or the debtor's lawyer or paralegal has sent a registered letter stating that they are disputing the debt and directing the collector to go to court;

8 *Ibid*, s 4(1).

9 *Ibid*, s 26.

10 *Ibid*, ss 21-24.

- communicating in such a manner or with such frequency as to constitute harassment;
- phoning the debtor on Sunday before 1 p.m. or after 5 p.m. (local time), on a statutory holiday, or on any other day other than between the hours of 7 a.m. and 9 p.m. local time in the place being called;
- giving false information about a debtor to anyone;
- failing to give full particulars of the debt when contacting a debtor;
- contacting the debtor more than three times in a seven-day period;
- contacting the debtor's spouse, family, relatives, friends, or acquaintances, unless that person is a guarantor or the debtor has granted consent to speak to them, or if the sole purpose of the contact is to find out the debtor's home address or home telephone number;
- contacting the debtor's employer, unless they are a guarantor or consent has been granted to speak to them by the debtor or if the sole purpose of the contact is to find out the debtor's employment, business title, and/or business address;
- publishing or threatening to publish the debtor's failure to pay;
- using threatening, profane, intimidating, or coercive language;
- using undue, excessive, or unreasonable pressure;
- collecting or attempting to collect a debt from a person who the collection agency or collector knows or reasonably ought to know is not liable for the debt;
- continuing to contact a person who has stated that they are not the same person as the debtor the agency is seeking, unless the agency takes all reasonable precautions to ensure that the person is, in fact, who the collection agency intends to contact;
- giving any person any false or misleading information;
- misrepresenting to any person contacted in respect of the debt the purpose of the contact or the identity of the creditor, collection agency, or collector;
- using, without lawful authority, any summons, notice, demand, or other document that states, suggests, or implies that it is authorized or approved by a court in Canada or another jurisdiction; and
- commencing proceedings in its own name, unless it has paid the creditor for the right to collect and keep the amount owing to the creditor.

In order to register as a collection agency, applicants must be 18 years of age or older (in the case of non-corporate applications), be a Canadian citizen or a permanent resident,[11] and must do the following:

- pay the required fees;
- state in the application an address for service in Ontario;

11 *Ibid*, s 12(1).

- operate out of a place of business in Ontario that is open to the public and is not in a private residence;
- post an initial bond of $5,000 with subsequent bonds posted in amounts based on the sum of money collected by the agency;[12]
- file copies of all forms and form letters sent to debtors and all contracts used with creditor-clients for review by the registrar;[13]
- achieve at least 75 percent on a written examination based on the Act and such further subject matters as the Registrar prescribes (if the agency is a corporation the active officers and directors must meet this examination requirement); and
- have at least two years' experience in the collections business or, in the opinion of the Registrar, equivalent related experience.

All monies collected by the agency are deemed to be held in trust for the creditor in accordance with the collection contract.[14] The required bonding of agencies is designed to provide some assurance that money collected for a creditor is turned over to the creditor. If an agency fails to do this, the bond may be forfeited and its proceeds used to pay creditors.

Collectors work for collection agencies. In order to be a collector under the Act, an individual must be at least 18 years of age and a Canadian citizen or have been lawfully admitted to Canada for permanent residence and must ordinarily reside in Canada.[15]

Catch 22: Complying with the Collection and Debt Settlement Services Act

The Act's requirement of two years' experience as a prerequisite for registration as a collection agency is a bit of a Catch-22 for paralegals: a paralegal cannot have a collections practice unless the paralegal has had two years' experience in a collections practice.

A person who makes an isolated collection and whose regular business is not collecting debts for others is exempt from the Act and its registration requirements,[16] but any paralegal who acts on behalf of creditors on a regular basis as part of a paralegal practice must register as a collection agency under the Act and have two years' experience in order to do this.

12 *Ibid*, s 2.

13 *Ibid*, s 21(1).

14 *Ibid*, s 17(1).

15 *Ibid*, s 12(2).

16 *Ibid*, s 2(f).

An alternative route would be to attempt to persuade the Registrar that because a paralegal is a member of a profession that is licensed and regulated by the LSO, subject to rules of professional conduct, audit controls over monies handled for others, and a prescribed educational program, additional control by the Registrar under the Act is not required. In effect, the argument is that paralegals should be treated like lawyers under the Act.

Another option is to work for an existing collection agency as a collector for a period of at least two years, and then apply for registration under the Act in the ordinary way.

It is clear, at present, that paralegals cannot ignore the Act if they wish to establish a Small Claims Court practice that includes collections. But note that a paralegal can act on behalf of debtors without having to register or do anything else under the Act.

Law Clerks and the Debt Collection Process

If the debt is for more than $25,000, then the matter must be heard in the Ontario Superior Court of Justice. If the debtor contests payment and wishes to have representation in court, a lawyer will be required to appear in court to handle the case because, although a debtor who is not incorporated may appear on their own behalf in any court—including the Supreme Court of Canada—non-lawyers may not appear in the Superior Court on behalf of paying clients. However, if the debtor has no defence and the plaintiff can obtain a **default judgment**, the matter does not require a court appearance, and it may be handled by a non-lawyer who can complete the procedures to obtain a default judgment. In this case, a lawyer should be supervising the work because non-lawyers have no independent standing in the Superior Court. For this reason, while debt collection for amounts of $25,000 and under can be an important part of a paralegal's practice, a claim in excess of $25,000 should be handled by a lawyer or by a law clerk or paralegal working under a lawyer's supervision.

default judgment
a plaintiff obtains a default judgment when the defendant takes no action and files no defence when they are sued, meaning the defendant is deemed to have admitted the debt and the plaintiff may apply to the court clerk, who, on behalf of the court, will sign a judgment for the amount claimed

Debt collection work is or can be a large part of a legal practice. It includes the collection of consumer debt, credit card debt, defaults on personal loans, and retail and wholesale customer accounts involving commercial debtors. Often this work can be done economically on a high-volume basis because the routine nature of most collection cases lends itself to standardized processing. Many law firms, however, still treat debt collection matters in the same way as more complex matters, which results in higher costs to the client and greater inefficiencies. This unnecessarily complicated approach creates opportunities for collection agencies, paralegal firms, and law firms that are organized efficiently and effectively to do debt collection work.

Such law firms may improve efficiency through the use of law clerks who have some legal training and can participate in the kinds of work done by lawyers, provided that they are supervised by lawyers and that they do not undertake work that only lawyers are allowed to do. An example of prohibited work is giving a legal opinion or legal advice to a client. This cannot be done by a law clerk. The prohibitions on legal work by a non-licensee are set out in the LSO's By-Law 7.1 (see the box below).

Summary of By-Law 7.1 of the LSO

In general, By-Law 7.1 requires that lawyers closely supervise the work of their non-lawyer staff. Specifically, law clerks and other unlicensed persons are prohibited from

- taking instructions from clients or giving undertakings on behalf of a lawyer, unless the lawyer provides express instructions and authorization to do so and closely supervises the work;
- giving legal advice to clients;
- negotiating with third parties without the client's specific approval and without the lawyer supervising the process;
- signing or sending correspondence, other than on routine or administrative matters, unless it is reviewed by a lawyer;
- using the lawyer's personalized key to access the electronic registration of title documents system;
- appearing as advocates—the LSO requires non-lawyers employed by lawyers who appear before tribunals and lower courts to be licensed paralegals, unless the appearance is limited to routine or administrative matters, such as setting dates for trial in criminal courts; and
- sending collection letters on behalf of a client, unless the letter is prepared under the direct supervision of the lawyer and reviewed, approved, and signed by the lawyer prior to being sent out.

There are other features of collection work that are of interest here. Obtaining a judgment against a debtor is often easy, since many debtors cannot pay what they owe. Because that is not a defence in an action for debt, debtors often do not bother to put forward a defence, and the creditor is able, with relative ease, to obtain a default judgment as an administrative act. The more difficult job is to enforce the judgment. A judgment is no more than a piece of paper containing an order to pay. It is not self-enforcing; if the debtor pays voluntarily when the order is made, that is the end of the matter. However, if the debtor does not pay, then the creditor must take steps to enforce the judgment, using a variety of legal procedures. Some of the more common procedures are as follows:

- *A writ of seizure and sale* (also called a writ of execution) allows the sheriff (in the case of land) or court enforcement officers (in the case of personal property) to manage the seizure and sale of land or goods belonging to the **judgment debtor** and apply the proceeds to the **judgment creditor**'s claim.[17]
- *Garnishment* allows the judgment creditor to have someone who owes money to the debtor pay some or all of that money to the creditor to satisfy the creditor's claim against the debtor.
- *Examination in aid of execution* allows the judgment creditor to demand that the debtor appear for questioning before the creditor's legal representative and

judgment debtor
a debtor against whom a judgment has been obtained

judgment creditor
a creditor who has obtained a judgment for debt against a debtor

17 As of June 2017, this is the case. However, the provincial government is considering privatization of the enforcement of court judgments. For an interesting article on this topic, see <http://www.blaney.com/articles/ontario-paves-road-to-improved-judgment-creditor-recovery-new-developments-could-expedite-enforcement>.

requires them to answer questions about what income or assets they have that can be seized to satisfy the debt.

execution debtor
a debtor who is the subject of enforcement proceedings by an execution creditor

execution creditor
a creditor who has obtained a judgment and is in the process of executing or enforcing a judgment for debt

The most difficult part of the collection work is enforcement. The tools available are cumbersome, expensive to use, and slow. A skillful **execution debtor** can delay matters, drive up costs, and, in general, make it difficult to seize assets to satisfy the debt. In many cases, the **execution creditor** will decide that the cost of collection exceeds the benefit to be obtained. At that point, the creditor may decide to "write off" the debt. This is not a dead loss for the creditor because they may deduct the loss from other income for tax purposes, thereby reducing the taxable income and the amount of overall income tax otherwise paid. Institutional lenders or creditors with large numbers of customer accounts usually track collection costs and, using formulas, determine in a rational and dispassionate way when to cease unsuccessful enforcement proceedings or when a compromise should be made with the debtor. Where a creditor is deciding to cut their losses, they will often accept some of what is owing, rather than the total amount, on the assumption that getting partial payment now is better than the risk of recovering less later.

How Creditors Administer Credit Transactions

When a person provides goods or services on contract where some or all of the payment is due in the future, there has been an extension of credit. While the parties may arrange special terms for payment, the customary business arrangement on the sale of goods and services is to offer payment terms of "net 30 days." This means that the debtor has 30 days, including the date of the invoice, to pay the invoiced amount without having to pay interest, and often with a discount of 5 to 10 percent on the invoiced amount to encourage prompt payment.[18] The invoice will usually provide that, starting on the 31st day, interest accrues at some percentage per month, usually in the range of 1 to 2 percent. Although that may not sound like much, it works out to between 12 and 24 percent per year, which adds substantially to the debt and makes it more difficult to pay off. As a matter of practice, a knowledgeable debtor may negotiate a late payment by trying to reduce or eliminate the interest component. A creditor may well accept this, knowing that the older a debt is, the harder it is to collect, and take what is offered rather than run the risk of collecting nothing.

Many creditors and some lawyers assume that if there is provision for interest in the invoice, the creditor is legally entitled to payment. This is usually not the case. Unless the debtor specifically agreed to the interest provision at the time of sale or extension of credit, simply including it on an invoice does not make interest an enforceable part of the contract. Contractual terms, such as the imposition of interest, cannot be unilaterally added to an invoice *after* the contract has been formed.

18 Some business owners start the net 30-day period on the day after the purchase has been invoiced; however, this text follows the more common business practice of using the date of purchase (invoice date) as day 1 of the net 30-day period as the vendor creditor generally wants the net 30-day period to end as soon as possible to ensure a regular cash flow and timely payment of invoices.

Note that if interest is payable on terms of less than a year (for example, if daily, weekly, bi-weekly, or monthly interest is payable), the contract must set out the yearly rate of interest. If the equivalent annual interest rate is not set out, section 4 of the *Interest Act*[19] sets out that interest is limited to 5 percent or less per year.

An Overview of the Debt Collection Process

1. The creditor is unable to collect the money owing and refers the matter to a lawyer or a paralegal.
2. A demand letter giving the debtor 10 days to pay should be sent by a collection agent, lawyer, or a paralegal who is also registered as a debt collection agent. Paralegals who occasionally handle debt cases are not licensed to send demand letters prior to commencing litigation. They may, however, send a paralegal letter to the debtor that sets out the amount owed and states that they have been retained to commence litigation. The letter may not demand payment but it may invite the debtor to contact the paralegal to discuss the matter.[20]
3. Asset and identification searches of the debtor are carried out.
4. The amount owing is calculated prior to commencing action.
5. At the expiry of the 10-day period, the pleadings are prepared, issued in the appropriate court, and served.
6. If the debtor does not defend within the time provided for filing a defence, default judgment is signed against the debtor.
7. When a judgment has been obtained, proceedings to enforce the judgment are commenced.
8. The lawyer or paralegal will file a writ of execution, issue a garnishment notice, and/or conduct an examination of the judgment debtor to determine the debtor's ability to pay.

Ideally, creditors should have debtors sign a contract setting out terms of repayment, including interest. Such a contract should also include consent from the debtor permitting the creditor to conduct a credit bureau search on the debtor. Except among sophisticated institutional lenders, however, this practice is rare. The lawyer or paralegal should consider recommending to clients who have collection issues that they obtain this consent when a debtor–creditor relationship is established. Privacy legislation requires that consent be obtained before conducting a credit bureau search, and it is easier to get such consent up front rather than when an account later goes into default. In general, a creditor should obtain as much information as possible about the debtor at the outset, when the parties are on good terms. The use of a customer information form should be considered to collect data that includes the debtor's full legal name and driver's licence number, as well as asset, debt, and banking information. The form should also secure the debtor's consent to a credit bureau search and release of information in accordance with the *Personal Information Protection and Electronic Documents Act*.[21] In the event of nonpayment, a driver's licence search may confirm the debtor's whereabouts. A credit

19 RSC 1985, c I-15.

20 The LSO, in practice audits of paralegals, has stated that unless they are also licensed under the CDSSA they cannot send demand letters prior to commencing litigation.

21 SC 2000, c 5.

bureau report on the debtor can provide information concerning the debtor's employment, other debts, and repayment history. Driver's licence and credit bureau searches are discussed in more detail in Chapter 3.

Most commercial extenders of credit will not immediately demand payment on the 31st day after the debt was incurred. Often there is a business relationship that has gone on for some time and is expected to go on in the future. In the interest of continuing the relationship, most creditors will allow the 31st day to pass without taking action. Instead, the overdue debt, called a **receivable**, begins to earn interest. Most businesses will review the receivable at the end of 60 days, and again at 90 days. Depending on the nature of the relationship, the extender of credit may automatically send a letter in the form of a gentle reminder that payment is due when 60 days have elapsed. When 90 days have elapsed, most lawyers and most businesses consider that there is a problem with the account and that there may be difficulties with collecting. Now is the time for the creditor to make personal contact with the debtor and find out why payment has not been made. Sometimes the reason is quite innocent—for example, the person responsible for payment has been ill or is on vacation, or the matter has simply been overlooked. At other times, the creditor may learn that the debtor has a cash flow problem—perhaps business has fallen off, other creditors are demanding payment, or the debtor's own customers have been slow to pay. In times of recession, this can have a ripple effect as one debtor fails to pay their creditor who, in turn, does not have the cash to pay their creditor, and so on. Whatever the reason, the creditor needs to make a decision to alter the terms of payment, extend further time to pay, or turn the matter over to a lawyer, paralegal, or collection agency. This decision requires a balancing of the desire to continue a commercial relationship with the desire to be paid. In the interests of preserving the relationship and profits from it over time, a creditor may choose to forgo all of the entitled interest and relax the payment terms.

receivable
money owing to a creditor (also called an account receivable); because it describes a right to future payment or income, a creditor can sell or assign its receivables as a way of paying others—a creditor thereby gives the purchaser or assignee the right to be paid the amount of the receivable by the debtor

To avoid debts that are difficult to collect, a creditor will, at the commencement of a commercial relationship, usually require cash on delivery (COD). Once the relationship is ongoing, credit may be extended by allowing payment on terms of net 30 days, as described earlier, or as the parties otherwise decide.

Another common way to advance credit, particularly in consumer transactions of "big ticket" items such as automobiles, is for the creditor (the seller) to lend the money to the purchaser to buy the seller's product. This is done with a **conditional sale contract** (also called an executory contract or an installment contract). For example, if a consumer buys a car and does not have all the cash to pay the purchase price, the seller may give the buyer credit, allowing the buyer to put a down payment on the purchase price and pay the balance of the purchase price plus interest in monthly installments over a period of time. Because this loan may be quite large, the seller may require the purchaser to pledge the car as security for repayment of the loan. This means that, if the purchaser misses an installment payment on the debt, the lender has the right to seize and sell the car and apply the sale proceeds to pay down the loan.[22] Usually, if the

conditional sale contract
also called an executory contract or an installment contract; the vendor finances the debtor's purchase, taking security in the item sold

22 Section 25 of the *Consumer Protection Act, 2002*, SO 2002, c 30, Schedule A provides that where a consumer under a conditional sale contract has paid two-thirds or more of their payment, the repossession/resale provisions of the Act are unenforceable except with leave of the Superior Court of Justice.

debtor still owes money after that happens, the seller has the right to then sue the debtor to collect any outstanding balance. A transaction where the debtor gives the creditor an interest in property of the debtor as a guarantee of payment to the creditor is referred to as a **secured credit transaction** or a secured debt.

secured credit transaction
a transaction where the debtor has put up some asset of value as collateral that the creditor may use as security for the unpaid debt; if the debtor defaults, the creditor can recover what is owing by seizing the collateral; the debt is secured by the creditor's rights in the collateral

personal property
consists of tangibles, such as consumer goods, other goods, inventory and equipment, and intangibles, including investments and securities

Secured Transactions Under the Personal Property Security Act

The Ontario *Personal Property Security Act* (PPSA)[23] applies whenever a debtor grants a creditor a secured interest using some or all of their **personal property** as collateral and registers notice of their interest under the Act.[24] The PPSA contains rules to determine and govern the priorities and rights of secured creditors and debtors.

The Personal Property Security Registration System

The Personal Property Security Registration (PPSR) system handles registrations and searches executed under the provisions of the PPSA. The PPSR also accepts registration of liens under the *Repair and Storage Liens Act* (RSLA).[25] The RSLA is most commonly used by motor vehicle repair shops to register a non-possessory lien against a motor vehicle to secure unpaid repair work. When a motor vehicle is repaired and a customer does not make full payment for properly authorized repairs, the repairer can either keep the vehicle until payment is made or release the vehicle to the customer upon receipt of an acknowledgment signed by the customer stating that the bill has not been paid in full. The repairer can then use the acknowledgment to register a non-possessory lien against the vehicle. The owner cannot legally sell the vehicle with the lien in place. Liens under the RSLA are effective for three years.

Registration Under the PPSA

In order to obtain priority under the PPSA, a creditor must achieve attachment of the collateral and perfect their secured interest.

Attachment of the Secured Collateral

For a secured interest to be enforceable under the PPSA against a third party, the interest must attach to the collateral. The most basic form of attachment is for the creditor to keep possession of the property. However, in most cases, a debtor requires possession of the property. When the secured property is to stay in the debtor's

23 RSO 1990, c P.10, s 51(1).

24 All common law provinces and territories have their own personal property security acts.

25 RSO 1990, c R.25.

possession, the parties will need to execute a security agreement to set out the terms of their agreement. In this case, attachment occurs when the agreement is signed.

Security Agreements

The parties may enter into either a specific security agreement or a general security agreement. The specific security agreement covers only a single asset. A general security agreement usually covers all present and future assets with the exception of real property, for which a mortgage is required.

Security agreements generally cover matters such as a description of the parties and the collateral, restrictions on the use of the collateral, the obligations of the debtor to maintain and insure the collateral, and remedies for breach of the agreement. An example of a general security agreement is appended to this chapter as Figure 1.1.

Perfection of the Security Interest Under the PPSA

Following attachment, in order to obtain priority under the PPSA, the creditor must perfect their interest. Perfection usually occurs upon registration of a financing statement.

Advantages of Registering Under the PPSA

- Registration provides notice of the creditor's secured interest to the public, allowing potential creditors to conduct searches against the debtor to determine whether the debtor has already granted security to another creditor.
- Registration, in most cases, provides the creditor with priority over unregistered interests and over interests registered subsequent to their interest.
- Future advances to a debtor can be secured under the initial registration; however, in the case of consumer goods, a financing statement must be registered after the execution of every security agreement.
- The Act sets out rules for realization of the security that may result in a faster and less expensive seizure of property.

Registering a Financing Statement Under the PPSR

The PPSR is a notice-based system. Security agreements themselves are not registered. Notice of the agreement, in the form of an electronically filed financing statement, is registered in the PPSR system. The financing statement contains the borrower's name, address, and date of birth. It also contains the lender's name and address, along with the registration period, the initial amount of the loan, its maturity date, and a description of the collateral.

A financing statement should be filled out very carefully and proofread thoroughly before registration. Neglecting to include the debtor's middle initial (if they have one), spelling their name incorrectly, or marking off the wrong box on the form may result in a loss of priority under the PPSA. Information on PPSA registrations is available online at <https://www.ontario.ca/page/frequently-asked-questions

-access-now-and-personal-property-security-registration-system>. There is a PPSA Assurance Fund to provide compensation for errors made by PPSR staff.

A financing statement must be registered online. Registration can be done online at <https://www.ontario.ca/page/register-security-interest-or-search-lien-access-now> or through a third party for hire. A creditor can register a financing statement for between one and 25 years, or for a perpetual period.[26] The registration fee is $8 per year for one to 25 years or $500 for a registration in perpetuity. Note that for consumer goods the registration period is a maximum of five years.

Within 30 days of registration the creditor must deliver a copy of the registered financing statement to the debtor.[27]

Priority Under the PPSA

There is only one registered secured creditor against a particular piece of property or inventory, then they have priority over unregistered creditors and trustees in bankruptcy. If, however, there is more than one registered security interest against the property, the PPSA sets out who has priority. A perfected security interest takes priority over an unperfected one. If, for example, the debtor has signed two security agreements and only one of the creditors has registered a financing statement under the PPSA, the registered security interest is the only perfected one and has priority over the unregistered, unperfected interest. If both creditors registered under the Act, the rule of "first in time, first in right" applies, so that the party who first registered a financing statement has priority. However, there is one category of registration, called the purchase money security interest (PMSI), that takes priority over other perfected interests, even those registered prior to the PMSI. A PMSI occurs, in some cases, when a creditor lends the debtor funds to purchase a specific item. The creditor then takes a secured interest, in the form of a PMSI, in that item. Under the PPSA, PMSIs are perfected by registration within 15 days after the debtor obtains possession of the purchased item.[28] PMSIs allow for multiple security on a debtor's property. For example, the debtor may have executed a general security agreement over their entire inventory with a creditor, and then contracted with another creditor to borrow money to buy a new item to add to inventory covered by the general security agreement. The new creditor will want to register a PMSI in order to take priority on that item against the other creditor, who has security under the general security agreement.

In some cases, with multiple registrations under the PPSA, priorities may be difficult to determine. The PPSA provides that the Superior Court of Justice can be called upon to establish priorities and also to make orders to protect the collateral in the interim. In some cases, a court-ordered injunction to refrain from selling or damaging the property may be of assistance to the creditor.

---

26 *Supra* note 22, s 51(1).

27 *Ibid*, s 46(6).

28 *Ibid*, s 20(3)(a).

Enforcement of PPSA Secured Interests

Part V of the PPSA sets out the rights and responsibilities of the parties when realizing upon security under the PPSA. The overriding general rule is that the parties must act in a commercially reasonable manner. Therefore, the creditor must give the debtor time to remedy the default. The Act permits the creditor to seize the secured item and even to render it unusable if it cannot be easily seized. If the collateral consists of consumer goods, under section 65(1) of the PPSA, if the debtor has paid at least 60 percent of the indebtedness secured, the secured party must dispose of or contract to dispose of the collateral within 90 days of taking possession. Once 66.66 percent or more of the amount outstanding on consumer goods has been paid, in accordance with Schedule A of the *Consumer Protection Act, 2002*, the goods cannot be seized. The PPSA also provides for the granting of injunctions by the court, and for the appointment of a receiver where appropriate. In all cases, a creditor should avoid using violence when realizing upon the security because charges of assault and trespass against the creditor could result. Once the creditor gains possession of the collateral, they must use reasonable care to preserve it. The creditor can charge the debtor reasonable repair, storage, and insurance costs. The creditor must notify the debtor and other creditors with an interest in the collateral of the seizure and must provide 15 days' notice of any sale of the property. All sales must be at fair market value as determined by two appraisers. The creditor must account to the debtor and the other creditors and must pay any surplus after the sale to the debtor. If there is a shortfall, the creditor may sue for recovery against the debtor.

Example of Priority Ranking Among Secured and Unsecured Creditors of a Debtor

A debtor owes $4,000 to Sedate Motors Ltd on a conditional sale contract. The debtor's car is collateral for payment to Sedate. The contract was made in 2012 and registered under the PPSA. In 2011, the debtor bought an exercise machine for $1,000 from Bulko Wholesale Ltd (Bulko). The debtor didn't pay for it and was sued in 2013; Bulko obtained judgment and filed a writ of execution against the debtor in 2014. In 2015, the debtor pledged his car to Fly-By-Night Enterprises for a $2,000 loan. Fly-By-Night registered its interest in the car under the PPSA in 2015.

Priority Ranking

1. Sedate, having registered its interest in the collateral in 2012 under the PPSA, has first priority with respect to a claim by the other creditors against this asset.
2. Fly-By-Night, having registered its interest in the same collateral as Sedate, but after Sedate, is in the second priority position with respect to the car. This means that Sedate is entitled to seize and sell the car and take $4,000 from the proceeds to satisfy the debt. If there are any proceeds of sale left over, Fly-By-Night is entitled to take its share from those proceeds.
3. Bulko, as an unsecured creditor, can levy execution on any sale proceeds left over from the sale of the car and against any other assets that are not held as collateral for a secured debt. Although Fly-By-Night's interest arose after Bulko's, Bulko has a lower priority because a registered interest in specific collateral takes priority over any unsecured interest.

Creditor Approaches to Extending Retail Credit

Consumer credit is remarkably easy to obtain. Many retail sellers offer credit to finance purchases or allow payments on easy terms. Although many of these credit transactions may go into default and require collection, retail sellers rely on the high volume of such sales to generate profits. In the absence of a downturn in the economy with rapidly rising unemployment, this approach has usually worked. However, even in the best of times, many consumers take on a debt load that they cannot discharge and find themselves being sued or having their secured property seized. A retail seller who does not want to be in the debt collection business will often sell their right to be repaid, at a discount, to a finance company or other financial institution. This means that the seller will sell the right to collect the debt at a price that is less than the full amount owing to them. Although the seller has not gotten the full purchase price, they have gotten rid of the cost of collecting the debt, as well as the risk that the debtor will default. And, of course, the cost of discounting a receivable will often have been factored into the price charged to the retail consumer to begin with. At the present time, someone purchasing overdue credit is not subject to the provisions of the CDSSA.[29]

29 As at June 2017, the Ontario government is studying potential amendments to the CDSSA—along with their study of possible changes to the *Payday Loans Act*—that may require such persons to be regulated under the CDSSA. The white paper on this topic can be found at <http://www.ontariocanada.com/registry/showAttachment.do?postingId=18882&attachmentId=28331>.

CHAPTER SUMMARY

This chapter introduced the nature of a debt collection practice, beginning with the reasons debtors do not pay debts when they are due. The reason for nonpayment often drives the strategies and approaches to collection taken by both parties to the debt. Jurisdictional controls over paralegals and law clerks were then discussed. Under the CDSSA, paralegals running a collection practice must register as a collection agency. Paralegals are also limited to certain types of debt collections, in particular those within the limit of the Small Claims Court's monetary jurisdiction. Paralegals must also refrain from making payment demands prior to litigation, unless they are also registered as collection agents under the CDSSA. Law clerks, provided that they are working under a lawyer's supervision, may have more varied work, but may not operate independently. The chapter continued with a discussion of how creditors administer credit transactions, including how interest is determined and charged; how creditors decide when they need to take action to collect a debt; and how creditors decide when a debt is not worth pursuing. Secured transactions under the PPSA and PPSR were then discussed. The chapter concluded with a brief discussion of consumer credit and in what situations retail sellers will sell to a finance company or other financial institution their right to collect on a debt.

KEY TERMS

assignment in bankruptcy, 4
collection agent, 6
conditional sale contract, 14
consumer proposal, 4
counterclaim, 5
debt settlement service provider, 6
default judgment, 10
execution creditor, 12
execution debtor, 12
judgment creditor, 11
judgment debtor, 11
personal property, 15
receivable, 14
secured credit transaction, 15
unsecured credit, 4

REVIEW QUESTIONS

1. Bulko Wholesale Ltd (Bulko) sells exercise machines to fitness clubs and to individual consumers. The machines range in price from $600 to $10,000.
   a. What kind of sale arrangement might Bulko make with a first-time wholesale (commercial) customer?
   b. What kind of sale arrangement might Bulko make with an established wholesale customer?
   c. Suppose that an individual consumer wishes to buy a $6,000 machine, but cannot pay the sale price immediately. What kind of arrangement might Bulko make to sell the machine to the consumer?
   d. If Bulko isn't paid after 30 days, should it sue immediately? After 60 days? After 90 days? Explain your answer.
2. Identify the usual reasons for which a debt remains unpaid.
3. Describe two limitations on the right of paralegals to conduct a debt collection practice.
4. What are the limitations on a law clerk's involvement in the debt collection process?
5. Name two persons, other than a lawyer or a paralegal, who can represent someone in Small Claims Court on a debt collection matter.

6. Define
   a. secured and unsecured transactions
   b. judgment creditor
   c. execution creditor
   d. judgment debtor
   e. execution debtor
   f. conditional sale contract
   g. assignment in bankruptcy
7. Give two reasons why a creditor would register a financing statement under the PPSA.
8. Explain two ways in which attachment under the PPSA can take place.
9. How is a security interest perfected under the PPSA?
10. Explain which secured creditor has priority in each of these circumstances:
    a. one creditor who has perfected their interest and one who has not perfected their interest
    b. two perfected interests
    c. a creditor with a perfected interest and one with a PMSI

FIGURE 1.1 Example of a General Security Agreement

SECURITY AGREEMENT

Crazy Car Parts Manufacturing (the "Company"), the secured party, and Auto Parts Dealer (the "Dealer"), as debtor, agree to the following terms:

1. INDEBTEDNESS SECURED

The Dealer contracts to pay the Company, when due, all debt now owed to the Company and all additional debt later incurred by the Dealer to the Company.

2. COLLATERAL

The collateral that is to be subject to the security interests created under this agreement consists of the Dealer's entire stock of goods, including, but not limited to, all cars, parts, and accessories supplied to the Dealer by the Company and that form part of the Dealer's inventory.

3. GRANTING OF SECURITY INTEREST

As security for payment of the indebtedness and in consideration of this agreement, the Dealer grants to the company a security interest in all paid and unpaid for items of collateral, both of which are referred to in this agreement as the "security interest." Such collateral shall remain as security for the Dealer's entire indebtedness until payment in full is made. The security interest extends to collateral presently in the Dealer's possession and collateral subsequently acquired along with proceeds from the sale or lease of such collateral and any returned or repossessed collateral.

4. ATTACHMENT

The security interest attaches upon execution of this agreement in regard to all collateral that the Dealer has at that time and shall attach to future collateral upon acquisition of same.

5. PROTECTION OF COLLATERAL

The Dealer shall properly store collateral and protect it from injury or damage. The Dealer shall not release, surrender, or abandon possession of the collateral. The Dealer shall keep the collateral insured with all risk coverage satisfactory to the Company. The Dealer shall provide details of such coverage to the Company. If coverage is not in place, the Company may purchase its own and charge it to the Dealer.

The Dealer shall pay all taxes associated with the collateral.

The Dealer shall keep the collateral free from liens and encumbrances unless it has the prior written authorization of the Company to lien the property.

The dealer shall not sell, lease, or assign, or otherwise dispose of or deal with, the collateral outside of the ordinary course of business.

6. DEFAULT

The following shall be considered defaults by the Dealer:

a) the Dealer's authority to sell the Company's goods is cancelled,
b) the Dealer defaults in the payment or performance of any obligation owed to the Company,
c) the Dealer fails, upon request, to hand over proceeds or provide further information,
d) the Dealer disposes of the collateral without first obtaining the written consent of the Company,
e) the Dealer enters into bankruptcy or a bankruptcy order is made against the Dealer,
f) a receiver is appointed on behalf of a secured creditor of the Dealer,
g) an application is made under the *Companies' Creditors Arrangements Act* or a proposal or notice to make a proposal is filed under the *Bankruptcy and Insolvency Act*.

7. RIGHTS ON DEFAULT

If default occurs, the Company may:

a) accelerate all debt owed by the Dealer to the Company along with reasonable legal expenses,
b) take possession of any or all collateral,
c) stop delivery of any collateral,
d) commence legal action to enforce payment and/or performance of the Dealer's obligations,
e) appoint a receiver of the collateral to carry on the Dealer's business,
f) exercise all rights and remedies of a secured party under the *Personal Property Security Act*,
g) sell, consign, or lease, or otherwise dispose of, the collateral in a commercially reasonable manner.

8. REPOSSESSION

For repossession purposes, the Company, to the extent permitted by law, may enter the Dealer's premises to repossess the collateral.

9. SALE OF THE COLLATERAL

The Company may sell the repossessed collateral privately or by public auction. The proceeds of any sale are to be applied to the Company's expenses, then to the Dealer's indebtedness, and, third, to any subordinate security interest where notice has been received by the Company. Any surplus shall be paid to the Dealer, and if there is a shortfall, the Dealer is liable to pay it forthwith.

10. SUCCESSORS AND ASSIGNS

This agreement enures to the benefit of the heirs, executors, successors, and assigns of the Company.

11. AGREEMENT

This agreement becomes effective immediately upon execution by the parties and will continue in effect until replaced by a new agreement.

DATED at ______________________ this ____________ day of ______________________, 20____________.

______________________________ ______________________________

Dealer Witness

______________________________ ______________________________

Company Witness

Steps to Take Before Commencing Proceedings

2

LEARNING OUTCOMES

After reading this chapter, students will:

- Know how to obtain information from a client.
- Understand what information they need to obtain from a client.
- Recognize the importance of client identification and verification.
- Know how to explain the uses of retainers and retainer agreements.
- Recognize the various ways in which a client file can be organized and managed via paper-based or electronic-based storage methods.
- Know how to set up a "tickler system" and understand why it is important to do this.
- Recognize and understand the importance of limitation and notice periods and "bring forward dates" connected with the client's case.

This chapter is concerned with setting up and organizing collection litigation files and with client identification and verification procedures.

Obtaining Information from the Client

Most debt collection cases rely on documents rather than on oral evidence. It is important to obtain all of the documents that the client relies on to support their claim. These are likely to include documents that create indebtedness, such as sale contracts, promissory notes, invoices, account records, and correspondence. When possible, it is important to obtain and retain in the file the *original* documents—if it is necessary to prove a fact in court with the use of a document, rules of evidence generally require that the original document, rather than a copy of it, be produced. If documents have been produced electronically, the hard drive or any flash drive used should be available, if required, to authenticate the document sent or produced from it. The use of electronic records, as evidence in Ontario courts, is covered in section 34 of the *Evidence Act.*[1] If only copies, rather than originals, are available, the copies may be allowed as evidence. Courts generally follow the "best evidence" rule: the best evidence should be submitted. In other words, use originals if at all possible.

Client Identification and Verification

Summary of By-Law 7.1 of the Law Society of Ontario

There have been a number of situations where lawyers and paralegals have been retained by clients using false identities to engage in fraud or other unlawful activities.[2] To combat this, By-Law 7.1 requires lawyers and paralegals to identify and, in most cases, verify a client's identity. If a lawyer or paralegal fails to take steps to identify and, where required, verify a client's identity, that failure could result in the lawyer or paralegal being subjected to discipline by the Law Society of Ontario (LSO). By-Law 7.1 is summarized in the following points:

- When a lawyer or paralegal is retained by an individual they must identify the client by obtaining the client's full name, address, home telephone number, and occupation(s).
- If a lawyer or paralegal is retained by a business, they must obtain the client's legal business name, address, telephone number, incorporation number or business identification number and place of issue of the number, information on the nature of the business, the name(s), position(s), and contact information for the individual(s) who gives instructions on behalf of the business, and in the case of a corporation, the legal service provider must also make reasonable efforts to obtain the name(s) and occupation(s) of each director and the name(s), address(es), and occupation(s) of any person who owns 25 percent or more of the shares of the corporation.
- In receiving, paying, or transferring funds, reasonable steps must be taken to verify a client's identity using a reliable, independent source document such as a driver's licence, passport, or

1 RSO 1990 c E. 23.

2 See, for example, Lawyers Professional Indemnity Company, "Don't Get Duped: 20 Red Flags of a Bad Cheque Fraud You Should Recognize," LAWPRO Magazine, online: <http://www.practicepro.ca/lawpromag/20_red_flags_of_bad_cheque_fraud.pdf>

birth certificate for an individual and, in the case of a corporation, a corporate status certificate.

- The legal service provider[3] must keep client identification and verification information for a minimum of six years.
- By-Law 7.1 identification and verification procedures do not apply if the client is the legal service provider's employer or a financial institution.[4]

Clients may provide the legal representative with useful background information about the debtor, including address, email address, phone number(s), assets owned, banks where the debtor does business, and whether the debtor is in financial difficulty. This information allows the legal representative to locate the debtor when it is time to sue; it will also provide information as to what assets may be available to satisfy the debt owed to the client and help the legal representative to decide what strategy to take in pursuing the claim. When interviewing the client, a checklist should be used (see Figure 2.1 for an example) to be sure that all of the relevant information and documents have been obtained. A checklist can be used to help the lawyer or paralegal meet their obligations concerning client identification and verification under By-Law 7.1 of the LSO. In most cases, a client must be identified, and if a transfer of money is involved (which is the case in most debtor–creditor situations), the client's identity must also be verified. As explained in the box above, the client identification and verification process was implemented to try to reduce the possibility that a legal service provider might be duped by an unknown client into carrying out fraudulent activities. For more information on By-Law 7.1, refer to the box.

In addition to recording information received from the client and identifying and verifying the client's identity, a checklist can also be used to track steps taken and progress made on a collection file. The sample checklist found in Figure 2.1 can be used for these purposes.

After obtaining the information required to open and set up the new client file, the lawyer or paralegal will need to work with the client to determine the amount owed to them. The client can provide the necessary information because they will have kept track of the accounts, know how the calculations were done, what the balance is, what payments have been missed, what interest has accrued, and so on. The client may have a computerized accounting or bookkeeping system that does calculations, and there is no reason not to use this information; however, it is important to check the calculations and understand how they were done, in case the debtor argues that the calculations or the creditor's data are in error.

After the legal representative has determined with the client what is owing to a given date, they must ensure that there is enough information to calculate how much the balance will increase from that date because of accruing interest or further

3 The term "legal service provider" is used because both paralegals and lawyers are licensed to provide legal services in Ontario. The term "legal representative" is also used to include both lawyers and paralegals.

4 See sections 22 and 23 of By-Law 7.1 made under the *Law Society Act*, RSO c L.8.

installment payments that have become due.[5] The balance actually owing at the time of judgment or payment must be calculated. In order to do this, the lawyer or paralegal will have to know what the interest rate is and how it is being calculated. Calculation of the balance owing is discussed in more detail in Chapter 4.

Once the legal representative has met with the client and it has been agreed that they will do the work, the contractual relationship should be formalized by having the client sign a **retainer**. Usually, the retainer agreement records that the legal service provider has been hired to do the work specifically described in it and that a cash deposit has been paid (see the example on page 30). The retainer agreement may also set out when the client may next expect to be billed and when the client may expect to receive a progress report, among other things.[6]

retainer
a document that records the contractual relationship between legal service provider and client, usually stating that the legal service provider acts for the client and stipulating generally what the legal service provider has been retained to do; also used to describe an amount of money that the client pays the legal service provider as a down payment for services to be rendered—in this case, the legal service provider is required to account for how this money is used on the client's behalf; also used to describe a situation where a client does not hire a legal service provider for anything specific, but simply wants the legal service provider to be available to them to perform legal work for a specified period—in this case, the legal service provider does not have to account for the money and may use it for their own purposes; they are deemed to be entitled to the money for making themselves available to the client, although they may charge for any services actually performed during the period of the retainer

A letter should be sent to the client as a follow up to the meeting. The letter should acknowledge receipt of the account, set out the basic facts of the account (amount owing, interest rates, and due dates), as well as the billing and reporting structures, and should reiterate the client's instructions. The letter should set out what action(s) the client has authorized. For example, in some cases the client may only have authorized the lawyer or paralegal to conduct searches and send a demand letter. In other cases the client may have authorized court action to be taken through to a judgment and its enforcement. Enclose a copy of the retainer agreement with the letter if a copy was not given to the client at the initial meeting. Although this letter is not mandatory, it promotes a more positive and constructive relationship with the client.[7] The letter might also prove useful to protect a legal service provider in the event that a client files a complaint against a lawyer or paralegal for allegedly carrying out and charging a fee for work that was not authorized by the client. If a client's instructions are oral and not in writing, and there is a disagreement about what those instructions were, there is a presumption in law that the client's version is correct. That presumption is rebuttable, however, if there is evidence of written instructions.

File Organization

Once the client has retained the legal representative, it is important to organize the client file in a rational way so that documents can be easily accessed, filed, and

5 This may happen on a "running account," where the debtor runs up debt with continuous transactions and pays down the debt at stated intervals. In some cases, purchases have been made with payment not yet due, when the creditor decides to take action against the debtor for previous defaults. As recent debts become due after default, those debts will be added to the claim. In many cases this problem is avoided if the creditor, in the contract extending credit, inserts an "acceleration clause." An acceleration clause provides that, when there is one act of default by the debtor, all amounts outstanding are deemed to be due and owing immediately rather than on the date they were originally due.

6 Use of a retainer agreement permits a lawyer to sue a client in small claims court for collection on an unpaid account. This has been confirmed by the Divisional Court in *Gilbert's LLP v David Dixon Inc*, 2017 ONSC 1345.

7 One of the most frequent causes of complaints to the LSO about lawyers and paralegals is that they fail to communicate with clients.

stored. Although filing practices vary from office to office, most use a format similar to the one described here:

- *Case file folder.* Each case or matter should have a separate retainer agreement and a separate case file, even if there are multiple case files for the same client. Once a case file is set up, all subfiles go inside the case file. The case file folder contains the name of the client—for example, "SMITH v Slippout"[8]—and should contain on the inside file cover a form with the client's name, address, email address, phone and fax numbers, and other essential information. It should also contain a checklist (see Figure 2.1) where steps in the proceedings are checked off, so that anyone picking up the file for the first time will know the stage the proceedings have reached. The file name will also have a file number assigned by the file clerk or accounting clerk—the file number can include codes for the type of file, the lawyer, paralegal, or staff person responsible for the file, the date it was opened, and so on. Some offices use different colours of file folders for different types of legal work.
- *Correspondence subfile.* All correspondence related to the file should be here, with the most recent on top. A quick glance at this file should reveal what the matter is about, how it has progressed, the stage the proceedings have reached, and what problems need to be dealt with. At one time this file consisted of letters sent and received, but it is now more likely to be composed of printouts of emails and any texts sent and received. While emails can and should be stored electronically on the office computer system, keeping hard copies is a useful way of ensuring that there are copies if there is a system failure.
- *Notes subfile.* Notes that the legal representative or others in the office take should be filed here. If the client later hires someone else to finish the matter, the legal representative may remove notes from any materials returned to the client or transferred to the new lawyer (if authorized by the former client to transfer the file).
- *Client documents subfile.* Client documents, including copies, should be kept separate from other documents because they may be required to be filed as evidence in the proceedings. These documents are the property of the client and must be returned to the client when the matter is concluded. It is good practice to store original documents in plastic sleeves in the file in order to protect them from spills and stains, and being inadvertently written upon by anyone handling the file.
- *Client identification and verification.* In order to meet the requirements of By-Law 7.1 and to be organized for a possible LSO audit, it can be useful to maintain copies of client identity verification documents in a subfile.
- *Pleading subfile.* All court documents, including copies, should be kept in this file.

8 Where the client is the debtor (or defendant) rather than the creditor, for filing purposes the client's name should still be first. In this case, the file name would be written: "SMITH ats Snoggle"; "ats" means "at the suit of" and indicates that the client, Smith, is being sued by Snoggle. Uppercase letters are used so that it can be quickly identified which party is the client. This format allows the client's name to be first whether the client is plaintiff or defendant.

- *Miscellaneous subfile.* Documents that do not fit into the preceding categories should be placed here. When this file gets crowded, consider whether additional specific subfiles should be created.

Sample Retainer Agreement

Date: May 23, year 0[9]

To: Just and Coping

From: I.M.A. Client

Re: Debt Collection from U.R. Scapegrace Ltd

I retain Just and Coping to act as my lawyers and to take all necessary steps to collect a debt owing to me in the approximate amount of $45,000 from U.R. Scapegrace Ltd.

This retainer is your authority to proceed to take all necessary steps to collect this debt, including authorization to take legal proceedings and obtain and enforce a judgment. I also authorize you to engage on my behalf any expert you believe is required in this matter, and I acknowledge that I am responsible for payment of the expert's fees.

I agree to pay a deposit of $__________ now, and I understand that you will deduct legal fees and expenses incurred on my behalf from this deposit. I also agree to pay further deposits in anticipation of further legal fees and expenses not covered by the initial deposit. I understand that no work will be done until a deposit demanded by you has been paid.

I understand that the following members of the firm may work on the file and that their hourly rates are as follows:

- I.M. Just—$450
- Carl Coping—$350
- Dan Lawclerk—$150

I understand that these rates may increase annually, and I agree to pay them upon receiving written notice of the increase from you.

I understand that I must pay HST on fees and expenses.

I agree that I will pay interest at the rate permitted by the *Solicitors Act* on accounts that are paid later than 30 days after the date they were sent by you.

I acknowledge receipt of this contract.

By my signature below I authorize Just and Coping or their delegate to search my credit bureau record now or in the future for the purposes of collecting information for any lawsuits brought on my behalf or against me and for the enforcement of any judgments or debts against me. I understand that Just and Coping will protect my personal information and use it only for the purposes referred to in this retainer. If I require any further information about the use of my personal information, I agree to contact I.M. Just.

Date: __________________

__________________ per __________________

I.M.A. Client I.M. Just

9 Year 0, in examples in this text, is used in place of the present year. By way of an example, if the reader is using this book in 2018 they can replace Year 0 with 2018. Year 1 stands in place of the following year so in this example it would be 2019. Year −1 is used to represent the previous year, which in this example would be 2017. Be aware, however, in the case of calculations, that leap years such as 2016 and 2020 have an extra day in February so calculation examples may have to be adjusted when using a leap year.

Care should be taken with the storage of files. File storage can become an important issue in an office with a large volume of cases. In large firms, files, like library books, may be checked in and out by staff from a central filing area. In this way, a file can be located easily, and centrally stored when not in use. When a matter has been completed, original documents belonging to the client should be returned to the client along with the final reporting letter and account. The file should be purged of any unnecessary documents such as file copies of routine letters sent to clients. The material remaining should then be stored among the inactive files. Because further work may need to be done, or in case a client becomes dissatisfied and sues for negligence, the file should not be destroyed. Many lawyers used to keep closed files indefinitely. The LSO currently suggests that there is no fixed rule regarding file retention. However, By-Law 7.1 requires that client identification verification documents be kept for a minimum of six years.[10] In determining file retention policies, there are a number of factors to consider. Certainly closed files should be kept until after the limitation period for negligence has expired. Other factors include the nature of the actual legal work performed, the working life of the legal document(s), the outcome of the case, and the attitude and capacity, or lack thereof, of the client.[11] Note that storage may not require vast physical space because most parts of a file may now be stored electronically. Many law firms get advice from technical experts in deciding on the type of e-storage system they will use.

The Paperless Law Office

Many business documents are now exchanged and stored electronically without ever being printed. Some law firms have made the move to paperless or, more commonly, almost paperless offices. A law office that aspires to go paperless may still elect to maintain some documents in a paper format, including client identification and verification documents required by the LSO. If such documentation is kept in a paper format, it may be easier to access quickly in the event of a spot audit by the LSO. The office may also elect to keep hard copies of other documents, such as signed retainer agreements.

Although the initial transition to a paperless office may be somewhat costly and time consuming, there are advantages to operating a paperless office, and the LSO is supportive of the paperless storage of files.[12]

---

10 By-Law 7.1, s 23(14).

11 The LSO's website provides guides to retention and destruction of closed client files. See The Law Society of Upper Canada, "Guide to Retention and Destruction of Closed Client Files, For Lawyers," online: <http://lsuc.on.ca/with.aspx?id=2147499150> for the guide for lawyers and <http://www.lsuc.on.ca/with.aspx?id=2147499378&langtype=1033> for the paralegal guide.

12 To read an interesting article presented by the Law Society on suggestions for a paperless office, see Donna Neff, "The Paperless Office" *Ontario Lawyers Gazette* (Summer 2009), online: <http://www.lsuc.on.ca/media/olg_summer09_paperless.pdf>.

Some Advantages of a Paperless Office

1. Files can be viewed from anywhere that a user can access them electronically.
2. Files can be accessed by more than one user at a time.
3. Time lost in tracking down missing paper files is minimized, particularly as electronically stored files have backup copies available.
4. The cost of printing—including printers, paper, ink, and fax machines—and storage of paper-based material is greatly reduced.
5. Files can be more quickly and easily searched compared to paper files.
6. While working on one file, it is easier to access other files, making it faster and easier to use precedents from other files.
7. In the event of a disaster such as a fire, flood, or tornado, client files will still be maintained.
8. Reduction in the use of paper and space required to store paper benefits the environment.
9. Electronically stored files can utilize a greater variety of security features compared to paper-based files.

While the paperless office is the direction most law and paralegal firms are heading in, there are some disadvantages. As noted, setting them up can be expensive and require the use of an IT consultant. As well, hardware and software change constantly, and system upgrades may be required from time to time. Lastly, there are security issues, particularly when outside "cloud" storage sites are used, raising the risk of hackers gaining access to a file system.

Like paper files, electronically stored files should be organized in a clear and complete system with information stored in various subfiles as previously described. Various types of software, including Microsoft Office, can be utilized to set up an electronic filing system. Adhering to an organized filing system, whether by paper or electronically, makes it easier to search and find information in a file and allows for proper review of a file by the LSO in the event of an audit or a review based on a client complaint. Reflecting the importance of having a reliable system in place, most law offices considering the move to a paperless or near paperless environment will hire a consultant to assist them with the transition. Generally the purchase of a reliable scanner and software to convert documents to pdf is the starting point of the transition; from there, firms move forward with new files being stored electronically and old paper files being phased out over time.[13] In addition to scanning and conversion tools, a law office needs to consider the most secure way to store and share documents and files. Many offices use a cloud service such as Dropbox or Google Drive for the secure storage and sharing of electronically stored documents.

13 Many firms use the Fujitsu Image Scanner ScanSnap to convert paper documents to electronic ones. In order to convert documents into the commonly used pdf format, and to manage such documents, many firms rely on Wondershare PDFelement, Adobe Acrobat, or Microsoft Office software. For taking notes and sharing ideas, Evernote is a popular tool.

"Tickler" Systems, Limitation Periods, Notice Periods, and "Bring Forward Dates"

In any litigation, deadlines must be carefully noted in the file and in a "tickler" system. A tickler system is a date-recording system that alerts a legal representative to upcoming deadlines. It can be a datebook, calendar, computer system, hand-held device, or phone app that provides alerts. In order for these systems to work, the relevant deadlines need to be diarized or entered in the tickler system. The careful and methodical use of a tickler system is absolutely essential, because a missed deadline can be damaging to a client's case. A missed limitation period can cause a client to sue a legal representative for professional negligence.[14]

There are a number of deadlines that can be very important in debt collection proceedings. The first deadline involves **limitation periods**. Limitation periods are found in federal and provincial legislation, including the Ontario *Limitations Act, 2002*.[15] A limitation period is the time period in which a legal procedure must be commenced. If the procedure is not begun during the specified time period, it cannot be done at all. If plaintiffs do not start a proceeding, by issuing a claim within the time period, they are "statute barred" and may not proceed with the lawsuit. The limitation period begins when the right to sue (sometimes called a "cause of action") arises.

limitation period
a time period in which a legal procedure must be commenced—after the time period has expired, a party is barred from commencing a proceeding

Under the *Limitations Act, 2002*,[16] the basic limitation period for almost all causes of action, including actions in debt, is two years from the time the debt was past due (s 4) or could reasonably be determined to be past due (s 5). There are some exceptions to this general rule that may affect a debt action:

- *Minors and persons under disability:* The limitation period begins to run only when a litigation guardian is appointed (ss 6 to 9).
- *Debt actions not subject to any limitation period:* Proceedings to enforce a family law domestic agreement for support; and proceedings by the Crown to collect taxes, reclaim welfare benefits, or recover on defaulted student loans (s 16(1)).
- *Actions by debtor that extend the limitation period:* If the debtor acknowledges the debt or makes a partial payment on the debt, the limitation period restarts for an additional two-year period.

14 The Ontario Lawyers' Professional Indemnity Company (LawPro) reports that a leading cause of insurance claims against lawyers for professional negligence arises from missed limitation periods—an insurance loss that is almost wholly preventable if a law office is operating efficiently. See Debra Rolph, "'Repairing' Lawyers' Mistakes," LawPro Casebook (July 2002), online: <http://www.lawpro.ca/LawPRO/Casebook_July2002.pdf>.

15 SO 2002, c 24, Schedule B.

16 *Ibid.*

If a limitation period is set out in another Act, it does not apply unless it is set out as an exception to the general provisions of the *Limitations Act, 2002* in the schedule to the Act (s 19).

There are a number of reasons for having limitation periods. By requiring an action to be commenced within a specific time period, the defendant does not have the threat of litigation constantly hanging over them. Also, in an action brought soon after the events giving rise to it, witnesses' memories are fresher and evidence is probably more reliable than it would be if recalled long afterwards.

In addition to limitation periods, there are also notice periods that should be diarized or noted in the tickler system. For example, when a statement of claim is issued by the Superior Court of Justice, it must be served within six months of the issuing date.[17] Unlike a limitation period, where failure to observe the timelines will be fatal to the action, missing a notice period may be merely a procedural irregularity that can be rectified. Overcoming such an irregularity will, however, result in a delay and increased costs for the client.

In addition to limitation periods and notice periods, there are other important deadlines or dates that need to be "brought forward" so that tasks can be accomplished before the time for doing so has passed. Many of these dates are based on common sense rather than on rules. Of particular importance is the timing of the demand letter and the commencement of proceedings. The older a debt is, the harder it is to collect. If the client did not send a letter demanding payment as part of its initial collection efforts, one should be sent as soon as possible. A demand letter should indicate the date on which payment is required. If payment is not made by that date, diarize commencement of a proceeding for the next day, and issue the claim on that date. If the action is not defended, diarize the date for signing the default judgment, and submit the default judgment for signing by the court on that date. It is important to diarize and to adhere to a litigation schedule. Delay does not favour a creditor, because the debtor's assets may be shrinking rapidly. Also, sticking firmly to dates sends a psychological message to the debtor that the creditor is determined to pursue the matter diligently and that the matter is not going to fade away.

---

17 Rules of Civil Procedure, RRO 1990, Reg 194, r 14.08.

CHAPTER SUMMARY

Once it has been determined that a debt is overdue, there are a number of tasks that must be completed before commencing proceedings, the first of which are being retained by the client and opening a client file. This chapter discusses the various ways in which a file can be organized, whether through a paper-based system, a paperless electronic-based system, or a combination of both systems. In particular, attention is drawn to the use of tickler systems and to the need to keep track of limitation and notice periods. The requirements of client identification and verification under By-Law 7.1 are also explained in the chapter.

KEY TERMS

REVIEW QUESTIONS

1. Why are client documents important in collection cases?
2. What information about the debt collection matter would you expect the client to provide?
3. What is a retainer agreement? Why is it advisable to have one signed by the client?
4. Explain the steps to be taken in the process of opening a collection file.
5. Explain three advantages that a paperless file storage system may have over a paper-based one.
6. Are there disadvantages to a paperless file storage system?
7. What is a "tickler system" and how is it useful?
8. What is a limitation period?
9. Give four potential exceptions to the standard limitation period in a debt collection matter.
10. Why is it important not to delay work on a collection file?
11. Explain what information a legal service provider must collect when being retained by (a) an individual client, and (b) a corporate client.

FIGURE 2.1 Client Information Checklist

Client information:

1. Client's full name and any other names client is known by:

____

2. Address (home and business): _______________

____

3. Telephone number(s): _______________
4. Fax number: _______________
5. Email address: _______________
6. Occupation and employer's address (list all that apply):

____

____

7. Bank and address: _______________
8. Credit card—type, number, and expiry date: _______________
9. Date of birth and place of birth: _______________

List and copy driver's licence information and one other piece of identification to verify client information:

(Note: In all cases, obtain the client's driver's licence number (if they have one) along with one of the following documents (documents should be reviewed and copied): an original government-issued identification that is valid and has not expired, such as a birth certificate or passport. If non–face-to-face instruction is provided from a client in Canada, then the review and verification of the identification documents can be provided by attestation from a person listed under By-Law 7.1, including a commissioner of oaths or a guarantor (doctor, pharmacist, lawyer, etc.). If the client is outside Canada, an agent who can provide an attestation must be retained—see the By-Law 7.1 for details and/or call the Law Society at 416-947-3315, ext 3315 for confidential assistance.)

____

Date identity verified and by whom: _______________

For clients that are a business or organization:

10. Incorporation or business identification number: _______________
11. Place of issuance of incorporation/business identification number:

____

12. Type of business: _______________
13. Name, position, and contact information for those individuals authorized to give instructions with respect to the matter for which the licensee is retained (in the case of an organization, reasonable efforts must be made to record the names, addresses, and occupations of all directors and of those persons who own 25 percent or more of the shares of a corporation):

____

____

____

14. Give details of identification reviewed and copied to verify client information:

(Note: The following documents, where applicable, should be reviewed and copied: a certificate of corporate status issued by a public body for corporations, articles of incorporation, or a trust or partnership agreement, or any other similar record that confirms the unincorporated organization's existence. For directors' information, consult corporate minute books or online corporate registry services.)

____

____

Where the client is acting for or representing a third-party beneficiary or a principal:

15. Information about the beneficiary or principal as set out in paragraphs 1 to 14, as applicable:

Information about the debtor/defendant:

16. Full name/business name:
17. Business type (sole prop., corp., partnership), if applicable:
18. Defendant's address:
19. Defendant's phone number:
20. Fax/email of defendant
21. Defendant's representative (if any) and their contact information:
22. Marital status of defendant and name of spouse, if applicable:
23. Defendant's employer:

Defendant's assets:

24. Real estate (address, lot, plan number, if known):
25. Vehicle(s) (licence, VIN, description):
26. Bank account numbers and bank addresses:
27. Investments (type, number, company, address of company):

Details of claim:

28. Type of case (tort, collections, etc.): __________

If collection matter:

29. Original amount: __________
30. Terms, including interest: __________
31. Evidence of debt (contract, invoice, note, security agreement): __________
32. Payment history/default history: __________
33. Co-signors or guarantor information (name, address, phone number): __________
34. Collateral given as security (if any, and type, location): __________

Documents delivered by client (obtain and secure originals and make copies):

35. Invoices: __________
36. Account records: __________
37. Promissory notes: __________
38. Guarantees: __________
39. Security agreements: __________
40. Demand letters sent by client: __________
41. Other documents (list): __________
42. Searches carried out by client: __________

Client retainer, instructions, and action taken:

43. Name of lawyer/paralegal assigned to case: __________
44. Retainer agreement reviewed and signed (write date and copy for file, put retainer funds into trust account): __________
45. Reporting frequency (monthly or details of other): __________
46. Billing frequency (monthly or details of other): __________
47. Conflicts check carried out: __________
48. Tickler date system established: __________
49. Client account opened: __________
50. File number assigned: __________

51. Details of searches carried out (credit bureau, driver's licence, business name, etc.): ____________

____

52. Demand letter sent and date of letter: ____________
53. Time given for payment in demand letter: ____________
54. Authority given to discuss settlement and details as to what client will accept:

____

____

55. Authority to commence litigation: ____________
56. Authority to retain outside counsel: ____________
57. Authority to retain experts: ____________
58. Date statement of claim issued: ____________
59. Date statement of claim served: ____________
60. Date default judgment may be requested: ____________
61. Pre-trial deadline: ____________
62. Case management deadlines: ____________
63. Judgment date: ____________
64. Examination in aid of execution date: ____________
65. Date writ of seizure and sale obtained: ____________
66. Date for renewal of writ of seizure and sale: ____________
67. Date garnishment obtained: ____________
68. Date for renewal of garnishment: ____________
69. Final reporting and letter to client: ____________
70. Client documents and any property on hand returned to client: ____________

____

71. Date file closed: ____________

NOTE: This form and copies of any identification verification documents must be kept on file for six years following completion of the matter.

Searches to Carry Out Before Commencing Proceedings

3

LEARNING OUTCOMES

After reading this chapter, students will:

- Know why it is necessary to conduct background searches prior to commencing proceedings and how to use search information that they discover.
- Know what search sites will help them verify the legal name of a party.
- Know what search sites will help them locate a party.
- Know what search sites can be used to locate and identify a party's assets.
- Be able to gather information to properly conduct searches.
- Know how to conduct searches online.

This chapter is concerned with how to carry out the necessary background investigation and information gathering required before commencing collection proceedings. These searches have two purposes. First, they are used to verify the identity and legal name of a party and determine where the party can be found so that they can be served with court documents. Second, searches can be used to determine whether assets can be identified and located in order that they may be used by a creditor to satisfy a judgment.

Obtaining Information from the Client

The legal representative should ask the client to provide all of the information that they have on the debtor. They may already have information on the debtor's legal name, address, and credit status. In some cases, a client will have the debtor's driver's licence number in their file. The legal representative will usually need to verify and update this information and can do so by carrying out public and private record and database searches.

Obtaining Background Information: Public Record Searches

When creditors come to a lawyer or paralegal, it is because they have tried and failed to collect a debt and expect the legal representative to do it for them, usually by suing the debtor. However, that may not be the best strategy if the debtor

- has fled the jurisdiction;
- has recently transferred or encumbered assets that might otherwise be available to satisfy the debt;
- has been sued by other creditors who have been unsuccessful in collecting on their judgments;
- had assets seized by other creditors;
- has tried to hide assets;
- has suffered personal or business financial losses recently; or
- had assets seized by secured creditors who have a collateral interest in those assets and a right to seize them to satisfy the debt when there is default.[1]

1 Recall from Chapter 1 that secured creditors are those who, in exchange for giving credit, ask for an interest in an asset of the debtor (called collateral) to secure payment of the debt. If the debtor defaults, instead of just suing the debtor, the creditor may seize or repossess the collateral without suing or getting a judgment, sell it, and use the proceeds of sale to satisfy the debt. Usually the secured creditor has a prior right to collateral as against an unsecured creditor, who has no right to seize the assets of the debtor until after a judgment is obtained. The secured creditor usually also has the right to bring in a receiver to manage the debtor's business.

In these circumstances, there may be little or no purpose in suing the debtor because there may be no assets available to satisfy the debt or no hope of payment. To obtain the necessary information about the debtor or to confirm information supplied by the client, there are a number of public and private searches and databases that can yield useful information to help the legal representative decide whether to sue or to pursue another strategy. Today, these searches can be done online, although some can still also be done by phone, fax, mail, or in person.

Identifying and Locating the Debtor

Name Search: Consumer Debtors

If an individual consumer is being sued, the legal name of the debtor should be verified. Suing in the wrong name can result in an unenforceable judgment.

For example, if Murray Benek is being sued and a judgment is obtained in that name, the judgment will be useless if it turns out that Murray's legal first name is really Miroslav, but that he informally changed it to Murray years ago. Most people use their formal legal name for title deeds, banking documents, and other "official" documents such as driver's licences. Legally, and certainly for formal purposes, Miroslav Benek exists, but Murray Benek does not, at least for the purposes of obtaining and enforcing a judgment. Getting the debtor's name right at the outset is important both to obtaining a judgment against the debtor in the right name, and to conducting searches to determine whether the debtor is worth suing.

There are several ways to verify a debtor's correct legal name.

Statement of Driving Record

If the legal representative has the debtor's driver's licence number, a Statement of Driving Record can be requested, which provides a three-year history of the driver, including their name, licence status information (including a physical description and date of birth), and a record of driving offence convictions. The person's driving record can help with verification of the name of the debtor and confirmation that the legal representative has the right person. The information about height, gender, and date of birth might be useful in performing other searches. For example, having the date of birth makes it easier to verify who a debtor is on a *Personal Property Security Act* (PPSA)[2] search. A driving record search may be especially useful with someone who has a common last name, like Singh, Smith, or Wong. Note, however, that this search will not provide an address for the licence holder—privacy restrictions keep addresses out of the public record. However, an authorized user may obtain the driver's address by ordering a driver's license history. A legal representative may become an "authorized" user if

1. they apply for authorization and enter into an agreement with the Ministry of Transportation, and

2 RSO 1990, c P.10.

2. the search is conducted for one of the purposes for which authorization will be granted, such as debt collection, litigation, claims, and accidents. Authorized investigators may include private investigators, security guards, lawyers, paralegals, and others acting for the noted purposes. For the complete list of authorized users and uses and further details about becoming an authorized user, see <https://www.apps.rus.mto.gov.on.ca/edtW/documents/cbt-module1/M1-AuthorizedUses.html>.

Information about becoming an authorized Ministry of Transportation (MTO) user may also be obtained by contacting the Supervisor of the Driver Vehicle Licensing Call Centre by mail or by phone:

Supervisor,
Driver and Vehicle Licensing Call Centre
Licensing Administration Office
Ministry of Transportation
2680 Keele Street
Downsview, ON M3M 3E6

Tel: 416-235-2999
Toll free: 1-800-387-3445

Driver's searches may be conducted online, paying by credit card. The search site for driver and automobile related searches is the ServiceOntario site on the Ontario government website, which can be found at: <https://www.ontario.ca/page/order-drivers-record>.[3]

To see what a Statement of Driving Record abstract looks like, see Figure 3.1.

Vehicle and Plate History Abstracts

The Vehicle Identification Number (VIN) or the licence plate number for a vehicle that may be owned by the debtor, can be used to carry out either a plate or VIN history search, either of which will provide, to registered authorized users, the name of the owner, their driver's licence number, the date the vehicle was registered, and whether it has changed owners recently. The certified abstract may be ordered online but will be shipped by Canada Post. For information on ordering a Certified Plate Search—Recent Owner, see <https://www.apps.rus.mto.gov.on.ca/jtips/plSearchRecOwner.do?method=view&lang=EN&certified=true>.

While it used to be possible for anyone to conduct these searches, an increasing focus on privacy concerns has led to the restrictions discussed here, which limit access to personal information to authorized users.

---

3 Because online sites are relatively easy and inexpensive to change compared with paper systems, websites are often altered, usually for the better, to facilitate searches. As well, among commercial and private search sites there is much competition, so sites are frequently transformed with the result that URLs come and go with some frequency. The reader may have to search and experiment with links or use Google or another search engine to find a site that seems to have disappeared or is not where it last was. This may be frustrating, but that is the nature of the Internet.

An example of a Certified Plate Search—Recent Owner can be seen in Figure 3.2. The VIN search record is similar.

Online Searches

Various search engines and other online sources allow the legal representative to submit the name of a debtor to obtain addresses, telephone numbers, and other information about an individual that can help verify a name, obtain other identifying information, and locate the person. These searches can be used to find both individual consumer debtors and business debtors operating under a business name. A **reverse search** can be carried out on many of these sites by submitting a telephone number, address, email address, or other information that will help the legal representative to obtain the correct name and address of a debtor, as well as other information. Reverse searches of phone numbers will often identify the subscriber of unlisted landlines and cell phones. Many sites are free, but some charge for information, in which case payment can be made by credit card. The following websites were useful at the time of writing in summer 2017:

reverse search
a reverse search allows someone to submit an address, telephone number, or email address to obtain the name of a resident or subscriber

- *Canada411:* <http://www.canada411.ca> Submitting a name to this site can turn up a telephone number. Reverse searching is also available.
- *WhitePages.ca:* <http://www.whitepages.ca> Names can be searched on this site to obtain addresses, phone numbers, and email addresses in the United States, although some of that information is not free and requires payment. The site also allows reverse directory searches of addresses and phone numbers to be conducted to identify and locate individuals.
- *CanPages:* <http://www.canpages.ca> This site can be used to find the telephone number of an individual or a business along with their address. Reverse searches are possible.
- *Yellow Pages:* <http://www.yellowpages.ca> This site can be used to find the telephone number of a business along with their address. Reverse searches are possible.
- *Pipl:* <http://www.pipl.ca> This site is a gateway to a wide variety of databases and record systems to help find references to any name submitted. It accesses databases in many countries, including Canada. Some searches are free and some come with a fee.
- *NetTrace:* <http://www.nettrace.com.au/resource/search/people.html> This Australian site is another gateway to a variety of search sites that allow searches to be carried out in various countries, including Canada, by inputting phone numbers, addresses, email addresses, names, and other data. Many of the sites will search various public and private databases, including many in Canada. Some charge fees.
- *ReversePhoneLookup.com:* <http://www.reversephonelookup.com> This site can be used to do reverse phone searches, particularly for cellphone numbers, and provides subscriber's names and contact information.
- *Intellius:* <http://www.intellius.com> This site is a gateway to various people-finding sites, including reverse phone searches and criminal record

and background searches. It provides quite detailed information and charges a fee to access its databases.

- *Lycos Search:* <http://www.whowhere.com> This site can find individuals with a name search for locations in the United States. Reverse searches can also be carried out. The results will yield information about who has the phone or email account, or who owns premises or lives at an address. It may also provide other personal information.
- *Google:* <http://www.google.ca> This well-known general search engine can draw information from all kinds of databases, including some the legal representative may not have thought of. If the name of an individual is typed into a Google search box, the legal representative may discover quite a lot of information about the person, some of which may then be used to do some of the more specific and precise searches already discussed here.
- *Yahoo!:* <https://ca.yahoo.com/> This is similar to Google and works the same way. Searching an individual debtor's name in Yahoo! or by "Googling" them is a good first step in conducting a search.

Name Search: Business Debtors

If the debtor is a business debtor, it is important to know the form of business organization used by the debtor. The debtor may be an individual (referred to in law as a natural person) carrying on business in their own name. In that case, the consumer name search techniques discussed in the previous section can be used to verify the name of the debtor. However, if the individual carries on business using a trade name (Mary Ann Chen carrying on business as Mary's Golf Driving Range, for example) or as a partnership or a corporation, it may initially be difficult to determine what the debtor should legally be called in the lawsuit.

- If the business is incorporated, the corporation must be sued in its legal corporate name.
- If the business is a sole proprietorship, the individual may be sued, or the sole proprietorship may be sued in the name in which it carries on business. The *Rules of Civil Procedure* and the *Rules of the Small Claims Court* make it easy to sue in the business name, and then expand enforcement rights against the individual who is the sole proprietor, allowing for the seizure of assets in both the business name and in the name of the individual.[4]
- If the debtor is a partnership, the partnership may be sued in the partnership's name. Some or all of the partners may be sued in their own names. Again, the *Rules of Civil Procedure* and the *Rules of the Small Claims Court* make it easy to sue the partnership in the partnership name, and then identify the partners and expand enforcement rights to include the personal assets of the partners.

---

4 Rule 8 of the *Rules of Civil Procedure*, RRO 1990, Reg 194 made under the *Courts of Justice Act* and Rule 5 of the *Rules of the Small Claims Court*, O Reg 258/98, also made under the *Courts of Justice Act*.

For example, if the creditor's business has been with Mary Ann Chen's golf driving range and the business is incorporated as Chengolf Ltd, the creditor must sue in the correct corporate name. If Mary Ann Chen is sued personally or the lawsuit is brought against Mary's Golf Driving Range, a defence is likely to be made that either of those defendants has no liability because it is the corporation that is legally liable, not Mary Ann Chen as an individual or as an individual carrying on business as Mary's Golf Driving Range. In this example, Chengolf Ltd must be sued.

Similarly, if Mary's Golf Driving Range is operated as a business partnership between Mary Ann Chen and John Parten, the legal representative will need to know the name the partnership uses to carry on business, as well as who the partners are. While the lawsuit can be brought against the partnership name, that judgment will only bind partnership assets, such as the golf balls and clubs used in the business. In order to gain access to the assets of each individual partner, such as their real property, cars, and personal bank accounts, the legal representative needs to know the correct name of each partner so that they can be sued as well, or can be given notice that the creditor intends to go after their assets as well as those of the business in order to satisfy the judgment. Rule 8 of the *Rules of Civil Procedure* of the Superior Court and Rule 5 of the *Rules of the Small Claims Court* provide a complete code for the procedure to sue partners. This includes provisions to obtain disclosure of the names of those who were partners at the relevant time, in order that they can be given notice of the lawsuit as a prerequisite to enforcing a judgment against their personal assets, as well as against any assets in the partnership name.

Any business being carried on in Ontario in a name other than the owner's name must register its business name with the Central Production and Verification Services Branch, Ministry of Government and Consumer Services (Companies Branch).[5] To identify individuals who may be liable as business debtors, submission of a business name search will result in the identification of the individual person if the business is a sole proprietorship. The business may be sued by suing the individual sole proprietor, or the lawsuit may be brought against the business's name. If the business is a partnership, submission of the business name will result in identification of the partners. A partnership can be sued by suing in the partnership's name, suing the individuals who are partners, or suing both. This broadens the range of assets available to satisfy the judgment against the partnership. Because some members of a partnership may leave after its initial registration, and some may join, a demand can be made on the partnership to disclose who the partners were at the relevant time when the debt was incurred. Both the *Rules of the Small Claims Court* and the *Rules of Civil Procedure* explicitly allow for this, and the information is available through pre-trial procedures.

Conducting a search of the name under which a corporation carries on business will result in the correct corporate name. Unlike the position with sole proprietorships and partnerships, remember that when suing a corporation, its legal name must be used. For example, if Mary Ann Chen had incorporated her golf driving range business, the corporation must be sued, not Mary Ann Chen (even though

5 See the *Business Names Act*, RSO 1990, c B.17.

she may be the sole officer and shareholder of Mary's Golf Driving Range). Do not be surprised if the corporate name that turns up has nothing to do with the golf driving range business. The name may well be an assigned registration number given by the Companies Branch, and it may appear, for example, as something like "192356 Ontario Limited." This is sometimes referred to as a "numbered company." There is nothing particularly sinister about a numbered company. For example, if Henry Gold (Gold) decides to buy and operate a McDonald's franchise, Gold may run the franchise business as a corporation. If so, there is no point in getting a business name for the company, because it will be carrying on business under the well-known and highly marketable name of the franchiser. In this case, Gold may simply use the number that the Companies Branch assigns to the company when it is incorporated without a name.

A business name search can be done in two ways. A search can be carried out in person at the public search office of the Central Production and Verification Services Branch, Ministry of Government and Consumer Services (MGCS), 375 University Avenue, 2nd floor, Toronto, Ontario M5G 2M2, where there are computer terminals at which a search can be conducted. Alternatively, an online search can be conducted remotely by accessing the MGCS search site at ServiceOntario at <https://www.services.gov.on.ca/sf/#>. This link is a gateway to numerous online services that are useful for various business searches discussed in this chapter. If "business" is entered in the service finder search box at the top of the screen, links to a number of useful search sites are listed, including sites for various types of business searches, including business names searches.

A business names report will identify persons using a business name and will show their address. If the business name is not registered, a certificate of non-registration showing that a business name that may be in use has not been registered can be obtained. (There are penalties for failing to register a business under the *Business Names Act*, although this will not directly affect a creditor's lawsuit against the debtor. However, if the creditor is suing in a name that is not registered, their lawsuit may be **stayed** until the name is registered.)

stayed
a legal proceeding may be stopped from proceeding further by a judge, until one of the parties does something they are obliged to do; for example, a plaintiff who is suing using an unregistered business name may have the proceedings stayed until they prove that they have registered the name as they are legally required to do

If a business name search shows that the business is actually a corporation, or the legal representative knows that they are dealing with a corporation, a search of the Initial Return/Notice of Change filing of the corporation can be carried out to verify that the legal representative has the correct corporate name, and to obtain the corporation's address for service, and the names and addresses of the officers and directors of the corporation. An Initial Return/Notice of Change form must be filed by every corporation incorporated in Ontario. A sample of a completed Initial Return/Notice of Change is set out in Figure 3.3.

An online search can be inexpensively done, provided that the name being searched has been registered with the Companies Branch. At the ServiceOntario website, <http://www.serviceontario.ca>, follow the links online for business services and select "Search, register and renew business names" to order an Enhanced Business Name Search. An example of an Enhanced Business Name Search online form can be found in Figure 3.4. Searches can be carried out using the exact business name, words within the name, or the business identification number that all businesses are given when their names are registered (if the legal representative has it). A credit card can be used to pay for the search online. Searching can also be done, for a fee, online or by telephone through private search companies, such as Carswell Legal Solutions (formerly Cyberbahn), Corporate Searchers, or Oncorp, which are all recognized service providers to the Ontario government. Oncorp's search services and samples of documents such as a Corporation Profile Report (which contains a corporation's address and the names of its directors) can be viewed online at <http://www.oncorp.com/home/services_onbis_corp.asp>. Note that not all business registration documents are available from the government website. Documents such as a Corporation Profile Report are available only through private search sites such as Carswell Legal Solutions or Oncorp. To view a sample Corporation Profile Report, see Figure 3.5. This report is useful because it sets out the corporation's legal name and the names of the directors. If a business client does not have the information required to fulfill the legal service provider's client identification and verification requirements under By-Law 7.1 (as discussed in Chapter 2), a Corporation Profile Report can be obtained, at the client's expense, to verify information concerning the business, such as the legal business name, address, incorporation number or business identification number, and place of issue of the number.

If a document is required that is not available through the government website or the legal representative does not have the time or expertise to search on their own, there are companies that will conduct searches for a fee. Online searches can also be carried out by using private search and registration services, such as the previously mentioned Oncorp (<http://www.oncorp.com>) or Carswell Legal Solutions (<http://www.carswelllegalsolutions.com/due-diligence-searches>). These search sites will also allow the legal representative to conduct a variety of other searches of public business records maintained by the federal and provincial governments. The cost of the search can be passed on as a disbursement to the client that requires the search on their matter. Note that if a corporation is carrying on business in Ontario but is incorporated in another province or is a federally incorporated company, an Ontario corporate search will not be useful. However, either of the above-mentioned private search sites can be used to obtain information about companies incorporated federally or in other provinces.

Information About the Debtor's Assets and Debts

The debtor has now been identified by its proper name for the purposes of naming the debtor in a lawsuit, and information has been obtained to locate the debtor for service. An accurate name for the debtor can now be used to carry out a second set of searches in order to answer some important questions:

- Is this debtor worth suing?
- Does the debtor have any assets worth seizing to satisfy a judgment?
- Are there secured creditors that will get all the valuable assets before a client can get near them with their judgment?

- Is the creditor the only creditor suing, or are there 15 others, all hounding the debtor?
- Has this debtor a long history of defaulting on debts where creditors have had little success in recovering anything on their judgments?
- Has the debtor filed for bankruptcy or been declared bankrupt?

The answers to these questions may indicate that the creditor should be advised that the best course of action may be to obtain a judgment, hopefully by default, but not to spend too much time or money trying to enforce it. Or the legal representative might advise the client not to waste money by suing, but simply to write the debt off as a business loss for tax purposes. If the debt is written off for tax purposes, the taxpayer must be able to document the reasons for doing so, especially if they decided not to sue.

In order to properly advise a client, some or all of the following searches should be conducted to determine whether there are likely to be assets to seize and whether collection efforts are likely to be successful.

Execution Search

writ of seizure and sale also called a writ of execution; allows the sheriff to seize and sell goods or land belonging to the judgment debtor and apply the proceeds to the judgment creditor's claim

exigible assets assets that are available to be legally seized under a writ of seizure and sale; non-exigible assets are those that are exempt from seizure under the *Execution Act*, RSO 1990, c E.24, or under the provisions of another statute

When a plaintiff obtains a judgment in a lawsuit, the judgment orders the defendant to pay money, but the judgment is not self-enforcing. If the defendant does not pay, it is necessary for the plaintiff to file a **writ of seizure and sale** (also referred to as a "writ of execution") with the sheriff of the county or district where the defendant has **exigible assets**.[6] Unfortunately, the province still has no easily accessed centralized file of all writs of seizure and sale. This means that duplicate writs of execution may have to be filed in sheriff's offices in more than one county or district if the defendant may have assets in more than one county or district. Once filed, a writ of execution can be used in one of two ways: (1) if the judgment creditor knows of an asset that can be seized and sold, so that the proceeds of sale can be used to satisfy the judgment, they can direct the sheriff to seize and sell the goods; or (2) the judgment creditor can simply leave the execution sitting on file. Others who do business with the debtor, or who may be lending the debtor money, often search executions to assure themselves that the person they are dealing with is a good credit risk. They may be reluctant to lend or extend credit to a business once they learn of an outstanding writ of execution. In these circumstances, the debtor may be pressured to pay off the execution creditor. Another advantage of filing an execution is that if another judgment creditor enforces their writ, the client will be entitled to share, on a pro rata basis, in the amount collected.[7] The writ, once filed, is enforceable for six

6 As noted in the preface to this edition, in 2016 the province began to look at changing the way civil court orders are enforced, primarily by privatizing the enforcement process. This would involve taking enforcement out of the hands of sheriff's officers, who are public officials, and transferring it to private bodies with the judgment creditors paying the full cost of enforcement. As at July 2017, this process had not gotten past the discussion stage, but if it does, there may be changes to some of the enforcement procedures found in this text.

7 See the *Creditors' Relief Act, 2010*, SO 2010, c 16, Schedule 4.

years and can be renewed. Sheriff's offices used to send renewal notices, but now they do not. The renewal date will need to be entered into the lawyer or paralegal's tickler system. Writs may now also be issued and filed electronically, saving a trip to the sheriff's office.

It is a good idea to do an execution search against the name of the debtor, as a means of collecting a lot of useful information. For example:

- It can be used to verify the debtor's name or the spelling of the name.
- A number of outstanding writs of execution may indicate that the debtor has been sued before and, if the writs are still on file, that the judgment creditors have not been able to collect on the judgment.
- Several writs of execution filed recently may indicate that all of the creditors are closing in and that the debtor may be "**judgment proof**," with little likelihood that assets will be available to satisfy the judgment. This pattern may also indicate that the debtor has just gone, or is about to go, bankrupt. Suing may be a waste of time, as an action commenced against someone who is in bankruptcy proceedings is automatically stayed. The creditor may recover more money by registering a claim with the Trustee in Bankruptcy. Bankruptcy procedure is discussed in detail in Chapter 14 of this text.
- Many outstanding writs that are several years old may indicate that the debtor has successfully avoided paying creditors for some time and either has no assets or is adept at hiding them.
- No executions may indicate that there are no prior unsatisfied judgments and that there will be assets available to seize; it may also indicate that the debtor's assets are not located in the county or district where executions were searched.

judgment proof
describes a debtor against whom a judgment may be obtained, but where the judgment will be unenforceable because the debtor has no assets to pay the judgment or has hidden or encumbered assets preventing easy seizure; a judgment in these circumstances is sometimes described as a "paper judgment"—that is, it is worth no more than the paper it is printed on because it cannot be enforced in any practical way

Even where a number of writs are found on file, it may still be useful to try to obtain a judgment and add a writ of execution to those on file. The reason for this is that the *Creditors' Relief Act, 2010*[8] requires that execution creditors (all those who have filed writs of execution in that county) share on a pro rata basis if any execution creditor succeeds in seizing and selling assets. When assets are seized and sold, the sheriff is obliged to distribute a share of the money to each of the execution creditors in proportion to what they are owed. This means that execution creditors with large judgments receive a larger share of the money than those who have judgments for smaller amounts (as the box on the next page shows). There are some exceptions to the rule about pro rata distributions. Support creditors and the Crown in respect of unpaid taxes take priority over other judgment creditors, for instance.

To conduct a search of executions against the name of a debtor, a legal representative can attend at the sheriff's office and request a certificate indicating whether there are writs of seizure and sale on file in that office. The sheriff's office is usually located in the local Superior Court of Justice courthouse. Superior Court addresses can be found online at <http://www.attorneygeneral.jus.gov.on.ca/english/courts/Court_Addresses/index.php>.

8 *Ibid*, s 2(1).

In Toronto, execution searches at the Sheriff's Office are done online after payment of the prescribed fee. Users key in the same kind of information they would provide for the certificate, and the system produces an onscreen response, and, if desired, a printout of that response. In time, this system will extend to other parts of Ontario, and may one day be available online from an office computer.

The legal representative should give the full name of the debtor; if the debtor is an individual, middle names as well as the first name should be provided, if possible. If the debtor is a business, the legal representative should be sure to give the business's proper legal name. With sole proprietorships and partnerships, it is wise in most cases to list the name of the individual who is the sole proprietor or the names of the partners. The search should be conducted in the sheriff's office for the county or district where the debtor is likely to have assets, lives, or carries on business. Once the search results have been obtained, copies of the writs may be requested to find out the particulars, such as the name of the judgment creditor, the amount owing, and the length of time the debt has been unsatisfied. The judgment creditor's lawyer, whose name appears on the writ, may be contacted to find out about any attempts to collect the debt that have been made.

Illustration of a Pro Rata Distribution of the Proceeds of Execution

Amount owing to execution creditor A	$500
Amount owing to execution creditor B	$200
Amount owing to execution creditor C	$100
Total	$800

Execution creditor C levies execution and recovers $300 as a net amount after the costs of execution have been deducted from the gross amount.

Formula:

$$\text{amount recovered on levy} \times \frac{\text{amount owing to creditor}}{\text{amount owing to all creditors}} = \text{share paid to creditor}$$

A will receive	$300	×	500/800	=	$187.50	(62.5%)
B will receive	$300	×	200/800	=	$ 75.00	(25.0%)
C will receive	$300	×	100/800	=	$ 37.50	(12.5%)

An online writ of execution search can be ordered through the writs search service provided by Teranet. A search can be conducted in one or more counties or districts, or an Ontario-wide search (OWL—Ontario Writs Locator) can be ordered through Teranet. To access this service, the legal representative must register as a member (for free) at <https://www.teranetexpress.ca/csp>. Execution searches can also be carried out on the Carswell Legal Solutions site, at <http://www.carswelllegalsolutions.com/due-diligence-searches>.

Personal Property Security Act Searches

Once the legal representative has the proper name of the debtor, a search can be conducted under the PPSA. The PPSA allows creditors, who have taken an interest in property of the debtor, to secure repayment and register notice of their interest in the property so that anyone conducting a search will learn about it. When a creditor has registered, they are said to have "perfected" their interest. When the property is pledged as security for a loan, it is sometimes referred to as "collateral." Registration of a Financing Statement that makes reference to a security agreement between the creditor and the debtor is notice to the world that the creditor has an interest in the debtor's property, which the creditor may seize if the debt is not repaid. The PPSA also determines priority among secured creditors. Generally, the first to perfect a security interest in the debtor's property has the right to seize property ahead of other creditors whose interest was perfected later.

At this stage, a PPSA search will reveal what assets the debtor owns that are pledged as collateral to other creditors. The nature and range of assets will reveal something about the debtor's business or, if the debtor is a consumer, their spending habits. It will also identify assets that may not be available for seizure once a judgment has been obtained, because the secured creditor has priority over judgment creditors. If the amount of secured debt is very high, so that none of the assets appear to be available for seizure, it may not be advisable to sue at all because there may be no assets available to be seized and sold to satisfy a judgment. Because the secured creditor is likely to have priority over a later judgment creditor, proceeds of sale after seizure by an unsecured judgment creditor would be used first to pay the secured creditor before proceeds would be available for an ordinary judgment creditor.

After judgment has been obtained, the judgment creditor obtains the right under the PPSA to ask the secured creditor questions about the security agreement with the debtor, including how much the debtor owes the creditor. The legal representative may also write to the secured creditor and ask questions before a judgment has been obtained, but the secured creditor does not have to answer such questions. However, asking questions at this stage sometimes causes the secured creditor to contact the debtor, which may cause the debtor to pay the client.

In order to conduct a PPSA search, the full name of the debtor, including, if possible, the person's middle name must be known. Supplying the debtor's birth date will narrow the search. A search under the name "John Smith" without an accompanying birth date will result in a report with all the registrations against every John Smith in the system. Having the right birth date will help eliminate the John Smiths that the client is not interested in. A search may be conducted for automobiles owned by the debtor, that have been pledged as security, by supplying the VIN.

Filing a PPSA inquiry request results in a report that will identify the category of asset secured along with the secured creditor's name and address. To obtain details about the asset and the debt, it is necessary to contact the secured creditor identified in the report. PPSA searches may be conducted online at the ServiceOntario site at <http://www.ontario.ca/en/services_for_business/access_now/STEL01_086165.html>. There is a fee for the search that varies depending on whether a certified report (one that can be filed as evidence in court) or an uncertified report is ordered.

Payment is by credit card. If the legal representative carries out many PPSA searches, an account can be opened with ServiceOntario. PPSA searches can be conducted online for a fee through Carswell Legal Solutions and Oncorp at the URLs set out previously in this chapter.

Several types of PPSA searches may be carried out:

- *Individual non-specific:* The last name and the first name must be submitted. A legal representative may search for all possible registrations, or registrations within a specific time period.
- *Individual specific:* The last name, first name, and middle initial along with the birth date are submitted.
- *Business debtor inquiry:* The business name is submitted.
- *Motor vehicle inquiry:* The VIN is submitted. This is for the tracking of a vehicle given as collateral no matter who owned the car, or what licence plate was on it.

See Figures 3.6 to 3.9 for completed samples of these forms.

Bank Act Search

In section 427 of the federal *Bank Act*,[9] there are provisions under which a business can borrow from a chartered bank and pledge its property or future property (for example, future crops) as security by giving the bank a section 427 security interest in the property. This results in a transfer of **title** of the debtor's property to the bank until the loan is repaid. During this time, the debtor remains in possession of the collateral and may use it in the ordinary course of business. For example, a fish processor may pledge its fleet of delivery trucks as collateral under section 427. The bank has title and is the legal owner; the debtor continues to use the trucks to deliver goods without interference by the bank unless the loan goes into default. When the loan is repaid, title in the trucks passes back to the debtor.

title
the legal ownership of something; often refers to a document that indicates ownership or an ownership interest—to say someone has title to a car usually means that the car is registered with the province in the name of that person

Bank Act searches are not used for most consumer debtors or small businesses. They are likely to be used in a case where a large business has borrowed significant sums over a long period of time to finance its operations and is in the business of agriculture, aquaculture, or forestry. These are the circumstances that give rise to a section 427 security. A *Bank Act* search is done by examining the registers under the name of the business debtor at the offices of the Bank of Canada. In Ontario, such a search is done through the Canadian Securities Registration Systems office (CSRS) operated by D+H CollateralGuard RC. *Bank Act* searches can also be conducted through Carswell Legal Solutions or ESC Corporate Services (<http://www.eservicecorp.ca/index.php/searches/security-searches/>). There is a fee for the search report, which may be paid by credit card. An entry in the register will give a file number that can be used to obtain further particulars of the loan. If most or all of the business's assets are pledged as security under section 427, there may be very few assets

9 SC 1991, c 46.

available to satisfy the claims of an ordinary judgment debtor, such that suing the business may not be worthwhile.

Section 427 provides for a secured credit registration system similar to that of the PPSA. In fact, assets may be pledged as collateral under both systems. If it is advisable to conduct a *Bank Act* search, it is probably a good idea to do a PPSA search as well; the reverse, however, is not necessarily true, because a PPSA search may be used with consumer debtors and small businesses, whereas a *Bank Act* search would usually be unnecessary for those classes of debtors.

Because creditors may register against the same debtor in both systems, there can be problems in sorting out which creditor has priority over the other. Where two creditors use the PPSA, for example, the PPSA's internal priority ranking rules will determine which of two PPSA creditors of the same debtor has priority. There is, however, no national statutory solution to resolve a priority conflict between a PPSA registration and a *Bank Act* registration, which has its own separate rules for determining priorities among competing section 427 registrants.[10]

Bankruptcy and Insolvency Act Searches

There are two ways to go bankrupt: (1) in certain circumstances, an unpaid creditor who is owed $1,000 or more can put a debtor into bankruptcy using a petition for bankruptcy, or (2) the debtor can make an assignment in bankruptcy. As an alternative to bankruptcy, a debtor who owes up to $250,000 (excluding a mortgage) may make a consumer proposal to their creditors through a trustee in bankruptcy.

A bankruptcy search is useful to determine whether the debtor has gone bankrupt or is about to go bankrupt. If a debtor is bankrupt, there is no point in suing them because any action would be automatically stayed. Instead, the creditor will file a proof of debt claim with the debtor's trustee in bankruptcy. The trustee will review the claim and, if it is in order, the creditor may recover some of the money owing but is unlikely to ever see all of it. Secured creditors are entitled to seize their secured property to satisfy the debt owing to them and to do so ahead of the claims and rights of unsecured creditors claiming through the trustee. Unsecured creditors, which include ordinary judgment creditors, get what is left over. After all of the bankrupt's creditors, both secured and unsecured, have had their interests attended to, the debtor is usually discharged from bankruptcy, free and clear of the debts incurred before bankruptcy, with some exceptions.[11]

As a result of the bankruptcy rules, there is often little of value left for unsecured creditors of the bankrupt. For this reason, unsecured creditors may recover no more than 10 or 20 cents on each dollar owed, because the secured creditors have already taken all the major assets.

---

10 In the case of *Bank of Montreal v Innovative Credit Union*, 2010 SCC 47, the Supreme Court of Canada held that, although a province cannot legislate to oust a bank's rights, it can alter a law as it relates to property and civil rights. A province can, therefore, as Saskatchewan has done, add priority provisions to its provincial PPSA legislation.

11 Although most debts are extinguished on the discharge of the bankrupt, some, such as child support debts and some unpaid student loans, are not.

All bankruptcy searches are done through the Office of the Superintendent of Bankruptcy. All bankruptcies and proposals filed in Canada since 1978 are on file. The Office of the Superintendent of Bankruptcy is represented in each province by its Offices of the Official Receiver. Official Receivers are individuals authorized to handle various functions under the *Bankruptcy and Insolvency Act*.[12] There are four offices of the Official Receiver in Ontario. Their locations are set out below. The toll-free phone number for all locations is 1-877-376-9902.

- 55 Bay Street North, 9th Floor, Hamilton, Ontario L8R 3P7; fax: 905-572-4066.
- 451 Talbot Street, Suite 303, London, Ontario N6A 5C9; fax: 519-645-5139.
- 160 Elgin Street, 11th Floor, Suite B-100, Ottawa, Ontario K2P 2P7; fax: 613-996-0949.
- 25 St. Clair Avenue East, 6th Floor, Toronto, Ontario M4T 1M2; fax: 416-973-7440.

The bankruptcy and insolvency records database, which includes information on bankruptcies, proposals, and receiverships, may be searched online through the Office of the Superintendent of Bankruptcy at <http://www.ic.gc.ca/app/scr/bsf-osb/ins/login.html> or by calling 1-877-376-9902 (toll free) instead. In order to conduct searches the legal representative must establish a Name Search Account with the Office of the Superintendent of Bankruptcy. Registration may be done online at <https://www.ic.gc.ca/cgi-bin/allsites/registration-inscription/mainScreen.cgi>.

A bankruptcy search will also reveal whether the debtor is in receivership. This may happen when a business debtor has defaulted on a loan, which, in some circumstances, gives the creditor the right, on default, to appoint a receiver to run the debtor's business or take it over to liquidate assets. Unless the client has some priority right over the secured lender in this situation, they are unlikely to recover any money, because the secured lender will dispose of virtually all of the assets free of any claim by the client. The Office of the Superintendent of Bankruptcy maintains online records of receiverships nationwide since 1993.

Bankruptcy is discussed in more detail in Chapter 14.

Credit Bureau Searches

Licensed credit bureaus, which can be found online, can provide their members with information on the debtor, including their address, past and present employers, outstanding loans, credit cards, and repayment history. Credit reports will reveal whether the debtor has applied for further credit or been given further loans, and may set out judgments against the debtor as well as information on past bankruptcies and consumer proposals. Only members of a credit bureau can order a report. The debtor must have consented to the search. The client may have obtained the debtor's consent to a credit bureau search if they had the debtor complete a credit application.

---

12 RSC 1985, c B-3, as amended. This Act and other federal legislation are available online at <http://laws.justice.gc.ca>.

Legal service providers can join a credit bureau as a business member. Existing creditors make reports on the debtor's payment record. With this information, creditors can be contacted to obtain more detailed information. Credit bureaus depend on their members to report information about loans, defaults, and payments made by a debtor to get an accurate sense of what kind of credit risk the borrower is. Some credit bureaus have inexpensive online services available to members that allow a search to be done online for a fee. Equifax and TransUnion are good examples, and can be found at <http://www.consumer.equifax.ca/home/en_ca> and <http://www.transunion.ca>, respectively.

Credit bureaus can provide commercial or consumer credit reports. Reports can be ordered online for a business name or an individual's name. As with all searches, the more identifying information that can be supplied about the debtor, the more likely it is that the legal representative will obtain an accurate credit report. A credit report provides broader and more detailed information than the other searches examined so far. However, the information in the report comes from a variety of sources, some of which may be less than accurate, so caution should be observed with respect to the contents of such reports.

Commercial Credit Reports

The following are among the types of information that commercial credit reports, sometimes called business credit reports, will likely provide (these details are from an Equifax commercial credit report). A sample Equifax commercial credit report, using the elements discussed here, is set out in Figure 3.10.

- *Identification:* The debtor is identified by name, address, phone number, the date the file was established, and the reporting agency's file number.
- *Summary:* This provides an overview of the degree of risk and the contents of the report. It may include how creditors have been treated and describe negative information, if any. This part can be quite subjective and should be used with caution. Debtors have the right to have errors corrected by the reporting agency. Information on how to correct a credit record is available on the agency's website.[13]
- *Creditor Information:* This section identifies the industry or reporting creditors for this debtor. It should include when the information was posted. It often provides information about the "aging" of receivables, which describes how long it takes a debtor to pay creditors. The most recently posted information comes first.
- *Payment Trends:* The speed with which payments are received is reported over a two-year period. This allows creditors to view trends and cyclical fluctuations in payment delays that can result from cash flow fluctuations as a result of the nature of the business.

13 Information on correcting a credit bureau report on Equifax can be found at <http://www.consumer.equifax.ca>.

- *Returned Cheques:* This provides details on non sufficient funds (NSF) cheques.
- *Collections Claims:* This reports creditors' collection claims for a five-year period.
- *Legal Information:* This sets out legal information about lawsuits and judgments over a five-year period. Note that not every lawsuit has to do with debts.
- *Information on Bankruptcy:* Information from the Superintendent of Bankruptcy about the debtor for a five-year period is noted here.
- *Banking Information:* When available, information about bank accounts, loans, and lines of credit is reported here.
- *Company Information:* The date of incorporation and information about officers and directors are reported here, if available.
- *Other Files:* If the business has had name changes, or is linked to other business entities, any previous credit files about predecessor business entities will be included here, providing a longer historical payment trail. However, assumptions about current behaviour based on the behaviour of predecessors is risky, because past behaviour may be only remotely linked to present behaviour due to changes in the nature of the business and its management.
- *Recent Inquiries:* There will be a record here of recent inquiries by other creditors about this debtor.
- *Scoring:* From all the details in the report, a credit reporting agency will provide a credit information score indicating overall risk in dealing with the debtor, and a payment index score indicating the percentage of the total amount owing that is past due. These scores are important to creditors when determining the steps they take with respect to a debtor and how quickly they take them. Discussed below is how these two scores are used by Equifax. Other credit reporting agencies use similar scoring techniques.
    - *Credit Information Score:* The higher the score, the greater the risk factor. The lowest possible risk score is zero. A zero score is characteristic of less than 1 percent of all businesses, and would describe a business that pays all debts when accounts are presented. A company with a score of more than 40 is considered to be a high risk. Only about 1.06 percent of all businesses score over 40.

      New companies automatically default to a factor of 20, indicating they are neither very safe, nor very risky. As time goes by, and there are few or no negative reports, the risk factor will drop. If there is a bad payment history, the risk factor will rise.

      If a company is reported by the Superintendent of Bankruptcy, it automatically gets a score of 70, indicating the presence of insolvency proceedings.

      A company that scores between 1 and 10 is considered a very good risk. Only about 15 percent of all businesses fall into this low-risk group. A score of 20 represents a "neutral" risk assessment, and a score of over 20 represents increased risk.

      The score is calculated using the seven factors shown in the score detail section (see page 2 of Figure 3.10).

- *Payment Index Score:* This index takes the amounts owed in the current, first, second, third, and fourth payment periods past due and calculates them as percentages of the total amount owed. It then uses a formula to work out the average number of days that payment is past due. In Canada, the average score is 22. Accounts are often sent to collection when they reach a score of 60. The highest score would be 100, which would mean that everything owing would have to be in the third period past due. This would mean that all the amounts owing have been unpaid for months, which would be evidence of insolvency. The lowest score would be zero, indicating that all bills are paid before the due date. Note that the long-term trend of the scores is more important than the score at the moment. Of interest is whether the risk is increasing, which indicates financial problems, or decreasing, which indicates that the business is doing well. Equifax provides nine quarters, or just over two years' worth of scores.

Consumer Credit Reports

Among the types of information that consumer credit reports will likely provide are the following (details on what an Equifax consumer credit report provides are described here). A sample Equifax consumer credit report that presents the elements discussed here is set out in Figure 3.11.

- *Information on Inquires by Third Parties:* This tells the consumer when inquiries have been made of Equifax and by whom. It also sets out the Equifax contact telephone number.
- *Subject Categories:* This states which subject categories Equifax has received and reported information about the consumer. Only subject categories that contain information about the consumer are included in the report.
- *Consumer Alert and Risk Scores:* Set out here is information about incorrect consumer identification data and alerts about potential fraud. It also sets out scores measuring the consumer's risk of default with some information about details that negatively impact on the risk score.

  Risk of default is measured by a scoring system called "R" ratings, which are known as North American Standard Account Ratings. The "R" represents accounts with revolving credit (such as credit cards, which may have varying balances from month to month). The best possible rating is R1, which indicates that the consumer has always paid this creditor on time. The lowest rating is R9, which indicates a bad debt, such as one that has gone into collection. The spectrum of available "R" designations is as follows:

  R0 There is no information to report. For example, a new account may have been approved but not yet used.

  R1 The debtor pays within 30 days of the due date or has had only one payment past due.

  R2 The debtor pays between 31 and 60 days from the due date or has had two payments past due.

R3 The debtor pays between 61 and 90 days from the due date or has had three payments past due.
R4 The debtor pays between 91 and 120 days from the due date or has had four payments past due.
R5 The debtor is at least 120 days overdue.
R7 The debtor is making regular payments under a special arrangement to settle debts.
R8 Indicates repossession.
R9 Indicates a bad debt, often one placed for collection or in bankruptcy, and may indicate that the debtor moved without giving a new address.

- *Consumer ID:* This section sets out data or information, such as a Social Insurance Number that will help to definitively identify the debtor, including present and past location information such as previous phone numbers.
- *Inquiries:* Persons making inquiries about the consumer's record are recorded here if there are three or more inquiries within 90 days, possibly indicating heightened concerns by creditors of the consumer that there may be payment problems.
- *Employment Information and History:* Information is provided here about who the current employer is, as well as the position held and salary. An employment history is also included.
- *Public Records Relevant to Consumer's Credit:* Included here is information of previous or current bankruptcy, collection agency attempts to recover debts for third parties, lawsuits, and outstanding judgments and financing statements indicating the debtor has pledged property as security under the PPSA.
- *Trade Information:* Recorded here is information about credit granted to the debtor as reported to Equifax, including the history and outcome of the credit transaction, the type of account, and manner of repayment.
- *Banking Information:* Information is provided here about the banks or other financial institutions the debtor deals with, including the type of account, the balance in the account, and other information on account activity.
- *Consumer Statement:* This indicates whether the consumer has reported being the victim of fraud or attempted fraud, and will contain any statement the consumer has filed with Equifax to explain any of the reports in the section.

Credit Score

Each file is assigned a credit score. Lenders rely on this score to assess credit risks. The score is based on payment history, number of debts, balances outstanding, how long accounts have been open and used, and any bankruptcies, consumer proposals, or debt management plans. The amount of credit that has been granted or applied for is factored in as well. The best possible score is 900, 800 is very good, and 600 is good. The lowest score is 300. More information about credit scores can be found on the Financial Consumer Agency of Canada's website at <http://www.fcac-acfc.gc.ca>. Anyone can obtain a copy of their credit bureau report from Equifax or TransUnion for free if it is sent to them by mail; it will be received quicker if it is ordered online, but there is fee for this. Credit scores can only be obtained online. Both Equifax and TransUnion will provide anyone with their credit score for a fee.

Post-Search Strategies

After completing the searches, the information obtained should be reviewed with the client, and instructions about how to proceed should be sought. Usually, legal proceedings to recover the debt will be commenced, but sometimes other remedies are called for.

If it appears that the debtor has recently been transferring assets to others because creditors are closing in, it is advisable to consider some quick steps to prevent further transfer of these assets before suing to collect the debt. It is possible to apply to the courts to "tag" the property so that others will know ownership rights are in dispute, and that the current "owner" may not have good title to the asset and would be unable to transfer it successfully. There is a common law rule that says that people cannot give a better title or greater ownership interest to a purchaser than they themselves have. For example, if a debtor is being sued and transfers their car to their mother for $10, which is well below market value, their mother may not acquire good title. If so, no one will knowingly buy it from the mother because they know that the mother's title is likely to be challenged by someone who has a superior interest, such as the creditor. There are a number of things a creditor in this example can do to "tag" the asset with its superior title interest so that no innocent but careful purchaser would buy the car.

In this situation, the creditor could obtain, in a fairly streamlined and simple procedure, an interim preservation order without notice to the debtor under the *Courts of Justice Act*,[14] section 104, and Rule 45 of the *Rules of Civil Procedure*.[15] The creditor would have to show lawful entitlement to the asset or a right to possess it with which the debtor or others have interfered.

If the property is real property (land) in which the creditor claims an interest, the creditor could obtain a certificate of pending litigation. When the certificate is registered on title, it is notice to the world of the creditor's interest, and the debtor would be unable to transfer any interest to a stranger. In the registration system, a potential purchaser is deemed to have notice of the creditor's interest when the certificate of pending litigation is registered, even if the potential purchaser does not search title. In this situation, a purchaser cannot be a **purchaser in good faith** because they are deemed to know about the creditor's interest and cannot acquire any title to the land that could eliminate the creditor's interest.

If a debtor is about to leave Ontario with their assets to hinder or defeat creditors, it is possible to obtain an injunction to prevent the removal of assets from Ontario.

purchaser in good faith
also called bona fide purchaser; describes an individual who has bought something in circumstances where there is nothing to tell them that the seller is trying to unload the asset quickly for cash before creditors manage to seize the asset or its proceeds; in a bad-faith sale there are usually signs that tip off a reasonable and prudent buyer—for example, a price below fair market value, secrecy in the transaction, undue haste, insistence on payment in cash—so that a purchaser would be presumed to be on notice that the seller's title is flawed or questionable and the purchaser is deemed to acquire ownership subject to the claims of creditors

14 RSO 1990, c C.43.

15 *Supra* note 4.

If the creditor has a security interest in assets of the debtor, it may not be necessary to sue at all. In most secured transactions, the creditor retains the right to seize and sell an asset if there is a default by the debtor, without going to court. Examples include:

- repossessing an automobile using a licensed, private bailiff;
- starting private power of sale proceedings under a land mortgage where the mortgagor (debtor) has defaulted on payments; or
- seizing a commercial tenant's goods using the landlord's remedy of distress on premises where the tenant is in arrears of rent, or evicting the tenant from the premises.

A creditor who has entered into a general security agreement with a debtor usually has the right to privately appoint a receiver. They could also bring an application under the *Bankruptcy and Insolvency Act* for a court-appointed receiver.[16]

Although these private law remedies are attractive because they are fast and inexpensive, those using them must comply with both the letter and spirit of the law. Because the courts do not supervise the process and allow the creditor to run it, if it is not done properly, the debtor can apply to the court for **relief from forfeiture**. If the court finds unfair or inequitable treatment, oppressive behaviour, or failure to comply exactly with required procedure, the court may order return of the asset to the debtor and stay further proceedings.

relief from forfeiture
a remedy granted to a debtor whose property has been seized by a creditor who has acted in an oppressive or capricious manner

In conclusion, if the searches show that the debtor's affairs are hopeless, and there is no chance of recovery of the debt by suing, the creditor may be able to petition the debtor into bankruptcy. This prevents further dissipation of assets. However, if most assets are subject to the interests of secured creditors because they have been given as collateral, there may be very little left to liquidate and use to pay unsecured creditors—but it still may be more than an unsecured creditor would otherwise get if they did nothing. As well, if there is evidence that the debtor is paying some creditors but not others or transferring assets to relatives or friends, then petitioning the debtor into bankruptcy may be advisable because there are provisions available under the Act that can provide remedies for bona fide creditors of the bankrupt that would be otherwise unavailable.

16 RSO 1985, c B-3, s 243, as amended.

CHAPTER SUMMARY

Once it has been determined that a debt is overdue and a client file has been opened, there are a number of things that must be done before commencing a proceeding. In this chapter various searches that should be carried out prior to commencing litigation were reviewed. Such searches can provide the debtor's legal name and address and provide information concerning their assets and liabilities to help determine whether or not they are worth suing. Driver's licence and vehicle searches can be conducted online through ServiceOntario to verify a name and an address, as can online searches through either general search engines like Google, or specialized paid search providers, such as Carswell. Execution, bankruptcy, and PPSA searches can reveal whether the debtor has assets that can be seized to pay the judgment. These searches may also show whether other creditors are trying to collect from the debtor and, if so, whether they have had much success. A credit bureau search may be carried out to obtain information about the debtor's credit history. Once information has been obtained about the debtor's identity, assets, and credit history, the legal representative should speak to the client to determine whether the sensible course of action is to sue or to take other measures.

KEY TERMS

exigible assets, 50
judgment proof, 51
purchaser in good faith, 61
relief from forfeiture, 62
reverse search, 45
stayed, 48
title, 54
writ of seizure and sale, 50

REVIEW QUESTIONS

1. Describe searches that can be used to identify the debtor.
2. Suppose I want to do a driver's licence search to get the debtor's address. Can I go online and get that information?
3. Why is it important to identify the debtor accurately as a legal entity before suing?
4. Explain who can be sued if the debtor is a sole proprietorship, a partnership, or a corporation.
5. What does it mean to "expand enforcement rights" when suing a sole proprietorship or partnership?
6. Describe the searches that can be used to find out information about the debtor that is relevant to the conduct of collection litigation.
7. How does an unsecured credit transaction differ from a secured credit transaction?
8. What problem arises if an asset is pledged as security to two different creditors and one creditor registers its interest under the *Bank Act* while the other creditor registers its interest under the PPSA?
9. What can be done if a creditor finds that the debtor is transferring assets to relatives?
10. In what circumstances is a credit bureau search useful?
11. What is the significance of a credit information score of 35 in a commercial credit report?
12. If a consumer credit report gives the consumer an "R" rating of R1, is this a high or low credit risk?

DISCUSSION QUESTIONS

1. Carol Creditor has come to you with a collection matter. She makes stained glass ornaments and was hired by the Tea for Two Restaurant to create a stained glass canopy depicting lettuce heads to go over the salad bar in the restaurant. She has been dealing with Don Dafoe, the restaurant's manager, who ordered the work done and signed the order form. Carol has heard rumblings that the restaurant may have been sold and that there are other creditors lurking in the wings.

   In this situation, what searches would you perform and why would you perform them? What searches would you not perform?

2. On behalf of a creditor you have done some searches that reveal the following:

   > The debtor carries on the business of a lumber yard. It has given a section 427 security to the Caring Bank for a $100,000 loan, with the security being all of its lumber inventory and all of its vehicles. In addition, it has borrowed from Monopoly Trust and pledged all of its vehicles as collateral for a second loan in the amount of $75,000. A check with the credit bureau indicates that it has not defaulted on any debts, but that payments are often late. There are three executions against the business that were filed five years ago. They total $43,000 and have yet to be paid. Your client has sold supplies to this business on a running account. The account is now at $72,000 and no payments have been made for 65 days. Usually, a payment is received after 40 days.

   a. What options does the client have in this case?
   b. What advice would you give to the client on which option to take and why they should pursue that option?
   c. In pursuing the option you and your client have chosen, what steps do you have to take to achieve your client's goal?

FIGURE 3.1 Statement of Driving Record

Transportation Information Productions System (TIPS) 17/08/11 3:24 PM

Ministry of
Transportation

| central site | feedback | search | site map | français |

Location: Ministry Home > Drivers & Vehicles > Ministry Online Service > Order

Back

Ontario

Ministry of Transportation | Ministère des Transports | Road User Safety Division | Division de la sécurité des usagers de la route

Ministry No./No. Du Ministère Search Date/Date de recherche (Y/A M D/J)
0000-0000-0 1994/08/19

5 YEAR DRIVER RECORD SEARCH/RECHERCHE DANS LE DOSSIER DU CONDUCTEUR DES 5 DERNIÈRES ANNÉES. PAGE 01

DRIVER INFORMATION/DONNÉE DE CONDUCTEUR

Name/Nom **PUBLIC, JOHN, Q.**
Address/Adresse *

Reference No. or Driver's Licence No./
No de référence ou du permis de conduire **P0000-00000-00000**
Date of Birth/Date de naissance (Y/A M D/J) **1990/04/30**
Sex/Sexe **MALE/HOMME**
Height/Taille **175**
Class/Catégorie **G*****
Condition/Restriction ***
Earliest Licence Date Available/Date d'obtention du permis de conduire 2006/08/17
Expiry Date/Date d'expirition (Y/A M D/J) **2019/04/30**
STATUS/STATUT **UNLICENCED/PERMIS DE CONDUIRE EXPIRÉ**
UNRENEWABLE/NON RENOUVELABLE
SUSPENDED/SUSPENDU

DATE CONVICTIONS, DISCHARGES AND OTHER ACTIONS
Y/A M D/J CONDAMNATIONS, LIBÉRATIONS ET AUTRES ACTIONS

13/04/07 REINST - SUSP. EXPIRED OR RESCINDED 1128705
REMIS EN VIGUEUR - SUSP. EXPIRÉE OU ANNULÉE

13/07/06 UNSAFE MOVE
MANOEUVRE DANGEREUSE

15/07/20 SUSPENDED RE UNPAID FINE
SUSPENDU, AMENDE IMPAYÉE
SUSPENSION NO./NO DE SUSPENSION 3050140 EXPIRY DATE: 1994/02/01
DATE D'EXPIRATION: 15/09/01

15/09/01 REINST - SUSP. EXPIRED OR RESCINDED 3050140
REMIS EN VIGUEUR - SUSP. EXPIRÉE OU ANNULÉE

| central site | feedback | search | site map | français |

Page 1 of 2

FIGURE 3.2 Certified Plate Search—Recent Owner

Transportation Information Productions System (TIPS) 17/08/11 3:44 PM

Ministry of Transportation

| central site | feedback | search | site map | français |

Location: Ministry Home > Drivers & Vehicles > Ministry Online Service > Order

Back

Ontario

Ministry of Transportation | Ministère des Transports | Road User Safety Division | Division de la sécurité des usagers de la route

MINISTRY CONTROL NO./NO. DE CONTRÔLE DU MINISTÈRE SEARCH DATE/DATE DE RECHERCHE
000000 12/07/13

SEARCH TYPE/TYPE DE RECHERCHE INQUIRY KEY/ CRITÈRE DE RECHERCHE

PLATE/PLAQUE PLATE/PLAQUE - **AAAAAA**
==
REGISTRANT/CONDUCTEUR
NAME/NOM - **PUBLIC, JOHN, Q.**
ADDRESS/ADRESSE - * STAGGER/ÉCHELONNER - **0930**

-VEHICLE/VÉHICULE
VEHICLE IDENTIFICATION NO./NO D'IDENTIFICATION DU VÉHICULE - **OAOAAOOAOAAOOOOOO**
CLASS/CATÉGORIE - **PASSENGER/VOITURE PARTICULIÈRE** MAKE/MARQUE - **PONT**
MODEL/MODÈLE - **FRS**
BODY TYPE/TYPE DE CARROSSERIE - **2 DOOR SEDAN/COUPÉ**
NO. OF CYLINDERS/NO DE CYLINDRÉE-**04**
MOTIVE POWER/FORCE MOTRICE - **GASOLINE/ESSENCE**
COLOUR/COULEUR - **WHITE/BLANC** YEAR/ANNÉE - **84**
STATUS/STATUT - **FIT/EN ÉTAT DE MARCHE** WEIGHT EMPTY/POIDS À VIDE -
NO. OF AXLES/NO D'ESSIEUX -
ODOMETER ON (YYMMDD)/COMPETUER KILOMÉTRIQUE LE (AAMMJJ) - 00125000 KM 10/01/27

-PLATE/PLAQUE
PLATE/PLAQUE - **000YYY** YEAR/ANNÉE -
SERIES/SÉRIE - **PASSENGER/ VOITURE PARTICULIÈRE**
STATUS/STATUT - **ATTACHED/FIXÉE**
FORMAT -
PLATE REGISTRATION DATE/DATE D'ENREGISTREMENT DES PLAQUES - **910122**
--VALTAG
NO./NO DE VIGNETTE - **0000000** REGISTERED WEIGHT/POIDS ENREGISTRÉ -
DECLARATION/DÉCLARATION -
START/DÉPART - **11/10/01** EXPIRY/EXPIRATION - **12/09/30**
PERMIT NO./NO DE CERTIFICAT - **49815715** DATE ISSUED/DATE DE DÉLIVRANCE - **12/06/25**

Click here to view Application Form

To return to the Product Order, click the back button on your browser.

Pour revenir à la page de commande de produits, cliquez sur le bouton de retour en arrière de votre logiciel de navigation Web.

Page 1 of 2

FIGURE 3.3 Initial Return/Notice of Change

Ontario **Ministry of Government Services**
Central Production and Verification Services Branch
393 University Ave, Suite 200
Toronto ON M5G 2M2

Ministère des Services gouvernementaux
Direction des services centraux de production et de vérification
393, av University, bureau 200
Toronto ON M5G 2M2

For Ministry Use Only
À l'usage du ministère seulement
Page/Page 1 of/de ______

Form 1 - Ontario Corporation Initial Return / Notice of Change
Formule 1 - Personnes morales de l'Ontario Rapport initial / Avis de modification
Corporations Information Act / Loi sur les renseignements exigés des personnes morales

Please type or print all information in block capital letters using black ink.
Prière de dactylographier les renseignements ou de les écrire en caractères d'imprimerie à l'encre noire.

1.

	Initial Return Rapport initial	Notice of Change Avis de modification
Business Corporation/ Société par actions	☐	☐
Not-For-Profit Corporation/ Personne morale sans but lucratif	☐	☐

2. Ontario Corporation Number / Numéro matricule de la personne morale en Ontario: 114836

3. Date of Incorporation or Amalgamation/ Date de constitution ou fusion
Year/Année 2018 Month/Mois 12 Day/Jour 11

For Ministry Use Only
À l'usage du ministère seulement

4. Corporation Name Including Punctuation/Raison sociale de la personne morale, y compris la ponctuation
CHENGOLF LTD.

5. Address of Registered or Head Office/Adresse du siège social
c/o / a/s: MARY CHEN
Street No./N° civique: 60 Street Name/Nom de la rue: CENTRE ST. Suite/Bureau: #3
Street Name (cont'd)/Nom de la rue (suite):
City/Town/Ville: TORONTO **ONTARIO, CANADA**
Postal Code/Code postal: M6Z 3A5

For Ministry Use Only/
À l'usage du ministère seulement

6. Mailing Address/Adresse postale
☑ Same as Registered or Head Office/ Même que siège social
☐ Not Applicable/ Ne s'applique pas
Street No./N° civique
Street Name/Nom de la rue Suite/Bureau
Street Name (cont'd)/Nom de la rue (suite)
City/Town/Ville
Province, State/Province, État Country/Pays Postal Code/Code postal

7. Language of Preference/Langue préférée
English - Anglais ☑ French - Français ☐

8. **Information on Directors/Officers must be completed on Schedule A as requested.** If additional space is required, photocopy Schedule A./**Les renseignements sur les administrateurs ou les dirigeants doivent être fournis dans l'Annexe A, tel que demandé.** Si vous avez besoin de plus d'espace, vous pouvez photocopier l'Annexe A.
Number of Schedule A(s) submitted/Nombre d'Annexes A présentées ☐ (At least one Schedule A must be submitted/Au moins une Annexe A doit être présentée)

9. (Print or type name in full of the person authorizing filing / Dactylographier ou inscrire le prénom et le nom en caractères d'imprimerie de la personne qui autorise l'enregistrement)
I/Je MARY CHEN
certify that the information set out herein, is true and correct.
atteste que les renseignements précités sont véridiques et exacts.

Check appropriate box
Cocher la case pertinente
D) ☑ Director/Administrateur
O) ☐ Officer /Dirigeant
P) ☐ Other individual having knowledge of the affairs of the Corporation/Autre personne ayant connaissance des activités de la personne morale

Note/Remarque : Sections 13 and 14 of the *Corporations Information Act* provide penalties for making false or misleading statements or omissions. Les articles 13 et 14 de la *Loi sur les renseignements exigés des personnes morales* prévoient des peines en cas de déclaration fausse ou trompeuse, ou d'omission.

07200 (2011/06) Page 1 of/de 3

FIGURE 3.3 Initial Return/Notice of Change (*continued*)

Form 1 - Ontario Corporation/Formule 1 - Personnes morales de l'Ontario
Schedule A/Annexe A

For Ministry Use Only
À l'usage du ministère seulement
Page/Page ____ of/de ____

Please type or print all information in block capital letters using black ink. Prière de dactylographier les renseignements ou de les écrire en caractères d'imprimerie à l'encre noire.	Ontario Corporation Number / Numéro matricule de la personne morale en Ontario	Date of Incorporation or Amalgamation / Date de constitution ou fusion (Year/Année Month/Mois Day/Jour)
	114836	2006 12 11

DIRECTOR / OFFICER INFORMATION - RENSEIGNEMENTS RELATIFS AUX ADMINISTRATEURS/DIRIGEANTS

Full Name and Address for Service/Nom et domicile élu

Last Name/Nom de famille: CHEN
First Name/Prénom: MARY
Middle Names/Autres prénoms: A
Street Number/Numéro civique: 60
Suite/Bureau: #3
Street Name/Nom de la rue: CENTRE ST.
Street Name (cont'd)/Nom de la rue (suite):
City/Town/Ville: TORONTO
Province, State/Province, État: ON
Country/Pays: CANADA
Postal Code/Code postal: M6Z 3A5

*OTHER TITLES (Please Specify) / *AUTRES TITRES (Veuillez préciser)
Chair / Président du conseil
Chair Person / Président du conseil
Chairman / Président du conseil
Chairwoman / Présidente du conseil
Vice-Chair / Vice-président du conseil
Vice-President / Vice-président
Assistant Secretary / Secrétaire adjoint
Assistant Treasurer / Trésorier adjoint
Chief Manager / Directeur exécutif
Executive Director / Directeur administratif
Managing Director / Administrateur délégué
Chief Executive Officer / Directeur général
Chief Financial Officer / Agent en chef des finances
Chief Information Officer / Directeur général de l'information
Chief Operating Officer / Administrateur en chef des opérations
Chief Administrative Officer / Directeur général de l'administration
Comptroller / Contrôleur
Authorized Signing Officer / Signataire autorisé
Other (Untitled) / Autre (sans titre)

Director Information/Renseignements relatifs aux administrateurs

Resident Canadian/Résident canadien: ✔ YES/OUI ☐ NO/NON
(Resident Canadian applies to directors of business corporations only.)/
(Résident canadien ne s'applique qu'aux administrateurs de sociétés par actions)

Date Elected/Date d'élection (Year/Année Month/Mois Day/Jour):
Date Ceased/Date de cessation (Year/Année Month/Mois Day/Jour):

Officer Information/Renseignements relatifs aux dirigeants

	PRESIDENT/PRÉSIDENT (Year/Année Month/Mois Day/Jour)	SECRETARY/SECRÉTAIRE (Year/Année Month/Mois Day/Jour)	TREASURER/TRÉSORIER (Year/Année Month/Mois Day/Jour)	GENERAL MANAGER/DIRECTEUR GÉNÉRAL (Year/Année Month/Mois Day/Jour)	*OTHER/AUTRE (Year/Année Month/Mois Day/Jour)
Date Appointed/Date de nomination	2018 12 11				
Date Ceased/Date de cessation					

DIRECTOR / OFFICER INFORMATION - RENSEIGNEMENTS RELATIFS AUX ADMINISTRATEURS/DIRIGEANTS

Full Name and Address for Service/Nom et domicile élu

Last Name/Nom de famille: PARTEN
First Name/Prénom: JOHN
Middle Names/Autres prénoms: E.
Street Number/Numéro civique: 25
Suite/Bureau:
Street Name/Nom de la rue: STIPPARD RD.
Street Name (cont'd)/Nom de la rue (suite):
City/Town/Ville: TORONTO
Province, State/Province, État: ON
Country/Pays: CANADA
Postal Code/Code postal: M4R 1M6

*OTHER TITLES (Please Specify) / *AUTRES TITRES (Veuillez préciser)
Chair / Président du conseil
Chair Person / Président du conseil
Chairman / Président du conseil
Chairwoman / Présidente du conseil
Vice-Chair / Vice-président du conseil
Vice-President / Vice-président
Assistant Secretary / Secrétaire adjoint
Assistant Treasurer / Trésorier adjoint
Chief Manager / Directeur exécutif
Executive Director / Directeur administratif
Managing Director / Administrateur délégué
Chief Executive Officer / Directeur général
Chief Financial Officer / Agent en chef des finances
Chief Information Officer / Directeur général de l'information
Chief Operating Officer / Administrateur en chef des opérations
Chief Administrative Officer / Directeur général de l'administration
Comptroller / Contrôleur
Authorized Signing Officer / Signataire autorisé
Other (Untitled) / Autre (sans titre)

Director Information/Renseignements relatifs aux administrateurs

Resident Canadian/Résident canadien: ✔ YES/OUI ☐ NO/NON
(Resident Canadian applies to directors of business corporations only.)/
(Résident canadien ne s'applique qu'aux administrateurs de sociétés par actions)

Date Elected/Date d'élection (Year/Année Month/Mois Day/Jour): 2018 12 11
Date Ceased/Date de cessation (Year/Année Month/Mois Day/Jour):

Officer Information/Renseignements relatifs aux dirigeants

	PRESIDENT/PRÉSIDENT (Year/Année Month/Mois Day/Jour)	SECRETARY/SECRÉTAIRE (Year/Année Month/Mois Day/Jour)	TREASURER/TRÉSORIER (Year/Année Month/Mois Day/Jour)	GENERAL MANAGER/DIRECTEUR GÉNÉRAL (Year/Année Month/Mois Day/Jour)	*OTHER/AUTRE (Year/Année Month/Mois Day/Jour)
Date Appointed/Date de nomination		2018 12 11			
Date Ceased/Date de cessation					

07200 (2011/06) Page 2 of/de 3

FIGURE 3.4 Enhanced Business Name Search—Search Criteria

ServiceOntario

Integrated Business Services Application

Enhanced Business Name Search - Search Criteria

Caution: The Integrated Business Services Application does not support the Browser's Back button. Changes to information can be done at the Summary Screens.

Help With This Page

You must enter either a Business Name or the Ontario Business Identification Number.

Note: It will take approximately 45 seconds to process your search.

Business Name	Fly-By-Night Enterprises
City	BARRIE
Ontario Business Identification Number	
Type of Search *(Required)*	◉ Enhanced Search ○ Exact Search
Type of Report	Detailed Business Names Report

FIGURE 3.5 Corporation Profile Report

Request ID:	000177620	Province of Ontario	Date Report Produced:	2018/10/21
Transaction ID:	12871109	Ministry of Consumer and Business Services	Time Report Produced:	14:38:07
Category ID:	UN/E	Companies and Personal Property Security Branch	Page:	1

CORPORATION PROFILE REPORT

Ontario Corp Number	Corporation Name	Incorporation Date
1990004	TEST	1993/02/25
		Jurisdiction
		ONTARIO
Corporation Type	**Corporation Status**	**Former Jurisdiction**
ONTARIO BUSINESS CORP.	ACTIVE	NOT APPLICABLE

Registered Office Address

2 QUEEN STREET

Suite # 222
TORONTO
ONTARIO
CANADA M6M 6M6

Mailing Address

2 QUEEN STREET

Suite # 222
TORONTO
ONTARIO
CANADA M6M 6M6

Date Amalgamated	Amalgamation Ind.
NOT APPLICABLE	NOT APPLICABLE
New Amal. Number	Notice Date
NOT APPLICABLE	NOT APPLICABLE
	Letter Date
	NOT APPLICABLE
Revival Date	Continuation Date
NOT APPLICABLE	NOT APPLICABLE
Transferred Out Date	Cancel/Inactive Date
NOT APPLICABLE	NOT APPLICABLE
EP Licence Eff.Date	EP Licence Term.Date
NOT APPLICABLE	NOT APPLICABLE

Number of Directors Minimum	Number of Directors Maximum	Date Commenced in Ontario	Date Ceased in Ontario
UNKNOWN	UNKNOWN	NOT APPLICABLE	NOT APPLICABLE

Activity Classification

NOT AVAILABLE

FIGURE 3.5 Corporation Profile Report (*continued*)

Request ID: 000177620
Transaction ID: 12871109
Category ID: UN/E

Province of Ontario
Ministry of Consumer and Business Services
Companies and Personal Property Security Branch

Date Report Produced: 2018/10/21
Time Report Produced: 14:38:07
Page: 2

CORPORATION PROFILE REPORT

Ontario Corp Number	Corporation Name
1990004	TEST

Corporate Name History	Effective Date
TEST	1993/02/25

Current Business Name(s) Exist: YES

Expired Business Name(s) Exist: YES - SEARCH REQUIRED FOR DETAILS

Administrator: Name (Individual / Corporation)	Address
ADAM EVE	77 5TH STREET KINGSTON ONTARIO CANADA N5N 5N5

Date Began	First Director	
2017/07/01	NOT APPLICABLE	
Designation	**Officer Type**	**Resident Canadian**
DIRECTOR		Y

FIGURE 3.5 Corporation Profile Report (*continued*)

Request ID:	000177620	Province of Ontario	Date Report Produced:	2018/10/21
Transaction ID:	12871109	Ministry of Consumer and Business Services	Time Report Produced:	14:38:07
Category ID:	UN/E	Companies and Personal Property Security Branch	Page:	3

CORPORATION PROFILE REPORT

Ontario Corp Number	Corporation Name
1990004	TEST

Administrator:
Name (Individual / Corporation)

ADAM

EVE

Address

77 5TH STREET

KINGSTON
ONTARIO
CANADA N5N 5N5

Date Began	First Director	
2017/07/01	NOT APPLICABLE	
Designation	**Officer Type**	**Resident Canadian**
OFFICER	GENERAL MANAGER	Y

Administrator:
Name (Individual / Corporation)

JANE

JANENE

Address

99 15TH AVENUE

OTTAWA
ONTARIO
CANADA L7L 6K5

Date Began	First Director	
2016/02/28	NOT APPLICABLE	
Designation	**Officer Type**	**Resident Canadian**
DIRECTOR		Y

FIGURE 3.5 Corporation Profile Report (*continued*)

Request ID: 000177620	Province of Ontario	Date Report Produced:	2018/10/21
Transaction ID: 12871109	Ministry of Consumer and Business Services	Time Report Produced:	14:38:07
Category ID: UN/E	Companies and Personal Property Security Branch	Page:	4

CORPORATION PROFILE REPORT

Ontario Corp Number: 1990004

Corporation Name: TEST

Administrator:
Name (Individual / Corporation)

JANE
JANENE

Address

99 15TH AVENUE

OTTAWA
ONTARIO
CANADA L7L 6K5

Date Began	First Director	
2016/02/28	NOT APPLICABLE	
Designation	**Officer Type**	**Resident Canadian**
OFFICER	PRESIDENT	Y

Administrator:
Name (Individual / Corporation)

JAMES
JONES

Address

2 KING STREET WEST

TORONTO
ONTARIO
CANADA M7M 7M7

Date Began	First Director	
2012/05/05	NOT APPLICABLE	
Designation	**Officer Type**	**Resident Canadian**
DIRECTOR		Y

FIGURE 3.5 Corporation Profile Report (*continued*)

Request ID:	000177620	Province of Ontario		Date Report Produced:	2018/10/21
Transaction ID:	12871109	Ministry of Consumer and Business Services		Time Report Produced:	14:38:07
Category ID:	UN/E	Companies and Personal Property Security Branch		Page:	5

CORPORATION PROFILE REPORT

Ontario Corp Number	Corporation Name
1990004	TEST

Administrator: Name (Individual / Corporation)		Address
JOHN P. SMITHEX		88 QUEEN STREET NORTH TORONTO ONTARIO CANADA L7L 5M5
Date Began	**First Director**	
2017/07/01	NOT APPLICABLE	
Designation	**Officer Type**	**Resident Canadian**
DIRECTOR		Y

Administrator: Name (Individual / Corporation)		Address
JOHN P. SMITHEX		88 QUEEN STREET NORTH TORONTO ONTARIO CANADA L7L 5M5
Date Began	**First Director**	
2017/07/01	NOT APPLICABLE	
Designation	**Officer Type**	**Resident Canadian**
OFFICER	SECRETARY	Y

FIGURE 3.5 Corporation Profile Report (*continued*)

Request ID:	000177620	Province of Ontario	Date Report Produced:	2018/10/21
Transaction ID:	12871109	Ministry of Consumer and Business Services	Time Report Produced:	14:38:07
Category ID:	UN/E	Companies and Personal Property Security Branch	Page:	6

CORPORATION PROFILE REPORT

Ontario Corp Number	Corporation Name
1990004	TEST

Last Document Recorded

Act/Code	Description	Form	Date
CIA	CHANGE NOTICE	1	2018/08/30 (ELECTRONIC FILING)

THIS CORPORATION HAS RECEIVED A NOTICE OF INTENTION TO DISSOLVE ON THE DATE INDICATED IN THE "NOTICE DATE" FIELD AND IS SUBJECT TO CANCELLATION.

THIS REPORT SETS OUT THE MOST RECENT INFORMATION FILED BY THE CORPORATION ON OR AFTER JUNE 27, 1992, AND RECORDED IN THE ONTARIO BUSINESS INFORMATION SYSTEM AS AT THE DATE AND TIME OF PRINTING. ALL PERSONS WHO ARE RECORDED AS CURRENT DIRECTORS OR OFFICERS ARE INCLUDED IN THE LIST OF ADMINISTRATORS.

ADDITIONAL HISTORICAL INFORMATION MAY EXIST ON THE COMPANIES AND PERSONAL PROPERTY SECURITY BRANCH MICROFICHE.

The issuance of this report in electronic form is authorized by the Director of Companies and Personal Property Security Branch

FIGURE 3.6 **PPSA Search—Individual Non-Specific**

ServiceOntario

Login New Enquiry

Individual Non-Specific Enquiry

File Currency: **23JUL 2017** Help

Fields marked with an asterisk (*) are mandatory.

First Name:	MARY
Last Name:	CHEN
Retrieve Registrations:*	◉ All Registrations ○ Starting From: Day Month Year
Report format:*	◉ View online ○ Order a certificate

Cancel Submit

FIGURE 3.7 **PPSA Search—Individual Specific**

ServiceOntario

Login New Enquiry

Individual Specific Enquiry

File Currency: **23JUL 2017** Help

Fields marked with an asterisk (*) are mandatory.

First Name:	MARY
Middle Initial:	A
Last Name:	CHEN
Date of Birth:*	Day 17 Month OCT Year 1958
Retrieve Registrations:*	◉ All Registrations ○ Starting From: Day Month Year
Report format:*	◉ View online ○ Order a certificate

Cancel Submit

FIGURE 3.8 PPSA Search—Business Debtor Enquiry

ServiceOntario

Login New Enquiry

Business Debtor Enquiry

File Currency: **23JUL 2017** Help

Fields marked with an asterisk (*) are mandatory.

Business Name:*	MARY'S GOLF DRIVING RANGE
Retrieve Registrations:*	◉ All Registrations ○ Starting From: Day [ ] Month [ ] Year [ ]
Report format:*	◉ View online ○ Order a certificate

Cancel Submit

FIGURE 3.9 PPSA Search—Motor Vehicle Enquiry

ServiceOntario

Login New Enquiry

Motor Vehicle Enquiry

File Currency: **23JUL 2017** Help

Fields marked with an asterisk (*) are mandatory.

Vehicle Identification Number:*	84321AA6021C62
Select Enquiry Type:*	◉ Exact ○ Exact & Similar ○ Condensed
Retrieve Registrations:*	◉ All Registrations ○ Starting From: Day [ ] Month [ ] Year [ ]
Report format:*	◉ View online ○ Order a certificate

Cancel Submit

FIGURE 3.10 Sample Commercial Credit Report

EQUIFAX — COMMERCIAL INFORMATION SOLUTIONS

BUSINESS CREDIT REPORT

Business information

Company name	EQUIFAX-PRD TEST FILE 8	Requestor ID	GTREM
Legal name		Reference number	
Address	8888888 NOTAREALADDRESS KIMMIRUT JAPAN X0A0N0	Report date	2015-04-01
		File in database since	2012-09-14
		File-number	0105766807
Phone	(514) 493-7590	Subject number	EFF284
Fax	(514) 493-7590		

Reported Date	Owner/Principal Name	Reported Date	Owner/Principal Name
2015-03-27	ROBERT BRENNAN	2014-02-13	ELSTON JOHN GREG AMORLIAN

Additional business information and firmographics

Other known tradestyles

EQUIFAX-PRD TEST FILE 6

Additional information may be included in the "Other files included" section.

Reported	Business contact/title	Incorporation number/ Effective date
2015-03-31		1010101 2010-12-28

Reported	Employee size	Reported	Sales volume
2015-03-27	Full Time 1000	2015-03-27	Sales $10.00B

SIC	NAICS
79960000-Amusement Parks	71311000-Amusement &Theme Parks

Score summary

CI 25 (scale 0 10 20 30 40 50 60 70) — Will I get paid?

CDS 241 (scale 700 600 500 400 300 200 100 0) — Likelihood of severe delinquency

PI 19 (scale 0 10 20 30 40 50 60 70 80 90 100) — When will I get paid?

BFRS 1318 (scale 1800 1600 1400 1200 1000 800) — Likelihood company will cease business

Report Highlights and Alerts

	Financial	Non Financial		Alerts
Number of Accounts Reporting	4	4	# of Collections	1
Number of Delinquencies	1	3	**Total Amount**	$223,333
Delinquency Amount	$1,000	$101,500	**Most recent date**	2013-09-09
Most Severe Status	Period 2 Past Due Am	Bad Debt	# of Legal items	1
			Total Amount	$50,000
Date	2015-03-27	2015-02-27	**Most recent date**	2011-11-11
Single Highest Credit			# of Judgments	1

FIGURE 3.10 Sample Commercial Credit Report (*continued*)

90 Day Single Highest Credit	$20.00M	$500,000	**Total Amount**	$50,000
13 Month Single Highest Credit	$20.00M	$500,000	**Most recent date**	2012-12-12
All Lines Single Highest Credit	$20.00M	$500,000	# of Returned cheques	1
Credit Limit			**Total Amount**	$50,000
90 Day Credit Limit	$20,000	$1.03M	**Most recent date**	2014-03-03
13 Month Credit Limit	$38,000	$1.03M	# of Liens	1
All Lines Credit Limit	$38,000	$1.03M	**Total Amount**	$10,000
Charge Offs			**Most recent date**	2015-04-01
Number of accounts charged off	0	1	Bank report on file	2014-12-12
Total amount charged off	$0	$4.00M	Corporate search on file	2015-03-31
Largest charge off amount	$0	$4.00M	# of inquiries on file	0
Date	-	2014-12-31	**# financial lines guaranteed**	2
Total Current Credit Exposure	$50,200	$411,000	**Excess of limits financial line**	0
Total Outstanding	$1.01M	$411,000	**% Utilization of Revolving financial lines**	13%
Total Current Balance	$1.00M	$309,500		
Total Past Due	$1,000	$101,500	**% Utilization Fixed Financial Lines**	5%

Principal/Guarantor Associated Businesses

Principal(P)/Guarantor(G)	Subject Number	Company Name	Address	Date In Database Since
ELSTON JOHN GREG AMORLIAN(P)	EFF284	EQUIFAX-PRD TEST FILE 2	CE2222222 NOTAREALADDRESS KIMMIRUTJAPAN X0A0N0	2012-09-14

Score detail

CI 25

Long-term secured debt is NOT included in the Credit Information calculation.

The Credit Information score for this business was determined based on the following*:

	Score
Active in Equifax credit database for 03 years	6
Current Payment Index is 19	0
Number of Supplier references on file is 2	8
On 2015-04-01 the Payment Index was 0 points higher than 2014-04-01	0
Number of derogatory items on file in the past 2 years is 2	3
The most recent derogatory item was recorded 13 months ago	0
Derogatory item amounts as a % of dollars owed suppliers is 88	8

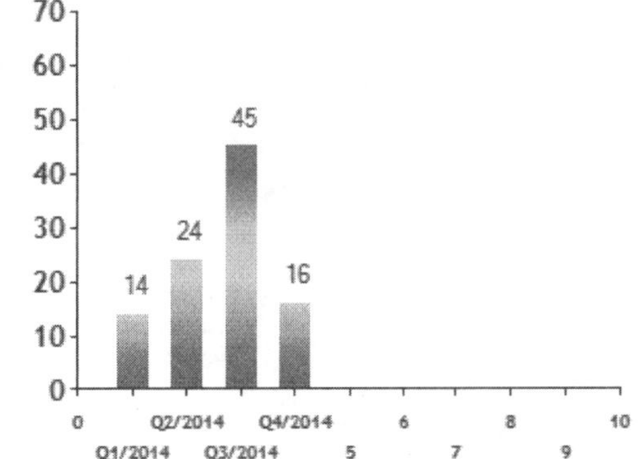

PI 19

Long-term secured debt is NOT included in the Payment Index calculations.

FIGURE 3.10 Sample Commercial Credit Report (*continued*)

The Payment Index is similar to "days beyond terms." The following ranges were calculated as benchmarks:

	Payment index	% of database
All suppliers reported being paid within terms	0	62
Average to pay is slightly beyond terms	1-10	11
Average pay is 10 to 20 days beyond terms	11-20	8
Average pay is 20 to 30 days beyond terms	21-30	5
Average pay is 30 to 40 days beyond terms	31-40	6
Only 1% of businesses fall into this range	41-90	5
All suppliers reported being paid in the third period past due or not at all	91-100	3
No suppliers reported in this time period	NA	NA

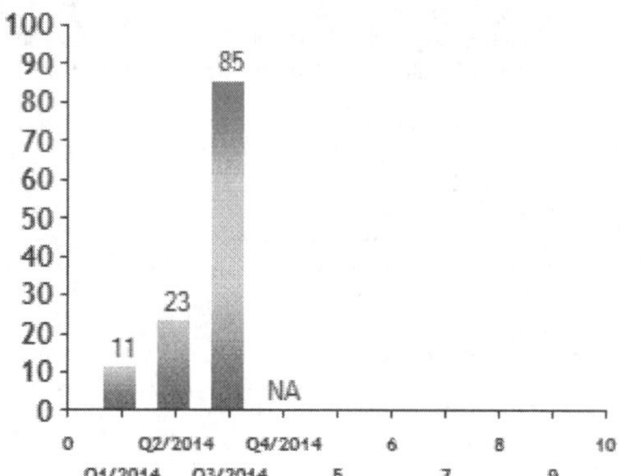

CDS 241

11 Percentage of Period 3 Accounts Suggests Higher Risk
5 Evidence of Returned Cheque(s)
7 Percentage of Satisfactory Accounts Suggests Higher Risk
17 Current Balance Trend Suggests Higher Risk

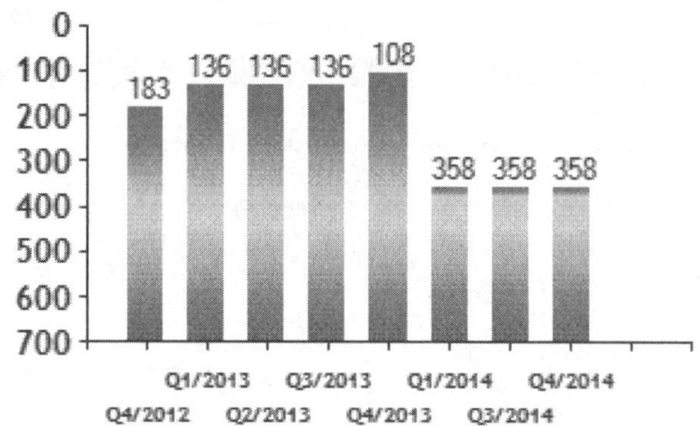

BFRS 1318

31 All Lines Period 3 Amount Suggests Higher Risk
4 Evidence of Suit(s) or Judgment(s)
5 Evidence of Derogatory Items
45 Number of Inquires in Last 12 Months Suggests Higher Risk

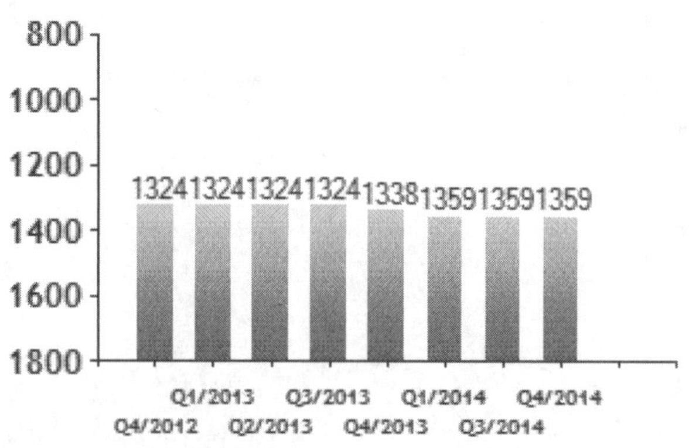

FIGURE 3.10 Sample Commercial Credit Report (*continued*)

Industry trade summary

	PI score	Number of credit references	High credit	Total owing	Current	Period 1	Period 2	Period 3
90 Day	19	2	$525,000	$310,000	$209,000	$51,000	$25,000	$25,000
13 Month	19	3	$526,000	$311,000	$209,500	$51,100	$25,200	$25,200
All References	14	4	$726,000	$411,000	$309,500	$51,100	$25,200	$25,200

Industry trade detail — Tabular View

In some situations, payments beyond terms can be a result of misplaced invoices or disputed accounts. Equifax reports trade items as they are received and as such they represent an historical experience. An outstanding amount on this report is not necessarily still outstanding today.

# indicates long term secured debt, which is NOT included in the Payment Index and Credit Information Score calculation.

Date Reported 2015-02-27

SIC	73000000-Business Services		
Terms	Net 60 Days	Account opened	2010-12-28
Pay habits	Bad Debt	Total past due	$100,000
Status	Written Off	Write off amount/ date	$4.00M 2014-12-31
	Takes Discount		

Original credit limit/date	High credit/ date	Total balance	Current balance	Balance amount: Period 1	Period 2	Period 3
$1.00M 2010-12-28	$500,000	$300,000	$200,000	$50,000	$25,000	$25,000

Date Reported 2015-01-01

SIC	60000000-Deposit Institutions		
Terms	Net 30 Days	Account opened	2003-01-01
Pay habits	Slow 1	Total past due	$1,000
Status	Account Secured		

Original credit limit/date	High credit/ date	Total balance	Current balance	Balance amount: Period 1	Period 2	Period 3
$0	$25,000	$10,000	$9,000	$1,000	$0	$0

Date Reported 2014-03-27

SIC	73000000-Business Services		
Supplier	EQUIFAX INDUSTRY GRP	Account opened	2013-03-20
Phone	(514) 493-7894	Total past due	$500
Terms	Net 30 Days		
Pay habits	Satisfactory		

Original credit limit/date	High credit/ date	Total balance	Current balance	Balance amount: Period 1	Period 2	Period 3
$0	$1,000	$1,000	$500	$100	$200	$200

Date Reported 2012-03-27

SIC	73000000-Business Services		
		Total past due	$0

Original credit limit/date	High credit/ date	Total balance	Current balance	Balance amount: Period 1	Period 2	Period 3
$0	$200,000	$100,000	$100,000	$0	$0	$0

Quarterly industry payment trend

Year/ quarter	Payment index	Credit information score	Number of references	Total amount	Current amount	Trend amount: Period 1	Period 2	Period 3
2014/4	NA	16	0	$0	$0	$0	$0	$0
2014/3	85	45	3	$5,000	$0	$0	$2,000	$3,000
2014/2	23	24	2	$1,000	$0	$1,000	$0	$0

FIGURE 3.10 Sample Commercial Credit Report (*continued*)

2014/1	11	14	1	$1,000	$1,000	$0	$0	$0

Financial Trade Details

#	SIC# / Supplier Name / Guarantor indicator Date Reported DLA	Date Opened Date Closed	Credit Limit High Credit	Schd Pymnt Amt Actual Pymnt Amt	Balance Past Due	Account Type Rating	Payment Type Freq 1, Freq2	30/60/90 Trade Pymnt Profile
1	73000000 / Business Services / 1							
	2015-03-27	2014-03-20	$20,000	$0	$4,000	CREDIT CRD		00001/00000/ 00000
	2015-03-20	2015-03-27	$10,000	$200	$1,000	R2	Mthly, -	2BBBBBBBBBBB BBBBBBBBBBBB BBBBBBBBBBBB
2	73000000 / Business Services / 2							
	2015-02-01	2014-01-03	$0	$50,000	$1.00M	Secured		00000/00000/ 00000
	2015-01-30		$20.00M	$50,000	$0	I1	BWkly, -	*BBBBBBBBBBB BBBBBBBBBBBB BBBBBBBBBBBB
3	61000000 / Lending Institution / 0							
	2014-10-16	2003-03-31	$10,000	$0	$0			00000/00000/ 00000
			$0	$0	$0	R1	Mthly, -	*****1BBBBBB BBBBBBBBBBBB BBBBBBBBBBBB
4	60000000 / Deposit Institutions / 0							
	2014-10-16	2008-04-17	$8,000	$0	$0	Overdraft		00000/00000/ 00000
			$0	$0	$0	R1	Mthly, -	*****1BBBBBB BBBBBBBBBBBB BBBBBBBBBBBB

	Credit Limit High Credit	Schd Pymnt Amt Actual Pymnt Amt	Total Balance Past Due
Total	$38,000 $20.01M	$50,000 $50,200	$1.01M $1,000
% Utilization – revolving credit		13%	
% Utilization – fixed credit		5%	

Guarantor Information

Financial Trade #	Number of the Guarantor	Guarantor	Additional Names	Address Information
1	1.1	JOHN P GEORGE		
2	2.1	TEST REALLY TES T EQUIFAX		
2	2.2	EQUIFAX PRD TES T GUARANTOR	EFX CA TEST	

Returned cheque details

The data presented here represents returned cheque information as reported by the creditor. If you are interested in submitting your returned cheque data, you may do so by contacting 1-877-227-8800 or 416-227-8800.

Bank date	Cheque amount	Bank	Creditor name	Reason	Status	Comment
2014-03-03	$50,000	BANQUE ROYALE		NSF	Not Replaced	

Collection detail

The data presented here represents collection information as reported by the collection agency noted. In some situations, accounts are sometimes placed for collection even though the account is disputed.

FIGURE 3.10 Sample Commercial Credit Report (*continued*)

Reported	Creditor		Collection agency	EQUIFAX CANADA TEST
2015-03-27	Debtor	EQUIFAX-PRD TEST FILE 8	Status update	2013-09-09
Claim placed	Claim amount	$223,333	Date paid	2013-02-08
2013-09-09	Amount paid	$22	Closed	
	Account balance	$223,311		
	Status	Disputed Account		

Legal details

Legal Information - suits

Reported	Counter Claim		Court	Court of Appeal
2015-03-27	Defendant	EQUIFAX-PRD TEST FILE 8		Calgary
Claim date/number	Plaintiff	JON'S LUNCH		NUNAVUT
2011-11-11	Amount	$50,000	Security	
08121212	Reason	Breach of Agreement		

Legal Information - judgments

Reported	Calculation-Deficiency Judg.		Court	Bank of Canada
2015-03-27	Defendant	EQUIFAX-PRD TEST FILE 8		Calgary
Claim date/number	Plaintiff	JON'S LUNCH		NUNAVUT
2012-12-12	Amount	$50,000	Security	
3323423	Reason	Agreement		

Other legal information

Reported	Affidavif of Deficiency		Court	Court of Appeal
2015-03-27	Defendant	EQUIFAX-PRD TEST FILE 8		Abitibi
Claim date/number	Plaintiff	NUB'S BOATS		NUNAVUT
2015-03-20	Amount	$9.00M	Security	
3232323	Reason	Agreement of Sale		

Corporate search and additional business information

Verified	Registration number/type	Jurisdiction location/type	Effective date
2015-03-31	1010101 Incorporation	Nunavut Provincial Charter	2010-12-28

Reported	Registration number/type	Jurisdiction location/type	Effective date
2015-03-31	6756343 Incorporation	Quebec Provincial Charter	2014-02-14

Reported	Business contact	Title	Shares owned
2015-03-27	ROBERT P BRENNAN SR	President	100

Reported	Business contact	Title	Shares owned
2014-02-13	ELSTON JOHN ELSTON JOHN GREG AMORLIAN MR	President	100

Reported	Ownership/source	Property covered/address	Property value/ evaluation date
2015-03-27	Owned Officer of Company	Buildings and Land 284 DALLAS,KIMMIRUT, NU	500000 2015-02-20

Date	Employee size	Date	Sales volume
2015-03-27	(R) Full Time 1000	2015-03-27	(R) Net Worth $10,000 (R) Sales $10.00B

FIGURE 3.10 Sample Commercial Credit Report (*continued*)

(R) Total Liabilities $33,234
(R) Account Receivable $3.25M
(R) Accounts Payable $354,233
(R) Total Assets $3,412
(R) Net Income $3,223
(R) Net Income $2,312
(R) Revenue $3.22M
(R) Budget $2.13M
(R) Subsidy $134,123
(R) Information Declined $123,341
(R) New Business $321,421
(R) Not Available $23,123

Banking report detail

Reported 2014-12-12	Name	ROYAL BANK OF CANADA HALIFAX NS ALMON ST BR Branch:003 Transit:02533	Last change date	2015-03-27
	Address	5805 ALMON ST HALIFAX, NOVA SCOTIA, B3K1T7 CANADA	Reference phone	(902) 332-3333
	Phone		Reference fax	(902) 222-2222
	Fax		Signing officer/special comment	

Open date 2013-12-28	Number of accounts		Account type	Canadian account
	Balance	Number of returned cheques	Frequency	Reason
	$400,000 to $1.00M			

Open date 2010-12-12	Number of credit lines		Credit line type	Credit letter
	Secured by	Rating	Authorized amount	Utilization
	Farm	Paid as agreed	$1.00M to $2.00M	5%

Open date 2010-12-12 — Number of loans

Loan type	Rating	Terms	Secure by	Authorized amount	Balance owing
Alberta farm development loan	I1		Assignment of accounts receivable Assets	$1.00M to $2.00M	$500,000 to $2.00M

** ** Bank Information Updates are available at a reasonable cost – Tel. 1-877-254-3263

Liens detail

Reported 2015-04-01	Lien number	54589796	Date registered	2015-04-01
	Caution filing	None Reported	Amendment date	
	Principal amount	$10,000	Maturity date	
	Lien period	20	Renewal period	20
	Collateral class/ description	Consumer Goods		
	Debtor name	EQUIFAX DQ TEST	Secured party	EQUIFAX TEST
	Address	5689 GALERIE D'ANJOU KIMMIRUT NUNAVUT CANADA	Address	7100 JEAN TALON ANJOU QUEBEC H1M0A3

FIGURE 3.10 Sample Commercial Credit Report (*continued*)

	CANADA
Party assignor	ROBERT BRENNAN VP

VIN	Year/make/body type
S59687X5689R754	2010/KIA CANADA INC/SEDAN

Other files included

Equifax has received information that the following names and addresses are related to this business. These could be: Different spelling of the business name, former addresses or names, branch location whose invoices are paid from on central locations, PO Box addresses, etc. Regardless of which address you've chosen to pull this report for, the information is identical.

Company number	Subject number	Company name	Address
0105766785	EFF282	EQUIFAX-PRD TEST FILE 6	6666666 NOTAREALADDRESS KIMMIRUT X0A0N0 JAPAN

Inquiries

An inquiry is registered when a report on this business is ordered by an Equifax Customer. Few or no inquiries may indicate that a business is not an active credit seeker. Numerous inquiries indicate that the business is an active credit seeker. However, you may want to consider the following in your review:

- Does the number of inquiries seem appropriate for a business that size?
- Is this business shopping around for better supplier arrangements?
- Are they having problems paying their current suppliers and looking for credit from others unaware of their problems?
- Are they expanding, moving locations or opening another office?
- Are their current suppliers not meeting their current needs?

The most recent inquiries in the past 24 months are listed here:

Inquiry date	Requestor SIC	Company name	Phone
2015-04-01	73000000-Business Services	EQUIFAX INDUSTRY GRP	514-493-7894

Customer service — If you have any questions about this report, please call Equifax Business Service at 1-877-227-8800 or 416-227-8800. If you are concerned about the content of this report, please contact the Equifax Commercial Disclosure department by email at commercial.disclosure@equifax.com.

FIGURE 3.11 Sample Consumer Credit Report

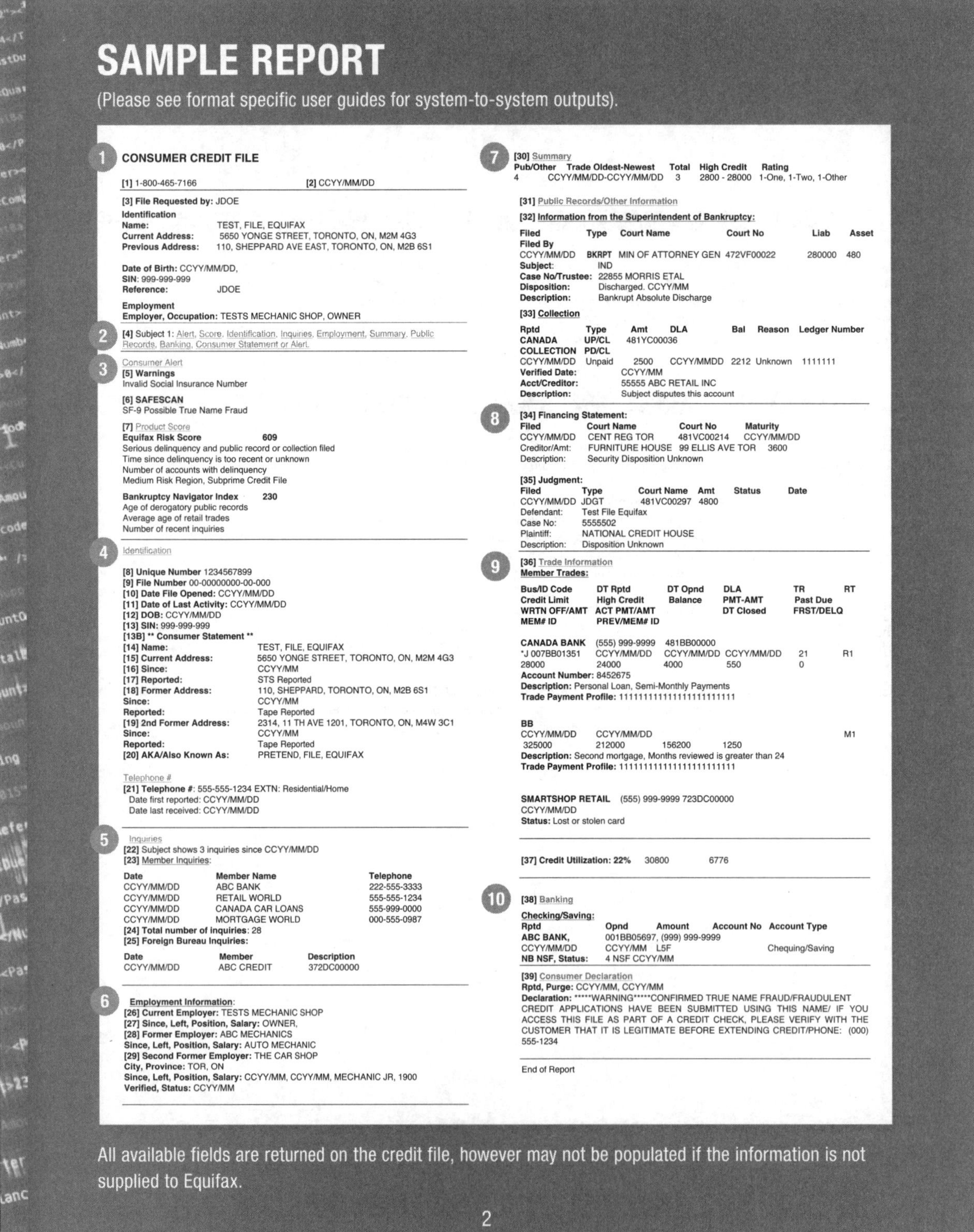

SAMPLE REPORT

(Please see format specific user guides for system-to-system outputs).

1 **CONSUMER CREDIT FILE**

[1] 1-800-465-7166 [2] CCYY/MM/DD

[3] File Requested by: JDOE

Identification
Name: TEST, FILE, EQUIFAX
Current Address: 5650 YONGE STREET, TORONTO, ON, M2M 4G3
Previous Address: 110, SHEPPARD AVE EAST, TORONTO, ON, M2B 6S1

Date of Birth: CCYY/MM/DD,
SIN: 999-999-999
Reference: JDOE

Employment
Employer, Occupation: TESTS MECHANIC SHOP, OWNER

2 [4] Subject 1: Alert, Score, Identification, Inquiries, Employment, Summary, Public Records, Banking, Consumer Statement or Alert.

3 Consumer Alert
[5] Warnings
Invalid Social Insurance Number

[6] SAFESCAN
SF-9 Possible True Name Fraud

[7] Product Score
Equifax Risk Score **609**
Serious delinquency and public record or collection filed
Time since delinquency is too recent or unknown
Number of accounts with delinquency
Medium Risk Region, Subprime Credit File

Bankruptcy Navigator Index **230**
Age of derogatory public records
Average age of retail trades
Number of recent inquiries

4 Identification

[8] Unique Number 1234567899
[9] File Number 00-00000000-00-000
[10] Date File Opened: CCYY/MM/DD
[11] Date of Last Activity: CCYY/MM/DD
[12] DOB: CCYY/MM/DD
[13] SIN: 999-999-999
[13B] ** Consumer Statement **
[14] Name: TEST, FILE, EQUIFAX
[15] Current Address: 5650 YONGE STREET, TORONTO, ON, M2M 4G3
[16] Since: CCYY/MM
[17] Reported: STS Reported
[18] Former Address: 110, SHEPPARD, TORONTO, ON, M2B 6S1
Since: CCYY/MM
Reported: Tape Reported
[19] 2nd Former Address: 2314, 11 TH AVE 1201, TORONTO, ON, M4W 3C1
Since: CCYY/MM
Reported: Tape Reported
[20] AKA/Also Known As: PRETEND, FILE, EQUIFAX

Telephone #
[21] Telephone #: 555-555-1234 EXTN: Residential/Home
Date first reported: CCYY/MM/DD
Date last received: CCYY/MM/DD

5 Inquiries
[22] Subject shows 3 inquiries since CCYY/MM/DD
[23] Member Inquiries:

Date	Member Name	Telephone
CCYY/MM/DD	ABC BANK	222-555-3333
CCYY/MM/DD	RETAIL WORLD	555-555-1234
CCYY/MM/DD	CANADA CAR LOANS	555-999-0000
CCYY/MM/DD	MORTGAGE WORLD	000-555-0987

[24] Total number of inquiries: 28
[25] Foreign Bureau Inquiries:

Date	Member	Description
CCYY/MM/DD	ABC CREDIT	372DC00000

6 Employment Information:
[26] Current Employer: TESTS MECHANIC SHOP
[27] Since, Left, Position, Salary: OWNER,
[28] Former Employer: ABC MECHANICS
Since, Left, Position, Salary: AUTO MECHANIC
[29] Second Former Employer: THE CAR SHOP
City, Province: TOR, ON
Since, Left, Position, Salary: CCYY/MM, CCYY/MM, MECHANIC JR, 1900
Verified, Status: CCYY/MM

7 [30] Summary

Pub/Other	Trade Oldest-Newest	Total	High Credit	Rating
4	CCYY/MM/DD-CCYY/MM/DD	3	2800 - 28000	1-One, 1-Two, 1-Other

[31] Public Records/Other Information

[32] Information from the Superintendent of Bankruptcy:

Filed Filed By	Type	Court Name	Court No	Liab	Asset
CCYY/MM/DD	BKRPT	MIN OF ATTORNEY GEN	472VF00022	280000	480

Subject: IND
Case No/Trustee: 22855 MORRIS ETAL
Disposition: Discharged. CCYY/MM
Description: Bankrupt Absolute Discharge

[33] Collection

Rptd	Type	Amt	DLA	Bal	Reason	Ledger Number
CANADA	**UP/CL**	481YC00036				
COLLECTION	**PD/CL**					
CCYY/MM/DD	Unpaid	2500	CCYY/MMDD	2212	Unknown	1111111

Verified Date: CCYY/MM
Acct/Creditor: 55555 ABC RETAIL INC
Description: Subject disputes this account

8 **[34] Financing Statement:**

Filed	Court Name	Court No	Maturity
CCYY/MM/DD	CENT REG TOR	481VC00214	CCYY/MM/DD

Creditor/Amt: FURNITURE HOUSE 99 ELLIS AVE TOR 3600
Description: Security Disposition Unknown

[35] Judgment:

Filed	Type	Court Name	Amt	Status	Date
CCYY/MM/DD	JDGT	481VC00297	4800		

Defendant: Test File Equifax
Case No: 5555502
Plaintiff: NATIONAL CREDIT HOUSE
Description: Disposition Unknown

9 [36] Trade Information
Member Trades:

Bus/ID Code Credit Limit WRTN OFF/AMT MEM# ID	DT Rptd High Credit ACT PMT/AMT PREV/MEM# ID	DT Opnd Balance	DLA PMT-AMT DT Closed	TR Past Due FRST/DELQ	RT
CANADA BANK	(555) 999-9999	481BB00000			
*J 007BB01351	CCYY/MM/DD	CCYY/MM/DD	CCYY/MM/DD	21	R1
28000	24000	4000	550	0	

Account Number: 8452675
Description: Personal Loan, Semi-Monthly Payments
Trade Payment Profile: 1111111111111111111111

BB					
CCYY/MM/DD	CCYY/MM/DD				M1
325000	212000	156200	1250		

Description: Second mortgage, Months reviewed is greater than 24
Trade Payment Profile: 1111111111111111111111

SMARTSHOP RETAIL (555) 999-9999 723DC00000
CCYY/MM/DD
Status: Lost or stolen card

[37] Credit Utilization: 22% 30800 6776

10 [38] Banking

Checking/Saving:

Rptd	Opnd	Amount	Account No	Account Type
ABC BANK,	001BB05697, (999) 999-9999			
CCYY/MM/DD	CCYY/MM	L5F		Chequing/Saving
NB NSF, Status:	4 NSF CCYY/MM			

[39] Consumer Declaration
Rptd, Purge: CCYY/MM, CCYY/MM
Declaration: *****WARNING*****CONFIRMED TRUE NAME FRAUD/FRAUDULENT CREDIT APPLICATIONS HAVE BEEN SUBMITTED USING THIS NAME/ IF YOU ACCESS THIS FILE AS PART OF A CREDIT CHECK, PLEASE VERIFY WITH THE CUSTOMER THAT IT IS LEGITIMATE BEFORE EXTENDING CREDIT/PHONE: (000) 555-1234

End of Report

All available fields are returned on the credit file, however may not be populated if the information is not supplied to Equifax.

2

FIGURE 3.11 Sample Consumer Credit Report (*continued*)

1

[1] 1-800-465-7166 **[2]** CCYY/MM/DD

[3] File Requested by: JDOE
Identification
Name: TEST, FILE, EQUIFAX
Current Address: 5650 YONGE STREET, TORONTO, ON, M2M 4G3
Previous Address: 110, SHEPPARD AVE EAST, TORONTO, ON, M2B 6S1

Date of Birth: CCYY/MM/DD,
SIN: 999-999-999
Reference: JDOE

Employment
Employer, Occupation: TESTS MECHANIC SHOP, OWNER

[1] **CONSUMER REFERRAL TELEPHONE NUMBER:** Consumers to be provided referral telephone number for Equifax as required.

[2] Date of file request by the member.

[3] **INQUIRY DATA:** Data submitted to EFX by the member to request the file.

2

[4] Subject 1: Alert, Score, Identification, Inquiries, Employment, Summary, Public Records, Banking, Consumer Statement or Alert.

[4] **SUBJECT 1:** Sections of the current file that are populated and displayed.

3

Consumer Alert
[5] Warnings
Invalid Social Insurance Number

[6] SAFESCAN
SF-9 Possible True Name Fraud

[7] Product Score
Equifax Risk Score **609**
Serious delinquency and public record or collection filed
Time since delinquency is too recent or unknown
Number of accounts with delinquency
Medium Risk Region, Subprime Credit File

Bankruptcy Navigator Index **230**
Age of derogatory public records
Average age of retail trades
Number of recent inquiries

[5] **CONSUMER FILE ALERT:** Information input on inquiry does not match file or is invalid.

[6] **SAFESCAN WARNING:** Fraud alert message warns you of potential application fraud. *(Available only to SafeScan subscribers)*

[7] **SCORES AND REASON CODES:** A risk score accompanied by up to three reason codes and score card indicator. Provides details on what information on file had a negative impact on the score (even if minimal impact). *(Available only to risk score subscribers).*

3

FIGURE 3.11 Sample Consumer Credit Report (*continued*)

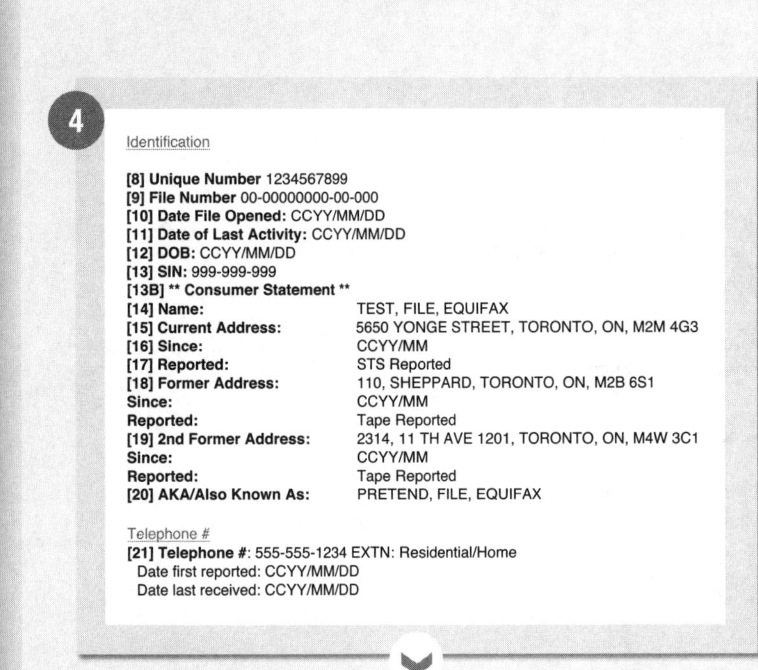

4

Identification

[8] Unique Number 1234567899
[9] File Number 00-00000000-00-000
[10] Date File Opened: CCYY/MM/DD
[11] Date of Last Activity: CCYY/MM/DD
[12] DOB: CCYY/MM/DD
[13] SIN: 999-999-999
[13B] ** Consumer Statement **

[14] Name:	TEST, FILE, EQUIFAX
[15] Current Address:	5650 YONGE STREET, TORONTO, ON, M2M 4G3
[16] Since:	CCYY/MM
[17] Reported:	STS Reported
[18] Former Address:	110, SHEPPARD, TORONTO, ON, M2B 6S1
Since:	CCYY/MM
Reported:	Tape Reported
[19] 2nd Former Address:	2314, 11 TH AVE 1201, TORONTO, ON, M4W 3C1
Since:	CCYY/MM
Reported:	Tape Reported
[20] AKA/Also Known As:	PRETEND, FILE, EQUIFAX

Telephone #

[21] Telephone #: 555-555-1234 EXTN: Residential/Home
Date first reported: CCYY/MM/DD
Date last received: CCYY/MM/DD

IDENTIFICATION SECTION:

[8] **UNIQUE NUMBER:** Reference number for consumers regarding their own file.

[9] **FILE NUMBER:** for internal use only.

[10] Date file was established.

[11] Date of last activity on file.

[12] Date of birth or age of Subject: (CCYY/MM/DD)

[13] **SIN:** Social Insurance Number: (will only display if provided on input and corresponds with the SIN on file)

[13B] **Consumer Statement:** Indicates declaration or alert on file (refer to section 10, line 39)

[14] Subject name.

[15] Current address.

[16] Since: Date the address was first reported to the file.

[17] Reported: Indicates how the information was reported to EFX STS: direct link customer, Tape: electronic reporting customer, DAT: Direct Access Terminal.

[18] Former address - Previous address of subject.

[19] Second former address.

[20] **AKA OR ALSO KNOWN AS:** The credit report contains all information under the names provided. (combined reports)

[21] Telephone #: Maximum 3 iterations of telephone #/extension, including type (home/business/cellular), date first reported to EFX, date last received at EFX.

4

FIGURE 3.11 Sample Consumer Credit Report (*continued*)

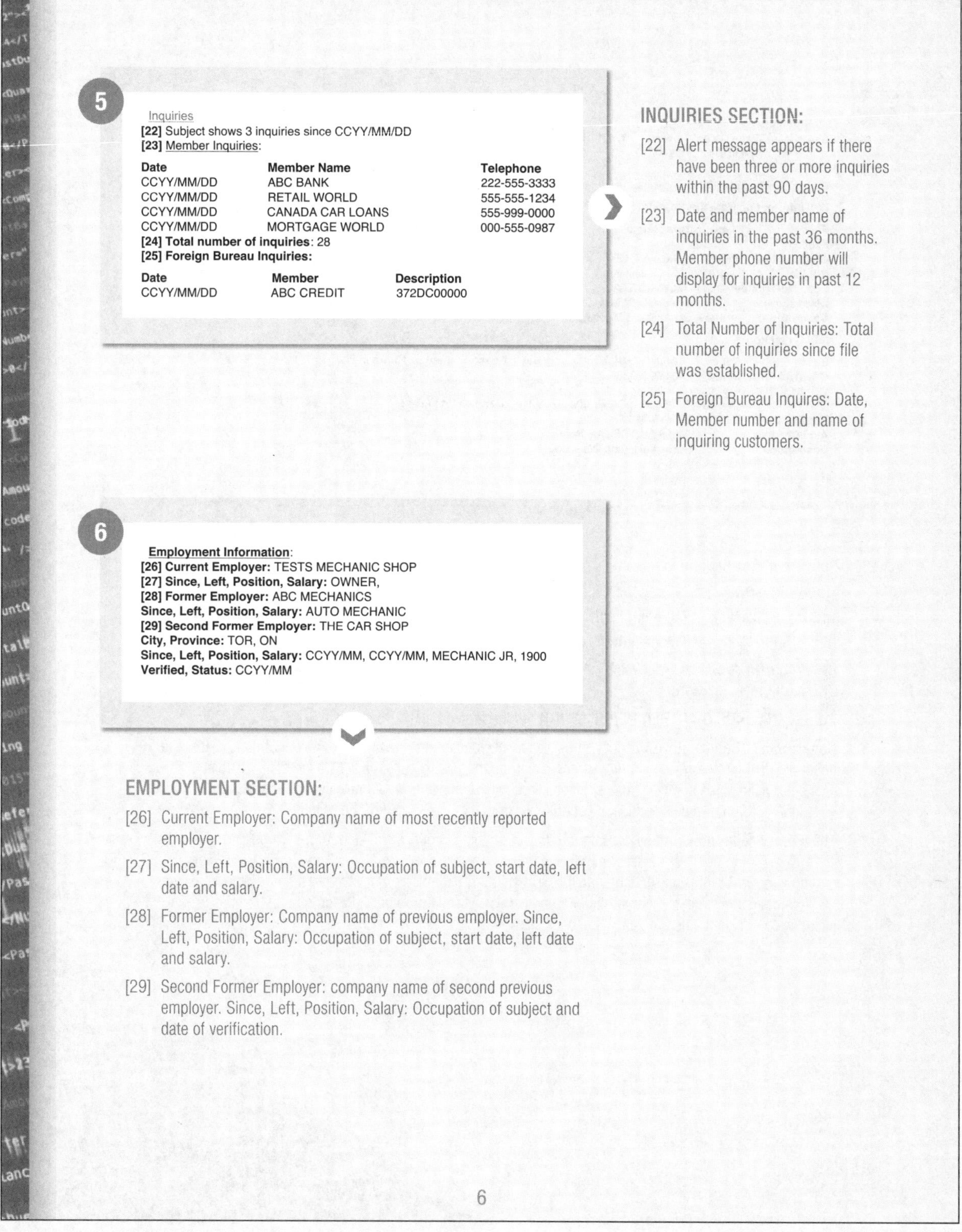

5

Inquiries

[22] Subject shows 3 inquiries since CCYY/MM/DD

[23] Member Inquiries:

Date	Member Name	Telephone
CCYY/MM/DD	ABC BANK	222-555-3333
CCYY/MM/DD	RETAIL WORLD	555-555-1234
CCYY/MM/DD	CANADA CAR LOANS	555-999-0000
CCYY/MM/DD	MORTGAGE WORLD	000-555-0987

[24] Total number of inquiries: 28

[25] Foreign Bureau Inquiries:

Date	Member	Description
CCYY/MM/DD	ABC CREDIT	372DC00000

INQUIRIES SECTION:

[22] Alert message appears if there have been three or more inquiries within the past 90 days.

[23] Date and member name of inquiries in the past 36 months. Member phone number will display for inquiries in past 12 months.

[24] Total Number of Inquiries: Total number of inquiries since file was established.

[25] Foreign Bureau Inquires: Date, Member number and name of inquiring customers.

6

Employment Information:

[26] Current Employer: TESTS MECHANIC SHOP

[27] Since, Left, Position, Salary: OWNER,

[28] Former Employer: ABC MECHANICS

Since, Left, Position, Salary: AUTO MECHANIC

[29] Second Former Employer: THE CAR SHOP

City, Province: TOR, ON

Since, Left, Position, Salary: CCYY/MM, CCYY/MM, MECHANIC JR, 1900

Verified, Status: CCYY/MM

EMPLOYMENT SECTION:

[26] Current Employer: Company name of most recently reported employer.

[27] Since, Left, Position, Salary: Occupation of subject, start date, left date and salary.

[28] Former Employer: Company name of previous employer. Since, Left, Position, Salary: Occupation of subject, start date, left date and salary.

[29] Second Former Employer: company name of second previous employer. Since, Left, Position, Salary: Occupation of subject and date of verification.

6

FIGURE 3.11 Sample Consumer Credit Report (*continued*)

7

[30] Summary

Pub/Other	Trade Oldest-Newest	Total	High Credit	Rating
4	CCYY/MM/DD-CCYY/MM/DD	3	2800 - 28000	1-One, 1-Two, 1-Other

[31] Public Records/Other Information

[32] Information from the Superintendent of Bankruptcy:

Filed Filed By	Type	Court Name	Court No	Liab	Asset
CCYY/MM/DD	BKRPT	MIN OF ATTORNEY GEN	472VF00022	280000	480

Subject: IND
Case No/Trustee: 22855 MORRIS ETAL
Disposition: Discharged. CCYY/MM
Description: Bankrupt Absolute Discharge

[33] Collection

Rptd	Type	Amt	DLA	Bal	Reason	Ledger Number
CANADA COLLECTION	UP/CL PD/CL	481YC00036				
CCYY/MM/DD	Unpaid	2500	CCYY/MMDD	2212	Unknown	1111111

Verified Date: CCYY/MM
Acct/Creditor: 55555 ABC RETAIL INC
Description: Subject disputes this account

[30] **Pub/Other:** Number of Public Records or Other information

Trade Oldest-Newest: Oldest trade open date-most recent trade reporting date

Total: Total number of trades on the file.

High Credit: High credit range of trades on file.

Rating for R/O/I/L/C/M: R: Revolving account, O: Open account, I: Installment account, L: Lease Account, C: Line of Credit, M: Mortgage.

[31] **PUBLIC RECORDS OR OTHER INFORMATION:** Information obtained from Public Court Records.

[32] **Bankruptcies/Bankruptcy Category:** A person legally declared to be unable to pay debt (date filed, type of action, [IND for personal; BUS for business], court name, court code, liability, assets, filer [subject, spouse or both], case number, trustee, disposition and description of the bankruptcy). Segment may contain non-bankruptcy information including: Orderly payment of debt or Credit Counselling.

[33] **Third party collections:** A debt which a creditor is unable to collect, transfers to a third party (name of collection agency, collection agency member number, reported date, type of collection [UP CL: unpaid collection or PD CL: paid collection], original debt amount, date of last activity with credit grantor, balance as of date reported, reason, ledger number, verified date, Credit grantor and account number, description). Includes collections related to Family Responsibility.

7

FIGURE 3.11 Sample Consumer Credit Report (*continued*)

8

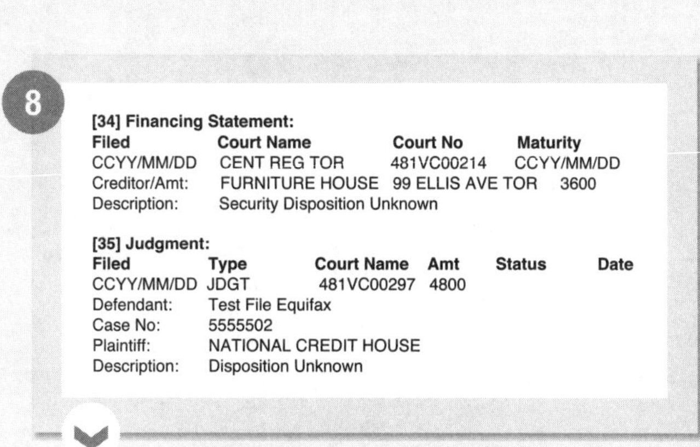

[34] Financing Statement:

Filed	Court Name	Court No	Maturity
CCYY/MM/DD	CENT REG TOR	481VC00214	CCYY/MM/DD

Creditor/Amt: FURNITURE HOUSE 99 ELLIS AVE TOR 3600
Description: Security Disposition Unknown

[35] Judgment:

Filed	Type	Court Name	Amt	Status	Date
CCYY/MM/DD	JDGT	481VC00297	4800		

Defendant: Test File Equifax
Case No: 5555502
Plaintiff: NATIONAL CREDIT HOUSE
Description: Disposition Unknown

[34] Financing Statement: A chattel mortgage, registered loan, or registered lien is a loan where the debtor has given personal property as collateral and the loan is registered with the provincial government under PPSA. This is not derogatory information. (Secured loans are not extended in the province of Quebec.) [Date reported; name of reporting government agency; member number of reporting agency, maturity date of the loan, name and address of creditor; amount of loan; Description of loan status].

[35] Judgments: A court order against a debtor for payment of monies owing (date judgment granted or date filed; judgment status [ST JD: satisfied judgment,JDGT: judgment]. Court identification number/ name of court; amount of judgment; defendant; judgment number; plaintiff; status of judgment [satisfied, unsatisfied or disposition unknown] and date, when applicable).

9

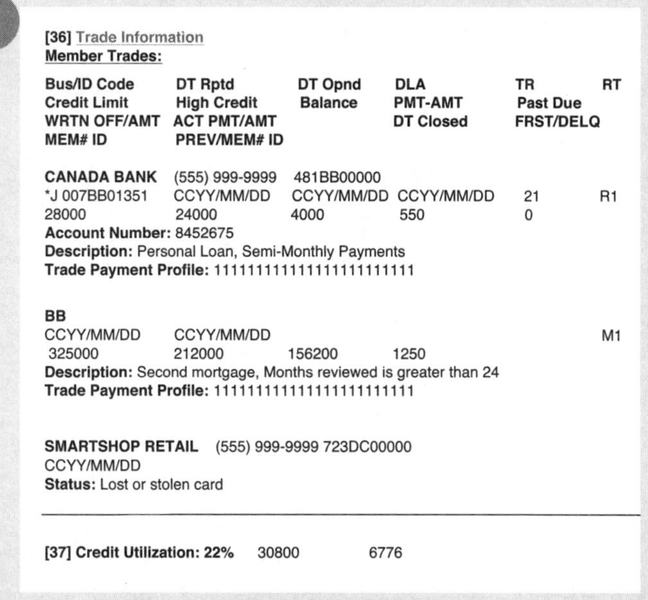

[36] Trade Information
Member Trades:

Bus/ID Code / Credit Limit / WRTN OFF/AMT / MEM# ID	DT Rptd / High Credit / ACT PMT/AMT / PREV/MEM# ID	DT Opnd / Balance	DLA / PMT-AMT / DT Closed	TR / Past Due / FRST/DELQ	RT
CANADA BANK	(555) 999-9999	481BB00000			
*J 007BB01351	CCYY/MM/DD	CCYY/MM/DD	CCYY/MM/DD	21	R1
28000	24000	4000	550	0	

Account Number: 8452675
Description: Personal Loan, Semi-Monthly Payments
Trade Payment Profile: 111111111111111111111111

BB					
CCYY/MM/DD	CCYY/MM/DD				M1
325000	212000	156200	1250		

Description: Second mortgage, Months reviewed is greater than 24
Trade Payment Profile: 111111111111111111111111

SMARTSHOP RETAIL (555) 999-9999 723DC00000
CCYY/MM/DD
Status: Lost or stolen card

[37] Credit Utilization: 22% 30800 6776

[36] **TRADE INFORMATION:**

Bus/ID Code: Company name/ telephone/ member number.

DT RPTD: Date item was reported to Equifax.

DT OPND: Date account was opened with the credit grantor.

DLA: Date of last activity on the account by the consumer.

TR: Number of times the credit grantor has reported an account update.

RT: Type of account and manner of repayment: (See Trade Information Descriptions and Manner of Payment for detailed rating descriptions).

8

FIGURE 3.11 Sample Consumer Credit Report (*continued*)

10

[38] Banking

Checking/Saving:

Rptd	**Opnd**	**Amount**	**Account No**	**Account Type**
ABC BANK,	001BB05697, (999) 999-9999			
CCYY/MM/DD	CCYY/MM	L5F		Chequing/Saving
NB NSF, Status:	4 NSF CCYY/MM			

[39] Consumer Declaration
Rptd, Purge: CCYY/MM, CCYY/MM
Declaration: *****WARNING*****CONFIRMED TRUE NAME FRAUD/FRAUDULENT CREDIT APPLICATIONS HAVE BEEN SUBMITTED USING THIS NAME/ IF YOU ACCESS THIS FILE AS PART OF A CREDIT CHECK, PLEASE VERIFY WITH THE CUSTOMER THAT IT IS LEGITIMATE BEFORE EXTENDING CREDIT/PHONE: (000) 555-1234

[38] BANKING INFORMATION SECTION:
Type of account, name and telephone number of institution; date item was reported to Equifax; Type of account; customer's member number; date account was opened with credit grantor; balance of account (approximate range); additional information on account. Ex: L4F=low 4 figures, ($1-2K), H5F= high 5 figures, ($70K-99K).

[39] CONSUMER STATEMENT: Rptd, Purge: Date reported and date information will be deleted. At the request of the consumer, EFX will add one of the following to the file:

True Name Fraud: Consumer is a true victim of fraud.

Identity Verification Alert: Consumer has not been a victim of fraud: cautionary alert added (available to Ontario and Manitoba residents only).

Consumer Statement: Statement provided by the consumer in order to explain items/information on file.

Credit Limit: Maximum credit amount assigned to the credit product.

High Credit: Highest amount ever owed on the product.

Balance: Amount owed at time of reporting.

PMT AMT: Actual dollar amount of most recent payment by the consumer.

PMT TERMS: Frequency of required payments to be made by the consumer.

Past Due: Past due amount as of date reported.

WRTN OFF/AMT: Actual dollarm amount written off by the credit grantor.

ACT PMT/AMT: Actual last payment amount by the consumer.

DT Closed: Date of closure of the account.

FRST/DELQ: Date of first payment delinquency by the consumer.

MEM#ID: Equifax Member number.

PREV/MEM# ID: Previous Equifax Member number.

Description: Provides additional information about the account.

Trade Payment Profile: Numeric summary of up to 36 months of previous ratings. Read left to right: recent rating to historical ratings.

Mortgage Trade line: Industry code is displayed (Example: BB): mortgage issuer name/date opened are masked.

[37] Credit Utilization

Provides the percentage of all available credit that is currently utilized by the consumer as of report date (total of current balances owed divided by total credit limits). The total of all open credit limit amounts and all open account balances are also displayed. *(Available to internet customers only).*

9

Determining the Amount Owing on a Claim

4

LEARNING OUTCOMES

After reading this chapter, students will:

- Understand and identify the types of interest charged when credit is extended.
- Know how to calculate the amount of interest owing on a claim.
- Know how to track and calculate interest on a running account.
- Know the difference between simple and compound interest and how to calculate each type of interest.
- Know how to explain the difference between and the relationship between prejudgment and postjudgment interest.
- Know how to determine prejudgment and postjudgment interest rates and how to calculate prejudgment and postjudgment interest from a contract or under the *Courts of Justice Act*.
- Know how to determine the number of days of interest from the time interest begins to run until judgment or payment.

This chapter explains how to calculate simple interest, compound interest, and interest on running accounts for the purposes of sending a demand letter and making a court claim.

In most cases a creditor will be owed an amount that consists of three parts: the principal amount of the debt that is outstanding; the accrued interest on that amount (which becomes prejudgment interest once a judgment is granted); and the legal costs incurred in making a claim for the debt. Once a judgment is granted, postjudgment interest is usually awarded. This interest continues to accrue until the judgment is paid. Some postjudgment legal costs are also added to the outstanding judgment as enforcement efforts are made.

Determining the Amount Owing

Before preparing a demand letter or drafting a claim, the amount that will be owing as of the date of the letter or claim must be determined. The basis for determining how that amount grows as interest accrues must be set out in the claim, so that when judgment is obtained or a payment is made, the legal representative will easily be able to tell how much is owing. Note that as the matter proceeds, legal costs may be added to the amount of the debt, and interest will also accrue on the costs on a judgment.

The chapter begins with a discussion of the differences between prejudgment interest and postjudgment interest. Particular attention is given to how to count the number of days for each type of interest. The formulas used to calculate simple and compound interest are explained, followed by instructions on how to calculate simple interest on a running account. This discussion is not exhaustive, and the reader may wish to consult a business math text for more detail. Also note that the calculation of compound interest can be tedious, but scientific calculators, software programs such as Excel, and specialized websites can help to do the calculations quickly and accurately.

Prejudgment and Postjudgment Interest

interest
the amount of money (usually expressed as a percentage of the amount of money borrowed or the amount financed to purchase an item) charged by the creditor to the debtor to compensate the creditor for advancing the funds or for selling the item to the debtor on a conditional sale contract

Interest is the amount of money (usually expressed as a percentage of the amount of money borrowed or the amount financed to purchase an item) charged by the creditor to the debtor to compensate the creditor for advancing the funds or for selling the item to the debtor on a conditional sale contract.

Prejudgment interest is the interest that is charged from the first day that the money is to be repaid with interest. Prejudgment interest continues to accrue up to and including the day that payment in full is made, or the court makes a judgment in favour of the creditor.

Postjudgment interest is the interest that is awarded by the court on a judgment. Postjudgment interest is payable on the judgment, including prejudgment interest, and on the legal costs awarded with the judgment, as well as on some legal costs incurred in attempts to collect the judgment. Postjudgment interest continues to accrue up to and including the day that the judgment and all postjudgment interest and costs are paid in full.

Determining the Rate of Prejudgment and Postjudgment Interest

The *Courts of Justice Act* (CJA)[1] in sections 127 to 129, sets out the rules for calculating prejudgment and postjudgment interest. Parties, particularly commercial business parties, have often entered into an agreement concerning financing arrangements. The agreement will usually set out the rate of interest to be charged. The parties' agreement should be reviewed in detail to determine any preset interest rate. If the parties have not addressed the issue of interest in an agreement in advance, the creditor is permitted to claim prejudgment and postjudgment interest under the provisions of the CJA. Note that in some cases interest has deliberately not been charged in accordance with religious beliefs or for other reasons. In those cases, the creditor will decline interest on the outstanding amount. In the event that interest has not been agreed upon but is being permitted under section 127, the section sets out the formula for determining prejudgment and postjudgment interest rates. The rate is calculated for each quarter of the year by a person designated by the deputy attorney general. The rate for each quarter is posted on the attorney general's website at <https://www.attorneygeneral.jus.gov.on.ca/english/courts/interestrates.php>. The given rate is simply applied.

Calculation of Prejudgment and Postjudgment Interest

Below are step-by-step instructions for calculating prejudgment and postjudgment interest on a debt. A sample calculation follows on pages 99 and 100. If the legal representative is required to do frequent prejudgment and postjudgment interest calculations, there is an online service that, for a monthly fee, will do the calculations. The service's website is at <http://www.judgmentcalculator.com/on>.

1. Determine whether there is a right to interest in the contract.

If there is a written agreement between the parties, it should be reviewed in detail to determine if it includes any references to interest. In some cases, the loan agreement may state in writing that it is interest-free. On occasion, for example, a family member may make a loan to another family member on an interest-free basis. In other cases, the parties may agree that for religious reasons no interest shall be charged.

If the agreement does provide for interest, then the interest rate in the contract will be used to calculate the outstanding amount.

If the contract is silent on interest, then interest can be claimed under sections 127 to 129 of the CJA.

2. If a claim for interest is based on a rate in the contract, interest under the CJA should be claimed in the alternative.

If contractual interest is disallowed for some reason—for example, if the interest rate clause in a contract is deemed to be unenforceable—then the creditor may still

1 RSO 1990, c C.43.

get interest under the CJA in the alternative, provided it is claimed. If the creditor claims only contract-based interest and fails to get it, they may end up getting no interest at all.

The creditor's claim for relief in their statement of claim should then read:

> *The plaintiff claims prejudgment and postjudgment interest under the terms of the contract and in the alternative under the provisions of the* Courts of Justice Act.

3. If the contract provides for an interest rate, use that rate; otherwise, establish the prejudgment interest rate using sections 127 and 128 of the CJA.

a) Interest Rate Contained in the Contract

If the parties' contract contains an agreed upon interest rate, then that rate should be used in the calculation of prejudgment interest. However, as noted above, interest under the CJA should be claimed in the alternative as sometimes a contract, or an interest provision in a contract, may be struck down by the court.

b) Interest Rate Under the CJA

If the parties do not have an agreement, or their agreement is silent as to interest, or their agreement or the interest provision of the agreement is struck down by the court, the creditor may claim interest under the CJA.

The rule under the CJA is that the *rate of interest to be used is the rate for the quarter in which the action was commenced.* An action commences when it is **issued** by the court.

issue
the act whereby the court office, for a fee, assigns the action a file number, signs the claim, and affixes a court seal to it; the act of issuing stops the limitation period from running out

This should not be confused with the quarter in which the cause of action (or right to sue) arose. The right to sue arises earlier than the day the creditor acts on that right by having their legal representative commence an action. Often the rate on the day the cause of action arose will be different from the rate on the day when the action was commenced, because the two dates are in different quarters.

The Relationship Between the Date the Cause of Action Arose and the Date the Action Commenced

debt past due: June 12	action commenced: November 4
> June 12 is the date the cause of action arose 2nd quarter, rate 2%	> November 4 is the date the action commenced 4th quarter, rate 1%

The rate of interest that applies is 1 percent, and it applies to the principal amount of the debt as of June 12. Accordingly, prejudgment interest commences June 12 and runs up to and including the day of judgment.

4. Having established the rate, calculate the prejudgment interest.

The next step is to determine the date on which interest began to run. On a debt, interest is calculated from the day after the debt was due and not paid. If, for example, a borrower agreed to pay back a loan from a friend on June 30 and did not do so, interest would be calculated commencing July 1. With respect to business transactions, terms of **net 30**, meaning 30 interest-free days commencing with the date of purchase, is a common arrangement. If a term of net 30 was granted to the debtor and the 30th day was today, then interest would start tomorrow, which is the first day the debt is past due.

net 30
used in contracts to indicate that the principal amount can be paid, without interest, within 30 days of the start of the billing period (which begins the date of purchase), after which interest is charged on the principal amount; this interest-free period is sometimes also described as a grace period

Date from Which Interest Runs

debt incurred	*debt due*	*interest runs*
day 1	day 30	from and after day 31 when debt is past due

Having determined the date on which interest began to run (the day after the principal amount of the debt was due), the end date of the prejudgment interest period must be calculated. In order to do so, the number of days starting with the day after the debt is due up to and including the day the judgment or order is made, must be counted. If the prejudgment interest period covers several months, it is much easier to calculate the number of days using a "Number of Each Day of the Year" chart (see Figure 4.1). To use the chart, identify the number of the date of judgment and the number of the date one day *before* interest began. Subtract the date before the interest began from the judgment date to calculate the number of days that qualify for prejudgment interest. (As noted below in Figure 4.1, a simple adjustment will need to be made for leap years.) Whether or not the chart is used, the result is the same. When counting the days using a calendar, note must be taken, of course, that some months have 30 days, some have 31, and February has 28. In the case of leap years, a leap day will need to be added into the calculations if February 29 falls within the calculation period. Prejudgment interest is calculated below by using the following formula:

the prejudgment interest calculation formula (simple interest) is

$I = P \times R \times T$

where

I = interest

P = principal amount of the claim

R = rate of interest from the rate for the quarter when the action was commenced (if no contract rate is given). The rate is set out with the decimal in place. For example, 5% interest would be shown as .05. Twenty percent would be .2.

T = number of days of interest commencing the count from the day after the principal amount of the debt is due (which is when interest starts) up to and including the day of the judgment. This is expressed as a fraction of a year—32 days, for example, is expressed as $^{32}/_{365}$.

5. Determine the amount of the judgment, including prejudgment interest.

The judge will make the judgment at the end of the trial or on default if there is no defence. The judgment amount will include:

the amount of the principal debt + prejudgment interest + court costs = amount due under the judgment

6. Determine the postjudgment interest rate.

In making a judgment, the judge will indicate whether postjudgment interest has been awarded in accordance with an agreed-upon rate. If there was not an agreement, then the judge will usually grant postjudgment interest in accordance with the CJA. Once judgment has been signed, postjudgment interest must be calculated on the amount of the judgment that includes the principal amount on the debt, prejudgment interest to the date of judgment, and costs. The interest rate that applies under the Act, for postjudgment interest, is the rate for the quarter in which the order or judgment was made. Note that, unless the order specifically disallows postjudgment interest, the court clerk will automatically insert the rate into the following standard wording, which should be added to the bottom of a judgment:

> THIS JUDGMENT BEARS INTEREST at the rate of ____________ percent per year commencing on ____________________.

7. Calculate postjudgment interest.

Calculate postjudgment interest using the following formula:

the postjudgment interest calculation (simple interest) is

$$I = P \times R \times T$$

where

I = postjudgment interest owing on amount of judgment

P = total amount of judgment (amount of principal debt + prejudgment interest + costs) + postjudgment enforcement costs

R = rate of interest from the rate for the quarter in which judgment was made

T = number of days of postjudgment interest commencing the day after judgment up to and including the day of payment (if using the Number of Each Day of the Year chart (Figure 4.1), start the count with the date the judgment was made)

Summary of How to Use I = P × R × T

	Prejudgment Interest	Postjudgment Interest
Principal	Principal debt owing	Judgment amount (principal debt plus prejudgment interest plus costs awarded) plus postjudgment enforcement costs
Rate	Use contract rate, if applicable • If not, use CJA rate for quarter in which action was commenced	Use contract rate, if applicable • If not, use CJA rate for quarter in which judgment was made
Time	Start with the date cause of action arose up to and including date of judgment	Start with the day after judgment up to and including date of next step (e.g., date of payment, date of enforcement document)

8. Calculate the total amount due and owing to the plaintiff.

The total amount due equals the amount of the judgment (claim for principal debt, prejudgment interest, and costs) plus postjudgment interest up to and including the date of payment.

Set out below is an example that illustrates how to calculate prejudgment interest and postjudgment interest on the judgment and on any costs incurred in enforcing the judgment.

The Year Zero system used in examples in the text:

Yr 0 = the current year

Yr 1 = the year after the current year

Yr 2 = two years after the current year, etc.

Yr −1 = the year before the current year

Yr −2 = 2 years prior to the current year, etc.

Sample Calculation of Prejudgment and Postjudgment Interest

Facts

Arnold enters into a contract with Bartolo to deliver goods by July 11, year 0; the price was $10,000 and payment was due on August 10, year 0. No payment was received, and an action was commenced on August 21. Judgment was obtained by default on September 11, year 0 and satisfied (paid) on September 30, year 0.[2]

Assume that prejudgment interest rates have been set as follows under the CJA*:*

1st quarter	Jan. 1 to Mar. 31	2.5%
2nd quarter	Apr. 1 to June 30	2%
3rd quarter	July 1 to Sept. 30	2%
4th quarter	Oct. 1 to Dec. 31	1.5%

Postjudgment interest rates have been set as follows under the CJA*:*

1st quarter	Jan. 1 to Mar. 31	4%
2nd quarter	Apr. 1 to June 30	3%
3rd quarter	July 1 to Sept. 30	3%
4th quarter	Oct. 1 to Dec. 31	2.5%

1. *Determine the basis for claiming prejudgment interest.* There is no indication that the parties agreed to an interest rate for overdue payments in the contract. As the contract does not state that the transaction was interest-free, the creditor may use the prejudgment and postjudgment interest rates prescribed by the CJA.

   Because the action commenced on August 21, in the 3rd quarter, the applicable interest rate is the rate for the 3rd quarter—2 percent.

2. *Calculate prejudgment interest.*
   a. *Determine the date on which interest begins to run.* This is the date on which the cause of action arose. The cause of action arose on the day after the debt was due—August 11 (if the prejudgment interest period is being calculated using the Table of Days, however, remember to use the day *before* this as the lower number (see Figure 4.1)).

---

2 The reader should note that in this and most examples in the book Year 0 is used as the base year to represent the current year. If, for example, this book is being read in the year 2018, then Year 0 would be 2018. Year 1 would be year 0 plus 1 (2019) and Year −1 would be one year in the past (2017).

b. *Determine the date on which judgment is given and count the days between the two dates.* Because the debt was due on August 10, prejudgment interest runs from August 11 until and including September 11, the day judgment was given—32 days.
c. *Calculate prejudgment interest:*

$$I = P \times R \times T$$
$$10{,}000.00 \times .02 \times {}^{32}/_{365} = \$17.53$$

3. *Determine the amount of the judgment*—assume that costs of $180.00 were awarded on the judgment:

$$\$10{,}000.00 + \$17.53 + \$180.00 = \$10{,}197.53$$

As payment was not made on the day of judgment, postjudgment interest must be calculated.

4. *Determine the postjudgment interest rate.* Because there is no rate set by the contract, the rate that applies is the rate under the CJA for the quarter in which the order or judgment was made. The judgment was given on September 11, which is in the 3rd quarter, for which the interest rate is 3 percent.

5. *Calculate the postjudgment interest:*
   a. *Determine the day on which postjudgment interest begins to run.* Interest begins the day after the judgment or order was made. The order was made on September 11. (If the Number of Each Day of the Year chart is being used (Figure 4.1), then use September 11 as the lower number. This is the day *before* the postjudgment interest begins.) September 12 will be the start date if the Number of Each Day of the Year chart is not being used.
   b. *Count the days from the day after the order is made until and including the date of payment.* The day after the order is made was September 12, and payment was made on September 30, which is 19 days.
   c. *Calculate the postjudgment interest:*

$$I = P \times R \times T$$
$$\$10{,}197.53 \times .03 \times {}^{19}/_{365} = \$15.92 \text{ postjudgment interest}$$

6. *Calculate the amount due on the date of payment, including postjudgment interest:*
   a. $10,197.53 (judgment) + $15.92 (postjudgment interest) = $10,213.45

Calculation of Simple and Compound Interest

In the Sample Calculation of Prejudgment and Postjudgment Interest beginning on page 99, simple interest was applied—interest that is calculated on the principal amount of the debt only. Simple interest is calculated during the interest period on the principal amount and added to the accumulated interest. Compound interest is calculated on the principal amount as well as on previous interest. The following examples, using the same principal amount and interest rate, show how the calculations are done with simple and compound interest. The effect of using compound interest is that the amount of earned interest is greater than it would be using simple interest. With large amounts of principal, compound interest results in significantly higher total amounts. A determination can be made as to whether compound interest is due by examining the payment and interest provisions in the contract. When the contract or loan agreement describes interest as being "compounded monthly" (or annually, or quarterly, or daily), or states that "interest is calculated on previous arrears of principal and interest," there is cause to compound interest.

Sample Simple Interest Calculation

Calculate the total amount owing on a debt of $10,000 that is 1 month, 2 months, 3 months, and 15 months overdue. The interest rate is 21 percent **per annum**.

per annum
Latin for "per year"

Solution
Use the formula $I = P \times R \times T$

Because the number of months the debt is overdue has been provided, rather than the number of days, the figures, $^1/_{12}$, $^2/_{12}$, $^3/_{12}$, and $^{15}/_{12}$ have been used for the measurement of time for the formula. This represents time as months as a fraction of the year.

Interest for 1 month	=	$10,000	×	.21	×	$^1/_{12}$	=	$175
Interest for 2 months	=	$10,000	×	.21	×	$^2/_{12}$	=	$350
Interest for 3 months	=	$10,000	×	.21	×	$^3/_{12}$	=	$525
Interest for 15 months	=	$10,000	×	.21	×	$^{15}/_{12}$	=	$2,625

Therefore, the total amount of principal and interest would be:

1 month $10,175
2 months $10,350
3 months $10,525
15 months $12,625

Sample Compound Interest Calculation

Calculate the total amount owing on a debt of $10,000 that is 1 month, 2 months, 3 months, and 15 months overdue. The interest rate is 21 percent per annum and the debt is compounded monthly.

Solution
Note: Amounts have been rounded off.
Use the following formula for compound interest:

$$S = P(1 + i)^n$$

where

S = amount owing (principal and interest)
P = principal (amount of the claim without interest)
i = interest rate for each compounding period
n = number of compounding periods

Note: Because the compounding period is one month, the monthly rate of interest needs to be calculated. It is $.^{21}/_{12} = .0175$.

The amount owing (S) at the end of month 1 is:
$\$10{,}000(1 + .0175)^1 = \$10{,}175.00$

The amount owing at the end of month 2 is:
$\$10{,}000(1 + .0175)^2 = \$10{,}353.06$

The amount owing at the end of month 3 is:
$\$10{,}000(1 + .0175)^3 = \$10{,}534.24$

The amount owing at the end of month 15 is:
$\$10{,}000(1 + .0175)^{15} = \$12{,}972.28$

With compound interest the total amount paid is always higher than with simple interest.

Determining the Amount Owing from the Contract

The terms of the contract and the creditor's accounting records usually form the basis for determining the amount due and owing. Often the creditor will provide the calculations up to a certain date. In such cases, the legal representative need only check the client's calculations and update the interest from that date to the date that payment is demanded in the demand letter, or to the date on which judgment is granted. If the creditor is claiming interest under the contract, the contract must be reviewed to confirm that it contains a contractual basis for interest to be charged; mere reference to interest in the invoice or bill is not enough by itself. It has to have been agreed to by the parties in the contract itself.

Running Accounts

A running account is one where the debtor is a regular customer and has a fluctuating balance from time to time. This happens where the debtor charges purchases to their account and makes payments periodically. A debtor may not pay off the full amount due at the end of a payment period. The creditor will carry that amount forward into the next payment period, when the debtor will pay some or all of it off. It is possible for a creditor's customer to always have a balance due greater than zero, in which case the creditor is "carrying" the debtor by carrying an unpaid amount that is due and owing. Of course, if interest is charged on overdue amounts, then the debtor is being "carried" at some cost to themselves.

When determining what is owing on a running account, go back through the debits and credits until a nil balance is found and start calculating from there. Calculate the interest on the balance from the time it is due until there is a change in the principal balance because of a further debit or credit. When a payment is received, it is first allocated to outstanding interest, and then to outstanding principal.

An example of a running account and how to determine the amount of a claim is set out below.[3]

Sample Calculation of Amounts Owing on a Running Account

Facts

We act for Artemis Plumbing Supply Ltd. One of its customers, Personable Plumbers Ltd, has a running account for orders that the office manager from Personable phones in to Artemis. There was some activity in July, year 0, but there has been no activity since. The transactions are as follows:

DATE	INVOICE	DEBIT	CREDIT	BALANCE
June 3	0113	20,000		$20,000.00
June 4			20,000	0.00
June 15	0893	32,000		32,000.00
June 21	0896	20,000		52,000.00
July 28			20,000	32,199.89*

* This is the result of applying the July 28 payment first to the interest owing on overdue amounts and then to the principal owing—see solution below.

No further orders have been placed or payments received. The original agreement stated that payments were due on terms of net 30 (within 30 days of billing), after which interest would be charged at the rate of 12 percent per annum.

Assume that it is September 15, year 0. Calculate the amount owing for inclusion in a demand letter that requires the debt to be paid by September 25, year 0.

Solution

Note: Amounts have been rounded off.

1. *Determine if interest applies in this situation. Then determine the rate of interest and type of interest to use.* Interest does apply in this example as the parties agreed to it in advance. The agreement indicates that there is a contractual interest rate of 12 percent per annum; there is no clear indication that compound interest is required, so assume that it is simple interest and use the simple interest formula, $I = P \times R \times T$.

2. *Calculate the prejudgment interest on the first debit.* Because there is a nil balance on June 4, start with the debit of $32,000 on June 15. Interest runs from July 15 (the 30-day interest-free period ended on July 14) to the date when payment is made on July 28, which results in 14 days' interest:

   $\$32,000 \times .12 \times {}^{14}/_{365} = \$147.29$ interest

3 In Chapter 5, the statement of claim on a running account in Figure 5.1 is based on the facts in this example. By reviewing Figure 5.1 and the calculations for interest set out in this chapter, the reader can see how a case progresses from a demand letter through to a statement of claim and the calculation of interest.

3. *Calculate the prejudgment interest on the subsequent debit(s).* Calculate interest on the next debit of $20,000 on June 21. Interest runs from July 21 (30-day interest-free period ended on July 20) to the date when the payment is made on July 28, which results in 8 days' interest:

   $20,000 × .12 × 8/365 = $52.60 interest

4. *Apply a credit for the amount paid to the outstanding interest.* From the payment of $20,000, subtract the outstanding interest:

   $147.29 + $52.60 = $199.89
   $20,000 – $199.89 = $19,800.11

5. *Apply a credit for the amount paid to the outstanding principal.* Allocate the remainder of the $20,000 payment to outstanding principal:

   $52,000 – $19,800.11 = $32,199.89,

   which is the outstanding balance as of July 28.

6. *Calculate the outstanding interest and costs.* Calculate the interest on the outstanding principal from July 29 to September 25 and add it to the outstanding principal to determine the amount owing as of September 25. This amount, plus a reasonable amount for costs, is the amount to claim in the demand letter.

Interest:	$32,199.89 × .12 × 59/365 =	$ 624.59
Add principal:		$32,199.89
Total due on September 25:		$32,824.48

CHAPTER SUMMARY

Chapter 4 has examined the various steps required to determine the actual amount of a claim. The chapter went into detail on the steps to take to calculate simple interest in order to determine prejudgment and postjudgment interest. The chapter also demonstrated how to determine the balance owing on a running account and how to calculate compound interest where compound interest can be claimed.

KEY TERMS

REVIEW QUESTIONS

1. How do you determine the amount to be claimed in a demand letter? What components should be included in determining the total?
2. What determines the rate of interest to be claimed in an action against a debtor?
3. If you are relying on the CJA interest rates for prejudgment and postjudgment interest:
   a. How do you determine the rate of interest to be used?
   b. How do you determine the date on which interest begins to run at that rate?
4. What is the difference between simple and compound interest?
5. Explain the steps in calculating the amount due on a running account.
6. Peter bought supplies from Retro Hardware on terms of net 30 days with interest of 8% to be charged per annum. It is 60 days since Peter bought the supplies, and he has not paid. On July 15, 2016, Retro issued a claim against Peter. Default judgment was signed on October 12, 2016. What are the prejudgment and postjudgment interest rates to be used?
7. Walter lent Adam $3,000 on February 14, Year 0. The money was to be paid back by October 31, Year 0. Adam signed a promissory note to pay it back by October 31, after which time interest of 18% per annum would commence. It is now May 20, Year 2, and Walter has not been paid. How much does Adam owe as of May 20, Year 2? Note that Year 2 is a leap year.
8. Phoebe sued Phyllis and was granted judgment on October 25, Year 1, totalling $9,741.62 inclusive of the judgment, prejudgment interest, and costs. Postjudgment interest in accordance with the CJA rate of 3% per year was awarded. It is now May 15, Year 2. Year 2 is a leap year. What does Phyllis owe including postjudgment interest?
9. Peter's Pickles purchased a peck of peppers from Pepper Ports. The charge for the pickles was $4,000 with interest of 24% per annum compounded monthly on all overdue accounts. Peter's bill is now 4 months overdue. How much does Peter owe Pepper's?
10. Jennifer obtained judgment in the amount of $10,000 inclusive of costs on February 24, year 0. Postjudgment interest in accordance with the CJA was awarded. Assume the CJA rate for postjudgment interest is 2%. It is now May 23, Year 2 and Jennifer would like to know what she is owed. Year 2 is a leap year.

FIGURE 4.1 The Number of Each Day of the Year

Day of Month	Jan.	Feb.	Mar.	Apr.	May	June	July	Aug.	Sept.	Oct.	Nov.	Dec.	Day of Month
1	1	32	60	91	121	152	182	213	244	274	305	335	1
2	2	33	61	92	122	153	183	214	245	275	306	336	2
3	3	34	62	93	123	154	184	215	246	276	307	337	3
4	4	35	63	94	124	155	185	216	247	277	308	338	4
5	5	36	64	95	125	156	186	217	248	278	309	339	5
6	6	37	65	96	126	157	187	218	249	279	310	340	6
7	7	38	66	97	127	158	188	219	250	280	311	341	7
8	8	39	67	98	128	159	189	220	251	281	312	342	8
9	9	40	68	99	129	160	190	221	252	282	313	343	9
10	10	41	69	100	130	161	191	222	253	283	314	344	10
11	11	42	70	101	131	162	192	223	254	284	315	345	11
12	12	43	71	102	132	163	193	224	255	285	316	346	12
13	13	44	72	103	133	164	194	225	256	286	317	347	13
14	14	45	73	104	134	165	195	226	257	287	318	348	14
15	15	46	74	105	135	166	196	227	258	288	319	349	15
16	16	47	75	106	136	167	197	228	259	289	320	350	16
17	17	48	76	107	137	168	198	229	260	290	321	351	17
18	18	49	77	108	138	169	199	230	261	291	322	352	18
19	19	50	78	109	139	170	200	231	262	292	323	353	19
20	20	51	79	110	140	171	201	232	263	293	324	354	20
21	21	52	80	111	141	172	202	233	264	294	325	355	21
22	22	53	81	112	142	173	203	234	265	295	326	356	22
23	23	54	82	113	143	174	204	235	266	296	327	357	23
24	24	55	83	114	144	175	205	236	267	297	328	358	24
25	25	56	84	115	145	176	206	237	268	298	329	359	25
26	26	57	85	116	146	177	207	238	269	299	330	360	26
27	27	58	86	117	147	178	208	239	270	300	331	361	27
28	28	59	87	118	148	179	209	240	271	301	332	362	28
29	29		88	119	149	180	210	241	272	302	333	363	29
30	30		89	120	150	181	211	242	273	303	334	364	30
31	31		90		151		212	243		304		365	31

Notes: (1) For leap years, February 29 becomes day 60 and the numbers in the table must be increased by 1 for all following days. (2) For debts, start counting on the day the debt is due, not on the day after it is due.

Commencement of Proceedings

5

LEARNING OUTCOMES

After reading this chapter, students will:

- Understand the nature and function of a demand letter.
- Be able to draft a demand letter to be sent to the debtor.
- Know which court to sue in based on the amount of the claim or other remedies required.
- Know how to make claims in foreign currency.
- Determine who the proper parties are to the proceedings.
- Know how to prepare and draft the statement of claim.
- Know the various ways in which a defendant can be served and what mode of service to use in a given situation.
- Know how to serve the claim and draft the necessary documentation to prove effective service.
- Understand when and how to make a motion for substitutional service.
- Understand the time frame for filing a notice of intent to defend and/or a statement of defence.

Chapter 5 explains how to start legal proceedings to collect a debt arising from a simple promise to pay. First, a letter should be written to the debtor. If the debtor does not respond, then the decision as to which court to sue in needs to be made. After the claim has been drafted, it must be filed with and issued by the appropriate court. The issued claim must then be served on the defendant debtor. In most cases the claim is personally served on the debtor or by an alternative to personal service as permitted under Rule 16 of the Rules of Civil Procedure.[1] If the debtor is evading personal service of the court documents, then approaches to substitutional service must be considered. This chapter focuses on proceedings in the Superior Court of Justice. Chapter 10 outlines proceedings in the Small Claims Court branch of the Superior Court of Justice.

Sending a Demand Letter

Typically, the creditor will have made a demand on the debtor for payment, threatening to turn the matter over to legal representatives if the demand has not been met. The client often wishes no further demand letters to be sent and, after discussion with the client, the legal representative may agree that this is a prudent course to take, particularly if the debtor's situation is rapidly getting worse. Where the debtor's situation is going from bad to worse, it may be advisable to move quickly and start a proceeding or take other action, rather than provide the debtor with any further opportunities to delay payment. However, if the client has not sent a demand letter in circumstances where one should have been sent, a letter should be sent (see page 109). Some debtors will ignore a creditor's demand letter, but will respond to the threat of civil legal action by the creditor's legal representative. There may also be some credit contracts that require the creditor to make a written demand for payment to the debtor before starting proceedings. In that case, a demand letter must be sent and will serve as the required notice. Paralegals who carry out collections work on a regular basis are required, under the *Collection and Debt Settlement Services Act* (CDSSA),[2] to send the debtor a written notice, such as a letter, prior to commencing any litigation. If a paralegal is not licensed under the CDSSA, they are restricted to sending a paralegal letter to the debtor. In a paralegal letter they cannot make a demand for payment unless litigation has already been commenced. For further details on paralegals and the CDSSA see Chapter 1.

A demand letter from a lawyer or a paralegal who is licensed under the CDSSA should

- be brief and businesslike;
- state that the writer is the agent of or is employed by the law firm or paralegal for the creditor and is instructed to collect money that is owing to the creditor;
- identify the debt owing and the fact of default in payment;

---

1 RRO 1990, Reg 194.

2 RSO 1990, c C.14.

- indicate how much is owing, including principal, interest, and costs, as of a date specified for payment, usually ten days to two weeks after the date of the letter;
- demand payment of that amount as of that date; and
- indicate that failure to pay what is due by the date given will result in civil proceedings being taken to collect what is owing to the creditor.

Example of a Demand Letter

JUST AND COPING
Lawyers
8701-365 Bay Street
Toronto, ON M3J 4A9, 416-762-1342
416-762-1343 (Fax)
justandcoping.ca

June 3, year 1

Edward Goodwheel
84 Spokes Blvd
Toronto, ON M6Y 3T4

Dear Sir:

Re: Whizzbang Automobile Financing Agreement

We are the lawyers for Pretentious Automobiles Ltd. We have been instructed to collect from you the outstanding balance on the financing agreement you entered into for the purchase of a year 0 Whizzbang automobile. The amount due and owing is $66,000 inclusive of interest and costs to June 3, year 1.

In order to avoid legal proceedings, please forward a certified cheque in the amount of $66,000 payable to Just and Coping, in trust, by June 13, year 1. If we have not received this amount by that date, we will commence a civil legal proceeding without further notice to you. Please note that, in addition to the amount of the debt, you will also be liable for further accrued interest and for court costs.

Kindly govern yourself accordingly.

Yours very truly,

JUST AND COPING
I.M. Just

IMJ/od

It is not necessary in this letter to set out the detailed basis for the calculation of the amount owing, but the total amount required should be set out clearly. It is permissible to include in the total an amount that reasonably reflects the cost to the client of collecting the debt, including things like legal fees and expenses paid to conduct various searches. It is recommended that payment be made to the law firm or paralegal firm in trust. This allows the legal representative to verify that the cheque will be honoured and that the money has actually been received.

The legal representative should require that the cheque be certified to ensure that it is honoured when it is presented for payment. When a cheque is certified, the bank guarantees that the money to honour it will be held in the account until the cheque is presented for payment.[3] Alternatively, the creditor can ask for payment by a bank or postal money order or by electronic transfer if that option is available. It is permissible to state that if payment is not made, a civil proceeding to collect the debt will be taken. Do not threaten the debtor by writing to tell them that if payment is not made, the creditor will bring criminal proceedings. To threaten criminal proceedings to collect a civil debt is **extortion**, which is a criminal offence. Although it is possible for the client to lay an **information** that leads to criminal charges against a debtor, this is not the usual course of action because the creditor is much more interested in getting paid than in getting involved in the criminal justice system. There may be times, however, as in debts involving serious fraud, where criminal charges may be appropriate. There is nothing to prevent a creditor from initiating criminal proceedings in respect of acts that are public wrongs, as well as a civil proceeding, to collect the debt.

extortion
the act of threatening, oppressing, or abusing authority over another person to obtain money or favours

information
a sworn written statement made before a justice of the peace that can initiate criminal proceedings against a person

guarantor
one who is obliged to pay a creditor when the principal debtor defaults

A demand letter (see the example above) should be sent to each debtor, if there is more than one, and to the **guarantor** of the debt, if there is one. The letter should be sent by registered mail, as the letter can be tracked online at Canada Post (<https://www.canadapost.ca>), and Canada Post will verify that it has been delivered and signed for. The letter should also be sent by ordinary mail, in case the debtor refuses to accept the registered mail version. A registered letter that cannot be delivered will be returned to the sender.

Jurisdiction

If the debtor ignores the demand letter, or the instructions from the client are to start a proceeding immediately once the date for payment in the letter has passed, the

3 LAWPRO, which is the errors and omissions insurance company for Ontario lawyers, has reported an increase in fraudulent activity involving phony certified cheques presented by clients for payment into lawyers' trust accounts. For more information, please read the articles at <http://www.practicepro.ca/Practice/fraud.asp>. Although a certified cheque will normally be honoured, a legal representative should also be aware that it is possible for the drawer of the cheque to ask its bank to put a "stop payment" on the certified cheque after it is issued, but before it is presented for payment. In this case, payment will not be made when the cheque is presented even though the cheque is certified. The debtor may do the same thing with a money order prior to the creditor presenting it for payment.

decision has to be made as to which court to sue in. If a personal debtor ordinarily resides in Ontario, a creditor will normally commence their action in the Ontario courts. In the case of a commercial debtor, the parties' contract should be reviewed concerning jurisdiction. In many cases the parties have agreed, in their contract, to a jurisdiction in which to file any required court actions. Also check to see if the contract requires disputes to be mediated or arbitrated. If there is such a requirement, you may be barred from commencing an action in the courts altogether.

If court action is to be commenced in Ontario, there are three possible choices when deciding in which court to sue:

1. *Small Claims Court jurisdiction is for matters of $25,000 or less*, exclusive of costs and interest. The plaintiff can reduce the amount claimed to $25,000 to proceed in this court if they wish, but the court will not award $25,001. Small Claims Court proceedings are discussed in Chapter 10.
2. *If the amount is between $25,001 and $100,000*, exclusive of costs and interest, the plaintiff must sue in the Superior Court of Justice, using the simplified procedure available under Rule 76 of the *Rules of Civil Procedure*. The discussion of the simplified procedure that follows is an overview; a detailed discussion is beyond the scope of this text.[4] The procedure is designed to reduce cost and delay by using a streamlined version of the standard civil process. To invoke the rule, it must be stated in the statement of claim that "the action is brought under the simplified procedure pursuant to Rule 76."

   If the plaintiff sues for more than $100,000 but recovers less than that amount, the plaintiff may be subject to severe cost penalties for not using the simplified procedure. However, a plaintiff suing for more than $100,000 can use the simplified procedure, unless the defendant objects. An objecting defendant should set out the objection in the statement of defence and ask that the proceedings continue under the ordinary procedural rules. The plaintiff must then either comply or abandon that part of the claim that exceeds $100,000.

   The advantage of the simplified procedure is that it speeds up the pre-trial process by shortening or eliminating some of the steps in the pre-trial stage, and speeds up the trial process by simplifying the presentation of evidence, notably by relying on the option of using **affidavits** rather than oral evidence.

   In the pre-trial stage, **examinations for discovery** are limited to a total of two hours for each party; however, many parties there are to be examined. Cross-examinations on affidavits used in support of court **motions** are not permitted. The parties must, as in all Superior Court of Justice cases, deliver

affidavit
a sworn or affirmed statement of facts that can be used as evidence in court proceedings in lieu of oral evidence

examination for discovery
a pre-trial process where lawyers get to ask the opposite party (plaintiff or defendant) questions about the allegations in the statement of claim or statement of defence

motion
a proceeding before the court within the main proceeding to settle a legal issue that has arisen in the main proceeding—for example, a plaintiff might bring a motion to court asking that the defendant provide more detail in the statement of defence; a motion is brought by a notice of motion, which states what remedy is sought and the reasons for it; the facts in support of the motion are usually presented in an affidavit

4 Watson and McGowan, *Ontario Civil Practice* (Toronto: Carswell, annual) contains a detailed narrative description with useful commentary on Rule 76, as well as the text of the rule. Because *Ontario Civil Practice* is published annually, be sure to use an up-to-date version.

affidavit of documents an affidavit in which a party identifies those documents that are relevant to the issues in the proceedings and that the party has in its possession, power, and control and can produce; the party must also identify those documents that it once had in its possession, power, and control but no longer has and those that it objects to producing; privileged documents, such as solicitor–client correspondence, will fall in the latter category; the documents being produced and relied on are usually contained in a document brief that may be filed as evidence in the proceedings and may be referred to in court

an **affidavit of documents**, which lists the documents they are relying on. They must also provide copies of the documents along with the names and addresses of potential witnesses.[5]

The pre-trial stage is further shortened by requiring settlement discussions to be held within 60 days after the first defence has been filed.[6] Of course, if the debtor does not file a statement of defence, the plaintiff may obtain a default judgment in the usual way.[7] The parties can have a summary trial or proceed with a regular trial. If the parties agree to a summary trial, it proceeds more quickly than does a trial under the standard rules due to the following factors:

a. evidence is given by affidavit rather than orally, although a party may examine the witness for no more than ten minutes on the affidavit;
b. the opposing party may cross-examine orally on notice, but total cross-examination of all witnesses by a party is limited to 50 minutes;
c. re-examination of the witness following cross-examination is limited to ten minutes; and
d. oral argument at the conclusion of the trial is limited to 45 minutes for each party.

3. *If the amount of the claim exceeds $100,000*, the claim is brought under the ordinary rules for civil trials in the Superior Court. The filing of a claim under these rules is discussed in the balance of this chapter.[8]

Rule 1.04(1.1) requires parties to an action to interpret the rules using the doctrine of proportionality. This means that the complexity of a proceeding must be proportional to the amount claimed in the lawsuit. Where a simpler, more expeditious, and less expensive way of proceeding is available and suitable, the parties are expected to use it.

Claims in Foreign Currency

The *Courts of Justice Act*, section 121, permits a creditor to sue for an amount expressed in a foreign currency. If the debt is expressed in a foreign currency, it must be converted to Canadian dollars, usually as of the date the creditor is paid on the judgment, following the directions in section 121(1). However, the court has discretion to specify a specific date and method for conversion, if the situation warrants.

5 Rule 76.03.

6 Rule 76.08.

7 Rule 76.12.

8 If the limitation period is set to expire shortly and the legal representative does not have sufficient facts to prepare the claim, they can have a Notice of Action issued by the court, which will halt the limitation period's expiry provided that within 20 days of issuance of the Notice a Statement of Claim is filed (Rule 14.03(2)). For further details on the use of Notices of Action, consult Laurence M Olivo and Mary Ann Kelly, *Civil Litigation*, 3rd ed (Toronto: Emond Montgomery Publications, 2014).

An exchange rate can be obtained by doing a search of exchange rates reported in the financial pages of a newspaper such as the *Globe and Mail*. Exchange rates can be also searched on a currency trading site such as <http://www.oanda.com/currency/converter> or by calling a currency trader.

Naming the Proper Parties to the Proceedings

Once the amount owing has been determined, who is liable for payment must be decided. The person (or persons) liable for payment is the proper party defendant to the claim. The legal representative must first determine who the debtor is and what its status is. For example, when an employee of a company is the person placing an order, it is not the employee who is liable for payment, because the employee did not order on their own account but was acting on behalf of their employer. It is the employer in this example who is liable for payment and who is the proper party defendant.

Once it has been determined who is liable, the next step is to determine what the status of the party is for the purpose of suing and then name the party appropriately. Chapter 3 addressed the importance of carrying out searches to determine or verify the type of business organization the debtor used (sole proprietorship, partnership, or limited liability company). It also made clear that it is important, once the type of business organization the debtor is using is known, that the business entity is correctly named in the lawsuit so that a judgment is obtained against an entity that legally exists.

- If an individual person carrying on business as a sole proprietor is being sued, it is best to sue the individual in their own name and in the business name: sue "Michael DeFalco" and "Michael DeFalco carrying on business as Swiftsure Accounting" or "Swiftsure Accounting." In this way, the sheriff will not hesitate to seize the assets of both the individual and the business.
- If a partnership is being sued, then sue the partners and the partnership: sue "Farrah Rahman, Shazlin Massa, and Premier Software Services." If only the partners are sued, judgment can only be recovered against the personal assets of the individual partners—for example, by seizing and selling Shazlin Massa's yacht—but if the partnership is named as well, partnership assets can also be recovered—for example, by seizing and selling the office computer system. Alternatively, under Rule 8 of the *Rules of Civil Procedure*, sue the partnership in the firm name alone, and give notice to the individual partners that the plaintiff will seek to enforce the judgment against their personal assets. If there is any uncertainty about the names of all of the partners, the partnership can be served with a notice, under Rule 8.05(1), to disclose the names and addresses of the partners as of the time of the cause of action.
- If a corporation is being sued, sue in the name of the corporation exactly as it appears in the public search records. If the search record identifies a company as a numbered company, then use the numbered company name, rather than any trade name under which it carries on business.

Preparing the Statement of Claim

Once it has been determined who the appropriate defendants are, the statement of claim can be drafted. An action for debt in the Superior Court commences with a statement of claim.[9] A sample statement of claim for payment of a debt is set out on pages 121 through 124. If the action is brought under the simplified procedure, in accordance with Rule 76.02(4), the following must be inserted just before paragraph 1 of the statement of claim:

> This action is brought against you under the simplified procedure pursuant to Rule 76 of the *Rules of Civil Procedure*.

Filing, Issuing, and Service of the Statement of Claim

Once the statement of claim is completed, it is necessary to start the action by having the statement of claim issued by the court office. In order to have the statement of claim issued, the claim along with an Information for Court Use form must be filed. A court clerk, acting on behalf of the registrar of the court, issues the claim.

Filing and issuing can be done in person at the court office or online. In order to file a claim electronically, the plaintiff must specify an email address at which they agree to accept documents from the court electronically.[10] If a statement of claim is filed and issued electronically followed by the filing of any other document in the action in paper format (with the exception of noting in default documentation set out in Rules 19.01(1) and (2)), the plaintiff must then file a paper copy of the statement of claim with the court. The court registrar has the authority under the rules to require anyone who has filed a document electronically to also file a copy in paper format.[11]

Whether a claim is filed electronically or in person,[12] a court clerk, acting on behalf of the registrar of the court, will, on payment of the prescribed fee, date, sign, and seal the document and assign it a file number.[13] The clerk will return a copy of the issued claim by email or, if filed in person, by handing the original document, signed and sealed, to the person attending at the court to file the proceedings. If the claim was issued in person at the court office, the person attending at the court may be asked to make a "true copy" of the claim for the court. In order to do this, they must write on a copy of the document the file number, date, and signature with quotation marks around it. This copy is called a "true copy" or "trued-up copy." It is then given back to the clerk, who will put it in the court file. Along with the statement of claim, Form 14F, Information for Court Use, found on pages 117 and 118, has to be filed, which indicates whether the action is brought as a "regular" proceeding, or brought as a simplified procedure under Rule 76. The person attending at court to

9 Rule 14.04(2).

10 Rule 14.04(4)(b).

11 Rules 14.04 and 14.07(3).

12 Rule 14.07.

13 Rule 19.01.

file the proceedings will take the original issued claim back to the office with them. Several photocopies should be made for the file and to serve on defendants. The original should be kept in the office file. It will need to be produced it at various times—for example, when signing a default judgment.[14]

In Toronto, there are often lengthy lineups to have claims issued in person. Therefore, in the Toronto area, sufficient time for the physical task of attending at the court office to issue claims needs to be allocated. The suburban court offices surrounding Toronto are also often quite busy.

Once a statement of claim has been issued, it must be served within six months of the date of issue.[15] Failure to serve the claim within the six-month time limit is an irregularity. However, the court, on a motion brought before it (the motion may be done in writing), may make an order giving the plaintiff extra time to serve the claim. A claim must be issued, but not necessarily served, by the time a statutory limitation period expires.

Serving the Proper Parties and Methods of Service

Once the statement of claim is issued, who is to be served with the statement of claim needs to be considered.

If an individual is being sued, then that is the person to be served by leaving a copy of the statement of claim with that individual. However, if a corporation is being sued, service is effected by leaving a copy of the claim with an officer of the company (for example, the president or the treasurer), a member of the board of directors, an agent of the company, or an individual who appears to be in control or managing the company's place of business. In addition to those at a head office, it is acceptable to serve persons in charge of branch offices.[16]

If the partnership only is being sued, and the individual partners are not named, anyone who appears to be in control of the partnership's main place of business may be served.[17] If the partners are named as well as the partnership (because the plaintiff wishes to be able to enforce a judgment against the partners' personal assets as well as the partnership assets), then each partner against whose assets the plaintiff wishes to enforce a judgment must be personally served.[18] As discussed in more detail in Chapter 3, there is also the option of suing the partnership and serving a Notice to Alleged Partner on each partner, putting them on notice that a judgment against the partnership may be enforced against both the partnership assets and the partner's personal assets.[19]

Rule 16 sets out a comprehensive code for service of documents. Generally, the first document, sometimes referred to as the "originating process" in a lawsuit, must be served on the defendant by personal service or an alternative to personal service. After the first document is served, the rules become more relaxed, permitting copies of subsequent documents to be mailed, couriered, emailed (provided the other lawyer has

14 Rule 14.08.

15 Rule 16.02(1)(c).

16 Rule 16.02(1)(m).

17 Rule 8.03.

18 Rule 8.03(1) and Form 8A.

19 Rules 16.01 to 16.06.

consented to service by email or a court order for such service has been made), or faxed to the party or their lawyer.[20] Once a document has been served, an affidavit of service should be prepared. This will be used later in the proceedings to prove service of the document. A sample affidavit of personal service is set out on pages 119 and 120.[21]

Service of a statement of claim by an alternative to personal service makes it easier to serve a defendant. However, it is best to use personal service, if possible, to avoid having a defendant ask that a default judgment be set aside because the defendant had no notice of the lawsuit. Motions to set aside default judgments in these circumstances are often successful, and a lot of time and money is wasted if the legal representative has to begin all over again.

Alternatives to personal service should be used in situations where the defendant and the defendant's lawyer know that the plaintiff will be suing and are prepared to be cooperative about moving the lawsuit along. An alternative method of service may be used where speed is required, and it is not possible to personally serve the defendant.

The alternatives to personal service are:

- Service of a document on the lawyer for the party, where it is known that the party has one, and the lawyer is prepared to accept service on behalf of the client. In this case, proof of service is shown by the lawyer, or an employee of the law firm, accepting a copy of the document and writing on the server's copy that they accept service of the statement of claim on behalf of their client; the lawyer or the law firm employee then writes in the date and signs their name on the document.
- Service by mail to the last known address of the defendant; however, to be effective, an acknowledgment of receipt card (Form 16A) must be sent to the defendant and received back by the plaintiff. Service is effective as of the date the plaintiff receives the acknowledgment of receipt card.
- Service by leaving a copy of the claim at the residence of the defendant is permitted provided an attempt is made to effect personal service at the residence. In this case, a copy must be left, in a sealed envelope addressed to the defendant, with a person who appears to be an adult member of the same household and, on the same or following day, another copy must be mailed to the defendant at that address. In this case, service is effected on the fifth day after mailing.
- If the defendant is a corporation, and its head office or business office in Ontario cannot be found, it may be served by mail at the last head office address or address of its agent in Ontario registered with the Ministry of Government and Consumer Services.[22]

---

20 Rule 16.03.

21 Rule 16.03(6).

22 The Ontario *Evidence Act*, RSO 1990, c E.23 permits affidavits to be either sworn or affirmed. In both cases the deponent is declaring, by their oath or affirmation, that what they have said in their affidavit is the truth and they are bound by their conscience and, in the case of an oath, by their religious beliefs. A sworn oath may be made with or without a religious text or icon in hand. An affirmation is taken without any texts or icons. See Ontario, Ministry of the Attorney General, "Guide for Newly Appointed Commissioners for Taking Affidavits," online: <https://www.attorneygeneral.jus.gov.on.ca/english/courts/notary_public/guide_for_newly_appointed_commissioners_for_taking_affidavits.html>.

Sample Information for Court Use (Form 14F)

ONTARIO

SUPERIOR COURT OF JUSTICE

BETWEEN:

PRETENTIOUS AUTOMOBILES LTD — Court file no.

Plaintiff

and

EDWARD GOODWHEEL

Defendant

INFORMATION FOR COURT USE

1. This proceeding is an: [x] action [ ] application

2. Has it been commenced under the *Class Proceedings Act, 1992*? [ ] yes [x] no

3. If the proceeding is an action, does Rule 76 (Simplified Procedure) apply? [x] yes [ ] no
Note: *Subject to the exceptions found in subrule 76.01(1), it is MANDATORY to proceed under Rule 76 for all cases in which the money amount claimed or the value of real or personal property claimed is $100,000 or less.*

4. The claim in this proceeding (action or application) is in respect of:

(Select the __one__ item that __best__ describes the nature of the main claim in the proceeding.)

Bankruptcy or insolvency law	[ ]	Motor vehicle accident	[ ]
Collection of liquidated debt	[x]	Municipal law	[ ]
Constitutional law	[ ]	Partnership law	[ ]
Construction law (other than construction lien)	[ ]	Personal property security	[ ]
Construction lien	[ ]	Product liability	[ ]
Contract law	[ ]	Professional malpractice (other than medical)	[ ]
Corporate law	[ ]	Real property (including leases; excluding mortgage or charge)	[ ]
Defamation	[ ]	Tort: economic injury (other than from medical or professional malpractice)	[ ]
Employment or labour law	[ ]		
Intellectual property law	[ ]	Tort: personal injury (other than from motor vehicle accident)	[ ]
Judicial review	[ ]	Trusts, fiduciary duty	[ ]
Medical malpractice	[ ]	Wills, estates	[ ]
Mortgage or charge	[ ]		

Sample Information for Court Use (Form 14F) (*continued*)

CERTIFICATION

I certify that the above information is correct, to the best of my knowledge.

Date: July 20, year 1

Signature of lawyer

JUST AND COPING
Lawyers
8701 - 365 Bay Street
Toronto, ON M3J 4A9

I.M. Just (12345A)
imj@justandcoping.ca

416-762-1342
FAX 416-762-1343

Lawyers for the Plaintiff

RCP-E 14F (November 1, 2008)

Sample Affidavit of Personal Service (Form 16B)

ONTARIO

SUPERIOR COURT OF JUSTICE

B E T W E E N:

PRETENTIOUS AUTOMOBILES LTD Court file no. 1234

Plaintiff

and

EDWARD GOODWHEEL

Defendant

AFFIDAVIT OF PERSONAL SERVICE

I, Henry James, of the City of Toronto, SOLEMNLY AFFIRM:

1. On Friday, July 25, year 1, at 2:00 p.m., at 84 Spokes Boulevard in the City of Toronto, I served the defendant in this proceeding, Edward Goodwheel, with a true copy of the statement of claim in this proceeding by leaving a copy with him.
2. I was able to identify the defendant by his acknowledgment to me that he was Edward Goodwheel.

AFFIRMED before me at the City of)
)
Toronto, this 2nd day of)

August, year 1 ______________________
Henry James

____

I.M. Just

A Commissioner, etc.

RCP-E 16B (May 1, 2016)

Sample Affidavit of Personal Service (Form 16B) (*continued*)

PRETENTIOUS AUTOMOBILES LTD
Plaintiff

and

EDWARD GOODWHEEL
Defendant

Court file no. 1234

ONTARIO
SUPERIOR COURT OF JUSTICE
PROCEEDING COMMENCED AT TORONTO

AFFIDAVIT OF SERVICE
OF HENRY JAMES
Sworn August 2, year 1

JUST AND COPING
Lawyers
8701 - 365 Bay Street
Toronto, ON M3J 4A9

I.M. Just (12345A)
imj@justandcoping.ca

416-762-1342
FAX 416-762-1343

Lawyers for the Plaintiff

RCP-E 4C (May 1, 2016)

Sample Statement of Claim for Debt: Price of Goods Sold and Delivered (Form 14A)

ONTARIO

SUPERIOR COURT OF JUSTICE

B E T W E E N:

PRETENTIOUS AUTOMOBILES LTD Court file no.

Plaintiff

and

EDWARD GOODWHEEL

Defendant

STATEMENT OF CLAIM

TO THE DEFENDANT

A LEGAL PROCEEDING HAS BEEN COMMENCED AGAINST YOU by the plaintiff. The claim made against you is set out in the following pages.

IF YOU WISH TO DEFEND THIS PROCEEDING, you or an Ontario lawyer acting for you must prepare a statement of defence in Form 18A prescribed by the Rules of Civil Procedure, serve it on the plaintiff's lawyer or, where the plaintiff does not have a lawyer, serve it on the plaintiff, and file it, with proof of service, in this court office, WITHIN TWENTY DAYS after this statement of claim is served on you, if you are served in Ontario.

If you are served in another province or territory of Canada or in the United States of America, the period for serving and filing your statement of defence is forty days. If you are served outside Canada and the United States of America, the period is sixty days.

Instead of serving and filing a statement of defence, you may serve and file a notice of intent to defend in Form 18B prescribed by the Rules of Civil Procedure. This will entitle you to ten more days within which to serve and file your statement of defence.

IF YOU FAIL TO DEFEND THIS PROCEEDING, JUDGMENT MAY BE GIVEN AGAINST YOU IN YOUR ABSENCE AND WITHOUT FURTHER NOTICE TO YOU. IF YOU WISH TO DEFEND THIS PROCEEDING BUT ARE UNABLE TO PAY LEGAL FEES, LEGAL AID MAY BE AVAILABLE TO YOU BY CONTACTING A LOCAL LEGAL AID OFFICE.

IF YOU PAY THE PLAINTIFF'S CLAIM, and $2,500.00 for costs, within the time for serving and filing your statement of defence, you may move to have this proceeding dismissed by the court. If you believe the amount claimed for costs is excessive, you may pay the plaintiff's claim and $400 for costs and have the costs assessed by the court.

TAKE NOTICE: THIS ACTION WILL AUTOMATICALLY BE DISMISSED if it has not been set down for trial or terminated by any means within five years after the action was commenced unless otherwise ordered by the court.

Date July 20, year 1 Issued by ....
Local registrar

Address of court office: 393 University Ave.
Toronto, ON M5G 1T4

TO: Edward Goodwheel
84 Spokes Blvd
Toronto, ON M6Y 3T4

Sample Statement of Claim for Debt: Price of Goods Sold and Delivered (Form 14A) (*continued*)

THIS ACTION IS BROUGHT AGAINST YOU UNDER THE SIMPLIFIED PROCEDURE PROVIDED IN RULE 76 OF THE RULES OF CIVIL PROCEDURE.

CLAIM

1. The plaintiff claims:
   a. the balance of the purchase price of a year 0 Whizzbang automobile in the liquidated amount of $66,000;
   b. prejudgment and postjudgment interest, as provided for by the *Courts of Justice Act*, at the rate of 21 percent per annum in accordance with the terms of the purchase contract commencing June 3, year 1 until payment;
   c. in the alternative, prejudgment and postjudgment interest at the rate of interest prescribed by the *Courts of Justice Act* commencing June 3, year 1 until payment;
   d. the plaintiff's costs of the proceeding including applicable HST; and
   e. such further relief as this Honourable Court deems appropriate.
2. The plaintiff is a corporation, with offices in Toronto, Ontario, and carries on business as a broker and seller of automobiles.
3. The defendant is an individual who resides in the city of Toronto, and is the purchaser from the plaintiff of a year 0 Whizzbang automobile.
4. The plaintiff's claim is for the balance of money owing from the defendant to the plaintiff on a contract for the purchase by the defendant of a year 0 Whizzbang automobile, VIN 398654321, which automobile was delivered to the defendant on June 1, year 1. The purchase price, inclusive of costs and taxes, was $76,000. The defendant paid a cash deposit of $10,000 against the purchase price. The balance of the purchase price, $66,000, was due and payable on June 2, year 1.
5. The defendant failed to pay the balance of the purchase price on June 2, year 1 and, despite demands for payment, has refused or neglected to pay the balance due to the plaintiff.
6. The balance due and owing as of June 3, year 1 is $66,000. The plaintiff also claims interest at the rate of 21 percent per annum pursuant to the terms of the contract governing interest on overdue payments, in accordance with the *Courts of Justice Act*.
7. Attached to this claim and marked as schedule A is a statement of account showing how the balance claimed is calculated.

July 20, year 1

JUST AND COPING, Lawyers
8701 - 365 Bay Street, Toronto, ON M3J 4A9
I.M. Just (12345A)
imj@justandcoping.ca
416-762-1342
FAX 416-762-1343
Lawyers for the Plaintiff

RCP-E 14A (June 9, 2014)

Sample Statement of Claim for Debt: Price of Goods Sold and Delivered (Form 14A) (*continued*)

SCHEDULE "A" TO THE STATEMENT OF CLAIM

DATE	DEBIT	CREDIT	BALANCE
May 15, year 1	$76,000		$76,000
May 15, year 1		$10,000	$66,000
June 2, year 1		nil*	$66,000

Balance due and owing as of June 3, year 1:

$66,000 with interest at 21 percent per annum until payment.

* A "nil" entry is made to show that the balance was due and unpaid, with interest running from the next day, June 3, on the balance due on June 2. With a simple unpaid account, as in this example, it is not necessary to include the account schedule, and you may omit it. It is provided here for illustrative purposes. It should certainly be included if the claim is on a running account, or is otherwise detailed or complex.

Sample Statement of Claim for Debt: Price of Goods Sold and Delivered (Form 14A) (*continued*)

PRETENTIOUS AUTOMOBILES LTD
Plaintiff

and

EDWARD GOODWHEEL
Defendant

Court file no.

ONTARIO
SUPERIOR COURT OF JUSTICE
PROCEEDING COMMENCED AT TORONTO

STATEMENT OF CLAIM

JUST AND COPING
Lawyers
8701 - 365 Bay Street
Toronto, ON M3J 4A9

I.M. Just (12345A)
imj@justandcoping.ca

416-762-1342
FAX 416-762-1343

Lawyers for the Plaintiff

RCP-E 4C (June 9, 2014)

Substitutional Service

If the defendant appears to have left town or disappeared, or is attempting to evade service, the plaintiff's legal representative may apply by **notice of motion** to the court for an order for substitutional service on the defendant. It must be demonstrated that any other method is impractical and that the mode of substitutional service being suggested would likely bring the matter to the attention of the defendant. The court does not have to be assured that this will happen. In some rare cases, the court may order that service be dispensed with—usually where it is unlikely that any mode of service will reach the defendant.

notice of motion
a court document used to initiate a motion that states what remedy is sought and the reasons for it

Substitutional service is often carried out by registered mail on the defendant's last known address, their workplace address, or someone, such as a close relative, who likely knows where the defendant can be located. It can also be accomplished by newspaper advertisement. This method can be quite expensive and should be avoided if possible. For service to be effected, it is necessary that the court's order is carried out precisely, with the document served in exactly the way the court ordered.

Sample Statements of Claim

All statements of claim include a standard first page and a backsheet, which are reproduced on pages 121 and 124, respectively. In the sample statements of claim reproduced in Figures 5.1 through 5.3, only those pages that illustrate the specific claim that must be drafted are included.

Statement of Defence

In Chapter 1, it was noted that often there is no defence in a debt action because the reason for nonpayment is inability to pay, which is not a defence. However, the defendant, depending on where they are served, has

- 20 days to file a statement of defence if served in Ontario;
- 40 days to file a statement of defence if served in other parts of Canada or in the United States; and
- 60 days to file a statement of defence if served elsewhere.[23]

A defendant may also file a notice of intent to defend (see Figure 5.4),[24] which extends the time for filing a statement of defence. The time for filing the statement of defence should be diarized. If none has been received, or nothing has been heard from the defendant, the legal representative should begin preparing documents to obtain a default judgment. Chapter 6 discusses how to do this. A sample statement of defence is shown in Figure 5.5.

23 Rule 18.01.

24 Rule 18.02(1).

CHAPTER SUMMARY

Chapter 5 goes through the various steps required to commence proceedings after the decision to sue has been made. If a demand letter has not been sent, one should be prepared, and there should be a discussion of what goes into such a letter. There should also be a discussion of which court to sue in, and, in the case of the Superior Court, whether or not to use the simplified procedure. The subject of naming the proper parties to the action is then addressed. There is a description of how to prepare a statement of claim, issue it, and serve it on the debtor, followed by what the debtor might do to defend the action.

KEY TERMS

affidavit, 111
affidavit of documents, 112
examination for discovery, 111
extortion, 110
guarantor, 110
information, 110
motion, 111
notice of motion, 125

REVIEW QUESTIONS

1. In what circumstances is it necessary for you to send a lawyer's demand letter to the debtor?
2. What points should be included in a lawyer's demand letter?
3. In what form should payment be demanded?
4. In the demand letter, can you threaten to bring criminal proceedings if the debt is not paid?
5. What courts can you use to sue a debtor? What factors determine the choice of court?
6. What are two advantages that come from using the simplified procedure?
7. Joe Smith, the office manager of Nokando Ltd, has always ordered materials from your client over the phone. The order is shipped to Joe at Nokando's factory, but is addressed to Joe Smith. Who is the proper party for your client to sue if the bills are not paid? Explain your reasons.
8. If Joe Smith was running an unincorporated business that he owned called "Smith Productions," whom would you sue?
9. If Smith Productions was jointly owned and operated by Joe Smith and his wife, Jill Montoya, whom would you sue? Explain your reasons.
10. What are the steps involved in issuing a statement of claim?
11. If you file the statement of claim electronically and the court issues it electronically, is there a requirement to file a paper copy of the claim?
12. Suppose you have tried to serve a debtor personally with a statement of claim, but they don't ever seem to be home when your process server attempts service. A person named Pat answered the door on the two occasions that the process server attempted service. Pat admitted to being the debtor's spouse and said that the debtor had just stepped out. Pat said that they didn't know when the debtor would be back. What options for service do you have in this situation? Among these options, which would you choose in these circumstances?

DISCUSSION QUESTIONS

1. Your client has received a demand letter that says among other things: "If you fail to make the payment required by the due date, we will take all available legal proceedings against you." Is it permissible for the creditor to take this position?
2. You are suing for Penumbuco SA, a Mexican company that is owed 3,000,000 pesos by a defendant in Ontario. You are told to sue in the Superior Court for the amount of pesos owing. How do you do this?

CASE STUDIES

Case Study 1

MEMO

DATE: December 3, year 0
TO: U.R. Clerk
FROM: I.M. Principal
RE: Foucault Collection

Our client, Umberto Ecco, the sole shareholder and president of Pendulum Artistics Ltd, has instructed us to collect an overdue debt from a customer, Henri Foucault. Foucault bought a silver pendulum to hang from his living room ceiling for the sum of $44,000 plus taxes and shipping for a total bill of $49,820. Foucault paid a deposit of $4,000 at the time of purchase on September 19, year 0. The pendulum was delivered to Foucault on September 23, year 0. The bill of sale is attached.

Bill of Sale

PENDULUM ARTISTICS LTD
2223 Yonge Street, Toronto, Ontario M4R 1V6 Tel. 416-234-5678

September 19, year 0

SOLD TO:
Henri Foucault
230 Rosedale Rd
Toronto, Ontario M6O 3B0

Item one silver pendulum 43″ diameter
w silver 1/2 inch chain @ 6 ft to be delivered.

Price $44,000 + HST + shipping = $49,820

Deposit $4,000

Total due $45,820

Terms: net 30 days from the date of billing. Overdue balances are subject to interest at the rate of 1.5 percent per month (18 percent per year) until payment.

Signed: *Umberto Ecco* Purchaser: *Henri Foucault*

As of November 15, year 0, no payments had been made; Ecco has heard Foucault is in financial difficulty; there has been no response to Ecco's calls.

Ecco has asked us to collect the amount owing.

1. Draft and send a demand letter requiring payment in full as of December 20, year 0.
2. Assuming that no money is received, draft a statement of claim to be issued on December 21, year 0.

Case Study 2

MEMO

DATE: April 30, year 0
TO: Law Clerk
FROM: I.M. Just
RE: Cookie Caldwell

Cookie Caldwell, the owner of Cookie's Cookies (Cookie), a sole proprietorship, called and told us that she has a problem. It seems she has been supplying Tina's Tearoom, a division of T Tuna Corp Ltd (Tina's), with chocolate chip cookies for several months. The manager of Tina's has signed a purchase order every month totaling $19,000 per month, with interest at the rate of 10 percent per annum on all overdue accounts. Payments are due 10 days after billing. Tina's has always been a slow payer, but the last two invoices, dated February 10 and March 10, year 0 and totalling $38,000, have not been paid at all as of this date.

1. Send a demand letter with payment to be made by May 20, year 0.
2. Assume that the demand letter produces no results. Draft a statement of claim.

Case Study 3

Assume the same facts as in Case Study 2 with the exception that Tina has come to you. She's been threatened with legal action by Cookie. She owes for two months but was reluctant to tell Cookie what has been happening. She is having some cash problems, but the primary cause of them is that the last three shipments of cookies from Cookie's have caused customers who eat the cookies to become violently ill—so ill that they "woof their cookies" all over the shop. It is getting to the point where Tina is thinking of handing out airline motion sickness bags to the customers that she has left. Her business has fallen off considerably in the last two months—business losses are estimated to be about 20 percent, or $32,000 so far. The situation could be worse, but she has other things on the menu that sell, and she isn't ordering any more cookies.

Draft a letter responding to Cookie's demand letter.

FIGURE 5.1 **Sample Statement of Claim on a Running Account (Form 14A)**

THIS ACTION IS BROUGHT AGAINST YOU UNDER THE SIMPLIFIED PROCEDURE PROVIDED IN RULE 76 OF THE RULES OF CIVIL PROCEDURE.

CLAIM

1. The plaintiff claims:
   a. the balance of the purchase price for plumbing supplies sold and delivered in the liquidated amount of $32,199.89;
   b. prejudgment and postjudgment interest, as provided for by the *Courts of Justice Act*, at the rate of 12 percent per annum in accordance with the credit agreement entered into by the parties commencing July 29, year 0 until payment;
   c. in the alternative, prejudgment and postjudgment interest at the rate of interest prescribed by the *Courts of Justice Act* commencing July 29, year 0, until payment;
   d. the plaintiff's costs of the proceeding including applicable HST; and
   e. such further relief as the Honourable Court deems appropriate.
2. The plaintiff, Artemis Plumbing Supplies Ltd, is a corporation with offices in the city of Toronto and carries on business as a wholesale plumbing supply company.
3. The defendant, Personable Plumbers Ltd, is a corporation with offices in the city of Toronto and carries on a plumbing business in the city of Toronto.
4. The plaintiff's claim is for the balance of money owing from the defendant to the plaintiff on a running account. The defendant executed under seal a revolving credit agreement on April 4, year 0, under which the defendant could make purchases on credit from time to time; the terms agreed to by the parties were that the defendant would pay each invoice within 30 days from the date of the invoice, after which interest would accrue at the rate of 12 percent per annum.
5. The defendant made payments from time to time, as set out in schedule A to this statement of claim. The defendant, however, has failed or neglected to make any payments on the balance due on the account from July 28, year 0 to the date of pleading.

FIGURE 5.1 Sample Statement of Claim on a Running Account (Form 14A) (*continued*)

6. The balance due and owing as of July 28, year 0 is $32,199.89. The plaintiff also claims interest on this amount at the rate of 12 percent per annum pursuant to the terms of the contract governing interest on overdue payments, in accordance with the *Courts of Justice Act*.
7. Attached to this claim and marked as schedule A is a statement of account showing how the balance claimed is calculated.

September 26, year 0

JUST AND COPING
Lawyers
8701 - 365 Bay Street, Toronto, ON M3J 4A9

I.M. Just (12345A)
imj@justandcoping.ca
416-762-1342
FAX 416-762-1343
Lawyers for the Plaintiff

RCP-E 14A (June 9, 2014)

FIGURE 5.1 Sample Statement of Claim on a Running Account (Form 14A) (*continued*)

SCHEDULE A TO THE STATEMENT OF CLAIM

DATE	INVOICE	DEBIT	CREDIT	BALANCE
June 3	0113	$20,000		$20,000.00
June 4			$20,000	0
June 15	0893	$32,000		$32,000.00
June 22	0896	$20,000		$52,000.00
July 28			$20,000	$32,199.89

FIGURE 5.2 Sample Statement of Claim on a Credit Card Balance (Form 14A)

THIS ACTION IS BROUGHT AGAINST YOU UNDER THE SIMPLIFIED PROCEDURE PROVIDED IN RULE 76 OF THE RULES OF CIVIL PROCEDURE.

CLAIM

1. The plaintiff claims:
   a. money owing to the plaintiff by the defendant under a "Rapacious Credit" cardholder agreement, in the liquidated amount of $29,123.45;
   b. prejudgment and postjudgment interest at the rate of 25 percent per annum as provided for by the cardholder agreement between the parties, pursuant to the *Courts of Justice Act*;
   c. in the alternative, prejudgment and postjudgment interest in accordance with the *Courts of Justice Act*;
   d. the costs of this action, including applicable HST; and
   e. such further relief as this Honourable Court deems appropriate.
2. The plaintiff is a financial services company, incorporated under the laws of Canada, with offices in Toronto, Ontario. The plaintiff is in the business of extending credit to persons such as the defendant through the use of credit cards.
3. The defendant is an individual who resides in the city of Toronto and who at all relevant times was a credit customer of the plaintiff.
4. On the defendant's application, the plaintiff opened a credit account for the defendant and issued the defendant a "Rapacious Credit" credit card. The card was issued subject to the terms and conditions set out in a cardholder agreement. The defendant was asked to read and sign the cardholder agreement by an agent of the plaintiff. The defendant signed the agreement on May 3, year 0. At that time, the defendant was issued with a credit card and given an account number—1904 569 3452.
5. By signing the cardholder agreement, the defendant promised to be bound by the terms of the agreement, which allowed him to purchase goods and services on credit and to obtain cash advances on credit by using the credit card provided by the plaintiff. The defendant agreed to pay all debts arising from the use of the credit card to the plaintiff.

FIGURE 5.2 Sample Statement of Claim on a Credit Card Balance (Form 14A) (*continued*)

6. The defendant, from and after May 3, year 0, used the credit card to purchase goods and services and make cash advances that were charged to his account with the plaintiff.

7. As a result of late payments or non-payment on the account, interest accrued on the outstanding balance from time to time, payable at the rate in effect from time to time as provided for in the cardholder agreement. At all relevant times, the defendant was given notice of the interest rate from time to time, as required by the cardholder agreement. At present, the rate of interest charged is 25 percent per annum.

8. The defendant has received full particulars of all transactions on his account in monthly statements sent by the plaintiff and from sales and transaction drafts delivered to him at the time of the transactions.

9. The balance of the account outstanding and due and owing by the defendant to the plaintiff is $29,123.45 as of June 15, year 1. The defendant is in default because he has failed to pay any amount since December 3, year 0, despite repeated demands that he pay the balance outstanding in accordance with the provisions of the cardholder agreement.

July 3, year 0

I.M. Weasel (88512B)
Lawyer
123 Finch Road
Toronto, ON M2J 2X5
iweasel@gmail.com
416-223-6789
FAX 416-223-6788
Lawyer for the Plaintiff

RCP-E 14A (June 9, 2014)

FIGURE 5.2 Sample Statement of Claim on a Credit Card Balance (Form 14A) (*continued*)

SCHEDULE A TO THE STATEMENT OF CLAIM

DATE	INVOICE	DEBIT	CREDIT	BALANCE
June 3	0113	$20,000		$20,000.00
June 4			$20,000	0
June 15	0893	$32,000		$32,000.00
June 22	0896	$20,000		$52,000.00
July 28			$20,000	$32,199.89

FIGURE 5.3 Sample Statement of Claim Against a Principal Debtor and Guarantor (Form 14A)

THIS ACTION IS BROUGHT AGAINST YOU UNDER THE SIMPLIFIED PROCEDURE PROVIDED IN RULE 76 OF THE RULES OF CIVIL PROCEDURE.

CLAIM

1. The plaintiff claims:
    a. money owing to the plaintiff by the defendants under a "Rapacious Credit" cardholder agreement in the liquidated amount of $39,123.45;
    b. prejudgment and postjudgment interest at the rate of 25 percent per annum as provided for by the cardholder agreement between the parties, pursuant to the *Courts of Justice Act*;
    c. prejudgment and postjudgment interest in accordance with the provisions of the *Courts of Justice Act*, in the alternative;
    d. the costs of this action, including applicable HST; and
    e. such further relief as this honourable court deems appropriate.
2. The plaintiff is a financial services company, incorporated under the laws of Canada, with offices in Toronto, Ontario. The plaintiff is in the business of extending credit to persons such as the defendant Alvin Profligate through the use of credit cards.
3. The defendant Alvin Profligate is an individual who resides in the city of Toronto and who at all relevant times was a credit customer of the plaintiff.
4. The defendant Petra Profligate is an individual who resides in the city of Toronto and who is the spouse of Alvin Profligate and guarantor of the payment obligations of Alvin Profligate to the plaintiff.
5. On the defendant Alvin Profligate's application, the plaintiff opened a credit account for him and issued him a "Rapacious Credit Inc" credit card. The card was issued subject to the terms and conditions set out in a cardholder agreement. The defendant Alvin Profligate was asked to read and sign the cardholder agreement by an agent of the plaintiff. The defendant signed the agreement on May 3, year 0. At that time, the defendant was issued with a credit card and given an account number, 1904 569 3452.
6. The defendant Petra Profligate executed a guarantor agreement on May 3, year 0 whereby she agreed to guarantee the debt of the defendant Alvin Profligate in the event that he defaulted on his payment obligations under the cardholder agreement.

FIGURE 5.3 Sample Statement of Claim Against a Principal Debtor and Guarantor (Form 14A) (*continued*)

7. By signing the cardholder agreement, the defendant Alvin Profligate promised to be bound by the terms of the agreement, which allowed him to purchase goods and services on credit, and to obtain cash advances on credit by using the credit card provided by the plaintiff. He agreed to pay all debts to the plaintiff arising from the use of the credit card.

8. The defendant Alvin Profligate, commencing and after May 3, year 0, used the credit card to purchase goods and services and make cash advances, which were charged to his account with the plaintiff.

9. As a result of late payments or non-payment on the account, interest accrued on the outstanding balance from time to time, payable at the rate in effect from time to time as provided for in the cardholder agreement. At all relevant times, the defendant Alvin Profligate was given notice of the interest rate from time to time, as required by the cardholder agreement. At present, the rate of interest charged is 25 percent per annum.

10. The defendant Alvin Profligate has received full particulars of all transactions on his account in monthly statements sent by the plaintiff and from sales and transaction drafts delivered to him at the time of the transactions.

11. The defendant Petra Profligate was given written notice of the default in payment of Alvin Profligate on January 16, year 1, and by this written notice, demand was made on her as guarantor to honour the obligations of Alvin Profligate.

12. The balance of the account outstanding and due and owing by the defendants to the plaintiff is $39,123.45 as of June 15, year 1. The defendants are in default because they have failed to pay any amount since December 3, year 0, despite repeated demands that they pay the balance outstanding in accordance with the provisions of the cardholder agreement and the guarantor agreement.

July 3, year 1

I.M. Weasel (88512B)
Lawyer
123 Finch Road
Toronto, ON M2J 2X5
iweasel@gmail.com
416-223-6789
FAX 416-223-6788
Lawyer for the Plaintiff

RCP-E 14A (June 9, 2014)

FIGURE 5.4 Sample Notice of Intent to Defend (Form 18B)

ONTARIO

SUPERIOR COURT OF JUSTICE

BETWEEN:

ARTEMIS PLUMBING SUPPLY LTD — Court file no. 6789

Plaintiff

and

PERSONABLE PLUMBERS LTD

Defendant

NOTICE OF INTENT TO DEFEND

The defendant intends to defend this action.

May 25, year 0

BLODGETT AND SNOGG
Lawyers

307 - 301 Cartway Road
Toronto, ON M3R 1P3

Susan Snogg (98714D)
SSnogg@outlook.ca
416-987-6543
FAX 416-987-6544
Lawyers for the Defendant

TO:

JUST AND COPING
Lawyers
8701 - 365 Bay Street
Toronto, ON M3J 4A9

I.M. Just (12345A)
imj@justandcoping.ca
416-762-1342
FAX 416-762-1343
Lawyers for the Plaintiff

RCP-E 18B (July 1, 2014)

FIGURE 5.5 Sample Statement of Defence (Form 18A)

ONTARIO

SUPERIOR COURT OF JUSTICE

BETWEEN:

ARTEMIS PLUMBING SUPPLY LTD Court file no. 6789

Plaintiff

and

PERSONABLE PLUMBING SUPPLIES LTD

Defendant

STATEMENT OF DEFENCE*

1. The defendant admits the allegations contained in paragraphs 2 and 3 of the statement of claim.
2. The defendant denies the allegations contained in paragraphs 1, 4, 5, 6, and 7 of the statement of claim.
3. The defendant did not execute a revolving credit agreement as alleged in paragraph 4 of the statement of claim. The defendant and the plaintiff orally agreed that credit would be extended to the defendant, and that accounts would be rendered from time to time and that the balance would be paid down from time to time. No rate of interest was agreed to in respect of overdue payments.
4. The defendant is obliged to make payments from time to time if the outstanding balance becomes excessively high. At no time has the balance due been excessively high.

---

*Based on the sample statement of claim on a running account in Figure 5.1 and calculation example of a running account in Chapter 4.

FIGURE 5.5 Sample Statement of Defence (Form 18A) (*continued*)

5. The defendant is not in breach of its obligations to pay the balance due, and is not in breach of its contractual obligations to the plaintiff.

6. The defendant asks that the action be dismissed, with costs.

October 15, year 0

BLODGETT AND SNOGG
Lawyers
307 - 301 Cartway Road
Toronto, ON M3R 1P3
Susan Snogg (98714D)
SSnogg@outlook.ca
416-987-6543
FAX 416-987-6544
Lawyers for the Defendant

TO:

JUST AND COPING
Lawyers
8701 - 365 Bay Street
Toronto, ON M3J 4A9

I.M. Just (12345A)
imj@justandcoping.ca
416-762-1342
FAX 416-762-1343
Lawyers for the Plaintiff

RCP-E 18A (July 1, 2014)

Default Judgment 6

LEARNING OUTCOMES

After reading this chapter, students will:

- Know when and in what circumstances a default judgment may be obtained.
- Know generally the procedure to be followed to obtain a default judgment.
- Know what to include in preparing a requisition for default judgment.
- Be able to draft a bill of costs.
- Be able to draft a default judgment.
- Be able to prepare a requisition for a Writ of Seizure and Sale.
- Be able to prepare a Writ of Seizure and Sale.

Once the statement of claim has been served, the defendant must serve the plaintiff or their lawyer with a statement of defence within the time provided for in the *Rules of Civil Procedure*.[1]

If no statement of defence is received, the defendant is deemed to have admitted the truth of the facts in the statement of claim and admitted liability and a judgment against the defendant in default of a defence may be obtained.[2] If the claim is a **liquidated amount**, there is a simple, quick, and relatively straightforward administrative process for obtaining a judgment for the amount due. Most debt collection cases are liquidated claims—for example, claims for payment for goods or services sold or supplied, credit card debts, unpaid loans, and unpaid running accounts. In addition to obtaining judgments for liquidated amounts, this quicker procedure is also available when no defence is filed in an action for the recovery of land or personal property or for the foreclosure, sale, or redemption of a mortgage.[3] However, in this chapter the discussion will focus on judgments for liquidated amounts.

liquidated amount
a specific sum of money that can be easily and objectively calculated; if a debtor borrows $1,000 for a one-year period at 10 percent interest per year, the amount owing —$1,100—would be a liquidated amount because it is precise and specific and the total is easily calculated using an objective standard or formula

If the claim is not liquidated, even though the defendant is deemed to have admitted the truth of the facts in the statement of claim and to have admitted liability, the plaintiff is obliged to prove the monetary value of damages in court. For example, a claim for general damages for loss of business arising from a breach of contract cannot be simply calculated using a formula. In this case, the plaintiff must lead evidence showing the extent of the business losses to allow a judge to exercise discretion in subjectively deciding how much money to award the plaintiff.

To obtain or sign default judgment on behalf of a plaintiff, the following documents must be prepared and then filed with the registrar of the Superior Court. If the documents are properly prepared and in order, the clerk, acting on behalf of the registrar, will sign judgment for the full amount of the claim, prejudgment interest, and costs. The clerk will also award postjudgment interest in accordance with the terms of a contract, or, if there is no contractual rate that applies postjudgment, in accordance with the terms of section 129 of the *Courts of Justice Act*.[4] The claim must be accurately stated and the calculations accurate; it is embarrassing and time consuming to have to change or amend a judgment later to correct an error.

Forms Required to Sign Judgment

The following forms are required to sign judgment:

1. Affidavit of service proving service of the statement of claim together with the original statement of claim.

1 RRO 1990, Reg 194, Rule 18.

2 *Ibid*, Rule 19.02.

3 *Ibid* s 19.04(1).

4 RSO 1990, c C.43.

2. Requisition for default judgment, noting the defendant in default (which has the effect of **noting the pleadings closed**),[5] stating that the claim is a liquidated claim, coming within the class of claims for which default judgment may be signed, and showing how much is owing, less payments made by the debtor, if any.
3. Draft bill of costs (original and two copies) to provide a basis for fixing the amount of costs to be included in the judgment.
4. Draft judgment (original and two copies). Note that there are different judgment forms for default judgment based on the type of claim: liquidated claim or demand (Form 19A); recovery of possession of land (Form 19B); and recovery of personal property (Form 19C).
5. Requisition for writ of seizure and sale, or writ of delivery if the claim is for return of personal property, or writ of possession if there is a claim to land.
6. Writ of seizure and sale or delivery or possession (original and two copies).
7. Cheque payable to the Minister of Finance to file the requisition for default judgment and to issue the writ of seizure and sale, delivery, or possession, as the case may be.[6]

noting the pleadings closed
the act of noting pleadings closed bars the parties from filing any further claims, defences, or other pleadings (without leave of the court); this act brings the pretrial stage to a close—in a defended proceeding, the matter then moves forward to the discovery stage and may then be listed for trial; in a default proceeding, the defendant is barred from filing a statement of defence and the plaintiff is free to have judgment signed

Procedure for Signing Judgment

Set out below is a step-by-step guide to signing default judgment on a liquidated claim or demand. There is a default judgment fact situation at the end of this chapter that shows the necessary forms, filled out as required by the court. The requisition for default judgment, the requisition for the writ of seizure and sale, the judgment and the writ of seizure and sale are court forms that are prescribed by the *Rules of Civil Procedure*. The bill of costs is a document that is drafted from precedents or word-processing templates. The statement of claim and affidavit of service, or other proof of service, will already be in the office file.

Prepare a Requisition for Default Judgment

The original statement of claim attached to the process server's affidavit of service is required, so that the clerk can see when the claim was served, where it was served,

5 The defendant may be noted in default by filing a requisition using Form 4E. In the blank space on the form where what administrative act the court is being asked to perform, state: "I require that you note the defendant in default in this action, on the ground that the defendant has failed to deliver a statement of defence within the time provided for in the rules" (or on other grounds, such as the defence being struck out without leave to amend). The usual practice, however, is to include the default in defence as part of the requisition for default judgment in Form 19D. The effect of noting the defendant in default is to note pleadings closed, which bars the late filing of a statement of defence. If there isn't time to complete the Requisition for default judgment, a simple noting in default can at least ensure that a statement of defence is not filed after the defendant's time to respond is up.

6 Items 5, 6, and 7 are not required to sign default judgment, but are often prepared when signing judgment so that the writ of seizure and sale (or delivery, or possession) can be filed as quickly as possible to catch assets before they are dissipated.

and that the time for filing a statement of defence has elapsed. When reading through the following steps, they are easier to understand if read with the Requisition for Default Judgment (Form 19D) in hand (see Figure 6.1).

1. On the requisition itself, after the words "TO THE LOCAL REGISTRAR AT ...," the location of the registrar should be noted—for example, Toronto. In the following line after the words, "I REQUIRE you to note the defendant..." the defendant's name should be inserted. Next, insert the defendant's name below "I REQUIRE default judgment to be signed against the defendant."
2. Check off the basis for signing default judgment.
3. Indicate whether any payments have been made on account with respect to the claim. If some payments have been made, complete Part A; if none have been made, complete Part B.
4. If some payments have been made, indicate the principal sum claimed, without interest; then show the payment on account and show how much of that payment is allocated to interest and to principal; then indicate the principal amount outstanding, after the allocations have been made. This is "Total A" on the form. Remember that any payment received after the claim has been issued has to be allocated first to accrued interest, and then to the principal amount claimed.
5. With respect to the calculation of prejudgment interest, indicate the date on which the claim was issued and the date on which the cause of action arose; this allows the clerk (and others) to determine how many days of interest the plaintiff is entitled to and what the appropriate rate is if interest is calculated under the *Courts of Justice Act* interest provisions.
6. Show how prejudgment interest is calculated. Calculate simple interest unless there is a contractual right to compound interest based on an agreement relied on and set out in the statement of claim. Calculate interest on the principal sum owing from the date of the last payment previously identified in the form. To calculate interest from the last payment, count the number of days from the last payment to the date on which judgment is to be signed ("End Date" in Part A of the form), multiply that number by the annual rate of interest, and multiply that result by the principal sum owing and divide by 365. This is "Total B" on the form.
7. From the calculations in Step 6, enter the amount of prejudgment interest on the "Total B" line and from the calculations in Step 4, enter the principal amount claimed on the "Total A" line. The totals from "A" and "B" are then added together in order to fill in the total amount for which to sign judgment.
8. If no payment was received, then complete Part B, indicating amount "A," the total amount of the claim without interest, and then provide the interest data, including the date on which the claim arose (i.e. the date from which prejudgment interest is claimed) and was issued. Then show the interest

calculations, using simple interest, unless there is a contractual right to compound interest, and this has been claimed in the statement of claim. Count the number of days from the time the cause of action arose to the date of judgment, and do the calculations as described previously for Part A. Add the sum claimed—"Total A"—to the interest claimed—"Total B"—to determine the amount for which judgment is to be signed.

9. Complete Part C—"Postjudgment Interest and Costs." Insert the rate of postjudgment interest that applies (this is either a contractually agreed-upon rate between the parties or the statutory rate, which is the rate for the quarter in which the judgment is signed) and indicate the basis for claiming interest. Then check off whether the plaintiff wishes the registrar to fix the costs or have them assessed later. The usual practice is to have the registrar fix the costs based on the lawyer's bill of costs, prepared in accordance with the *Rules of Civil Procedure*. This is much quicker and less expensive than coming back at a later date to have the costs assessed. A request might be made to have a bill of costs assessed if, for some reason, the costs to the plaintiff had been much higher than is usually the case for default judgment.

Prepare a Bill of Costs

A precedent of a Proposed Bill of Costs (Form 57A) can be found at the end of this chapter. In a default judgment situation, as in most civil cases, the loser pays some of the winner's legal costs on a **partial indemnity** scale. The basis for assessing a lawyer's fees on a bill of costs is Rule 57.01(1), which gives a broad discretion to the court when it determines the fee component of a costs award. However, costs used to be subject to a Notice from the Costs Subcommittee of the Civil Rules Committee, which established a costs grid. This grid was revoked in 2005, but in the absence of any other guidelines, the grid figures continue to be used by judges, lawyers, and law clerks, and are included here. The costs grid sets out the following *maximum* rates to be used:

partial indemnity
usual order for costs, based on a cost grid that establishes hourly rates for tariff items listed in the grid; provides less than full recovery of legal fees for the client

- law clerks: $80.00 per hour
- student-at-law: $60.00 per hour
- lawyer with less than 10 years' experience: $225.00 per hour
- lawyer with more than 10 but less than 20 years' experience: $300.00 per hour
- lawyer with 20 or more years of experience: $350.00 per hour.

However, for simpler matters, including obtaining a default judgment, the rates should be well below the maximums, although there is no prescription or formula to state with precision what they should be.

The lawyer's out-of-pocket expenses, or **disbursements**, are another story. These are covered in tariff A, part II, Disbursements. Here, cost recovery is usually on a dollar-for-dollar basis. For example, if $60.00 is paid to a process server to serve a statement of claim, then that is the amount that will be recovered in costs, although

disbursements
amounts paid out by the law office on its own account to third parties on behalf of a client

there are limits on some part II disbursements. Court fees and sheriff costs[7] can be recovered in full. The items usually included in the bill of costs on default judgment are as follows:

1. *Pleadings:* Hours spent multiplied by appropriate hourly rate from the cost grid.
2. *Court fees paid to issue statement of claim:* Fees are set by regulations made under the *Administration of Justice Act.*[8] The fees are scheduled to increase every three years, based on the increase in the Ontario Consumer Price Index. There is a list of fees in the Schedule of Fees that follows tariffs A and B in commercial editions of the Rules of Practice, such as the *Ontario Annual Practice.*
3. *Fees paid to serve statement of claim:* Part II of tariff A permits the recovery of a reasonable cost, backed by a receipt, for payment to a process server (the amount usually includes HST).
4. *Determination of costs and signing order (default judgment):* Hours spent multiplied by the appropriate hourly rate on the grid.
5. *Court fees paid to file requisition for default judgment:* As in item 2 above, these fees should be claimed in accordance with the Schedule of Fees.[9]

substantial indemnity costs scale usually used as a punitive costs award that results in near indemnity for the winner on a dollar-for-dollar basis

In the bill of costs, fees and disbursements are recorded in separate columns and totalled. Disbursements include tariff A, part II items, as well as court fees and sheriff fees. If for any reason the plaintiff wishes to recover costs on a **substantial indemnity** scale, this is a claim for a full recovery of costs and is best dealt with by being set down for a hearing before an assessment officer. Recovery on this scale is unusual in default situations, as this scale is usually only applied where a party has misconducted themselves in the course of the proceedings.

Draft a Judgment

Draft a judgment (see Figure 6.3) and make two copies of it. The judgment is a one-paragraph document in which the sum claimed must be inserted; the sum is composed of the principal amount and interest, taken from the requisition for default judgment, and the costs, taken from the total on the bill of costs. Remember to include a sentence stating that: "This judgment bears interest at the rate of _____

7 *Superior Court of Justice and Court of Appeal—Fees*, O Reg 293/92, as amended. The tariffs and court fees are set out in the Ontario *Rules of Civil Procedure*. These rules are regulations under the *Administration of Justice Act* (RSO 1990, c A.6) and can be found online at <http://www.e-laws.gov.on.ca>. To find these regulations at the e-laws website, click on Consolidated Law and choose "A," then click on the *Administration of Justice Act* entry in the list. Click on the Regulations under this Act's tab and scan the list for *Superior Court of Justice and Court of Appeal—Fees.*

8 O Reg 293/92, *supra* note 7.

9 Always check the tariff before preparing a bill of costs because the tariffs and court fees are amended from time to time. The latest amendment, as at July 2017, was in November 2016, and tariffs and fees will increase again on January 1, 2020.

percent per year from its date." If this statement is not present in the draft judgment, even though interest is claimed in the statement of claim and identified in the requisition for default judgment, the clerk may not insert the phrase, and the plaintiff will not obtain postjudgment interest. As a default judgment is a prescribed court form, Form 19A can be used as a guide for judgment on a liquidated sum.

Prepare a Requisition for a Writ of Seizure and Sale

While a requisition for a writ of seizure and sale and a writ of seizure and sale are not required to obtain default judgment, the documents are often prepared when obtaining default judgment because the lawyer may wish to file the writ of execution as quickly as possible to catch the debtor's assets before they are dissipated. The requisition (see Figure 6.4) should be directed to and filed with the sheriff of each county or area where it is thought the debtor has assets. If the debtor has assets in more than one area, the lawyer will, therefore, need to refer in the requisition to each sheriff's office in which they intend to file a writ of seizure and sale. Be sure to accurately set out the name of the debtor. Include the amount to be seized, the amount of costs claimed, and the applicable postjudgment interest rate, all of which can be copied from the judgment.

Prepare a Writ of Seizure and Sale

An original and one copy of the writ (see Figure 6.5) should be prepared for each sheriff's office in which it is planned to file the writ. When default judgment is obtained and the fee to issue the writ paid, file the original and one copy with the sheriff's office, along with a cover letter instructing the sheriff to file the writ in the land titles system. If the writ is not filed in the land titles system, the writ will not attach to the execution debtor's land registered in the system. Complete each writ, filling in the blanks, using the judgment and the requisition for a writ of seizure and sale as the source of the necessary information. Keep one copy of each writ for the office file. Remember to complete the backsheet by adding in the fee paid to issue the writ, and the lawyer's fee for issuing the writ. Rule 60.19(2)(a) sets the lawyer's fee for preparation of the writ at $50.00. The sheriff is entitled to add these costs to the amounts on the face of the writ that may be collected from the debtor in the future.

Lawyers, paralegals, and other persons who register to issue and file enforcement documentation electronically with the sheriff under Rule 60 are now able to file writs of seizure and sale online.[10] The ability to file documents electronically has greatly facilitated the filing of documents used to enforce judgments, particularly where the legal representative is filing in more than one location in Ontario. It is a good idea to watch for further developments with electronic filing as the Court Services Branch of the Ministry of the Attorney General works to increase the use of electronic documents in the court system. This will parallel the transition to "the paperless office" that has been occurring in law offices. There is also, as noted in the preface, a study underway by the Ontario government to privatize the court order

10 *Supra* note 1; O Reg 487/16, s 13.

enforcement system, with sheriff's officers replaced by for-profit agencies, with a view to making the process quicker and more efficient.

Pay a Fee to the Minister of Finance

There is a fee to cover the cost of requisitioning the default judgment and issuing each original writ of seizure and sale. The current tariffs for court and sheriff's fees should be consulted to determine the cost of obtaining default judgment and issuing a writ of seizure and sale. A cheque should then be prepared payable to the Minister of Finance or a payment should be made online if filing electronically.

Sample Illustration of a Default Judgment

This section and the figures that follow set out the instructions and documents required to obtain a default judgment. The documents were prepared using the facts in the Sample Calculation of Amounts Owing on a Running Account set out on pages 103 and 104 of Chapter 4. The facts are set out below. The statement of claim based on those facts is found in the sample statement of claim at the end of Chapter 5 in Figure 5.1, Sample Statement of Claim on a Running Account. When preparing court documents, remember that all of them must have a backsheet. See Rule 4 of the *Rules of Civil Procedure* for the general rules governing the format and content of court documents.

Facts

We act for Artemis Plumbing Supply Ltd; one of its customers, Personable Plumbers Ltd ("Personable"), has a running account for orders that the office manager from Personable phones in to Artemis. There was some activity in June, year 0, but there has been no activity since. The transactions are as follows:

DATE	INVOICE	DEBIT	CREDIT	BALANCE
June 3	0113	$20,000.00		$20,000.00
June 4			$20,000.00	0.00
June 15	0893	$32,000.00		$32,000.00
June 21	0896	$20,000.00		$52,000.00
July 28			$20,000.00	$32,199.89*

* This is the result of applying the July 28 payment first to interest on overdue amounts and then to principal.

No further orders have been placed, or payments received. The original agreement stated that payments were due within 30 days of billing, after which interest would be charged at the rate of 12 percent per annum.

On September 15, year 0, a demand letter was sent, but there was no response by the deadline in the demand letter, September 25. A statement of claim was issued and served on September 26. It is now October 16, year 0.

Documents were prepared on the assumption that default judgment would be signed on October 17, year 0. The cost of issuing a claim was $220 (2017). It was assumed that a process server was paid $60 (inclusive of HST) to serve the statement of claim and provide an affidavit of service as proof of service of the claim. It was also assumed that there were receipts to attach to the bill of costs for all disbursements and dockets to support the claim for fees in the bill of costs.

CHAPTER SUMMARY

In this chapter, the debt collection process moved on from the commencement of proceedings to what needs to be done if the debtor does not defend. At this point it is necessary for the plaintiff to move for default judgment if the debt is a liquidated claim or demand. For this, the following forms must be prepared: requisition for default judgment noting the defendant in default, a draft bill of costs, and a draft judgment. A requisition for a writ of seizure and sale and the writ itself should also be prepared. These documents are then filed with the court. If they are in order, the clerk will verify that the facts and calculations in the requisition for default judgment fit the claim in the statement of claim. The clerk will then assess the plaintiff's costs and sign judgment. The writ of seizure and sale may then be issued and filed with the sheriff's office(s) where the debtor has, or is likely to have, assets.

KEY TERMS

disbursements, 145
liquidated amount, 142
partial indemnity, 145
noting the pleadings closed, 143
substantial indemnity, 146

REVIEW QUESTIONS

1. Under what circumstances can you apply to sign default judgment?
2. Explain the difference between a liquidated claim and an unliquidated claim.
3. What documents must you prepare to sign default judgment?
4. Name the documentation to be used if you are preparing a default judgment that is *not* for a liquidated claim or demand.
5. What documents must you file with the court in order to sign default judgment?
6. Why is the registrar provided with a requisition for default judgment?
7. Suppose the defendant defaults on their defence, but pays some money on account of the amount set out in the statement of claim. How does this affect the process of signing default judgment?
8. What determines the interest rate used for prejudgment and postjudgment interest?
9. How do you determine the amounts that go into the bill of costs?
10. What is the difference between fees and disbursements?
11. What is the difference between partial indemnity costs and substantial indemnity costs?
12. Which scale of costs would you use in signing default judgment? Explain your answer.
13. What are the significant differences between assessing costs and fixing costs?
14. In what circumstances would you have to requisition more than one writ of seizure and sale on signing default judgment?
15. What do you need to tell the sheriff to do when you obtain a writ of seizure and sale to file with the sheriff's office?
16. Once the sheriff has the writ, can the sheriff collect more from the debtor than the face amount on the judgment, including accrued interest?

CASE STUDY

Prepare documents to sign default judgment in the following case:

B. Head
8701 – 365 Bay Street
Toronto, ON M5A 1J3
416-782-1234

MEMO

DATE: April 26, year 1
TO: U.R. Clerk
FROM: Bodley Head
RE: Default Judgment—Rapacious Lenders v Ophelia Foot

We issued a claim against Ophelia Foot on March 23, year 1. Foot had signed a promissory note to our client Rapacious Lenders Ltd for $60,000 on August 1, year 0. The note was due on December 1, year 0. It provided for interest at 12 percent per year from the time it was past due until payment. Interest has been claimed on this basis. The claim was thus for $60,000.00 plus interest on the overdue amount. On March 1, year 1, Foot paid $2,000 on account, but nothing has been paid since. Foot was served with the statement of claim on March 24, year 1; nothing has happened since.

Because Foot has not defended, and the time for filing a defence has passed, please prepare the necessary documents to sign default judgment on April 28, year 1. The original statement of claim and affidavit of service are in the file, together with a receipt for $60.00 (inclusive of HST) for service of the claim and a receipt for $220.00 from the court for the fee paid to issue the statement of claim. It is rumoured that Foot owns property in Toronto and Oshawa, so be sure to take that into account when requisitioning the writ of seizure and sale.

FIGURE 6.1 Requisition for Default Judgment (Form 19D)

ONTARIO

SUPERIOR COURT OF JUSTICE

BETWEEN:

ARTEMIS PLUMBING SUPPLY LTD — Court file no. 1234

Plaintiff

and

PERSONABLE PLUMBERS LTD

Defendant

REQUISITION FOR DEFAULT JUDGMENT

TO THE LOCAL REGISTRAR AT Toronto

I REQUIRE you to note the defendant Personable Plumbers Ltd in default in this action and that pleadings be noted closed against the defendant on the ground that the defendant has failed to deliver a statement of defence within the time provided for in the rules.*

I REQUIRE default judgment to be signed against the defendant

Personable Plumbers Ltd

Default judgment may properly be signed in this action because the claim is for:

[x] a debt or liquidated demand in money

[ ] recovery of possession of land

[ ] recovery of possession of personal property

[ ] foreclosure, sale or redemption of a mortgage

(Debt or liquidated demand)

[x] There has been no payment on account of the claim since the statement of claim was issued. *(Complete Parts B and C.)*

OR

[ ] The following payments have been made on account of the claim since the statement of claim was issued. *(Complete Parts A and C.)*

*Assume for the purposes of this chapter that Personable has not filed a defence.

FIGURE 6.1 Requisition for Default Judgment (Form 19D) (*continued*)

PART A — PAYMENT(S) RECEIVED BY PLAINTIFF

(Complete this part only where part payment of the claim has been received. Where no payment has been received on account of the claim, omit this part and complete Part B.)

1. Principal

Principal sum claimed in statement of claim (without interest) $ ....

Date of Payment	Amount of Payment	Payment Amount Principal	Applied to Interest	Principal Sum Owing
TOTAL	$..................................	$..................................	$	A $...............................

2. Prejudgment interest

(Under section 128 of the Courts of Justice Act, *judgment may be obtained for prejudgment interest from the date the cause of action arose, if claimed in the statement of claim.)*

Date on which statement of claim was issued ....

Date from which prejudgment interest is claimed ....

The plaintiff is entitled to prejudgment interest on the claim, calculated as follows:

(Calculate simple interest only unless an agreement relied on in the statement of claim specifies otherwise. Calculate interest on the principal sum owing from the date of the last payment. To calculate the interest amount, count the number of days since the last payment, multiply that number by the annual rate of interest, multiply the result by the principal sum owing and divide by 365.)

Principal Sum Owing	Start Date	End Date (Date of Payment)	Number of Days	Rate	Interest Amount
				TOTAL B	$.....................
		Principal Sum Owing (Total A above)			$.....................
		Total Interest Amount (Total B above)			$.....................
SIGN JUDGMENT FOR					$.....................

FIGURE 6.1 Requisition for Default Judgment (Form 19D) (*continued*)

PART B — NO PAYMENT RECEIVED BY PLAINTIFF

(Complete this part only where no payment has been received on account of the claim.)

1. Principal

Principal sum claimed in statement of claim (without interest) A $ 32,199.89

2. Prejudgment interest

(Under section 128 of the Courts of Justice Act, *judgment may be obtained for prejudgment interest from the date the cause of action arose, if claimed in the statement of claim.)*

Date on which statement of claim was issued: September 26, year 0

Date from which prejudgment interest is claimed: July 29, year 0

The plaintiff is entitled to prejudgment interest on the claim, calculated as follows:

(Calculate simple interest only unless an agreement relied on in the statement of claim specifies otherwise. To calculate the interest amount, count the number of days and multiply that number by the annual rate of interest, multiply the result by the principal sum owing and divide by 365.)

Principal Sum Owing	Start Date	End Date (Date of Payment)	Number of Days	Rate	Interest Amount
32,199.89	July 29, year 0	Oct. 17, year 0	81*	12%	857.42

TOTAL B	$ 857.42
Principal Sum Owing (Total A above)	$ 32,199.89
Total Interest Amount (Total B above)	$ 857.42
SIGN JUDGMENT FOR	$ 33,057.31

* When calculating the time (T) factor in interest calculations, the figure is rounded to four decimal places in all text examples. So, here, T = 81 /365 = .2219178, and .2219178 rounded off to four decimal places is .2219:

I = P × R × T = $32,199.89 × .12 × .2219 = $857.42 prejudgment interest.

FIGURE 6.1 Requisition for Default Judgment (Form 19D) (*continued*)

PART C — POSTJUDGMENT INTEREST AND COSTS

1. Postjudgment interest

The plaintiff is entitled to postjudgment interest at the rate of per cent per year,

[ ] under the *Courts of Justice Act,* as claimed in the statement of claim.

OR

[x] in accordance with the claim made in the statement of claim.

2. Costs

The plaintiff wishes costs to be,

[x] fixed by the local registrar.

OR

[ ] assessed by an assessment officer.

Date: October 17, year 0

I.M. Just

JUST AND COPING
Lawyers
8701-365 Bay Street
Toronto, ON M3J 4A9

I.M. Just (12345A)
imj@justandcoping.ca
416-762-1342
Fax: 416-762-1343
Lawyers for the plaintiff

RCP-E 19D (May 1, 2016)

FIGURE 6.1 Requisition for Default Judgment (Form 19D) (*continued*)

ARTEMIS PLUMBING SUPPLY LTD
Plaintiff

and

PERSONABLE PLUMBERS LTD
Defendant

Court file no. 1234

ONTARIO
SUPERIOR COURT OF JUSTICE
PROCEEDING COMMENCED at
Toronto

REQUISITION FOR
DEFAULT JUDGMENT

JUST AND COPING
Lawyers
8701-365 Bay Street
Toronto, ON M3J 4A9

I.M. Just (12345A)
imj@justandcoping.ca
416-762-1342
Fax: 416-762-1343
Lawyers for the plaintiff

RCP-E 4C (May 1, 2016)

FIGURE 6.2 Bill of Costs (Form 57A)

ONTARIO
SUPERIOR COURT OF JUSTICE

B E T W E E N:

ARTEMIS PLUMBING SUPPLY LTD — Court file no. 1234

Plaintiff

and

PERSONABLE PLUMBERS LTD

Defendant

BILL OF COSTS

AMOUNTS CLAIMED FOR FEES AND DISBURSEMENTS

FEES OTHER THAN COUNSEL FEES

1. Preparing and drafting statement of claim,

   I.M. Just, September 25, year 0   1.0 hour

2. Signing default judgment and assessing costs,

   I.M. Just, October 17, year 0   0.6 hour

1.6 hours × \$200 = \$320.00

TOTAL FEES \$320.00

HST ON FEES \$41.60

FIGURE 6.2 Bill of Costs (Form 57A) (*continued*)

DISBURSEMENTS*

1. paid to issue statement of claim	$220.00	
2. paid to serve claim (includes HST)	$60.00	
3. paid to file requisition for default judgment	160.00	
TOTAL DISBURSEMENTS		$440.00
HST (R0145892)**		______
TOTAL FEES AND DISBURSEMENTS		$801.60

STATEMENT OF EXPERIENCE

A claim for fees is being made with respect to the following lawyers:

Name of lawyer	Years of experience
I.M. Just (12345A)	12

THIS BILL assessed and allowed at $________ this _____ day of ____________, ______

____

Registrar, Ontario Superior Court of Justice

TO:

PERSONABLE PLUMBERS LTD

1256 Orfus Road

Toronto, ON M4R 1Y6

Defendant

RCP-E 57A (November 1, 2015)

* The court fees under disbursements here are based on the fees in O Reg 293/92, Superior Court of Justice and Court of Appeal — Fees Under the *Administration of Justice Act.* Note that these fees change from time to time—a reminder to always check tariffs and the schedule of fees. Note also that some lawyers will add in as a disbursement the litigation file levy they pay to LawPro.

** HST is paid on fees and disbursements paid out to third parties, which includes HST to serve the claim; however, HST is not paid on court and government fixed fees. Not all lawyers charge HST on bills of costs, although the better practice is to do so.

FIGURE 6.3 Default Judgment (Form 19A)

ONTARIO

SUPERIOR COURT OF JUSTICE

B E T W E E N:

ARTEMIS PLUMBING SUPPLY LTD Court file no. 1234

Plaintiff

and

PERSONABLE PLUMBERS LTD

Defendant

JUDGMENT

On reading the statement of claim in this action and the proof of service of the statement of claim on the defendant, filed, and the defendant having been noted in default,

1. IT IS ORDERED AND ADJUDGED that the defendant pay to the plaintiff the sum of $33,057.31 and the sum of $____________ for the costs of this action.

This judgment bears interest at the rate of ______ per cent per year from its date.

Date: ____________________________ Signed by: ____________________________

Local Registrar

Address of the court office:

393 University Avenue
Toronto, ON M5G 1T4

RCP-E 19A (November 1, 2015)

FIGURE 6.4 Requisition (Form 4E)

ONTARIO

SUPERIOR COURT OF JUSTICE

B E T W E E N:

ARTEMIS PLUMBING SUPPLY LTD — Court file no. 1234

Plaintiff

and

PERSONABLE PLUMBERS LTD

Defendant

REQUISITION

TO THE LOCAL REGISTRAR at Toronto

I REQUIRE a writ of seizure and sale pursuant to an order of this court made on

October 17, year 0 in favour of ARTEMIS PLUMBING SUPPLY LTD *(name of creditor)*

directed to the Sheriff of the City of Toronto

to seize and sell the real and personal property of

Surname of individual or name of corporation/firm, etc.
PERSONABLE PLUMBERS LTD *(name of debtor)*

First given name (individual only)	*Second given name (individual only) (if applicable)*	*Third given name (individual only) (if applicable)*

and to realize from the seizure and sale the following sums:

(a) $33,057.31 *(single payment)* and interest at 12 per cent per year commencing on October 17, year 0;

(b) $801.60 for costs together with interest at 12 per cent per year commencing on October 17, year 0; and

(c) your fees and expenses in enforcing this writ.

October 17, year 0

JUST AND COPING
Lawyers
8701-365 Bay Street
Toronto, ON M3J 4A9

I.M. Just (12345A)
imj@justandcoping.ca
416-762-1342
Fax: 416-762-1343
Lawyers for the plaintiff

RCP-E 4E (July 1, 2016)

FIGURE 6.5 Writ of Seizure and Sale (Form 60A)

ONTARIO

SUPERIOR COURT OF JUSTICE

BETWEEN:

ARTEMIS PLUMBING SUPPLY LTD — Court file no. 1234

Plaintiff

and

PERSONABLE PLUMBERS LTD

Defendant

WRIT OF SEIZURE AND SALE

TO: the Sheriff of the City of Toronto

Under an order of this court made on October 17, year 0, in favour of ARTEMIS PLUMBING SUPPLY LTD,

YOU ARE DIRECTED to seize and sell the real and personal property within your county or district of

Surname of individual or name of corporation/firm, etc.
PERSONABLE PLUMBERS LTD

First given name (individual only)	*Second given name (individual only) (if applicable)*	*Third given name (individual only) (if applicable)*

and to realize from the seizure and sale the following sums:

(a) $33,057.31 *(single payment)* and interest at 12 per cent per year commencing on October 17, year 0;

(b) $801.60 for costs together with interest at 12 per cent per year commencing on October 17, year 0; and

(c) your fees and expenses in enforcing this writ.

YOU ARE DIRECTED to pay out the proceeds according to law and to report on the execution of this writ if required by the party or lawyer who filed it.

Dated at ______________________ Issued by: ______________________

on October 17, year 0 Registrar

Address of court office: 393 University Avenue
Toronto, ON M5G 1T4

RCP-E 60A (July 1, 2016)

FIGURE 6.5 Writ of Seizure and Sale (Form 60A) (*continued*)

ARTEMIS PLUMBING SUPPLY LTD
Plaintiff(s)

and

PERSONABLE PLUMBERS LTD
Defendant(s)

Court file no. 1234

FEES		
Fee	Item	Officer
$70.00	Paid for this writ	
$50.00*	Solicitor's fee for issuing writ	
	First renewal	
	Second renewal	
	Third renewal	

RENEWAL	
Date	Officer

ONTARIO

SUPERIOR COURT OF JUSTICE

PROCEEDING COMMENCED at

Toronto

WRIT OF SEIZURE AND SALE

CREDITOR'S NAME
ARTEMIS PLUMBING SUPPLY LTD

Address
c/o JUST AND COPING
Lawyers
8701-365 Bay Street
Toronto, ON M3J 4A9

I.M. Just (12345A)
imj@justandcoping.ca
416-762-1342
Fax: 416-762-1343
Lawyers for the plaintiff

* As allowed by Rule 60.19(2)(a).

RCP-E 4C (July 1, 2016)

Summary Judgment

7

LEARNING OUTCOMES

After reading this chapter, students will:

- Understand why summary judgment can be a useful tool in debt collection cases.
- Understand and apply the procedure to obtain summary judgment.
- Be able to complete the necessary documentation for a motion for summary judgment.

Summary Judgment

Where either the plaintiff or defendant believes that the pleadings and the case of the opposite party do not disclose a genuine issue requiring a trial, the party may bring a motion for summary judgment.[1]

In order to succeed on a motion for summary judgment, the moving party must show that there is "no genuine issue *requiring* a trial." A responding party may not rest solely on the pleadings, but must set out, in affidavit material or other evidence, facts that show that there is a genuine issue that does require a trial.[2] A motion judge (but not a master) has the authority to go beyond the pleadings and may order a mini trial. The judge may weigh and assess evidence, make findings on credibility, and draw inferences from the evidence.

The regular costs provisions apply to summary judgment motions. In most cases, if costs are awarded they are awarded on a partial indemnity basis. Substantial indemnity costs are only awarded, as they are elsewhere, to punish unreasonable behaviour by either party.

The purpose of Rule 20 is to reduce the number of cases that proceed to trial unless a trial is really required, by allowing mini trials and extensive overview by a judge of the pre-trial paper record.[3] Clearly, many debt collection cases where defendants have mounted spurious defences can be cleared away under the amended Rule 20.

taking of accounts
a court may order that there be a taking of accounts where an issue involving complex financial transactions needs to be examined in some detail in a less formal process than a trial; accounts may be taken before a judge or other judicial officers, usually masters of the Superior Court; the process is similar to that used in a reference

reference
a judicial proceeding used where it is necessary to inquire into an issue in an action in great detail; rather than tie up the court's time in a formal proceeding, a judge may order a reference to be held before a judge or other judicial official, such as a master, with expertise or time, or both, to delve into the matter using a less formal process than the process used in a formal trial

Note that simplified proceedings under Rule 76 are also subject to Rule 20 motions for summary judgment.

Aside from an order for dismissal of the action, there are a variety of orders a court can make on a motion for summary judgment:

1. If the issue is a question of law alone, arising clearly from the pleadings, affidavits may not be necessary, and the court may dismiss the action or dismiss the motion, and in the latter case the action continues.
2. If the issue is the amount of damages owing, where liability is clear, the court may grant judgment with a **reference** for the **taking of accounts**.
3. If the court, having examined the issues, refuses to grant a summary judgment, it may make various orders to expedite the trial. For example, it may

1 *Rules of Civil Procedure*, RRO 1990, Reg 194, Rule 20. The language in the current rule changed in 2010 so that the test for whether a court could grant summary judgment changed from "no genuine issue for trial" to "no genuine issue *requiring* a trial." The Rules Committee was of the view that this change would make it much easier for a judge to hear and decide a matter using the summary judgment procedure. As of July 2017, there were no reported Court of Appeal cases that confirmed the view of the Rules Committee, but the Superior Court has indeed heard cases under Rule 20 that they likely would have rejected prior to 2010. In that context, when reading case law on summary judgment, the reader should ask whether cases decided prior to 2010 are still relevant.

2 *Ibid*, Rule 20.02(2).

3 As discussed in note 1 above, as of July 2017, the Court of Appeal had not handed down decisions that interfered with amended Rule 20 to prevent it from operating as the Rules Committee, which it intended when it introduced reforms to Rule 20 in 2010.

find that certain witnesses need not give oral evidence, and may file written statements instead, or that certain facts are deemed admitted and need not be proved.

4. The court may adjourn a motion for judgment, but payment of part of the disputed sum into court may be the cost of an adjournment, particularly for a defendant (an amount paid into court is held by the court until a judge gives judgment ordering it to be paid to the plaintiff or returned to the defendant).

Summary Judgments in Actions for Debt

Strategically, a motion for summary judgment can be a useful tool in debt actions because it allows a plaintiff to obtain judgment for all or part of a claim at an early stage in the pre-trial proceedings without the cost and delay of discovery and a formal trial. This is particularly useful if the dispute boils down to an argument over the amount of a debt that is actually owing, because a judgment can be given for a reference or to take accounts.

Procedure

In order to obtain summary judgment, the party seeking it must bring a **motion** before a judge or, in limited circumstances, a **master**.[4] Prior to bringing such a motion, it is a good idea to check local **practice directions** to see if there are special rules governing summary judgment motions. In support of the motion, an affidavit (Figure 7.3) setting out the evidence on which the moving party relies for the relief requested in the notice of motion (Figure 7.2) must also be served with the notice of motion. In response to the moving party's material, the responding party may serve an affidavit in reply. The moving party is then responsible for preparing and filing with the court a motion record (Figure 7.1), which contains all of the documents of both parties relevant to the issues arising on the motion. Before the hearing of the motion, both sides must file factums setting out concise statements of the facts and law that they are relying on. If either party wishes to cross-examine an **affiant** on their affidavit, it will probably be necessary to adjourn the hearing of the motion to conduct the cross-examination out of court, and then, by a supplementary notice of motion returnable on the date to which the original motion was adjourned, add the transcripts of cross-examination to the material to be used on the motion for summary judgment. Once all this has been done, counsel may appear before the judge

motion
a proceeding before the court within the main proceeding to settle a legal issue that has arisen in the main proceeding—for example, a plaintiff might bring a motion to court asking that the defendant provide more detail in the statement of defence; a motion is brought by a notice of motion, which states what remedy is sought and the reasons for it; the facts in support of the motion are usually presented in an affidavit

master
a judicial officer of the Superior Court who decides procedural issues on pre-trial matters and performs some other judicial functions

practice directions
instructions as to how court rules of procedure are supplemented by specialized procedures that apply within a judicial region, usually drafted by the Chief Justice of the Superior Court or the Regional Senior Judge; they can be found on the Superior Court of Justice website at <www.ontariocourts.ca/scj>

affiant
a person who swears to the truth of statements set out in their affidavit

4 Masters are not available in all judicial regions, but sit in Toronto, Ottawa, and London. The power of a master is more limited than that of a judge, and they generally hear certain classes of motions, which deal primarily with procedure rather than the merits of a case. The power of a master to grant summary judgment under Rule 20 is severely limited. A master cannot determine issues of law and does not have the authority to weigh and assess evidence and credibility, and to draw inferences from the evidence. A master could, perhaps, determine a summary judgment motion where the claim is based on an error concerning the quantum of damages where the quantum claimed is in fact based upon a typographical error. Where there is a choice, proceeding before a master may be quicker.

or master and make oral submissions, after which the judge may give a judgment dismissing the motion, or granting judgment in the ways described earlier. However, judges also have the power to hold mini trials and hear oral evidence, either from the maker of the affidavit or from other witnesses. This may have the effect of reducing the need to cross-examine on affidavits.

In a motion for summary judgment, the moving party, in this case the plaintiff, should focus on refuting with hard evidence the facts relied on by the defendant in the statement of defence. If there is reference to a contract, agreement, or other documents, those should be attached to the affidavit as exhibits, or relevant wording from them should be quoted directly in the affidavit. If there are complex or voluminous documents that are relevant to the issues, consider filing an **affidavit of documents** with a document brief as part of the evidence on which to rely. This would be done, for example, if there was no dispute that some debt was owing, but where there are complex financial records and there is some question about the accuracy of the records and about the amount owing. If necessary, file affidavits of other witnesses who have direct knowledge of evidence relevant to the issues, particularly where the plaintiff does not have direct knowledge. For example, if there is an issue about what payments were made on an account, the plaintiff's accounts receivable manager may be in a better position to give evidence than the plaintiff because the accounts receivable manager is likely to have direct knowledge of the relevant transactions. What is said here generally about organizing a case applies equally to a defendant who is moving for judgment to dismiss the action.

affidavit of documents an affidavit in which a party identifies those documents that are relevant to the issues in the proceedings and that the party has in its possession, power, and control and can produce; the party must also identify those documents that it once had in its possession, power, and control but no longer has and those that it objects to producing; privileged documents, such as solicitor–client correspondence, will fall in the latter category; the documents being produced and relied on are contained in a document brief that is filed as evidence in the proceedings and may be referred to in court

It is not possible here to do more than sketch the procedure for bringing a motion for summary judgment because it can be complex and is more properly covered in a civil procedure text. Reference should be made to the *Rules of Civil Procedure*, in particular to Rule 20 (summary judgment), Rule 37 (motions and motion procedure), and Rule 39 (evidence on motions and applications). In Toronto, if a debt action involves a commercial transaction, a motion for summary judgment would be governed by the procedure in *The Commercial List Practice Direction*.[5]

5 For a thorough guide to motion procedure see Laurence M Olivo & Mary Ann Kelly, *Civil Litigation*, 4th ed (Toronto: Emond, 2019).

CHAPTER SUMMARY

Chapter 7 identifies the general situations in which a lawyer would move for summary judgment and describes the standard to meet to obtain summary judgment. Likely situations in which there would be a motion for summary judgment in an action for debt are described. The procedure for obtaining summary judgment is set out together with suggestions of the contents required for affidavits and the kinds of documents to be relied on. At the end of the chapter the documentation for a typical motion for summary judgment is set out.

KEY TERMS

affiant, 165
affidavit of documents, 166
master, 165
motion, 165
practice directions, 165
reference, 164
taking of accounts, 164

REVIEW QUESTIONS

1. In what circumstances would a party to a debt action bring a motion for summary judgment?
2. What does a party have to show to obtain a summary judgment?
3. What sort of material should be used as evidence to support a motion?
4. What kinds of orders can a judge make on a matter for summary judgment?
5. In what circumstances would judgment with a reference be given?
6. In what kinds of situations is it advisable to serve, and require from the other party, an affidavit of documents?
7. Describe the procedure and procedural steps to be taken to apply for a summary judgment.

CASE STUDY

MEMO

DATE: March 16, year 1
TO: U.R. Clerk
FROM: I.M. Principal
RE: TALLIS ats Monteverdi

Joe Monteverdi sued our client Thomas Tallis for default on a written guarantee for a loan for his wife, Teodora Tallis. The loan for $100,000 was made on January 6, year 0. It was payable, together with interest at 10 percent per year, on January 6, year 1, the total then due being $110,000. Teodora didn't pay up. Monteverdi sued Teodora based on her failure to pay and our client based on his failure to honour the guarantee. We defended Thomas, and in the statement of defence said that Teodora and Monteverdi renegotiated the interest rate, raising it to 12 percent. No one told Thomas at the time, but Teodora mentioned it to him on December 15, year 0, when she told our client that she would have problems paying the note on January 6, year 1. Thomas was never given notice nor asked to agree to continue his guarantee on the new terms, even though it is well known that when the terms of a contract are altered, where there is a guarantor, the right to claim against the guarantor after the contract is altered is void, unless the guarantor is given notice of the change and consents to it.

Draft a notice of motion and affidavit in support of our client's motion for summary judgment dismissing the plaintiff's action against him.

FIGURE 7.1 Motion Record

ONTARIO

SUPERIOR COURT OF JUSTICE

BETWEEN:

ARTEMIS PLUMBING SUPPLY LTD — Court file no. 1234

Plaintiff

and

PERSONABLE PLUMBERS LTD

Defendant

MOTION RECORD

Lawyers for the plaintiff: I.M. Just

Lawyers for the defendant: H.E.S. Evasive

1. Notice of Motion, dated November 3, year 0 — Tab 1
2. Affidavit of Henry Freer, sworn October 28, year 0 — Tab 2
    a. Exhibit A — accounts payable records of Personable Plumbers Ltd — Tab A
    b. Exhibit B — cancelled cheque dated July 31, year 0 in the amount of $32,000 — Tab B
3. Statement of claim filed September 26, year 0 — Tab 3
4. Statement of defence filed October 15, year 0 — Tab 4

FIGURE 7.2 Notice of Motion (Form 37A)

ONTARIO

SUPERIOR COURT OF JUSTICE

B E T W E E N:

ARTEMIS PLUMBING SUPPLY LTD Court file no. 1234

Plaintiff

and

PERSONABLE PLUMBERS LTD

Defendant

NOTICE OF MOTION

The DEFENDANT will make a motion to a judge on Wednesday, November 15, year 0 at 11:00 a.m. or, or as soon after that time as the motion can be heard, at 393 University Avenue, Toronto, ON M5G 1E6.

PROPOSED METHOD OF HEARING: The motion is to be heard

[ ] in writing under subrule 37.12.1 (1) because it is on consent;

[ ] in writing as an opposed motion under subrule 37.12.1 (4);

[x] orally.

THE MOTION IS FOR summary judgment dismissing the action against the defendant pursuant to Rule 20 of the *Rules of Civil Procedure*, or for such other order as this court deems appropriate.

THE GROUNDS FOR THE MOTION ARE Rule 20 of the *Rules of Civil Procedure*.

FIGURE 7.2 Notice of Motion (Form 37A) (*continued*)

THE FOLLOWING DOCUMENTARY EVIDENCE will be used at the hearing of the motion:

1. The statements of claim and defence.
2. The affidavit of Henry Freer, sworn October 28, year 0.

Date: November 11, year 0

H.E.S. Evasive
LSUC No. 56785E
Barrister and Solicitor
1256 Orfue Rd
Toronto, ON M4R 1Y6
416-645-1267
FAX 416-645-1268
Lawyer for the Defendant

TO:

JUST AND COPING
Lawyers
8701 - 365 Bay Street
Toronto, ON M3J 4A9

I.M. Just (12345A)
imj@justandcoping.ca

416-762-1342
FAX 416-762-1343
Lawyers for the Plaintiff

RCP-E 37A (July 1, 2007)

FIGURE 7.3 Affidavit (Form 4D)

ONTARIO

SUPERIOR COURT OF JUSTICE

BETWEEN:

ARTEMIS PLUMBING SUPPLY LTD — Court file no. 1234

Plaintiff

and

PERSONABLE PLUMBERS LTD

Defendant

AFFIDAVIT OF HENRY FREER

I, Henry Freer, of the City of Toronto, MAKE OATH AND SAY:

1. I am the accounts payable manager of the defendant and, as such, have knowledge of the matters deposed to.

2. I have read the statement of claim and the statement of defence in this action.

3. I monitor all accounts payable, including those payable to the plaintiff. It is the defendant's policy to pay all debts as they become due and to pay down running accounts at regular intervals. Attached to my affidavit and marked Exhibit "A"* is a true copy of the accounts payable record, recording all payments made to the plaintiff for the last year, including the last payment made on July 31, year 0.

4. On July 31, year 0, I mailed a cheque, cheque no. 2345, dated July 31, year 0, payable to the plaintiff, in the amount of $32,000. This cheque was apparently cashed by the plaintiff's bank, and the cancelled cheque was returned to me in the ordinary course of business. Now attached to this affidavit and marked exhibit "B"* is a true copy of the cancelled cheque,

---

*Exhibits A and B have been omitted from the affidavit to save space. Typically, copies are attached at the end of the document.

FIGURE 7.3 Affidavit (Form 4D) (*continued*)

payable to the plaintiff, and dated July 31, year 0, showing both the front of the cheque and the back.

5. As of the date of the making of this affidavit, our account records show a credit balance in favour of the defendant and not an unpaid balance as the plaintiff maintains.

SWORN before me at the	)	
	)	
City of Toronto,	)	
	)	*Henry Freer*
on 28th day of October, year 0	)	Henry Freer
	)	
I.M. Just	)	
A Commissioner, etc.	)	

RCP-E 4D (July 1, 2007)

Defended Proceedings and Settlement

8

LEARNING OUTCOMES

After reading this chapter, students will:

- Know the sequence of steps to be taken by the plaintiff and defendant in a defended Superior Court proceeding.
- Know how to take the necessary steps, under a lawyer's direction, that are likely to lead to settlement.
- Know how to complete the documentation necessary to make a Rule 49 offer.
- Understand the strategies to be considered when making or receiving a Rule 49 offer.
- Know how to and be able to complete required settlement documentation before and after a proceeding has commenced, and after judgment.

Up to this point, debt proceedings where judgments have been obtained at an early stage of the proceeding either by default or by summary judgment have been examined. At this stage, much of the work that has to be done can be done by law clerks or paralegals;[1] a lawyer's involvement is often minimal.

However, if the action is defended with a serious and substantive defence, the proceeding may take a year or more to resolve through settlement or trial, and carriage and control is likely to be in the hands of lawyers. The handling of this type of litigation, in detail, is beyond the scope of this book, but set out below is a checklist of the steps to be taken for contested litigation in the Superior Court.

In all cases, both parties should consider the concept of proportionality, as courts are directed to apply the rules of procedure by making orders and giving directions that are proportionate to the issues, the complexity of the case, and the amount of money involved. Competent lawyers have long applied this concept, even before it was required under the Rules.[2]

Steps in a Defended Proceeding

The following are steps taken in a defended proceeding:

- the plaintiff files a Form 14F, Information for Court Use with the court along with the statement of claim, which is issued by the court and then served on the defendant;[3]
- the defendant serves and files a notice of intent to defend[4] (optional) and/or a statement of defence;[5]
- the plaintiff may serve and file a reply with respect to any issue raised in the statement of defence that the plaintiff did not deal with in the statement of claim;
- the pleadings are noted closed—that is, no further pleadings may be filed without the court's permission;
- the plaintiff and defendant are required to work together to develop a discovery plan for the discovery of documents including electronically stored information and for the scheduling of oral examinations for discovery. The requirement for a discovery plan includes specific directions for applying proportionality principles to discovery by requiring the parties to plan and stick to a discovery schedule and to focus on controlling the breadth and scope of discovery so that the time and expense of discovery is commensurate

1 A paralegal working on a Superior Court of Justice case must do so under a lawyer's supervision, unless the case is in the Small Claims Court where those matters can be done by a paralegal on their own.

2 *Rules of Civil Procedure*, RRO 1990, Reg 194. Rule 1.04(1.1) of the Rules requires parties to now consider proportionality in every case.

3 A sample of Form 14F can be found at page 117 in Chapter 5.

4 A sample notice of intent to defend can be found in Chapter 5 in Figure 5.4.

5 A sample statement of defence can be found in Chapter 5 in Figure 5.5.

with what is at stake for the parties.[6] This last point is a particular problem when it comes to dealing with e-discovery and the increasing volume of documents that arises because of the use of electronically stored information, which can dramatically increase the time and costs involved in a proceeding. Each party then prepares and serves their affidavits of documents and provides a document brief that contains copies of all documents relevant to the action and/or makes their original documents available for inspection;

- oral **discovery** of the plaintiff and defendant, where each answers questions orally under oath or affirmation on the facts and issues identified in the claim and defence;
- either party may set the case down for trial by preparing, serving, and filing a **trial record**, after which the party filing the record may take no further pre-trial proceedings; other parties may continue pre-trial proceedings right up until trial;
- 60 days after one of the parties has filed the record, the registrar places the matter on the trial list. Note that in Toronto there is a commercial trial list (the Commercial List) for commercial litigation that includes many debt actions; there are special rules that apply. Some regional court offices have issued **practice directions** that apply to the judicial region whose senior judge issued the direction. They can be found on the Superior Court of Justice website at <www.ontariocourts.ca/scj>. Generally, practice directions are found printed along with the particular rule of civil procedure to which they relate. They are also published as notices in *Ontario Reports*,[7] *Ontario Annual Practice*,[8] and other commercially published compilations of the *Rules of Civil Procedure*;
- the registrar schedules a pre-trial conference before a judge, during which the parties will explore settlement and narrow the issues for trial if no settlement is achieved. Pre-trial conferences are mandatory unless the court orders otherwise. A pre-trial conference brief must be served and filed by each party;
- both parties can serve requests to admit, in which they ask each other to admit facts or allegations, so that these do not have to be formally proved at trial;
- a party who intends to call an expert witness at trial must, 90 or more days before trial, serve the other parties with the expert's report that sets out the expert's name, address, and qualifications, as well as the substance of their proposed testimony. If the other party plans to call another expert to challenge the first expert they must serve that expert's report on the other side 60 or more days before trial;[9]
- the matter now proceeds to trial.

discovery
a process where each party is asked questions under oath or affirmation about the fact allegations in their pleadings and where the strength of the evidence with respect to the facts alleged can be tested; as well, credibility of the parties can be assessed and settlement options explored

trial record
a record filed with the court before trial; consists of pleadings, any pre-trial orders, a lawyer's certificate confirming that the record is complete, and, depending on the nature of the case, other documents as well

practice directions
instructions as to how court rules of procedure are supplemented by specialized procedures that apply within a judicial region, usually drafted by the Chief Justice of the Superior Court or the Regional Senior Judge; they can be found on the Superior Court of Justice website at <www.ontariocourts.ca/scj>

6 Rules 29.1 and 29.2 set out the requirements for discovery plans.

7 Law Society of Upper Canada Editorial Board, *Ontario Reports*, Third Series (Toronto: LexisNexis, 2017).

8 James J Carthy, WA Millar & Jeff G Cowan, *Ontario Annual Practice*, 2017-2018 ed (Toronto: Thomson Reuters, 2017).

9 Rule 53.03.

Settlement

Only a small fraction of all civil actions commenced in the Superior Court actually go to trial. Most settle along the way. In order to encourage settlement in debt collection proceedings, there are some things that should be done, particularly by plaintiffs:

- Stick closely to timelines and time limits set out in demand letters and the *Rules of Civil Procedure*. Adherence to deadlines sends the message that the creditor is serious and determined to collect the debt, and that there is no profit in delaying the matter in the hope that it will go away.
- Once the legal representative has determined with the client what their bottom line is, the client should consider making a formal offer to settle under Rule 49 of the *Rules of Civil Procedure*. A plaintiff who makes an offer that is as good as or more favourable than the judgment obtained at trial will be rewarded with a higher costs award than is usual; a defendant who makes an offer that is as good as or more favourable than the judgment will be insulated from some of the costs that a defendant normally bears if the defendant loses. It is the potentially punitive nature of a costs award that encourages parties to settle where they otherwise might not. The procedure involved in making an offer is discussed in more detail in the next section.

Formal Offers to Settle: Rule 49

An offer to settle that is made at least seven days before the trial or hearing and that remains open at least until the start of the hearing may be made under Rule 49, in writing, to the other side.

- If the plaintiff makes an offer and obtains a judgment that is as good as or more favourable than the offer, the plaintiff is entitled to partial indemnity costs to the date of the offer and substantial indemnity costs after the date of the offer.
- If the defendant makes an offer and the plaintiff obtains a judgment, but the judgment is only as favourable as the offer, or less favourable than the offer, then the plaintiff is entitled to partial indemnity costs to the date of the offer, and the defendant is entitled to partial indemnity costs thereafter.
- This treatment of the plaintiff also applies where the plaintiff's action is dismissed in its entirety at the end of the trial[10] (if no offer was made and the action was dismissed, the defendant would likely have received costs on a partial indemnity basis throughout).

10 Rule 49 is not explicit about this approach where a plaintiff's action is dismissed, but it is an approach sanctioned by the Ontario Court of Appeal: *Strasser Ltd v Richmond Hill* (1990), 1 OR (3d) 243 (CA).

Offers that fall under the Rule 49 costs provisions must be made at least seven days before the trial begins. An offer should be considered and made as early as possible, and certainly as soon as the strengths and weaknesses of the client's case and that of their opponent have been assessed. This forces the other side to look at settlement, and can result in a reasonable settlement with greatly reduced litigation costs for both parties. It may be possible to assess the case with respect to settlement at the close of pleadings, and it should be possible on completion of discovery—certainly by completion of the pre-trial conference.

A Settlement Timeline

An offer to settle, whether formal or informal, may be made at any time: before proceedings commence, during proceedings, or after judgment. Offers may be made informally, formally under Rule 49, "**with prejudice**," or "**without prejudice**." Depending on when an offer to settle is made, there are certain procedural steps that should be taken to safeguard the rights of both parties. The "Settlement Timeline" box below gives an overview of the documentation that must be considered when settling under various circumstances.

with prejudice
a phrase used to signify that the writer is prepared to disclose the contents of the document to the court during the trial because they believe that it will enhance their case by showing them to be reasonable

without prejudice
a phrase used to indicate that a document may not be disclosed to the court, even if it contains damaging statements or admissions; the use of this phrase allows for a free and frank discussion of settlement options

When negotiating a settlement, if a debtor misrepresents their affairs so that a creditor accepts less than what they are legally entitled to, the creditor may move to set aside the settlement and sue for false or fraudulent misrepresentation. Therefore, in all settlements for less than the full amount due, including interest and costs, whether before or after judgment, the plaintiff should require the debtor to furnish a statutory declaration (Figure 8.6) of the debtor's financial situation covering the last five years. This document should identify assets that have been conveyed and list all the assets of the debtor in that period.

Settlement Timeline

Before Proceedings Commence	*After Proceedings Commence*	*After Judgment*
• letter confirming terms of settlement • certified cheque or post-dated cheques • release for debtor • consent to judgment • statutory declaration	• minutes of settlement • consent to judgment (may be included in minutes of settlement) • certified cheque or post-dated cheques • consent to dismiss action (may be included in minutes of settlement) • release for debtor • statutory declaration	• letter confirming terms of settlement • satisfaction piece (accord and satisfaction) • file execution • certified cheque or post-dated cheques • lift execution when paid • statutory declaration

Settlement Before Proceedings Commence

If the debtor agrees to settle for the amount in the demand letter or a negotiated amount less than demanded, the creditor will require a lump-sum payment by certified cheque, or payment with a series of post-dated cheques. The debtor will want to have a release of liability and acknowledgment of payment of the obligation, particularly if the debtor has settled for less than the full amount owing. The creditor should be prepared to provide a release (Figure 8.1) once the payment is made. If payment involves post-dated cheques, the creditor should be prepared to acknowledge in writing that a release is held and will be provided to the debtor when the last payment has been made. The creditor should also hold a consent to judgment (Figure 8.2) in the event of default allowing the creditor to sue for the debt free of any defence by the debtor.

Settlement After Proceedings Commence

As above, the debtor should provide a certified cheque or post-dated cheques for the agreed amount. Because there is a lawsuit in existence, steps must be taken to conclude it. This can be achieved by both parties signing minutes of settlement (Figure 8.3) to dismiss the action, with or without costs; a consent judgment (Figure 8.4) dismissing the action must also be prepared and filed after the last payment is made. A release may also be required by the debtor.

The action, however, is not dismissed until the amount due is paid. In the event that the amount due is not paid, the plaintiff holds a consent to judgment (Figure 8.2), agreed to in the minutes of settlement or set out in a separate consent to judgment and signed by both parties. On default of payment, the plaintiff files, with the court, the consent to judgment, or the minutes containing the consent, and a judgment for the amount agreed to or for the original amount claimed and not paid. This should result in a default judgment because the debtor has no defence to the action. The plaintiff may then proceed to enforce the judgment in the usual ways. If no defence has been filed, once the plaintiff has been paid, a notice of discontinuance can be filed to terminate the action.

Settlement After Judgment

When the plaintiff has obtained a judgment and then settles with the judgment debtor, the debtor must provide a certified cheque or a series of post-dated cheques to the plaintiff. When this has happened and the payments have been made, the creditor provides the debtor with a satisfaction piece (Figure 8.5) (sometimes called an accord and satisfaction), which acknowledges payment of the agreed amount, even if it is less than the judgment. The satisfaction piece indicates that the judgment has been paid and is no longer enforceable. Although the debtor is making the payments, any writs of execution should be left in place and, if they have not been filed, they should be filed in any region or county where the debtor has assets. This will serve to give notice to the plaintiff if other creditors seek to enforce writs against the debtor, and will ensure that the plaintiff has a grip on some share of the assets of the debtor if enforcement by other creditors occurs.[11] Once the final payment has been made, the plaintiff should write to the sheriff to ask for withdrawal of the writ of seizure and sale.

For further assurance that there are assets belonging to the debtor that are available to support the settlement and that no other creditors are waiting in the wings to claim assets, the debtor may be required to provide a statutory declaration setting out the debtor's asset and liability situation. A sample statutory declaration by a debtor is set out in Figure 8.6.

11 As noted in Chapter 3, under the *Creditors' Relief Act, 2010*, SO 2010, c 16, Schedule 4, all execution creditors share ratably with respect to the proceeds where one creditor has successfully levied execution.

CHAPTER SUMMARY

Chapter 8 provides an overview of a contested action from commencement of proceedings to trial. The advantages of settlement are discussed, and formal offers to settle under Rule 49 are described, as are other less formal settlement procedures. Settlement is then discussed in terms of the stage of the action reached when settlement occurs. There are different legal requirements and safeguards reflected in the settlement documentation depending on whether settlement occurs before a proceeding is commenced, after a proceeding is commenced, or after judgment has been obtained.

KEY TERMS

discovery, 177
practice directions, 177
trial record, 177
with prejudice, 179
without prejudice, 179

REVIEW QUESTIONS

1. What are the steps taken in a defended proceeding?
2. What is the significance of the concept of proportionality?
3. What is the purpose of oral discovery and discovery of documents (affidavit of documents)?
4. What is the Commercial List?
5. Why should a plaintiff make a formal Rule 49 offer to settle? Why should a defendant make one?
6. What are the consequences if the defendant makes an offer under Rule 49 to settle and the plaintiff refuses the offer, goes to trial and wins, but obtains judgment for an amount that is less than the offer?
7. What documents do you need to prepare if a debt is settled after a demand letter is sent but before litigation starts?
8. What does "without prejudice" at the top of a letter mean?
9. If the debtor proposes to pay by a series of post-dated cheques and no action is commenced, what should the creditor do to safeguard their interests? What should the debtor require of the creditor once all payments have been made?
10. If the debtor pays the debt after proceedings have been commenced, what must be done to terminate the proceedings?
11. Suppose that the parties agree to settle the debt after judgment has been obtained. What documents will the creditor require? What documents will the debtor require?

CASE STUDY

MEMO

DATE: September 15, year 0
FROM: L.A. Principal
TO: U.R. Clerk
RE: Artesian Wells Ltd v Grumble

We sued Samuel Grumble on behalf of our client in June year 0 for $40,000 for drilling a water well on Grumble's lot. The $40,000 sum was to be paid on or before April 1, year 0. The action no. is 3423/year 0. The amount outstanding now with interest is $40,600. I have reviewed our costs to date, and they amount to about $500 in recoverable costs. The parties have agreed to a settlement where the defendant will pay $40,200 in total on September 25, year 0, for all of our client's claim, interest, costs, and expenses.

1. Draft all of the documents that the plaintiff's lawyer would prepare. Use September 16, year 0, as the date for the minutes. Assume that if payment is not received, then judgment will be signed on November 6, year 0, by the Honourable Mr. Justice Smith.

2. Suppose you are acting for the defendant. He has no debts and owns only the property on which the well was drilled—Part Lot 8, Concession 678, Township of Lutterworth, Haliburton County—which is worth $105,000. He has not sold any property, real or personal, since year −6. Draft the documents that the defendant is required to furnish in the proceeding.

FIGURE 8.1 Sample Release (Where No Court Action Has Been Commenced)

B E T W E E N:

ARTEMIS PLUMBING SUPPLY LTD

Creditor

and

PERSONABLE PLUMBERS LTD

Debtor

RELEASE

ARTEMIS PLUMBING SUPPLY LTD (ARTEMIS), on payment of $32,000 now made to Artemis, releases PERSONABLE PLUMBERS LTD from all liability arising from a debt on a running account #12345, comprising debits up to and including July 31, year 0. The parties agree that this account has, as of the date of this release, a nil balance.

Dated at Toronto this 6th day of September, year 0

ARTEMIS PLUMBING SUPPLY LTD

By: ______________________________ *(corporate seal)*

President*

* A corporation signs documents by the signature of those authorized by its articles or by-laws to sign on its behalf. If the corporation has a seal it should also be affixed to the document. Alternatively, the words "I have authority to bind the corporation" (under the signature) can be used.

FIGURE 8.2 Sample Consent to Judgment (Where No Court Action Has Been Commenced)

BETWEEN:

ARTEMIS PLUMBING SUPPLY LTD

Creditor

and

PERSONABLE PLUMBERS LTD

Debtor

CONSENT TO JUDGMENT

The parties consent to judgment in this action on the following terms:

1. The debtor acknowledges that it is indebted to the creditor in the amount of $32,000, including interest and costs in respect of a running account the debtor maintained with the creditor.

2. The debtor undertakes to pay this indebtedness by giving to the creditor four post-dated cheques, payable to the creditor in the amount of $8,000 each, on the first day of the following months: October year 0, November year 0, December year 0, and January year 1.

3. If the debtor defaults on any of the four payments referred to in paragraph 2 of this consent, the debtor shall be liable to pay the balance then outstanding, which becomes immediately due and owing, and the debtor hereby consents to the creditor obtaining a judgment for the balance then outstanding, and for a further $300 in costs.

Dated at Toronto this 6th day of September, year 0

PERSONABLE PLUMBERS LTD

By: ______________________________ *(corporate seal)*

FIGURE 8.3 Sample Minutes of Settlement

Court file no. 1234

ONTARIO

SUPERIOR COURT OF JUSTICE

BETWEEN:

ARTEMIS PLUMBING SUPPLY LTD

Plaintiff

and

PERSONABLE PLUMBERS LTD

Defendant

MINUTES OF SETTLEMENT

THE PARTIES TO THIS ACTION consent to the dismissal of this action without costs on the following terms:

1. The defendant shall pay to the plaintiff by certified cheque or money order the sum of $32,000 on or before January 1, year 1.
2. Upon receipt of payment from the defendant, the plaintiff shall, by these minutes, consent to dismiss the action without costs and obtain a judgment dismissing the action without costs. The parties consent to a judgment in the form attached hereto as "Schedule A."*
3. The parties, by their lawyers, hereby certify that the judgment being consented to does not affect the rights of any person under disability.
4. In the event that the defendant fails to make the payment referred to in paragraph 1 of these minutes, they shall, by these minutes, consent to the plaintiff obtaining a judgment for the sum of $32,000 and a further $500 for costs.

Dated at Toronto this 6th day of November, year 0

ARTEMIS PLUMBING SUPPLY LTD

By its lawyers: ______________________________

PERSONABLE PLUMBERS LTD

By its lawyers: ______________________________

* Schedule A is not attached to these minutes; however, Figure 8.4 is the draft judgment that would be attached here.

FIGURE 8.4 Sample Consent Judgment

Court file no. 1234

ONTARIO

SUPERIOR COURT OF JUSTICE

JUSTICE __________ ______day, the ___ day of _________, year 0

(court seal)

B E T W E E N:

ARTEMIS PLUMBING SUPPLY LTD

Plaintiff

and

PERSONABLE PLUMBERS LTD

Defendant

JUDGMENT

On reading the pleadings in this action and the minutes of settlement filed consenting to the dismissal of this action without costs,

1. IT IS ORDERED AND ADJUDGED that this action be dismissed without costs.

This judgment bears interest at the rate of ____ percent per year from its date.

____

FIGURE 8.5 Satisfaction Piece (Acknowledgment of Satisfaction of Judgment)

Court file no. 1234

ONTARIO

SUPERIOR COURT OF JUSTICE

BETWEEN:

ARTEMIS PLUMBING SUPPLY LTD

Plaintiff

and

PERSONABLE PLUMBERS LTD

Defendant

ACKNOWLEDGMENT OF SATISFACTION OF JUDGMENT

Satisfaction is acknowledged of the judgment dated Wednesday, December 16, year 0, in an action in the Ontario Superior Court of Justice, in which Artemis Plumbing Supply Ltd. was the plaintiff, Personable Plumbers Ltd. was the defendant, and it was adjudged that the plaintiff should recover from the defendant the sum of $32,000 for debt together with a further sum of $500 for costs.

FIGURE 8.5 Satisfaction Piece (Acknowledgment of Satisfaction of Judgment) (*continued*)

The plaintiff, Artemis Plumbing Supply Ltd., nominates its lawyer, Peter Pugnacious, to witness and attest the plaintiff's acknowledgment of satisfaction of this judgment.

(Signed by Henry Dorkin on
(behalf of the plaintiff on
(February 19, year 1 in
(the presence of Peter
(Pugnacious, a lawyer of
(the Ontario Superior Court
(of Justice.
(AND I, Peter Pugnacious,
(declare myself to be the
(lawyer for the
(plaintiff, expressly named
(by it, and attending at the
(plaintiff's request to
(inform the plaintiff and
(its designated
(representative of the
(nature and effect of this
(acknowledgment of
(satisfaction.
(I so informed the
(plaintiff's designated
(representative before he
(executed the accord and
(satisfaction on behalf of
(the plaintiff.
(In testimony whereof, I
(subscribe my name as
(solicitor for the plaintiff.

H. Dorkin

Artemis Plumbing Supply Ltd.
by its President, Henry Dorkin
I have authority to bind the
corporation.*

Peter Pugnacious

Peter Pugnacious

* Dorkin could also sign and use a corporate seal in lieu of the phrase "I have authority to bind the corporation."

FIGURE 8.6 Statutory Declaration

STATUTORY DECLARATION

CANADA

PROVINCE OF ONTARIO

IN THE MATTER OF A JUDGMENT AGAINST PERSONABLE PLUMBERS LTD. ON WEDNESDAY, THE 16TH DAY OF DECEMBER, YEAR 0 IN FAVOUR OF ARTEMIS PLUMBING SUPPLY LTD., COURT FILE NO. 1234

TO WIT:

I, I.M. Fitter

of the City **of** Toronto

DO SOLEMNLY DECLARE THAT:

1. I am a representative of the defendant in the action by Artemis Plumbing Supply Ltd. against Personable Plumbers Ltd. The defendant is indebted to the plaintiff pursuant to a judgment dated December 16, year 0 for the sum of $32,000 and $500 for costs.
2. The defendant has a 5-year commercial lease, which expires on February 1, year 4 for 15,000 sq. metres of warehouse space at 321 Daynor Dr., North York, ON, unit 25-27. The defendant has had no other interest in any real estate in Ontario or elsewhere since October, year –5.
3. Attached is a list of the assets of the defendant that are worth more than $1,000.
4. The defendant has not sold, transferred, conveyed, or otherwise disposed of any property, real or personal, other than inventory in the ordinary course of business since October, year –5.
5. Attached are corporate income tax returns of the defendant, with attached schedules and notices of assessment for the past 5 years.
6. Attached are audited financial statements of the defendant for the past 5 years.
7. Attached are a list of all the liabilities of the defendant.

AND I make this solemn Declaration conscientiously believing it to be true, and knowing that it is of the same force and effect as if made under oath.

DECLARED before me at the City
of Toronto
in the Province
of Ontario
this 28th **day of** December, year 0

____
A Commissioner, etc.

____
I.M. Fitter

FIGURE 8.6 Statutory Declaration (*continued*)

Dated December 28, year 0

In the matter of

A JUDGMENT AGAINST
PERSONABLE PLUMBERS LTD. ON
WEDNESDAY, THE 16TH DAY OF
DECEMBER, YEAR 0 IN FAVOUR OF
ARTEMIS PLUMBING SUPPLY LTD.,
COURT FILE NO. 1234

Statutory Declaration

of

I.M. Fitter

I.M. Just (12345A)
JUST AND COPING
Lawyers
8701 - 365 Bay Street
Toronto, ON M3J 4A9

416-762-1342
FAX 416-762-1343

Lawyers for the Plaintiff

Enforcement of Superior Court Judgments

9

LEARNING OUTCOMES

After reading this chapter, students will be able to:

- Recognize the various judgment enforcement remedies available to enforce a Superior Court judgment.
- Read, understand, and apply the procedures set out in Rule 60 of the *Rules of Civil Procedure*[1] that enable enforcement of a judgment.
- Understand recent changes that permit electronic filing of court documents related to enforcement.
- Understand future changes that will affect who will be authorized to carry out enforcement procedures.
- Know how to draft enforcement documentation and carry out enforcement procedures for:
  - examinations in aid of execution;
  - writs of seizure and sale;
  - garnishments; and
  - writs of sequestration.
- Know when and in what circumstances an injunction would be used to assist in enforcing a judgment by preventing the waste or disposal of assets.
- Know the circumstances in which a creditor may seek to appoint a receiver.
- Identify assets that may be exempt from seizure in whole or in part.

1 RRO 1990, Reg 194.

In collection matters where the debt is not secured, so that the creditor does not have the right to seize a particular asset to satisfy the debt, Superior Court judgments are usually enforced using some or all of the following enforcement techniques:

- examination in aid of execution, Rule 60.18;
- writ of seizure and sale, Rule 60.07;
- garnishment, Rule 60.08;
- writ of sequestration, Rule 60.09;
- injunctions;[2] and
- court appointment of a receiver, Rule 60.02.

The most commonly used of these methods in routine collection matters are discussed in some detail in this chapter: examinations in aid of execution (also called judgment debtor examinations), writs of seizure and sale, and garnishment. Rule 60 of the *Rules of Civil Procedure* governs the enforcement process and provides a detailed procedural guide to the use of enforcement remedies. It is wise when engaging in enforcement to refer to Rule 60 frequently.

Upcoming Changes to Enforcement Procedures in Ontario

There are two areas to watch with respect to changes in judgment enforcement procedures. First, electronic issuing and filing ("e-issuing" and "e-filing") of documents is expanding in terms of where it is permitted, and the list of persons who may issue and file documents electronically for enforcement under Rule 60 is likely to expand.

Second, Ontario is currently exploring different models to be used to enforce a civil judgment or order, with a view to making enforcement simpler, faster, and less expensive.

Electronic Issuing and Filing of Enforcement Documents (Rule 60.20)

Writs and other enforcement documents are usually issued and filed by going to the courthouse or the sheriff's office to issue a writ or to file one, as has been the case for centuries. However, some enforcement documents may now be issued and filed electronically, as will be discussed in this chapter. Further, Rule 60.20 provides some oversight as to who is entitled to electronically issue and file enforcement documents. Persons with broad power to electronically issue and file documents under Rule 60 include lawyers and paralegals. As well, *any* person may file a requisition with the court registrar to provide for the electronic issuance and filing of documents in relation to the enforcement of an order. This seems to permit others, including collection agencies and other "legal persons," to issue and file electronically,

2 An injunction is an equitable remedy that is not covered directly by Rule 60.

although there is oversight because they have to file a requisition with the court clerk. It follows from this that the court is screening applicants (other than licensed legal professionals), but there is no indication in the rule, at least at the time of writing, as to what the screening criteria are. Government agencies may also electronically issue and file Rule 60 documents.[3]

While e-filing is still a work in progress, the rule permitting e-filing reduces cost and delay. For example, because writs of execution may be filed in any judicial district, multiple filings are sometimes required, in which case it is far easier and less expensive to e-file enforcement documentation.

Proposed Changes to the Civil Enforcement Procedure

Currently when a judge orders money to be paid or property to be seized, sold, held, or delivered, those orders are carried out by public officials, primarily operating out of sheriff's offices located in the 49 Superior Court offices across Ontario. This method of enforcing civil court orders would be quite familiar to judicial officials staffing courts in England in the late Middle Ages.

The Ministry of the Attorney General decided that the current system is expensive, and neither quick nor efficient. Consequently, it set out some reform proposals to be considered in a public consultation process. As this book goes to press, the consultation process has ended, and the government is considering if and how it will change the enforcement process.[4]

The government is proposing to privatize this government service and is considering two service models: a delegated administrative authority (DAA) and local service providers.

A DAA is a private, non-profit corporation given authority by the government to carry out government services. If it is given the task of enforcing civil court orders, its powers and duties would be established by statute with provisions for government oversight, making it accountable to the provincial government. It would be self-funded from user fees, as well as from licensing fees paid by agents offering enforcement services under the DAA's supervision. Under this model, all aspects of enforcement would be handled by the DAA.

The second model being considered is local private service providers. Any individual or company or association of individuals interested in providing civil enforcement services within specific geographical areas for specific time periods could apply to do so, with applicants bidding for a licence. Once the licence period expired, the licence holder would have to apply again, competing with others to provide services in their specific area under a new licence. This model would be subject to legislation and regulations governing the conduct of licencees and their employees. A licencee's operations would be completely funded through user fees. In many

3 Rule 60.20, in force April 24, 2017.

4 The original government consultation document, "A New Approach to Providing Civil Enforcement Services in Ontario" (20 January 2016), can be found online at <https://www.attorneygeneral.jus.gov.on.ca/english/courts/civil/civil_enforcement_services_consultation_report.html>.

respects this model looks not all that different from existing private collection agencies in its proposed method of operation. Similar civil enforcement services operate in British Columbia and Alberta.

While there are a variety of ways to make enforcement more efficient, the models proposed here transfer the costs of enforcement directly to creditors with a focus on eliminating public expenditure. While it may make for more flexible and efficient service, it gives enforcement agencies under either model a strong incentive to do what is necessary to collect as much as possible as quickly as possible from debtors. Under the local private service provider model, operating under a profit motive, there will be real pressure to do what is necessary to collect on a debt for a creditor-client. While this may make for quick and efficient enforcement, it has a potential downside. The *Collection and Debt Settlement Services Act*[5] and its predecessor, the *Collection Agencies Act*, demonstrate just what kinds of questionable practices debt collectors might get up to in order to increase profits.

However, for now, the reader will have to watch and see how, and to what extent, the enforcement process changes.

Examination in Aid of Execution: Rule 60.18

The examination in aid of execution, or judgment debtor examination (the JD exam), is not usually considered an enforcement technique; rather, it is an investigative tool that provides assistance in finding what assets of the debtor are available to satisfy a judgment so that enforcement tools, such as writs of seizure and sale and garnishment, can be used to tap those assets to satisfy the judgment. However, the JD exam also presents an informal opportunity for the debtor to be persuaded to make arrangements to pay off the judgment on mutually acceptable terms.

A judgment creditor may examine a judgment debtor under oath or affirmation, once in any 12-month period,[6] asking the debtor questions about assets, liabilities, current obligations, expected future income, current income, and so on. The goal is for the creditor to find out as much as possible about the nature, extent, and location of the debtor's assets. The creditor may ask the debtor why the judgment has not been paid, what the debtor's assets consist of, what the debtor's income sources are, what other debts there are, whether the debtor has disposed of major assets in the last few years, whether assets have been transferred recently to relatives, and any other relevant questions. Cases indicate that the scope of questions is broad, and the court is permissive in allowing creditors a great deal of leeway in framing questions. Extensive notes should be taken on the debtor's answers about what assets they have. If proper notes are taken, transcripts, which can be quite expensive, may not be required.

---

5 RSO 1990, c C.14.

6 Rule 60.18(4).

If the defendant is a corporation, an officer or director of the company may be summoned for examination.[7] The choice of whom to summon is initially that of the creditor, who should choose an officer or director who the creditor knows is knowledgeable about the issues and the company's assets and liabilities. If the creditor simply summons "an officer or director," the defendant may very well send someone who is not knowledgeable and who ends up giving unhelpful answers, requiring motions for re-attendance or requests for undertakings to find out information. This delays the recovery of assets and raises costs.

Similarly, a partner may be summoned to answer questions on behalf of a partnership debtor, and an owner may be summoned to answer questions on behalf of a sole proprietorship.

If the judgment creditor has had difficulty in enforcing the judgment, has exhausted alternative enforcement options, and can show that some other person has relevant knowledge that will aid in enforcement, Rule 60.18(6) permits the creditor to ask the court for permission to summons a non-party to be examined. For example, if it appears that the debtor has recently transferred a substantial asset to a relative, an order may be obtained to examine this relative about the circumstances surrounding the transfer to see whether it is or appears to be a fraudulent conveyance. Remember, however, that this is an unusual remedy and that the court, in the case of a non-party, is reluctant to draw in non-parties to a proceeding without compelling reasons.

Where the judgment creditor has found that new circumstances have arisen since the last examination, the judgment creditor may also ask the court for permission to examine the judgment debtor more frequently than once a year. Consider the previous example where it appears that the debtor has transferred property to a relative. In addition to examining the relative, there may be grounds to re-examine the debtor on this transaction—in fact, both the debtor and the relative may be examined in these circumstances. But in order to carry out this examination, a motion must be brought and a court order obtained.

It is also worth noting that if, during the course of examining a debtor, it is discovered that the debtor has concealed or moved property to defeat or defraud creditors, a motion may be brought to hold the debtor in contempt.[8] The motion may be brought at the conclusion of the examination, or the examination may be adjourned in order to bring the motion for contempt, and the examination can be resumed after the contempt order is made.

If a judgment debtor does not attend when summoned, refuses to answer questions, or is otherwise uncooperative or obstructive, a motion to hold the judgment debtor in contempt of court may be brought, and, in the alternative, the court can be asked to require the judgment debtor to attend the JD exam again at the judgment debtor's own expense. A court will rarely jail someone for contempt on such a

7 Rule 60.18(3).

8 Rule 60.18(5).

motion. Rather, the usual order is for the judgment debtor to bear the cost of re-attending an examination to answer the outstanding questions. Because the court will likely give the debtor a chance to re-attend the examination before using the contempt power to imprison, asking for costs to be fixed and paid helps to drive home to the debtor that the creditor's rights are being seriously exercised. Ultimately, a judgment debtor who remains uncooperative can be jailed for contempt.

In situations where a judgment debtor is being uncooperative on the examination, it is best to avoid having to personally serve a second contempt motion if the judgment debtor fails to re-attend or answer questions or otherwise fails to purge the contempt. After all, an uncooperative judgment debtor already cited for contempt once on a motion is hardly likely to make it easy for the creditor to personally serve the debtor with a second contempt motion. In order to avoid having to bring and serve a further contempt motion if the judgment debtor continues to be uncooperative after the first contempt motion has been heard, ask the court at the first motion to adjourn the request to commit the debtor to jail for contempt, which will allow the adjourned part of the motion to be brought back to court on short notice if the court orders re-attendance and the debtor continues to be uncooperative. If the judgment debtor is still uncooperative, the judgment creditor can bring the adjourned part of the motion back before the court with minimal paperwork and in a relatively short time, and without the need to re-serve the debtor personally.

In order to summons a judgment debtor for examination, Rule 60.18(7) requires the judgment debtor to be served personally with a notice of examination (Figure 9.1), or by using an alternative to personal service. Ordinarily, if a party is represented by a lawyer, that party is served by serving the lawyer under Rule 34.04(1)(a).

The reason for using personal service is that personal service is required to be proved as a prerequisite to finding the judgment debtor in contempt for non-attendance. Some commentators[9] suggest that when serving the notice, a note can be attached to the notice of examination requesting that the person being examined produce detailed information and documents about certain assets or liabilities about which there is some knowledge that was obtained through investigations made at the start of proceedings or knowledge gained during the proceedings. Also, a standard checklist can be attached (see the box on page 199) to focus the judgment debtor's mind on assets or interests that are relevant.

The particular circumstances of the case should determine the questions asked, although most people working in this field follow the questionnaires developed by Frank Bennett[10] for individuals and corporations. For adapted versions of these questionnaires, see Figure 9.2.

9 Frank Bennett, *Bennett on Collections*, 6th ed (Toronto: Carswell, 2017) at 235-36.

10 *Ibid* at 262-77.

Standard Checklist to Be Attached to Notice of Examination of Judgment Debtor

To the judgment debtor: In preparing to attend a judgment-debtor examination touching upon your means and ability to pay what you owe to the judgment creditor, you are required to provide all documentation in your power, possession, or control, and to provide detailed information with respect to the following:

1. shares and stocks
2. bonds
3. accounts receivable
4. real estate
5. mortgages
6. leases
7. insurance policies
8. debts
9. furniture
10. motor vehicle licence plate and serial numbers
11. bank accounts—account numbers and balances
12. mutual funds—account numbers and current value
13. RRSPs
14. pensions
15. term deposits, GICs
16. jewellery
17. art collections
18. other collections of value
19. watercraft and aircraft
20. assets located outside of Ontario
21. assets located outside of Canada

Source: Adapted from a checklist suggested by F. Bennett, *Bennett on Collections*, 6th ed (Toronto: Carswell, 2017) at 236.

Writ of Seizure and Sale: Rule 60.07

Under the authority of the writ of seizure and sale (also called a writ of execution), the sheriff may seize the real and personal property of the execution debtor, subject to certain exceptions; sell the seized assets; and then distribute the net proceeds of sale ratably among all the judgment creditors who have filed writs of seizure and sale with the sheriff who has levied execution. Remember that sheriffs operate each within their own county. If a sheriff seizes property in Ottawa, execution creditors with writs filed in Toronto will not share in the proceeds, unless they have also filed duplicate writs with the sheriff in Ottawa.

The discussion in Chapter 6 about obtaining a default judgment shows that when a default judgment is obtained, the judgment creditor may then requisition the local registrar to issue a writ of seizure and sale. The writ is then filed with the sheriff in each county where there is reason to believe the debtor has property. The writ, when filed, could passively assist the creditor who might share in the proceeds of sale brought about by another execution creditor seizing assets of the debtor. The writ also serves as notice to other persons having dealings with the debtor of the creditor's judgment against that creditor. For example, a bank lending the debtor money on a mortgage will not advance funds if it discovers an **execution** filed against the debtor. It will require the execution to be paid off by the debtor before advancing mortgage funds.

execution
an act of the sheriff in enforcing a writ of seizure and sale (commonly referred to as a writ of execution), writ of delivery, or writ of sequestration; the word "execution" is also used to describe individual writs of execution on file; when lawyers "search executions" they are examining the sheriff's records to see if any writs of seizure and sale are filed with the sheriff

The Rules now provide, where available, for the electronic issuing of a writ of seizure and sale. However, special software is required to do this. See Rules 4.05(1), (1.1) to (1.3), (4.1), and 60.07(1.1) to (1.3). Remember: e-issuing and e-filing are rapidly evolving processes, and these rules may change, hopefully making these processes simpler and easier to use.

Although it is a common and recommended practice to automatically file a writ of seizure and sale on obtaining a judgment, the sheriff is not normally instructed to seize a particular asset unless the following has already been accomplished:

- the asset has been identified with sufficient particularity that the sheriff is able to locate it and verify its identity;
- a quote from the sheriff has been obtained as to the cost of seizure and sale and the deposit required to start the process and the client's consent to incur the expense have been obtained;
- it has been determined that the debtor has an interest in the asset that can be seized; and
- it has been determined where the asset is located so that the sheriff can be told where to go to seize it.

Note that the sheriff will not do research or carry out investigations to locate an asset. Provide as much information as possible about the asset that is going to be seized.

After acquiring this information, complete and send to the sheriff a direction to enforce (Figure 9.3). Provide the following information in a direction to enforce:

- the date of the judgment and the amount, including costs;
- the postjudgment interest rate;
- the cost of enforcement for issuing the writ of seizure and sale and for the sheriff's fees in filing and enforcing the writ (from the tariffs for court and sheriff fees, under the *Administration of Justice Act*[11]). Note that Rule 60.19(2)(a) limits the lawyer's preparation fee for a writ to $50;
- the dates and amounts of payments received since the date of judgment, if any; and
- the total amount owing including postjudgment interest to date.

This form does not give the sheriff any useful information to enforce the writ, so a letter should be attached that gives explicit directions about what should be seized, where it is located, and if there are any further issues involving seizure that a sheriff should know about. Also, the amount of the deposit required must be determined from the Sheriff's Office before the sheriff will seize a **chattel**. For the seizure of bank accounts, try to obtain the location of the branch and the account number. For the seizure of an automobile or any other chattel, provide information about where it can be found. It is useful to provide an up-to-date *Personal Property Security Act* (PPSA)[12] search report to show that assets being seized are either free of the claims of secured creditors or subject to the claims of secured creditors. For example, to seize a debtor's automobile, a Certified Plate Search—Recent Owner (Figure 3.2,

chattel
an item of tangible personal property (tangible means it is a thing, like a car); intangible personal property refers to a right to something of value—for example, a cheque, which is a right to payment

11 O Reg 293/92 and O Reg 294/92.

12 RSO 1990, c P.10.

at page 66) from the Ministry of Transportation should be provided, along with a PPSA Search—Motor Vehicle Enquiry (Figure 3.9, at page 77) in the name of the debtor, and information about where the car is likely to be found and when, so that the sheriff can have it towed away. If the information is correct, the sheriff will attend at the place where the asset is located and seize the asset. A sheriff who meets with resistance is entitled to call upon the police to assist the sheriff's officers in the execution of their duty. If the debtor raises legal objections to a seizure and sues or threatens to sue the sheriff, the sheriff will bring an interpleader motion. This motion asks for direction from the court as to what the sheriff is to do with the seized asset. The usual order is to dispose of it by sale and declare the sheriff to be without liability, but hold the proceeds until the court determines the rights of the disputants to the proceeds. Note that the sheriff is not immune from being sued. For example, if the sheriff disposes of assets at an abnormally low price, the sheriff could be held to have been negligent in not obtaining a reasonable and appropriate price.

Once a judgment is in hand, there is an absolute right to enforce it and requisition a writ of seizure and sale. If a writ is not issued immediately, it may be issued at any time within six years of the judgment. If a writ must be issued after six years have passed, or if there is a **condition precedent** to be fulfilled before a writ is issued (for example, where payment is specified for a future date), then a motion must be brought to the court that gave the judgment for leave to issue the writ. If an order giving leave to issue the writ is obtained, it may be issued at any time within a year of the date on which the order was made (Rules 60.07(2) and (3)). Note that the sheriff can decline to enforce a writ. It is important to give the sheriff as much information as possible to enforce a writ. If the sheriff is uncertain as to whether a writ is properly issued or filed, the sheriff may refuse to enforce it, at which point the creditor may bring a motion for directions. In the past, the sheriff's right of refusal to enforce was implicit (in that a motion could always be brought to get the judicial process to do something), but it is now explicit in Rule 60.07(13.1).

condition precedent
a situation where one must do A before one is allowed to do B—A is the condition precedent to the performance of the condition B

The process for filing and executing writs of seizure and sale is changing with the use of electronic filing. Normally under Rule 60.07, when requisitioning a writ of seizure and sale, a copy of the order for payment must be filed, and, in some cases, other supporting evidence entitling the creditor to payment must also be filed. However, when filing a requisition electronically, it is not necessary to file other material:

- Under Rule 60.07(1.1), a creditor is entitled to the electronic issue of one or more writs by electronically filing a requisition. A requisition or other document filed after regular business hours is deemed to be filed on the same day. The order on which the writ is based is deemed to have been entered as an order of the Superior Court. This should speed up and simplify the process of issuing a writ, saving both time and money.
- Under Rules 60.07(10) and (11.1), where a debtor uses an alias or a variation of the name on the writ, the writ may, on motion, be amended electronically.
- There is now a special rule for electronic filing of writs by the Workplace Safety and Insurance Board.

- If the address of a creditor or a creditor's lawyer changes, the change may be filed electronically under Rules 60.07(12.1) and (12.2).

Note that special software is required for electronic filing.

Because a judgment may be unsatisfied for years, and because a writ of seizure and sale expires six years after it is issued, it is necessary to apply to renew the writ. The Rules do not require the sheriff to give notice of expiry of the writ to the creditor's lawyer, so the renewal date must be diarized. If the creditor wishes to renew the writ, this may be done by filing a request to renew (Figure 9.4), in which case the writ is automatically renewed. If a writ has been obtained but not filed with the sheriff, the writ can be renewed at the end of six years by requisitioning renewal from the registrar. (Following Figure 9.4 is a sample letter to a client with regard to renewal of a writ of seizure and sale.) Under Rule 60.07(8.1), a request to renew a writ can now be filed electronically.

After suing and obtaining judgment, it may be discovered that the judgment debtor's name has been legally changed, the person goes by another name or alias, or they use a variation of the spelling of their name. If this is the case, bring a motion without notice to the debtor to the court that gave the original judgment, asking that the writ be amended, using the phrase "now known as" or "also known as" followed by the alias, new name, or spelling variation, as the case may be (Rule 60.07(10)). The same process may be followed if the address of the creditor or the creditor's lawyer changes from the time the writ was first issued (Rule 60.07(12)). Under Rule 60.07(11.1), the court may grant the creditor leave to file an amendment to the writ electronically under subrule 4.05(1.1)-(1.3) to show the new name, the alias, or the spelling variation.

Procedure Governing Sale

Once the sheriff has seized an asset—for example, the debtor's automobile—the sheriff must follow the procedure set out in Rules 60.07(16) to (24). Where personal property is seized, the sheriff must, if requested by the debtor, furnish a list of what has been seized within a reasonable time after the seizure. Before arranging a sale, the sheriff must give public notice of the time and place of the sale and give notice to the creditor and the debtor.

More stringent rules govern the sale of land by the sheriff. First, no step to sell land under a writ may be taken until the writ has been filed for at least four months, and no sale may take place until six months have passed since the writ was filed (Rules 60.07(17) and (18)). Notice of sale must be given in the *Ontario Gazette*[13] at least 30 days before the sale, and in a general circulation newspaper at least once each week in two successive weeks. The successive notices must start no earlier than three weeks before the sale and finish no later than one week before the sale. Notice

13 The *Ontario Gazette* (Toronto: Queen's Printer) can be found online at <http://www.ontariogazette.gov.on.ca>.

must also be given by mail to the creditor's lawyer and to the debtor. Notice must also be posted in the sheriff's office (Rule 60.07(19)). The contents of the notice are prescribed by Rule 60.07(20) and include:

- a short description of the land (lot and plan, and municipal address, if any);
- the short title of the proceedings (for example, *Smith v Jones*);
- the time and place of the intended sale; and
- the name of the debtor whose interest is being sold.

Although the sheriff is not obliged to get the top market price for land or personal property, there is an obligation to get the best price possible in the circumstances of a sheriff's sale. Buyers know that sheriff's sales are distress sales and that the seller's bargaining power is somewhat less than it would be on the open commercial market. If the sheriff considers it necessary to adjourn a sale to a later date to get the best price possible, that may be done with such further notice of the later sale as the sheriff deems appropriate. If property remains unsold because there are no buyers, the sheriff must inform the creditor of this fact. On receipt of this notice, the creditor can instruct the sheriff to proceed to sell in a way that will attract buyers and get the best price possible.

Normally, the sheriff will conduct sales by public auction, because that process permits anyone interested to see what prices are offered and that the best price was accepted. If the sheriff obtains an inordinately low price and accepts it rather than trying other sale times or methods, any party affected may be able to sue the sheriff successfully for negligence.

Garnishment (Rule 60.08)

If the judgment debtor does not have assets on which a creditor can levy execution, the debtor may have income from various sources that can be attached. These income sources can be tapped by a creditor using a procedure known as garnishment. With garnishment, the creditor (garnishor) obtains an order requiring a third party (garnishee) to pay money that the garnishee owes to the debtor to the creditor-garnishor instead. Funds attached in this way reduce the sum the debtor owes to the creditor. The garnishee is deemed to have paid what the garnishee owes to the debtor, even though the sum was diverted to pay the creditor.

Garnishment can be used to attach such things as:

- wages paid by an employer to the debtor;
- commissions earned and paid to the debtor—tips may also be garnisheed;
- cash surrender value of a life insurance policy owned by the debtor;
- pay out of moneys from an RRSP;
- joint bank accounts, up to one-half of the money in the account;
- bank accounts solely owned by the debtor;

- mortgage payments to the debtor;
- rental payments to the debtor;
- payments from a mutual fund;
- accounts receivable of the debtor; and
- payments to the debtor from a trust fund or an estate.

The garnishment process is primarily administrative. If neither the garnishee nor the debtor raises a defence to garnishment, there is no court appearance required, and the work can be done by a law clerk.

In order to garnish a debt, the following steps must be carried out in the court where the judgment was obtained.

Prepare and File a Requisition for Garnishment

The requisition for garnishment (Figure 9.5) will be used by the registrar to prepare the notice of garnishment (Figure 9.6) that will be served on the garnishee and the debtor. It is important that the requisition be accurate. The following information must be provided: the total amount of the garnishment (judgment, costs [including all costs of collection to date as allowed by Tariff A and the court and sheriff's fees], and postjudgment interest to date). Tariff A sets out rules and guidelines for determining fees and disbursements allowable under the *Courts of Justice Act* and Rules 57.01 and 58.05 of the *Rules of Civil Procedure*. Note that Rule 60.19(2)(a) limits the lawyer's fee for preparation of the requisition to $50.

Prepare an Affidavit in Support of a Requisition for Garnishment

An affidavit in support of a requisition for garnishment (Figure 9.7) may be sworn or affirmed by the creditor or by the lawyer for the creditor. The affidavit provides the evidence for the facts set out in the requisition. The affidavit should give the particulars of the judgment. A copy of the judgment, as **issued and entered**, should be attached to the affidavit. The affidavit should set out the payment history of the debtor since the judgment, as well as calculations showing how the present amount was determined, the principal amount, costs to which the garnishor is entitled, and postjudgment interest to the date of the affidavit. Lastly, it should set out the basis for the belief that the proposed garnishee is indebted to the debtor; the amount of the indebtedness, if known; and the last known addresses of the debtor, the garnishee, and anyone else to whom the notice will be sent. If the garnishee is outside Ontario, as a prerequisite to the garnishment, it must be set out that the garnishor would have a right to sue the garnishee for the debt in Ontario. If the garnishee is not yet indebted to the debtor, but will be indebted in the future, set out the circumstances of the debt and the date when it is payable. On receipt of the requisition for garnishment and the supporting affidavit, the registrar will issue a notice of garnishment, describing the persons identified as owing money to the debtor as garnishees. The registrar will send a copy of the notice of garnishment to the sheriff in the county or region where the debtor resides or, if the debtor resides outside Ontario, to the sheriff in the county or region in which the proceedings started.

issued and entered
a judgment or order is issued when it is signed by a judge or registrar and the court's seal is affixed to it; it is then entered (recorded) by the registrar, using a system for referencing and recording an issued judgment; an entered judgment or order will usually have a stamp on it, indicating the place of storage so that it can be found in court files

Garnishment of Joint Debts and Dealing with Co-Owners

In the past, where income was owed partly to the debtor named in the garnishment notice and partly to a co-owner, matters could be delayed while the share actually owing to the debtor was determined to be available for garnishment. Rule 60.08(1.1) now clearly specifies that one-half of the debt is presumed available for garnishment, or a greater or lesser amount if there has been an order under Rule 60.08(16) on a motion to determine the amount owing and available for garnishment. It is now clear under Rules 60.08(15.1) and (15.2) that, when a creditor is served with a garnishee's notice that a debt is owed to the debtor and a co-owner, a creditor must serve the co-owner with a notice to co-owners of a debt, which sets out the co-owner's rights and liabilities in the proceedings, and also serve a copy of the garnishee's statement. Service must be personal, or by an alternative to personal service. If any party or co-owner asks for a garnishment hearing under Rule 60.08(16), the notice of motion must be served on the sheriff. A co-owner wishing to dispute a proposed distribution to the creditor must bring a motion for a garnishment hearing within 30 days of service, failing which the co-owner will be presumed to not dispute payment of the full amount to the creditor.

Issuing and Renewing of Notices of Garnishment

Under Rules 60.08(6.1) to (6.5), a notice of garnishment is in effect for six years from the date of issue, and is renewable for an indefinite number of six-year terms. It shall name one debtor and one garnishee. One notice cannot be used to name several debtors. The notice may be renewed prior to its expiry by filing a requisition for renewal of garnishment where the garnishment was issued, together with a supporting affidavit. The registrar shall renew the garnishment notice, and notice of renewal shall also be served on the sheriff where the debtor resides or on the sheriff of the county or region where the proceeding commenced, if the debtor resides outside Ontario.

Service of Notice of Garnishment

Once the garnishment notice has been issued, the creditor should serve it along with a blank garnishee's statement (Figure 9.8), which the garnishee uses to report on payments to be made, or to report that nothing is due and owing to the debtor so that nothing will be paid. Service may be by mail, although service on the debtor should be by personal service, if possible, so that the debtor cannot complain later that they were not served and obstruct the garnishment process once it has begun. If serving a garnishee that is a financial institution or a business with more than one office or location, serve the branch or location where the account is located or where the payment is normally paid from. Remember that a garnishee at a location outside Ontario cannot be served unless it is a debt for which the garnishee could be sued in Ontario by the debtor.

If the garnishee is the **Crown in right of Ontario**, in respect of a debtor who is a provincial civil servant or a contractor with the government, a notice of garnishment is served on the garnishee with a statement of particulars attached (Figure 9.9),

Crown in right of Ontario the legal title used to refer to the government of Ontario and how the government is usually named when it is a party to a legal proceeding

setting out the details that will allow Crown officials to identify the debtor and the payment due to the debtor, so that they can comply with the notice of garnishment. Include a blank garnishee's statement with the documents for service. If it is desired that the federal Crown be the garnishee with respect to a debtor who is a federal civil servant, federally appointed judge, member of Parliament, employee of a Crown corporation (most of them), and others who are paid out of the Consolidated Revenue Fund, this may be done under the *Garnishment, Attachment and Pension Diversion Act* (GAPDA).[14] The statute and the regulations should be read carefully to determine whether the debtor falls under GAPDA, especially if the garnishment target is a federal Crown corporation. Generally, the regulations list the Crown corporations that come under GAPDA. (If the debtor is in receipt of money from Crown corporations that are not on the list, the debtor is governed by the usual provincial garnishment rules.) Once it has been determined that the federal Crown is an appropriate garnishee for the debtor, a garnishee summons must be served to garnishee Her Majesty. The federal Crown may dispute the garnishment and generally has all the rights to respond that an ordinary garnishee would have.

Illustration of Calculation of Garnishment of Wages

Gross wages:	$1,000	per week
Deductions from gross:	300	income tax deductions
	10	Canada Pension
	20	Employment Insurance
	50	pension plan
	20	health insurance
	30	group life insurance
	$ 430	TOTAL DEDUCTIONS

NET PAY: $1,000 – $430 = $570

AMOUNT AVAILABLE FOR GARNISHMENT: $570 × 0.20 = $114

Payments to the Sheriff

When the garnishee has been served, they are obliged to pay to the sheriff the sum set out in the notice, or the sum owed to the debtor if it is less than the sum claimed. The garnishee is also obliged to turn over any of the debtor's property that the debtor has a right to. Payment must be made within ten days after service of the notice of garnishment or ten days after payment is due, whichever is later.

14 RSC 1985, c G-2.

Effect of Garnishee Notice

The notice binds debts owed by the garnishee to the debtor at the time the notice is served, up to and including any debt due within six years after the notice is served. If there was a condition precedent to payment by the garnishee and if the condition is performed within six years of service of the notice, payment is deemed to have been made and is deemed to be attached and payable to the sheriff. The garnishee, on responding with payment, should send back the garnishee's statement indicating the payments that are being made and/or will be made in future unless the garnishee is paying the full amount owed to the creditor. The notice should be served on the garnishor and debtor and filed with the court within ten days of service of the notice of garnishment on the garnishee. Note that if the Crown is being served as garnishee, the Crown, under the *Proceedings Against the Crown Act*,[15] has 30 days from the actual or effective date of service[16] on the Crown to respond. If the garnishee fails to pay, or fails to respond with a garnishee's statement disputing the garnishment, within the time allowed for responding, the garnishor is entitled to serve a notice of motion on the garnishee, requesting an order that the garnishee pay the full amount owed by the debtor to the garnishor, as if the garnishee were liable directly to the garnishor for the debt.

Garnishment Hearing

If any party, including the garnishee, disputes the process, they may, by notice of motion, apply for a garnishment hearing. For example, if a bank account that appears to be jointly owned with a spouse is garnished, a garnishment hearing may be held to determine what the spouse's share of the account is. Note that all interested parties must be served with notice of a hearing and have a right to be heard and make submissions on the motion.

Payment Out by the Sheriff

The sheriff will make payments to the creditor, subject to the terms of the *Creditors' Relief Act*.[17] Recall that execution creditors shared ratably on any distribution by the sheriff. This is also the case in garnishment proceedings. The sheriff sends a distribution proposal to all execution creditors who have filed writs of execution or garnishment notices with the sheriff. In the distribution proposal, the sheriff records the details of all funds the sheriff has seized or otherwise received, and lists the execution creditors who are entitled to share in the proceeds, along with the amounts they are owed and their pro rata shares.

15 RSO 1990, c P.27.

16 "Effective date of service" is a reference to service by mail, where the document is deemed served five days after it is mailed. See Rule 16.06(2).

17 SO 2010, c 16, Schedule 4.

Garnishing Wages

When garnishing wages,[18] the *Wages Act*[19] allows for seizure of 20 percent of the debtor's *net* wages for a pay period. The box on page 206 shows how the amount is calculated.

Assets Exempt from Seizure

exigible
a word used to describe assets that the sheriff may seize when executing a writ of seizure and sale; if an asset is exempt from seizure it is referred to as a non-exigible asset

Some assets of the debtor are non-**exigible**—that is, they may not be seized by the sheriff under a writ nor may they be garnished. At common law, necessaries could not be seized as these were deemed necessary minimums for survival. For example, the clothes worn by the debtor cannot be seized, nor can damages paid to the debtor for pain and suffering. However, to these have been added a number of exemptions that are based on statute. Some of these exemptions reflect the concerns of an earlier age—for example, the detailed exemptions allowed to farmers in the *Execution Act*.[20] But the language now is a bit more general, describing categories of personal property. Note, however, that where a chattel that falls into an exempt category is the subject of the judgment, it is not exempt from seizure, whatever its value. For example, if a person bought some tools to use in their work and didn't pay for them, the seller could sue and recover the tools that were purchased, although the tools otherwise would fall into the exempt category. As well, if a chattel's value exceeds the exemption amount, it can be seized, though the debtor may be able to retain some of the sale proceeds up to the exemption limit.

Until 2010, the monetary amounts of exemptions were set out in the *Execution Act*. In October 2010, the *Open for Business Act, 2010*[21] amended the *Execution Act*, which resulted in a new regime governing personal exemptions. The fixed amounts were taken out of the statute and put into regulations where they could be changed more frequently and more easily without having to amend a statute. The current exemption rules are in O Reg 657/05 under the *Execution Act*. The last adjustment to the amounts, as of the time of writing, occurred in 2015.

The current exemptions in O Reg 657/05 are as follows:

1. The upper limit on necessary clothing for the debtor and dependants has been removed. Presumably, if the clothing can be described as "necessaries," it is exempt. The existing law governing "necessaries" for minors' contracts may be useful here to determine what is or is not a "necessary," and is therefore exempt or not from seizure.

18 The *Canadian Oxford Dictionary*, 2nd ed (Don Mills, Ont: Oxford University Press, 2004) notes that both "garnish" and "garnishee" are used to describe the act of a judgment creditor obtaining payment from someone who owes money to the judgment debtor. "He has garnisheed my wages" and "He has garnished my wages" are both acceptable use, although the latter form appears to be the more common usage in Canada.

19 RSO 1990, c W.1.

20 RSO 1990, c E.24.

21 SO 2010, c 16—Bill 68, *An Act to promote Ontario as open for business by amending or repealing certain Acts* (assented to October 25, 2010).

2. For household furnishings and appliances: $13,150.
3. For tools and other personal property used to earn income:
   a. in the case of a debtor engaged solely in the tillage of the soil or farming, $29,100 for livestock, fowl, bees, books, tools and implements, and other chattels ordinarily used by the debtor in the debtor's occupation, or
   b. in any other case, $11,300.
4. For a personal motor vehicle: $6,600.
5. For the principal residence of the debtor, the exemption is $10,000 or less in equity.
6. Any medical device or equipment used by a debtor or dependants for a disability or medical condition is exempt from seizure and sale.

The box below presents an overview of the current exemptions at common law and under provincial and federal legislation. Although most of the exemptions encountered arise with enforcement of writs of seizure and sale, remember that the exemptions also apply to garnishment proceedings.

Assets Exempt from Seizure

Provincial

PENSIONS, BENEFITS

Compensation for Victims of Crime Act — victim's compensation;
Welfare legislation — section 143 of the *Courts of Justice Act* prohibits garnishment of any benefit, allowance, or assistance payment;
Ontario Municipal Employees Retirement System Act — pensions are exempt except to satisfy a support order; and
Pension Benefits Act — pension benefits are exempt except to satisfy a support order.

INSURANCE BENEFITS

Workplace Safety and Insurance Act — injury insurance benefits and pensions; and
Insurance Act — rights of an insured in an insurance contract and insurance benefits are exempt if a beneficiary is designated who is a close family member.

WAGES

Wages Act — 80 percent of a worker's net wages are exempt from seizure, reduced to 50 percent if enforcement is in respect of a support order. These percentages may be varied upward or downward on application of either the debtor or the creditor.

OTHER ASSETS

Execution Act — exempt from seizure are tools of a trade or calling, up to $11,300 to permit a debtor to gain a livelihood; livestock, equipment up to $29,100, and other farming assets to permit a farmer to earn an income; necessary clothing, which is completely exempt from seizure; household furnishings up to $13,150; and vehicles up to $6,600.

If a debtor buys a chattel, fails to pay for it, and is sued by the creditor, the creditor may seize the chattel even though it might otherwise be exempt.

The exemptions are not available to corporations, but are available to partnerships and sole proprietorships.

Federal

PENSIONS, BENEFITS

Canada Pension Plan Act — pension benefits are exempt;
Canadian Forces Superannuation Act — pensions are exempt;

Government Annuities Act — annuities and income paid out are exempt under insolvency legislation;
Members of Parliament — pensions are exempt;
Old Age Security Act — benefits are exempt;
Pension Fund Securities Act — the interest of a member in the body of the fund is exempt, and may not be assigned to the creditor or others;
RCMP Superannuation Act — benefits are exempt;
Employment Insurance Act — benefits are exempt; and
War Veterans Allowance Act — allowances are exempt.

Note that most federal pensions are not exempt from garnishment with respect to enforcement of family support judgments under the *Garnishment, Attachment and Pension Diversion Act*.

OTHER ASSETS

Indian Act — real and personal property on a reserve can only be seized by an Indian or a band.

Other Enforcement Remedies: Writs of Sequestration, Injunctions, and Receiverships

Writs of sequestration can be obtained from the court if the creditor is able to show that other enforcement remedies are likely to be ineffective. This is difficult to do, and because the remedy is somewhat out of the ordinary, judges exercise discretion in making such orders. If such an order cannot be obtained, the effect is that, pending further direction by the court, the sheriff may seize and hold personal property and real estate of the debtor. For example, if a debtor is disposing of property to hinder or defeat creditors, property that might not be available for seizure may be available for sequestration and can be held as a form of security for the property that the debtor is trying to dispose of in order to prevent it from being seized.

Injunctions may be obtained on an interim or temporary basis to prevent the debtor from disposing of property before judgment. This goes against the general rule that the creditor may not enforce an unsecured right to payment against the property of a debtor until *after* obtaining a judgment. Because injunctions in these circumstances are extraordinary, they are used sparingly. They are resorted to primarily in cases where the *Fraudulent Conveyances Act*[22] cannot or will not be able to reach assets of the debtor.

Mareva injunction permits a creditor to obtain an injunction to secure the debtor's assets in a case where it is likely that the debtor will dispose of or remove all assets from the jurisdiction, before judgment, leaving no assets to satisfy the judgment debt

Where a creditor can show that there are some assets in Canada that belong to a debtor and that there is a strong risk that they will be removed so as to frustrate enforcement of a judgment, the creditor may be able to persuade the court to issue a **Mareva injunction**, which permits an asset to be seized and held to satisfy the judgment. For example, in the case that gave the Mareva injunction its name, the *Mareva* was the debtor's ship that had happened to dock at a port in the jurisdiction where an action against its owners had been brought and where there were no other assets. The creditor obtained an injunction to detain the ship and make it available to satisfy the debt, which would otherwise have been unenforceable if the ship had

22 RSO 1990, c F.29.

been allowed to leave port. In effect, a debtor who has no exigible assets in Ontario puts at risk any asset brought within the jurisdiction of Ontario courts.

Receiverships are orders of the court that allow for the appointment of a person to run a business enterprise owned by the debtor, with a view to managing it or selling it. They are often available to deal with property that is security for a debt, and some secured loan agreements will permit the creditor to appoint a receiver without a court order if the debtor is in breach of the loan agreement. Under the *Bankruptcy and Insolvency Act*,[23] it is possible to obtain an order for an interim receivership where there is a danger that an asset, otherwise available to creditors in bankruptcy proceedings, might be dissipated. If an order is made and an interim receiver appointed, the receiver can monitor the use of the asset and safeguard the value in it, but cannot exclude the debtor from using the asset.

As noted earlier, these remedies are exceptional in nature and rarely used, especially in a routine collection practice.

23 RSC 1985, c B-3, as amended.

CHAPTER SUMMARY

Chapter 9 examined the enforcement tools used in the Superior Court: examination in aid of execution, writs of seizure and sale, garnishment, writs of sequestration, injunctions, and court-appointed receivers. An examination in aid of execution is an investigative tool that provides information for more effective use of the other enforcement tools. It permits the creditor to question the debtor on the debtor's debts, assets, and means. A writ of seizure and sale can be filed with the sheriff. On receiving instructions to do so, the sheriff will seize and sell the judgment debtor's property and use the proceeds to pay all creditors who have filed writs in that court. If others owe the debtor money, the creditor may garnish payments owing to the debtor from third parties. If enforcement is proving difficult, in exceptional cases obtaining a sequestration order from the court will permit the sheriff to seize property pending further direction from the court. Injunctions can be used to prevent a debtor from disposing of or wasting property prior to judgment. If the debtor is an ongoing business, instead of seizing assets, the court may permit a receiver to be appointed to run the business and arrange to sell it. The remedies of injunction, receivership, and sequestration of assets are exceptional remedies that are not usually used in routine collections.

KEY TERMS

chattel, 200
condition precedent, 201
Crown in right of Ontario, 205
execution, 199
exigible, 208
issued and entered, 204
Mareva injunction, 210

REVIEW QUESTIONS

1. What are the principal methods of enforcing judgments?
2. What changes appear to be occurring in the filing of enforcement documents?
3. Describe the advantages that electronically filing and issuing documents has over physically filing and issuing hard copies of such documents.
4. What changes is the government of Ontario considering with respect to who handles the enforcement process?
5. What are some of the advantages and disadvantages of the current system and the proposed alternatives?
6. In what circumstances would each of the following be used? A Mareva injunction; a writ of seizure and sale; a writ of sequestration; an injunction; and garnishment proceedings.
7. How often can a judgment debtor be examined?
8. Is the judgment debtor the only person that can be examined in a JD exam?
9. What steps should be taken before conducting a JD exam of a corporation?
10. What can be done if, on a JD exam, the debtor goes on talking endlessly without answering the questions?
11. Why should a judgment debtor be personally served with a notice of examination?
12. Suppose a contempt motion is brought against a debtor who is obstructing a judgment debtor examination. On the motion, if the court orders

the judgment debtor to re-attend at their own expense, and the debtor does, but continues to be obstructive, how can the serving of a second contempt motion be avoided? And why is this important?

13. Should a direction to enforce a writ of seizure be filed with the sheriff every time a writ of seizure and sale is filed? Why or why not?
14. What is likely to happen if the sheriff is directed to seize a car and the debtor claims the car seized is not theirs?
15. How long after a writ of seizure and sale has been issued can it be filed?
16. What has to be done to prevent a writ of seizure and sale from expiring?
17. Suppose it is discovered that the judgment debtor is also known by an alias. Will this affect attempts to enforce the judgment? What steps should be taken to deal with this matter?
18. Can the creditor seize a judgment debtor's (a) car; (b) car, if she is a salesperson and uses the car in getting to her customers; (c) Canada Pension benefits; (d) clothing; and (e) set of wrenches if she is a mechanic and the judgment against her is for the unpaid price of the wrenches?
19. If the judgment debtor is a wage earner, can wages be seized to pay a judgment debt?
20. Suppose the creditor has just filed a writ of seizure and sale. Can the creditor direct the sheriff to immediately take steps to sell the debtor's house?
21. Suppose that, on the sale of an asset, the sheriff is offered a small fraction of what the seized asset is worth. Does the sheriff simply have to accept it? Should it be accepted?
22. Suppose that at a JD exam it is discovered that the judgment debtor has a joint bank account, a car, a house, income from employment, and income from a mortgage that a trustee owns and holds on the judgment debtor's behalf. What enforcement remedies would be used?
23. Suppose a garnishee is served with a notice of garnishment for $40,000. The garnishee owes the debtor, a building contractor, $10,000 for renovation work. What should the garnishee do in these circumstances? What would happen if the garnishee sat back and did nothing?
24. What happens if it is discovered that the debtor is an Ontario civil servant and the debtor's salary is the only asset? Would it make a difference if the debtor is employed by the federal government?
25. How long is the garnishee liable to make payments to the sheriff?
26. What can the creditor do if the garnishee serves a garnishee statement in which the garnishee says that there are no debts owing to the debtor and the creditor thinks this is untrue?
27. When the sheriff receives funds from a garnishee, can the sheriff simply turn that amount over to the creditor?
28. In what circumstances would an application to use a writ of sequestration be made?

CASE STUDY

MEMO

DATE: January 28, year 0
TO: U.R. Clerk
FROM: Fiona Anoif
RE: Judgment Against Snogglepus Apartments Ltd

Last week, on January 20, we obtained a judgment against Snogglepus Apartments Ltd for $36,000, plus prejudgment interest of $430 and costs fixed at $350, on behalf of our client Jerry's Janitorial Services Ltd. Postjudgment interest is at the rate of 10 percent per year. The plaintiff's address is 123 Main St., Toronto, ON M4Y 2P4.

Our investigations show that Snogglepus Apartments Ltd, not surprisingly, owns Snogglepus Apartments Ltd at 341 Victory Blvd., Toronto, ON M3R 1V6 and that its head office is in apt. 1 in that building. There are four tenants—G.F. Handel in apt. 2, J.S. Bach in apt. 3, L. Boccherini in apt. 4, and A. Corelli in apt. 5. All pay rent on the first of the month.

1. Complete the necessary documentation to file a writ of seizure and sale so that we can seize the ownership of the apartment building.
2. Complete the necessary forms to garnish rent paid by the tenants of the debtor.

FIGURE 9.1 Notice of Examination (Form 34A)

Court file no. 1234

ONTARIO

SUPERIOR COURT OF JUSTICE

B E T W E E N:

ARTEMIS PLUMBING SUPPLY LTD

Plaintiff

and

PERSONABLE PLUMBERS LTD

Defendant

NOTICE OF EXAMINATION

TO: Dagmar Johnson

YOU ARE REQUIRED TO ATTEND, on Friday, December 15, year 0 at 10:30 a.m. at the office of Suleman Kahn, CSR, 721 Bay Street, Suite 300, Toronto, ON M9R 3T4, tel. 416-762-1234 for:

[ ] Cross-examination on your affidavit dated (*date*)

[ ] Examination for discovery

[ ] Examination for discovery on behalf of or in place of (*identify party*)

[ ] Examination in aid of execution

[x] Examination in aid of execution on behalf of or in place of Personable Plumbers Ltd.

YOU ARE REQUIRED TO BRING WITH YOU and produce at the examination the documents the following documents and things:

all books, accounts, invoices, contracts, letters, emails, statements, records, bills, notes, securities, vouchers, plans, photographs, and copies of any of these things in your possession or under your control in any way relating to the matters that are within the scope of these proceedings or that have any reference to these proceedings.

Date: December 2, year 0

JUST AND COPING
Lawyers
8701 - 365 Bay Street
Toronto, ON M3J 4A9

I.M. Just (12345A)
imj@justandcoping.ca
416-762-1342
FAX 416-762-1343

Lawyers for the Plaintiff

TO: Dagmar Johannson
87 Pleasant Blvd.
Toronto, ON M3T 1A4

RCP-E 34A (July 1, 2007)

FIGURE 9.2 **Questions to Be Used in Examining Debtors**

QUESTIONS TO BE USED IN EXAMINING AN INDIVIDUAL DEBTOR

Date of Judgment: ______________

Date Writ of Seizure and Sale filed with Sheriff: ______________

Date Writ of Seizure and Sale filed with Land Titles Office: ______________

Date of Debt: ______________

I. PERSONAL DETAILS

A. Personal History

Full name: ______________ Birth date: ______________

Telephone: ______________ Email: ______________

Residence address: ______________

Are you the Mr./Ms. ______________ who owes money to ______________

according to this judgment dated ______________ ?

Do you ever use any other name? ______________

If so, what name(s)? ______________

Spousal Status

Married: ______________ Single: ______________ Divorced: ______________ Common Law: ______________

Living Apart: ______________

Family Information

Children: ______________ No.: ______________ Other Dependants: ______________

Total family group equals ______________ persons.

B. Employment Status

Unemployed: ______________ Employed: ______________ Self-Employed: ______________

Part-Time: ______________

What is your occupation? ______________ Who is your superior? ______________

Name and address of employer: ______________

Position: ______________ Present Wages: ______________

How long have you held this position? ______________

When are you paid (obtain day of week)? ______________

Bonus schemes (when paid etc.): ______________

Commissions: ______________

Are you in any way related to your employer? ______________

Previous Employers:

Name: ______________ Address: ______________

How Long? ______________

How you ever been in business on your own? ______________

When? ______________

Where? ______________

Inventory? ______________ What? ______________

Where kept? ______________

Have you ever had any employees? ______________

FIGURE 9.2 Questions to Be Used in Examining Debtors (*continued*)

Have you been involved in any partnership? ______________

When? ______________

Where? ______________

Have you ever carried on business under any trade or business name? ______________

If so, what name? ______________

Inventory? ______________ What? ______________

Where kept? ______________

Are you an Officer or Director of any corporation? ______________

If so, which corporation(s)? ______________

Have you any part-time jobs? ______________

If so, where? (*name and address*) ______________

If unemployed, are you subject to recall? ______________ When? ______________

II. DETAILS OF PLACE OF RESIDENCE

A. Type of Accommodation

Description of Property (e.g., 2-storey, garage, number of bedrooms):

____

Municipal address: ______________

Do you own it?

(absolute, beneficial, joint tenant, or tenant in common): ______________

Legal description: ______________

If yes, date of purchase: ______________

– reporting letter ______________

Amount paid: ______________

– present value ______________

– air conditioning ______________

– type of heating: oil, gas, or coal ______________

– number of square feet per floor ______________

– number of bathrooms ______________

– unfinished areas ______________

Who lives there? ______________

Particulars of mortgage including:

– amount: ______________

– balance owing: ______________

– terms: ______________

B. If Residence Is Not Owned

Name of building's owner: ______________

Address: ______________

Do you pay rent? ______________ How much? $ ______________

When is rent due? ______________

Is landlord related to you? ______________

FIGURE 9.2 Questions to Be Used in Examining Debtors (*continued*)

Is rent paid up to date? ________________

To whom do you give the rent? ____________________________

Do you pay rent by cash or cheque? __________________

Who signs the cheque? ____________________________

Is there a lease? ________________

Who signed the lease? ____________________________

III. DETAILS ABOUT DEBTOR'S SPOUSE

Full Name: ________________________________

Maiden Name (if wife): ________________________________

Address: ____

Age: __________ Telephone: _____________________

Employment Status

Unemployed: ________________ Self-Employed: __________________

Part-Time: ________________

Name of Employer: _______________________________

Address: ____

Position: _________________________ Salary: $ ______________

When paid: ____________________

How long has he/she worked there? _____________________

Where did he/she last work? ____________________________

Name: __________________________________

Address: ____

Moneys due: $_____________

How much: $_____________

Any support to other people: ___________________________

IV. PARTICULARS OF CHILDREN

Name	*Age*	*Address*	*Employed*
1.			Yes/No
2.			Yes/No
3.			Yes/No
4.			Yes/No
5.			Yes/No

FIGURE 9.2 Questions to Be Used in Examining Debtors (*continued*)

V. DETAILS OF PERSONAL BUDGET

Sources of Income and Expenses

Income (Per Month)		*Expenses* (Per Month)	
1. Weekly Salary	$	1. Food	$
2. Part-Time Income	$	2. Clothing	$
3. Room and Board from Others	$	3. Housing:	
		– Rent or Mortgage	$
4. Pensions	$	– Taxes	$
5. Employment Insurance	$	– Fuel	$
6. Workers' Compensation	$	– Phone/Cellphone/Internet	$
7. Family Allowances	$	4. Transportation	$
8. Annuities	$	5. Insurance	$
9. Inheritances	$	6. Education and Recreation	$
10. Other	$	7. Medical and Dental	$
		8. Bank Loans	$
		9. Other	$
Total	$		$

VI. ASSETS OTHER THAN INCOME

A. Real Estate

Do you own any real estate?

	Street Address	*City*	*Tenants*
1.			
2.			
3.			

[Obtain municipal address and legal description.]

Do you own other real estate? ____________________

If not, when did you last own real estate? ____________________

How did you transfer it? ____________________

When? ____________

To whom? ____________________ How much? $____________

Who was the solicitor acting on your behalf? ____________________

Do you own the furniture in your residence? ____________________

B. Vehicles

1. Do you own (and/or lease) a car or truck? ________ (Yes/No)

   Make ____________ Year ____________ Model ____________

   Licence No. ____________ Chassis No. ____________ Engine No. ____________

   Where is it kept? ____________ What use is made of it? ____________

   Value: $____________

   How much do you still owe on it? $ ____________

   To whom? ____________________ (Name)

   Address: ____

FIGURE 9.2 Questions to Be Used in Examining Debtors (*continued*)

Equity in owned auto? ______________

What type of security is there for this debt? ______________

Do you own any other automobiles? ______________

2. If you do not own an automobile, do you drive an automobile? __________ (Yes/No)

   [If yes, ask who owns the car and particulars under (1), above.]

   When did you last own an automobile? ______________

   To whom did you sell it? ______________

   For what amount? $ ______________

   Were there any liens on the car? __________ By whom? ______________

3. Do you own, lease, or have the use of a tractor; a snowmobile; an airplane; a motorcycle; or a motor boat? __________ (Yes/No)

   [If yes to one or more, ask particulars under (1), above.]

C. Bank Accounts

1. Do you have any bank accounts or trust company accounts? __________ (Yes/No)

   If yes, give the following information:

	Bank	*Address*	*Type and account number*	*Balance*
a.				
b.				
c.				
d.				

[Obtain statements and entry books if possible.]

If no, when did you last have a bank account?

Where? ______________

When did you close it? ______________

When did you last have any claim to or interest in any bank account in any name? ______________

When did you last draw a cheque? ______________

To whom was that cheque payable? ______________

Amount: $ __________ What was it given for? ______________

Have you ever had the right of access to any safe deposit box? ______________

Box No.: __________ Bank: ______________

Address: ______________

When was the last time you had a safe deposit box? ______________

Do you have any term deposits? __________ When was the last? ______________

FIGURE 9.2 Questions to Be Used in Examining Debtors (*continued*)

D. Specific Assets

	Yes	*No*	*Describe*
1. Mortgages			
2. IOUs			
3. Promissory notes			
4. Loan agreements			
5. Other security for payment of money			
6. Government bonds			
7. Other bonds			
8. Common stock in public and private corporations			
9. Preferred stock in public and private corporations			
10. RRSP			
11. RIF			
12. RHOSP			
13. RDSP			
14. RESP			
15. TFSA (Tax Free Savings Account and other tax savings and deferred financial instruments)			
16. Television set, electronic communication equipment			
17. Refrigerator			
18. Stove			
19. Washer and dryer			
20. Furniture			
21. Fur coats			
22. Jewellery			
23. Gold or silverware			
24. Works of art			
25. Horses and/or boats			
26. Any interest in any patent copyright, process, formula, invention, or royalties			
27. Pensions			
28. Lottery tickets			
29. Coins and stamps			
30. Liquor			

FIGURE 9.2 Questions to Be Used in Examining Debtors (*continued*)

E. Life Insurance

Do you carry life insurance on yourself? ______________ (Yes/No)

[Check whether term, group, or whole life.]

If yes, please give following information:

	Name of Insurance Company	*Policy No.*	*Amount of Policy*	*Beneficiary*	*Premium*	*Who Pays Premium*	*Cash Surrender Value*
1.							
2.							
3.							
4.							

Do you carry life insurance on your wife or any person in which you have an interest? ________________

If yes, please give following information:

	Name of Insurance Company	*Policy No.*	*Amount of Policy*	*Beneficiary*	*Premium*	*Who Pays Premium*	*Cash Surrender Value*
1.							
2.							
3.							
4.							

F. Moneys Owing to Defendant

Is there money owing to you? ________________ (Yes/No)

If yes, give the following information:

	Name of Debtor	*Address*	*Amount*	*Security Held*
1.				
2.				

G. Miscellaneous

1. How much money are you carrying right now? $ ____________________
2. Have you any income from any other source whatever? ____________________
3. Have you made a will? ________________
4. Have you any interest as beneficiary, remainderman, right of reversion, executor, administrator, trustee, guardian, or otherwise under any will or *inter vivos* of trust or in any estate? ____________________
5. Have you ever been a party to a trust agreement or other trust instrument? Did you at any time put any money or property of any kind in trust for yourself or anyone else? ____________________
6. Have you received any money or property of any kind under any will or by inheritance or from any estate? ________________
7. Do you have any business deals pending which will likely give you money? ____________________

FIGURE 9.2 Questions to Be Used in Examining Debtors (*continued*)

VII. ASSETS OF SPOUSE AND CHILDREN

A. Real Estate

Does your spouse own any real estate? ________________ (Yes/No)

Do your children own any real estate? ________________ (Yes/No)

Locations

	Street Address	*City*	*Tenants*
1.			
2.			
3.			

Where did they last own real estate? (give details above)

B. Automobiles

1. Does your wife own an automobile? ________________ (Yes/No)

   Make ________________ Year ________________ Model ________________
   Licence No. ________________ Serial No. ________________
   Where is it kept? ________________

   What use is made of it? ________________

   How much does she still owe on it? $________________

   To whom? ________________ (Name)

   Address: ________________

   Equity in owned auto? ________________

   What type of security is there for this debt? ________________

   Does she own any other cars? ________________

2. If she does not own an automobile, does she drive an automobile? ________________ (Yes/No)

   [If yes, ask who owns the car and above particulars.]

3. When did she last own an automobile? ________________ (Date)

   To whom did she sell it? ________________ (Name)

   Address: ________________

   Telephone: ________________

   Amount: $ ________________ Security taken: ________________

C. Bank Accounts

1. Do your wife or children have any bank accounts? ________________ (Yes/No)

   If yes, give the following information:

	Bank	*Address*	*Type and account number*	*Balance*
a.				
b.				
c.				
d.				

   Do you give them any money to put in the account(s)? ________________

   If yes, how much? ________________

   If no, where did they get it? ________________

FIGURE 9.2 Questions to Be Used in Examining Debtors (*continued*)

VIII. LIST OF CREDITORS

Present debts (approximate) $ ______________

Please list your debts for me, giving the following information:

	Name of Creditor	*Address*	*Amount*	*Security Held*	*Judgment*
1.					
2.					
3.					
4.					
5.					
6.					
7.					
8.					
9.					
10.					

Give details of payments to other creditors:

Who? ______________________________

How much? ______________________________

When? ______________________________

Why? ______________________________

What is the cause of your financial difficulty?

Explain briefly: ______________________________

Do you have any identification—for example, a driver's licence? ______________

1. Do you hold property in trust for anyone else? (particulars)

   ____

2. During the past year did you guarantee any indebtedness for anyone?

   ____

3. During the past year did you make or endorse any paper for anyone?

   ____

4. When did you last apply for or obtain a loan at any bank, finance company, or other lending institution or from any non-lender, corporation, or person whatsoever?

   ____

5. Are you holding in your name or possession for the benefit of anyone else any property of any kind whether real property, personal property, or otherwise?

   ____

6. Is anyone holding your property in trust for you?

   ____

FIGURE 9.2 Questions to Be Used in Examining Debtors (*continued*)

IX. MISCELLANEOUS MATTERS

1. Have you any judgment or interest in any judgment? ______________________________
2. Have you any claim of any kind against anyone? ______________________________
3. Have you any interest of any kind in any mortgage or any lease or interest in any leasehold on any real or personal property?

   ____
4. Are you a party to any agreement of any kind with anyone?

   ____
5. Are you a party to any action now pending in the courts?

   ____
6. Have you filed your income tax return for the last two years? ______________ [Obtain a copy.]

   Any tax refunds? ______________________________
7. Have you ever been bankrupt or made a proposal under the *Bankruptcy Act*? [If so, obtain particulars.]

   ____
8. When did you take your last vacation? ______________________________

   [If recently, obtain particulars. If some other person or corporation is in possession of the judgment debtor's property, examine that person or corporation. Ask questions that seek such information.]

X. DISPOSAL OF ASSETS

1. Have you sold any of the assets in the above questions from the debt date to present? ______________________________
2. Have you transferred any of the assets in the above questions from the debt date to present? ______________________________

   [A debtor should be able to account for every asset that he had at the debt date and every asset he acquired from that date to the present.]
3. Did you give your spouse presents for Christmas? Were the presents valuable? ______________________________
4. Have you allowed anyone to use your land or property free of charge? Nominal charge? ______________________________
5. Have you assigned or transferred any of your property to anyone by way of security? ______________________________

XI. PROPOSED SETTLEMENT

The amount owing to our client is $ ____________________. Is there any possibility that you may be able to get the money together to pay this debt? ___ (Yes/No)

If yes:

When? ______________________

What terms? ______________________

Suggested payment: $ ____________________ per week, month; payments to be made starting ______________________________.

What arrangements have you made for paying this judgment? ______________________________

Why has the judgment not been paid? ______________________________

FIGURE 9.2 Questions to Be Used in Examining Debtors (*continued*)

QUESTIONS TO BE USED IN EXAMINING AN OFFICER/REPRESENTATIVE OF A CORPORATE JUDGMENT DEBTOR

I. Introduction

1. Name of the officer.
2. Officer's address, telephone/cellphone numbers, and email addresses.
3. Is this the notice of appointment that was served upon you?
4. Are you aware of the amount owing to this creditor as a result of judgment?
5. What is your position with the company?
6. How long have you been with the company?

II. Minute Book

1. Location of minute book.
2. Would you make minute books available to me if I wanted to examine them?

III. Financial Statements

1. For present period: books of accounting, general ledger, etc.
2. For five years prior.
3. Particulars of revenues.
4. Particulars of expenses.
5. Particulars of loans, advances, or dividends to shareholders.
6. Salaries paid to officers and directors.
7. Any extraordinary expenses or revenues during period.
8. Has the company during the past five years returned any goods to creditors or paid creditors out of the normal course of business?
9. Copy of bank statements.
10. Who are the company's auditors/accountants/solicitors?

IV. Particulars of Corporation

1. Date of incorporation.
2. What kinds of shares were originally issued by the company? What was their original value? How many shares were originally issued?
3. Who were the original shareholders?
4. Who are the present shareholders?
5. Could you please give me the particulars of the transfer of shares?
6. Were the shares paid for in full?
7. Who were the original directors?
8. Who are the present directors?
9. Who were the original officers?
10. Who are the present officers?
11. Where is the company's head office?
12. Are the premises owned or leased?
13. Were premises ever owned by the company?
14. Could you please describe the type of business?
15. What was the cause for financial difficulties?

FIGURE 9.2 Questions to Be Used in Examining Debtors (*continued*)

V. Creditors of Company

1. Are there any other creditors?
2. What is the status of their claims—that is, do they have secured claims or judgments?
3. Do any creditors have any form of security on the company's assets?
4. If so, what type, when given, and circumstances at time when given?
5. Please provide a list of all the creditors.
6. Does the company owe the bank any money either on a loan or overdraft?
7. How does the bank secure its indebtedness (i.e., assignment of accounts receivable, section 178 security, personal guarantees, or security agreement)?
8. Are there any mortgages or liens against automobiles, equipment, furniture, trade fixtures, or general equipment or inventory of the company?
9. Are any of the company's goods taken on consignment or sold on consignment?

VI. Assets of Company

1. Furniture.
2. Office and plant equipment.
3. Vehicles—type, when acquired, how used.
4. Trade fixtures.
5. Inventory.
6. Accounts receivable—obtain list.
7. Lease for office or other leases owned by company.
8. Any holdings outside Canada.
9. If so, with whom did the company deal?
10. Did the company own any bonds?
11. Are any mortgages payable to the company?
12. Are any loan agreements payable to the company?
13. Are any securities payable to the company?
14. Did the company own any common stock in other corporations?
15. Does the company own any other personal property—for example, a TV or refrigerator?
16. Does the company own any real property?
17. Does the company own any other property?

FIGURE 9.3 Direction to Enforce Writ of Seizure and Sale (Form 60F)

Sheriff's file no. 12894

ONTARIO

SUPERIOR COURT OF JUSTICE

BETWEEN:

ARTEMIS PLUMBING SUPPLY LTD

Creditor(s)

and

PERSONABLE PLUMBERS LTD

Debtor(s)

DIRECTION TO ENFORCE WRIT OF SEIZURE AND SALE

TO: the Sheriff of the City of Toronto

Under an order of this court in favour of Artemis Plumbing Supply Ltd

made on October 17, year 0,

Personable Plumbers Ltd was ordered to pay the sum of $33,057.31

with interest at the rate of 12 percent per year commencing on October 17, year 0. Since the order was made, the creditor has received the following payments:

Date of payment		*Amount of payment*
	nil	

There remains owing today under the order:

Amount of Principal	*Due date*	*Accrued interest*
$33,766.91 (prejudgment interest and costs)	due immediately	$144.25* to October 30, year 0

* Postjudgment interest is calculated on the judgment plus costs being awarded:

$33{,}057.31 + 709.60 = 33{,}766.91 \times .12 \times .0356$ (which was $^{13}/_{365}$) $= 144.25$

FIGURE 9.3 Direction to Enforce Writ of Seizure and Sale (Form 60F) (*continued*)

Under Rule 60.19 of the *Rules of Civil Procedure*, the creditor is entitled to costs in the amount of

(a) $50.00 for the preparation of documents in connection with issuing, renewing and filing with the sheriff the writ of execution or notice of garnishment;

(b) $410.00* for disbursements paid to a sheriff, registrar, official examiner, court reporter or other public officer and to which the creditor is entitled under subrule 60.19 (1); *(Attach copy of all receipts.)*

(c) $ .... for an amount determined in accordance with Tariff A for conducting an examination in aid of execution; *(Attach affidavit confirming that examination was conducted.)*

(d) $ .... for any other costs to which the creditor is entitled under subrule 60.19 (1). *(Attach certificate of assessment.)*

YOU ARE DIRECTED to enforce the writ of seizure and sale issued on October 17, year 0 and filed in your office for a sum sufficient to satisfy the total of the amounts set out above, together with subsequent interest, and your fees and expenses.

Date October 17, year 0

I.M. Just

(Signature of party or lawyer)

(Name, address and telephone number of party or lawyer)

JUST AND COPING
Lawyers
8701 - 365 Bay Street
Toronto, ON M3J 4A9

I.M. Just (12345A)
imj@justandcoping.ca
416-762-1342
FAX 416-762-1343

Lawyers for the Plaintiff

RCP-E 60F (November 1, 2005)

* $70.00 to issue writ
$100.00 to file with sheriff
$240.00 to direct enforcement

FIGURE 9.3 Direction to Enforce Writ of Seizure and Sale (Form 60F) (*continued*)

ARTEMIS PLUMBING SUPPLY LTD
Creditor(s)

and

PERSONABLE PLUMBERS LTD
Debtor(s)

Sheriff's file no. 12894

ONTARIO
SUPERIOR COURT OF JUSTICE
PROCEEDING COMMENCED AT Toronto

DIRECTION TO
ENFORCE WRIT
(OF SEIZURE AND SALE)

JUST AND COPING
Lawyers
8701 - 365 Bay Street
Toronto, ON M3J 4A9

I.M. Just (12345A)
imj@justandcoping.ca
416-762-1342
FAX 416-762-1343

Lawyers for the Plaintiff

RCP-E 4C (July 1, 2007)

FIGURE 9.4 Request to Renew (Form 60E)

Court file no. 1234

ONTARIO

SUPERIOR COURT OF JUSTICE

B E T W E E N:

ARTEMIS PLUMBING SUPPLY LTD

Plaintiff

and

PERSONABLE PLUMBERS LTD

Defendant

REQUEST TO RENEW WRIT OF SEIZURE AND SALE

TO the Sheriff of the City of Toronto

YOU ARE REQUESTED TO RENEW the writ of seizure and sale issued on October 17, year 0 in this proceeding and filed in your office for a period of six years from the date of renewal.

DATE October 4, year 6 Signature I.M. Just

(Signature of party or lawyer)

JUST AND COPING
Lawyers
8701 - 365 Bay Street
Toronto, ON M3J 4A9

I.M. Just (12345A)
imj@justandcoping.ca
416-762-1342
FAX 416-762-1343

Lawyers for the Plaintiff

RCP-E 60E (July 1, 2007)

FIGURE 9.4 Request to Renew (Form 60E) (*continued*)

Just and Coping
Lawyers
8701 - 365 Bay Street
Toronto, ON M3J 4A9
416-762-1342
416-762-1343 (fax)

September 6, year 6

Henry Dorkin, President
Artemis Plumbing Ltd.
100 Laird Avenue
Toronto, ON M6Y 3A4

Dear Sir:

RE: Artemis Plumbing Ltd v Personable Plumbers Ltd

A writ of seizure and sale was filed against Personable Plumbers Ltd. on your behalf on October 17, year 0 for the amount of $33,057.31 together with assessed costs of $801.60. A writ of seizure and sale liens the property for a period of six (6) years, and must be renewed every six (6) years. The cost for the renewal of your writ will be $140 and this renewal must be filed before October 17, year 6.

We look forward to receiving your instructions regarding the renewal of the writ and if you do wish the execution to be renewed against the defendant, please forward the sum of $140 to our offices, payable to Just and Coping, in Trust.

Yours very truly,

JUST AND COPING
Per:

I.M. Clerk

I.M. Clerk
Law Clerk

FIGURE 9.5 Requisition for Garnishment (Form 60G)

Court file no. 1234

ONTARIO

SUPERIOR COURT OF JUSTICE

B E T W E E N:

ARTEMIS PLUMBING SUPPLY LTD

Creditor(s)

and

PERSONABLE PLUMBERS LTD

Debtor(s)

and

MURRAY HILL CONTRACTING LTD

Garnishee

REQUISITION FOR GARNISHMENT

TO: the local registrar at TORONTO

I REQUIRE a notice of garnishment to be issued in this proceeding, in accordance with the attached draft Form 60H. The total amount to be shown in the notice of garnishment is $34,603.16, made up as follows:

1. $33,057.31 for principal owing under the judgment or order, including prejudgment interest.
2. $801.60 for the costs of the action.
3. $50.00 for the preparation of documents in connection with issuing, renewing and filing with the sheriff a writ of execution or notice of garnishment.
4. $550.00* for disbursements paid to a sheriff, registrar, official examiner, court reporter or other public officer and to which the creditor is entitled under subrule 60.19(1). *(Attach copies of all receipts.)*
5. $ .... for an amount determined in accordance with Tariff A for conducting an examination in aid of execution. *(Attach affidavit confirming that examination was conducted, and a bill of costs.)*
6. $ .... for any other costs to which the creditor is entitled under subrule 60.19(1). *(Attach certificate of assessment.)*
7. $144.25 for postjudgment interest to today's date.

Date October 30, year 0

I.M. Just

(Signature of creditor or creditor's lawyer)

JUST AND COPING
Lawyers
8701 - 365 Bay Street
Toronto, ON M3J 4A9

I.M. Just (12345A)
imj@justandcoping.ca
416-762-1342 FAX 416-762-1343

Lawyers for the Plaintiff

RCP-E 60G (November 1, 2005)

* $70.00 to issue writ
$100.00 to file with sheriff
$240.00 to direct enforcement
$140.00 to issue garnishment

FIGURE 9.6 Notice of Garnishment (Form 60H)

Court file no. 1234

ONTARIO

SUPERIOR COURT OF JUSTICE

BETWEEN:

ARTEMIS PLUMBING SUPPLY LTD

Creditor

and

(Court seal)

PERSONABLE PLUMBERS LTD

Debtor

and

MURRAY HILL CONTRACTING LTD

Garnishee

NOTICE OF GARNISHMENT

TO MURRAY HILL CONTRACTING LTD
123 Dover St., Toronto, ON M1K 5E4

A LEGAL PROCEEDING in this court between the creditor and the debtor has resulted in an order that the debtor pay a sum of money to the creditor. The creditor claims that you owe a debt to the debtor. A debt to the debtor includes both a debt payable to the debtor and a debt payable to the debtor and one or more co-owners. The creditor has had this notice of garnishment directed to you as garnishee in order to seize any debt that you owe or will owe to the debtor. Where the debt is payable to the debtor and to one or more co-owners, you must pay one-half of the indebtedness or the greater or lesser amount specified in an order made under subrule 60.08(16).

YOU ARE REQUIRED TO PAY to the Sheriff of the City of Toronto,

(a) within 10 days after this notice is served on you, all debts now payable by you to the debtor; and

(b) within 10 days after they become payable, all debts that become payable by you to the debtor within 6 years after this notice is served on you,

subject to the exemptions provided by section 7 of the *Wages Act*. The total amount of all your payments to the sheriff is not to exceed $ $34,603.16 less $10 for your costs of making each payment.

EACH PAYMENT MUST BE SENT with a copy of the attached garnishee's payment notice to the sheriff at the address shown below.

IF YOU DO NOT PAY THE TOTAL AMOUNT OF $$34,603.16 LESS $10 FOR YOUR COSTS OF MAKING EACH PAYMENT WITHIN 10 DAYS after this notice is served on you, because the debt is owed to the debtor and to one or more co-owners or for any other reason, you must within that time serve on the creditor and the debtor and file with the court a garnishee's statement in Form 60I attached to this notice.

IF YOU FAIL TO OBEY THIS NOTICE, THE COURT MAY MAKE AND ENFORCE AN ORDER AGAINST YOU for payment of the amount set out above and the costs of the creditor.

IF YOU MAKE PAYMENT TO ANYONE OTHER THAN THE SHERIFF, YOU MAY BE LIABLE TO PAY AGAIN.

FIGURE 9.6 Notice of Garnishment (Form 60H) (*continued*)

TO THE CREDITOR, THE DEBTOR AND THE GARNISHEE.

Any party may make a motion to the court to determine any matter in relation to this notice of garnishment.

Date October 30, year 0 Issued by ____________________

Local registrar

Address of court office 393 University Avenue
Toronto, ON M5G 1T4

Creditor's address	Debtor's address	Sheriff's address
c/o JUST AND COPING Lawyers 8701 - 365 Bay Street Toronto, ON M3J4A9	#25-27 321 Daynor Dr., Toronto, ON M5X 3A1	393 University Avenue 19th Floor Toronto, ON M5G 1E6

telephone no. 416-762-1342

....

(The top portion of the garnishee's payment notice is to be completed by the creditor before the notice of garnishment is issued. Where it is anticipated that more than one payment will be made by the garnishee, the creditor should provide extra copies of the payment notice.)

GARNISHEE'S PAYMENT NOTICE

Make payment by cheque or money order payable to the Sheriff of the City of Toronto

and send it, along with a copy of this payment notice, to the Sheriff at
393 University Avenue
19th Floor
Toronto, ON M5G 1E6

Court Ontario Superior Court File no. 1234

Office at 393 University Avenue, Toronto, ON M5G 1E6

Creditor Artemis Plumbing Supply Ltd.

Debtor Personable Plumbers Ltd.

Garnishee Murray Hill Contracting Ltd.

TO BE COMPLETED BY GARNISHEE FOR EACH PAYMENT

Date of payment ____________

Amount enclosed $____________

RCP-E 60H (November 1, 2005)

FIGURE 9.6 Notice of Garnishment (Form 60H) (*continued*)

ARTEMIS PLUMBING SUPPLY LTD and PERSONABLE PLUMBERS LTD and MURRAY HILL CONTRACTING LTD
Creditor Debtor Garnishee

Sheriff's file no. 1234

ONTARIO
SUPERIOR COURT OF JUSTICE
PROCEEDING COMMENCED AT Toronto

NOTICE OF
GARNISHMENT

JUST AND COPING
Lawyers
8701 - 365 Bay Street
Toronto, ON M3J 4A9

I.M. Just (12345A)
imj@justandcoping.ca

416-762-1342
FAX 416-762-1343

Lawyers for the Plaintiff

RCP-E 4C (July 1, 2007)

FIGURE 9.7 Affidavit (Form 4D)

Court file no. 1234

ONTARIO
SUPERIOR COURT OF JUSTICE

BETWEEN:

ARTEMIS PLUMBING SUPPLY LTD

CREDITOR

and

PERSONABLE PLUMBERS LTD

DEBTOR

and

MURRAY HILL CONTRACTING LTD

GARNISHEE

AFFIDAVIT

I, Indigo M. Just, of the City of Toronto, MAKE OATH AND SAY:

1. I am a lawyer in the firm of Just and Coping, lawyers for the plaintiff, and as such have knowledge of the matters set forth in this affidavit.
2. Judgment was recovered in this action against the defendant on the 17th day of October, year 0, for the sum of $33,057.31 and the sum of $801.60 for costs. Attached to my affidavit and marked as exhibit "A" is a true copy of this judgment.
3. I have spoken with the accounts receivable manager of the Plaintiff, who advises me and I believe that no payments have been made with respect to this judgment.

FIGURE 9.7 Affidavit (Form 4D) (*continued*)

4. I believe that the amount owing at the present time is calculated as follows:

Judgment	$33,057.31
Costs	801.60
Writ of Seizure and Sale	
Fees	70.00
Disbursements	$410.00*
Notice of Garnishment	
Fees	140.00
Disbursements	.00
Subtotal	$34,478.91
Postjudgment interest at 12% from October 17 to October 30 (13 days)	144.25
Balance	$34,623.16

5. Based on the addresses to which the plaintiff shipped plumbing supplies to the defendant, I believe that Murray Hill Contracting Ltd., 123 Dover St., Toronto, ON M1K 5E4 is a customer of the defendant, and is indebted to the defendant in an amount that I am, at present, unable to name.

6. I have conducted a corporate search on the defendant that indicates that its head office is 1131 Fonthill Road, Toronto, ON.

SWORN before me at the)
City of Toronto,)
in the Province of Ontario)
this 30th day of October, year 0)

A. Coping
A Commissioner, etc.)

I.M. Just
I.M. Just

RCP-E 4D (July 1, 2007)

* $70.00 to issue writ
$100.00 to file writ
$240.00 to direct enforcement

FIGURE 9.8 Garnishee's Statement (Form 60I)

Court file no. 1234

ONTARIO

SUPERIOR COURT OF JUSTICE

BETWEEN:

ARTEMIS PLUMBING SUPPLY LTD

Creditor

and

PERSONABLE PLUMBERS LTD

Debtor

and

MURRAY HILL CONTRACTING LTD

Garnishee

GARNISHEE'S STATEMENT

1. I/We acknowledge that I/we owe or will owe the debtor or the debtor and one or more co-owners the sum of $, payable on , because

   (Give reasons why you owe the debtor or the debtor and one or more co-owners money. If you are making payment of less than the amount stated in line 2 of this paragraph because the debt is owed to the debtor and to one or more co-owners or for any other reason, give a full explanation of the reason. If you owe the debtor wages, state how often the debtor is paid. State the gross amount of the debtor's wages before any deductions and the net amount after all deductions and attach a copy of a pay slip.)

1.1 *(If debt owed to debtor and one or more co-owners, check here* ☐ *and complete the following:)*

Co-owner(s) of the Debt *(name, address)*

FIGURE 9.8 Garnishee's Statement (Form 60I) (*continued*)

2. *(If you do not owe the debtor money, explain why. Give any other information that will explain your financial relationship with the debtor.)*

3. *(If you have been served with any other notice of garnishment or a writ of execution against the debtor, give particulars.)*

Name of creditor	*Location of Sheriff*	*Date of notice or writ*	*Date of service on you*

4. *(If you have been served outside Ontario and you wish to object on the ground that service outside Ontario was improper, give particulars of your objection.)*

Date .... Signature of or for garnishee ....

Name of garnishee MURRAY HILL CONTRACTING LTD.

Address ....

....

....

Telephone number ....

RCP-E 60I (November 1, 2005)

FIGURE 9.8 Garnishee's Statement (Form 60I) (*continued*)

ARTEMIS PLUMBING SUPPLY LTD and PERSONABLE PLUMBERS LTD and MURRAY HILL CONTRACTING LTD
Creditor Debtor Garnishee

Sheriff's file no. 1234

ONTARIO
SUPERIOR COURT OF JUSTICE
PROCEEDING COMMENCED AT Toronto

GARNISHEE'S
STATEMENT

JUST AND COPING
Lawyers
8701 - 365 Bay Street
Toronto, ON M3J 4A9

I.M. Just (12345A)
imj@justandcoping.ca
416-762-1342
FAX 416-762-1343

Lawyers for the Plaintiff

RCP-E 4C (July 1, 2007)

FIGURE 9.9 Sample Statement of Particulars: Garnishment of Civil Servants and Those Receiving Funds from the Province of Ontario

IN THE MATTER OF A GARNISHMENT AGAINST A PROVINCIAL
CIVIL SERVANT AND IN THE MATTER OF THE
PROCEEDINGS AGAINST THE CROWN ACT

STATEMENT OF PARTICULARS

DEBTOR: Darius Milhaud
SIN: 123-45-6789

THIS STATEMENT OF PARTICULARS MUST BE SERVED WITH THE NOTICE OF GARNISHMENT IN ACCORDANCE WITH THE REGULATIONS MADE UNDER THE ACT.

____
Chief Financial Officer

____
Administrative Unit

1. Where the money payable to the debtor is salary, state:
   a. occupation: assistant deputy minister
   b. name of employer: Ministry of Training, Colleges and Universities
   c. section of employer: Community Colleges
   d. street address: 900 Bay Street, Toronto, ON M5G 1X7
2. Where the money payable to the debtor is remuneration for goods or services (other than wages), state:
   a. general description of the goods or services
   b. approximate date of delivery or performance
   c. location of delivery or performance
3. Is the attached notice of garnishment to enforce an order for support or maintenance?
   Yes ____ No ____

____
Signature of creditor

Date: October 18, year 0

[**NOTE:** The regulation under the *Proceedings Against the Crown Act* provides that a notice of garnishment issued against the Crown shall be deemed to be served on the 30th day after the actual date of service or on the 30th day after the effective date of service under the rules of the relevant court.]

Small Claims Court Proceedings 10

LEARNING OUTCOMES

After reading this chapter, students will:

- Understand the role of lawyers, law clerks, paralegals, and other persons in relation to Small Claims Court proceedings.
- Know what resources are available from the court and elsewhere to assist Small Claims Court litigants.
- Recognize the monetary and territorial jurisdictions of the Small Claims Court.
- Understand how and when to obtain a litigation guardian for a party under disability.
- Know how to file and serve a claim, a defence, and a defendant's claim.
- Understand the steps involved in obtaining a default judgment.
- Know how to set aside a default judgment.
- Know how to amend a claim.
- Understand the steps involved in a settlement conference and how to make offers to settle.
- Know the steps involved in motions and trials, including summoning witnesses and using documentary evidence.
- Understand costs awards and the impact of offers to settle on costs awards.
- Understand how the rules permit a motion for a new trial in limited circumstances.
- Recognize when a judgment may be appealed.

Introduction

Chapter 10 concerns actions for debt in Small Claims Court. Generally, the techniques and procedures covered in earlier chapters are applicable to Small Claims Court. In fact, the litigation and enforcement procedures are similar to, and are modelled on, the *Rules of Civil Procedure*[1] of the Superior Court of Justice, except that they are usually simpler and quicker to use than those of the Superior Court. Under a regulation to the *Courts of Justice Act*,[2] the Small Claims Court has its own rules, namely the *Rules of the Small Claims Court*.[3] Note that Small Claims Court fees, rules, forms, and procedural guides can be found online at <http://www.attorneygeneral.jus.gov.on.ca>. Choose Court Services and follow the links.

A paralegal may carry on a successful litigation practice in Small Claims Court. Because of the cost of lawyers' services relative to the amount in issue, and the limits on costs recovery in this court, lawyers are not seen as often as paralegals are in Small Claims Court. There has been a long tradition of having clients represented by court agents who regularly work in these courts, usually for creditors, and often on behalf of collection agencies. A paralegal with a high-volume caseload, where the cases are fairly routine, and often not defended, can operate economically and profitably in the Small Claims Court. Similarly, a law clerk working under a lawyer's supervision can produce and manage the paperwork for the law office's routine small claims collections process, making this part of a practice profitable for a law firm.

Lawyers and paralegals, as licensees of the Law Society of Ontario are permitted to appear in Small Claims Court. The Law Society has also authorized certain other groups of persons to appear as representatives in Small Claims Court, including Aboriginal case workers, articling students, and union representatives, among others. For information on these categories of permitted representatives, consult Chapter 1.

Small Claims Court Culture

Small Claims Court in one form or another has occupied a niche in the justice system of Ontario since the province's colonial beginnings. It was recognized early on that the lawyer-driven civil litigation process in the Superior Court was too expensive, too formal, and too slow to be of practical use where pursuit of a minor claim might cost more than the claim itself. If a small business person or consumer could litigate in a court that was quick, inexpensive, and relatively informal, then justice might be done.

Because of this court's perspective and unique position in the court system, it operates somewhat differently from other courts in Ontario.

- Small Claims Court clerks cannot provide advice to litigants. The Ministry of the Attorney General recognizes that many litigants in Small Claims Court

1 RRO 1990, Reg 194, as amended.

2 RSO 1990, c C.43.

3 O Reg 258/98, as amended.

are unrepresented. All of the Small Claims Court forms are available online, with instruction pages on each form to assist with their completion. In addition, there are several self-help guides available for litigants to access at no charge. The best starting point for such a search is the Ministry of the Attorney General's Small Claims Court Guides to Procedures, available at <https://www.attorneygeneral.jus.gov.on.ca/english/courts/guides>.

The guides and forms are designed for litigants who have no experience in conducting cases in this court. There are separate guides for the principal steps in a proceeding. Each guide explains the process and its purpose in plain language, identifies the relevant rules and forms, and gives detailed instructions on how to complete the forms and on how to carry out the court procedure in question.

There are several organizations that provide some free assistance to self-represented litigants. Pro Bono Law Ontario, for example, operates legal clinics in the Toronto and Ottawa Small Claims Courts. Litigants in other cities can contact Pro Bono Ontario for help. Their website is at <https://www.probonoontario.org>. Also, the Law Society of Ontario offers a lawyer/paralegal referral service that entitles individuals to a free 30-minute consultation. Details can be found at <www.findlegalhelp.ca.>. In some cases, litigants may qualify for assistance from a legal aid clinic for help in some matters, such as employment law, that may come under the jurisdiction of the Small Claims Court. For information on legal aid, consult <http://www.legalaid.on.ca/en/getting/typesofhelp.asp>. If litigants do not qualify for legal aid and need help in finding a lawyer or a paralegal, they can turn to JusticeNet at <http://www.justicenet.ca>.

- Small Claims Court judges tend to be more interventionist than judges in other courts, particularly when parties are self-represented; the judges will assist litigants in sticking to the real issues, and will sometimes guide the presentation of evidence to eliminate time-consuming efforts spent on legally irrelevant matters.[4] They will also suggest compromises and settlements, where these appear to be feasible, and will screen cases for settlement before they get on the trial list.

Jurisdiction

The court's authority and jurisdiction is found in the *Courts of Justice Act*, ss 22 to 33.1, and in the *Rules of the Small Claims Court*. The Small Claims Court is part of the Superior Court of Justice, although it maintains a separate identity and operates under its own rules.

The Small Claims Court has jurisdiction in most actions for the payment of money where the amount claimed is $25,000 or less, exclusive of costs and interest,

4 The Court of Appeal in *Moore v Apollo Health and Beauty Care*, 2017 ONCA 383, commented on the standards that a Small Claims Court judge should adhere to in assisting a self-represented litigant with the management of their case in court.

or where the plaintiff seeks recovery of personal property where the value of the property is worth $25,000 or less. No cause of action is specifically excluded, but may be implicitly excluded where the remedy claimed is one that is beyond the court's powers. If a plaintiff seeks more than money damages or recovery of property, they will have to bring their action in the Superior Court. Small Claims Court has no power to give a **declaratory judgment** or grant an injunction or an order for **specific performance**. At any time before trial, on consent of the parties, the registrar of the Superior Court can transfer a case to the Small Claims Court if it is in the latter court's jurisdiction.[5] Although the Superior Court has jurisdiction over all civil cases, whatever the amount of the claim, it is wise to use the Small Claims Court when within its monetary jurisdiction, because there is clear authority for denying a successful plaintiff their costs in the Superior Court when the claim is for $25,000 or less.[6]

declaratory judgment a judgment where the court declares the rights of the parties on some issue before it; also referred to as a declaration

specific performance a non-monetary remedy such as an order compelling a party to carry out completion of a contract

Territorial Jurisdiction

A plaintiff, under Rule 6.01(1),[7] may bring proceedings in the "territorial division" in which the cause of action arose, or where the defendant resides or carries on business. If there is more than one defendant, the plaintiff can bring the claim in the territorial division in which any one of the defendants resides or carries on business. The action may also be brought in the court nearest to a defendant's residence or business. This rule recognizes that a defendant may be closer to a court in an adjacent territorial division than they are to the court in the territorial division in which they reside.

Many credit card companies and institutional lenders specify in their loan contracts that any legal dispute can be heard in Toronto by declaring that the contract is entered into in the city of Toronto in the agreement itself. This means that a defendant who lives in Thunder Bay, who wishes to dispute the amount owing on a credit card, might be compelled to litigate the issue in Toronto and not in or near Thunder Bay. The courts, however, have interpreted these cases narrowly against the plaintiffs. In addition to the fact that the contract sets Toronto as the site of litigation, the court is entitled to look at all the factors, including where the parties entered into the agreement, where the defendant resides, and other factors, before permitting the plaintiff to have its way on the jurisdictional issues. Unless the plaintiff can show that the entire cause of action arose in Toronto, the court is entitled to determine jurisdiction on the basis of a defendant's residence.[8]

While the plaintiff chooses the territorial jurisdiction, the choice can be reviewed at any time by a defendant's motion, by the court on reviewing a request for default

5 *Supra* note 2, s 23(2).

6 *Supra* note 1, Rule 57.05(1).

7 References made to Rules in the text of Chapters 10 and 11 refer to the *Rules of the Small Claims Court*, not the *Rules of Civil Procedure*.

8 *Ingersoll Press Automation & Machinery v Tom Saab Industries* (1994), 46 ACWS (3d) 153 (Ont Sm Cl Ct); *Canada Trust MasterCard v Nowick* (1982), 27 CPC 183 (Ont Sm Cl Ct).

judgment, or where several defendants are served outside the court's jurisdiction, and at a settlement conference or trial.

Rule 6.01(2) provides that, on a motion, the court can order that the trial be held at a location other than those described in Rule 6.01(1) if "the balance of convenience" substantially favours holding the trial in another place. This is a common law test that looks at where the parties reside, where the witnesses reside, where the costs might be inordinately higher for one side rather than for the other because of location, and so on.

"Territorial division" is defined in Rule 1.02(1) as "a county, a district or a regional municipality," and also includes various geographical areas, including the City of Toronto. Some territorial divisions have more than one court. A small claims court **gazetteer** can be helpful in determining which court an action should be commenced in.[9]

gazetteer
a directory in which the entries are arranged by geographical location—various geographical places in the province are listed with the corresponding Small Claims Court to use, listed across from the geographical entry

Proper territorial jurisdiction is something the plaintiff has to prove; this may be done by setting out the facts that relate to the cause of action or the defendant's residence, as the case may be, in the claim. In the alternative, the plaintiff usually proves territorial jurisdiction by filing an Affidavit for Jurisdiction (Figure 10.1) setting out the facts relevant to jurisdiction. An affidavit will be required if:

- at the time the claim is filed, the address of the defendant is outside the court's territorial division;
- the defendant is served outside the court's territorial division and does not file a defence before the court grants default judgment; or
- the plaintiff has physically served all defendants outside the court's territorial division, whatever their address appears to be in the claim. A defendant may dispute territorial jurisdiction in the defence, may bring a motion contesting jurisdiction before filing a defence, or may raise the issue later.

Under Rule 6.01(3), at a settlement conference or a trial, a judge can change the place of trial if the judge finds that the trial was commenced in the wrong jurisdiction.

Commencing Proceedings

Before commencing proceedings, the usual investigations should be carried out, giving thought to the costs of doing this balanced against the size of the claim, and it should be confirmed that a lawyer's demand letter or a paralegal letter has been sent.[10] If there is no response to the letter, a Plaintiff's Claim (see Figure 10.7) should

9 The *Ontario Legal Directory*, published annually by the University of Toronto Press, contains a Small Claims Court gazetteer.

10 The Law Society of Ontario, in practice audits of paralegals, has stated that unless paralegals are licensed under both the Law Society of Ontario and the *Collection and Debt Settlement Services Act*, RSO 1990, c C.14, they may not send demand letters prior to commencing litigation.

be commenced. All Small Claims Court forms can be downloaded from the list of forms for the Small Claims Court at <http://www.ontariocourtforms.on.ca>.

Determining and Suing the Proper Parties

The proper parties to a lawsuit are those who have legal rights and obligations in issue. The issues canvassed in Chapter 3 cover these matters.

When suing unincorporated businesses, the *Rules of the Small Claims Court*, particularly Rule 5, are similar to those for the Superior Court. It is always wise, however, to cast the net as broadly as possible in order to enforce a judgment against those who own the business as well as the business itself. Rule 5 anticipates that the identities of the individuals who own a particular business may be unknown. While this information can usually be found using business name searches, Rule 5.04 can be used to avoid the cost of searches by requiring the business entity to divulge the name of the individual or individuals who comprise it.

With respect to suing an unincorporated business:

1. A partnership may be sued in the name of the partnership. If the partners Eli Smith and Jessica Jones owned SJ Enterprises, and the plaintiff only wanted to sue the partnership, they would sue SJ Enterprises.[11]
2. A partnership may not have enough assets to satisfy a judgment. Therefore, it is usually advisable to also sue the individual partners or to put them on notice that if there are not enough assets in the partnership to pay the judgment, it will be enforced against the assets of the individual partners. If the partnership and the partners are sued, the partnership is named as a defendant on the Plaintiff's Claim form and the partners are named as co-defendants on Form 1A, which goes behind page one of the Plaintiff's Claim and lists the other defendants. In the alternative, the partnership can be sued on the Plaintiff's Claim, and a Notice to Alleged Partner form (Figure 10.2) can be served on the individuals who are believed to be partners. An individual who is served in this manner is deemed to be a partner unless the person disputes that fact.
3. If the plaintiff successfully sued only the partnership, Rule 5.05(3) allows the plaintiff to bring a motion for leave to name the individual partners on the judgment so that it can be enforced against their personal assets.

There may be some situations where the plaintiff is not sure who the alleged partners were at the relevant time (usually when the cause of action arose), but wants to name them in the lawsuit. For example, if a partnership is sued where some partners have left and others have joined since the cause of action arose, the plaintiff may wish to narrow down the choice of partners to those who were partners when the cause of action arose, and may therefore be held personally liable. Under Rule 5.04(1), this information can be discovered by preparing and serving a notice

11 See Rule 5.01.

requiring the partnership to disclose in writing the names and addresses of all partners who were members of the partnership on a particular date (Figure 10.3).

Sole Proprietorships

Rule 5 applies, with necessary adaptations, to sole proprietorships. A lawsuit may be brought against an individual who carries on business in their own name—"Gina McLeod carrying on business as GM Financial Services"—or in the name of the sole proprietorship: "GM Financial Services."[12] It is almost always advisable to sue an individual in their own name. If the situation is such that the proprietor's name is unknown, but the name of the business is known when the claim is filed, Rule 5.04 can be used to find out who the individual sole proprietor is, or a business name search can be done on the sole proprietorship. The plaintiff may also sue in the business name and serve the sole proprietor in a manner analogous to the way a partner in a partnership would be served. If a sole proprietor or a partnership uses a business name without registering it, the business is not entitled to sue or defend a claim until the business name has been registered.[13]

Corporations

The rules for suing a corporation are the same as they are in the Superior Court. If the party is a corporation, then the claim must, in most cases, be brought against the corporation in its legal corporate name.

Litigants Who Are Under a Disability

If a party, whether plaintiff or defendant, is not of **full legal age and capacity** (a minor, someone who is mentally incapable of looking after their own affairs, or an absentee (a missing person)), they are deemed to be a party under a disability and must have a **litigation guardian** in order to sue or be sued. However, a minor, under Rule 4.01(2), may sue for an amount up to $500 without having a litigation guardian. Rule 4.01(3) requires that a plaintiff under a disability have a litigation guardian file a Consent to Act as a Litigation Guardian (Figure 10.4) with the claim, or as soon as possible after the claim is filed. The defendant, if under a disability, must do the same, with someone filing a Consent to Act as Litigation Guardian for the defendant (Figure 10.5) on filing a defence or when ordered to do so by the court. In the consents, the following information must be provided:

- a minor's date of birth;
- the nature of the disability;
- the relationship of the guardian to the party under a disability, if any;

full legal age and capacity
to sue or be sued, an individual usually has to have reached the age of majority and be mentally capable of taking part in a lawsuit; a person who is capable of participating and who is over 18 years of age is referred to as being of full age and capacity

litigation guardian
an individual who conducts a lawsuit and instructs counsel on behalf of a party who is under a disability or who is not of full age and capacity

12 See Rule 5.06(1).

13 *Business Names Act*, RSO 1990, c B.17, s 7(1).

- a statement that the guardian has no interest in the proceeding that is adverse to the party under disability; and
- *if appointed on behalf of a plaintiff*, an acknowledgement of personal liability to pay costs awarded against the litigation guardian, or against the party under a disability.

When a litigation guardian is used, the title of proceedings should take the form:

Gustave Flaubert, a person under disability, by his litigation guardian, Emma Bovary.

Children's Lawyer a public official whose legal staff looks after the financial and other interests of children who are involved in or have an interest in civil proceedings

Public Guardian and Trustee a government office whose staff are responsible for looking after the interests of mentally incapable persons (formerly called mentally incompetent) where no attorney under a power of attorney, guardian of the person, or guardian of property has been appointed

Rule 4.03 sets out who may be a litigation guardian. The person must not be under a disability. For a minor child, a parent or person with custody of the child shall be the guardian; if there is no person who can act as guardian, then the **Children's Lawyer** shall be the guardian.

If the person is mentally incapable but has a guardian or is a person with a power of attorney appointed under the *Substitute Decisions Act, 1992*,[14] the guardian or the attorney may act as a litigation guardian if the appointment grants the power to act as litigation guardian.

If a mentally incapable person has neither a person acting under a power of attorney nor a guardian appointed in accordance with the *Substitute Decisions Act, 1992*, then a "suitable person," one with no interest adverse to the mentally incapable person, may be appointed or, in the last resort, the **Public Guardian and Trustee** may be appointed.

In accordance with Rule 4.07, no person under a disability may enter into a settlement without court approval. For example, a minor's claim should never be settled without court approval. A release from parents or others in control of the minor will not prevent the minor, once they come of age, from suing the defendant—and in tort or contract they may have up to two years from the time they reach the age of majority to commence proceedings.

If a person under a disability is sued, the action must be defended by a litigation guardian. If one does not voluntarily appear when a defence is filed or after the time for filing a defence has passed, then a demand for a litigation guardian should be served (Figure 10.6) on the defendant; if that brings no response, a motion must be made to the court for an order appointing a litigation guardian for the defendant who is found to be under a disability. It is advisable to serve the motion on the Children's Lawyer in the case of a minor, or on the Public Guardian and Trustee in the case of a person who is mentally incapable and does not have an attorney or a guardian to look after their personal needs or property. The parent or the person having custody of a minor may file a defence and consent to act as litigation guardian, as may the attorney or the guardian of a person who is mentally incapable.

The duty of a litigation guardian, set out in Rule 4.04, is to diligently attend to the interests of the person under a disability and take all steps reasonably necessary for the protection of those interests, including the commencement and conduct of

14 SO 1992, c 30.

claims against others. A litigation guardian who fails in their duty may be removed by the court, whether or not a motion to do so has been brought. If a litigation guardian for a defendant has not been appointed where one is required, the court will set aside a default judgment.

Any money payable to a person under disability pursuant to an order or a settlement shall be paid into court unless the court orders otherwise.[15] A Form 4B affidavit should be used for motions concerning the payment of money under Rule 4.08.

Filing a Claim

A proceeding is commenced by filing a Plaintiff's Claim (see Figure 10.7) with the clerk, together with a copy of the claim for each defendant.[16] If the claim is filed in person, the clerk, on payment of the prescribed fee, will issue the claim by dating and signing it and putting a seal on it.[17] A court file number will be assigned to the claim. The setup of the claim form provides space to set out the reasons for the claim and has blank spaces to fill in the details of the amount claimed and the particulars of the interest claimed. The language used to draft the claim should be concise and non-technical. If the description of the claim requires it, additional pages can be attached.

If there is a document relevant to the claim—such as a promissory note, invoice, or contract—rather than describe it, it should be referred to in the claim and a copy of it should be attached to the claim. The original document should be kept to file in court as documentary evidence as part of the case. If, for example, the plaintiff was relying on a promissory note signed by the defendant, they would state in the reasons for claim that a copy of the promissory note was attached to the claim as Document "A." A copy of the promissory note would then be marked as Document "A" and attached to the claim. Documents attached to the claim should be referred to as "document" or "schedule." The term "exhibit" should not be used in a claim because a claim is not a sworn document, and the term "exhibit" refers to evidence such as sworn documents or other evidence entered into court on a hearing or at trial. (Again, see Figure 10.7 for an example of a Plaintiff's Claim.)

A claim may always be filed in person or by regular mail. In some cases a claim may be filed online. If filing by regular mail, send the claim and a letter to the court clerk along with the applicable fee and a self-addressed stamped envelope so that the clerk can send back a copy of the issued claim. When filing in person, attend at the applicable court office, bringing copies of the claim and the money to pay the fee. If the address of the defendant listed on the claim is located outside the court's territorial division, an Affidavit for Jurisdiction must also be filed. If the rate of interest

15 See Rule 4.08.

16 The term "plaintiff's claim" is used to distinguish it from a "defendant's claim," which can be used by the defendant in the plaintiff's action for a counterclaim against the plaintiff or a claim against another person whom the defendant thinks is liable (for example, a cross-claim against another defendant or a third-party claim bringing in another party).

17 As covered later in this chapter, many cases can now be filed and issued online.

sought in the claim is 35 percent per year or less, then the claim may be filed online, provided that none of the defendants are under a disability.[18] An account with Service Ontario is required to file court documents online. A ONe-*key* ID must be set up to pay for the claim. The plaintiff must have an email address that they advise the court office of so that they can be served at that address. A claim that is filed and issued electronically will not have the signature of a court clerk on it. If a defence to the claim is filed, the plaintiff must file paper copies of the claim with the court at least 14 days before a settlement conference.[19]

Service of the Claim

Service is governed by Rule 8. As in the Superior Court, the first document in the lawsuit, usually the plaintiff's claim, should be served personally using a process server.[20] Technically the plaintiff may serve the claim on the defendant; however, this should be avoided as there may be a dispute over whether the defendant was properly served. Where there is an issue of credibility, it is better to have a neutral, professional process server give evidence about the mode of service, rather than someone who has a personal interest in the matter.

The preferred method of service for a claim is personal service. An individual is personally served when the claim is handed to them. In the case of a sole proprietorship, a partnership, or a corporation, service may be made on a sole proprietor, a partner, or a director or upon any person who is or appears to be in control of the place of business.[21]

If an attempt to personally serve the claim has been unsuccessful, an alternative to personal service may be used.

Methods for alternatives to personal service are set out in Rule 8.03:

- Alternative service on an individual at a place of residence under Rule 8.03(2) may be carried out by leaving a copy of the document in a sealed envelope that is addressed to the defendant with an apparently adult member of the defendant's household *and*, on the same or next day, a copy of the claim must be mailed or sent by courier to the defendant at that address. Service is deemed to be effective on the fifth day after mailing or on verification of delivery by courier.
- In accordance with Rule 8.03(3), a corporation may be served by mail or courier at the last corporate address recorded with the Ministry of Government Services. Each listed director must be served at their address on file with the ministry by sending a copy by mail or courier. Service is deemed to be effective on the fifth day after mailing or on verification of delivery by courier. A Corporation Profile Report will reveal the last-known addresses of a

18 See Rule 7.02(1).

19 See Rule 7.02(5)1.

20 A summons to a witness and a notice of a contempt hearing must also be served personally.

21 Rule 8.02(1).

corporation and its directors. Corporate documents can be searched online at <http://www.oncorp.com/home/services_onbis_corp.asp>. OnCorp is recognized as a filing and search agency.

- A party's lawyer, paralegal, or an employee in the law office of the lawyer or the paralegal may acknowledge service by endorsing and dating a copy of the document. A lawyer, paralegal, or employee will not do this unless they have received instructions from the client to accept service.
- In accordance with Rule 8.03(7), an individual can be served by sending a copy of the document by registered mail or courier to the individual's residence. Such service is effective on the date the individual being served, or any person who appears to be a member of the same household, verifies by signature, on a Canada Post or courier delivery confirmation form, their receipt of a copy of the claim.

All documents that come after the claim may be served by mail, courier, or fax on a party, the party's paralegal, or the party's lawyer, unless the court orders otherwise. If served by mail or courier, a document should be sent to the party at the address given by that party on a previous court document. Once mailed, a document is deemed served on the fifth day after mailing. A document served by courier is deemed to be effective on the fifth day after the courier verifies that the document was delivered.[22] This should be taken into account when calculating the time for signing a default judgment or if serving motion documents.

The Rules set out the requirements for service by fax. If a fax under 16 pages long is served before 5 p.m., the document is deemed to be received on the day it is transmitted, if that day is not a holiday. If the fax is sent after 5 p.m., it is deemed to be received on the next day that is not a holiday. Rule 8.08(2) provides that faxes that are 16 pages or longer must be served between 5 p.m. and 8 a.m. unless consent from the other party to serve the document before 5 p.m. has been granted.

Rule 8 sets out the modes of personal service on a variety of entities. The rule should be consulted whenever an entity other than an individual of full age and capacity is being sued in order to see what is required to successfully serve the entity personally.

A claim should be served within six months of being issued.[23] If it is not, a motion must be brought to extend the time for service.

Service is proven by filing an Affidavit of Service (Figure 10.8), attested to by the process server, with the court after it has been served.

If a claim cannot be served personally or by an alternative to personal service, it is possible to serve the claim by substituted service. As in the Superior Court, this requires a motion to obtain a court order that must be complied with strictly. If a party outside Ontario must be served, it is wise to bring a motion to obtain court approval of the costs of service; otherwise, costs of service cannot be recovered by the successful party as part of court costs. Rule 19.01(3) limits the cost of service

22 See Rule 8.07.1(2).

23 Rule 8.01(2).

that can be recovered, without a court order, to $60 for each person served. Process servers can be found online. In order to find a process server for service outside Ontario, check the ServeNow.com website at <https://www.serve-now.com>. Note that claim and defence forms require that plaintiffs and defendants notify the court and all other parties of changes of address within seven days of the change.[24]

When calculating time periods for service or anything else in the Rules, note the Rule 1.02(1) definition of "holiday" and the provisions in Rule 3 that govern time computation.

In defining "holiday," which includes the expected statutory holidays, plus Saturdays and Sundays, Rule 1.02(1) provides the following details:

- holiday means any Saturday or Sunday;
- if New Year's Day, Canada Day, or Remembrance Day falls on a Saturday or Sunday, the following Monday is a holiday;
- if Christmas Day falls on a Saturday or Sunday, the following Monday and Tuesday are holidays; and
- if Christmas Day falls on a Friday, the following Monday is a holiday.

Rule 3 states that when the rules prescribe a time period, count the days required by *excluding the first day of the period, and including the last day of the period*. Where the last day of the period falls on a holiday, the time period is deemed to end on the next day after the holiday that is not itself a holiday. For example, if the last day was Labour Day (which is always the first Monday in September), the time would be extended to the next day, Tuesday. If the period ended on Christmas Day, when Christmas day fell on a Friday, then the application of the definition of "holiday" in Rule 1.02(1) requires that the time period be extended to the following Tuesday.

Filing Fees for Frequent Plaintiffs

A plaintiff who files more than ten claims in a particular Small Claims Court in a calendar year is termed a "frequent claimant." To issue claims, obtain default judgment, or set matters down for trial or assessment hearings, frequent claimants must pay a higher filing fee as set out in the regulation, *Small Claims Court—Fees and Allowances*,[25] made under the *Administration of Justice Act*.[26] Clients who are frequent claimants will be given, in advance, pre-assigned court file numbers that they must use. The lawyer or paralegal should keep track of large-volume clients who are required to pay higher fees and use pre-assigned court file numbers. Clients with a large volume of collection work should be asked whether they have been classed as frequent claimants. This information can also be obtained from the court.

---

24 See Rule 8.09.

25 O Reg 332/16.

26 RSO 1990, c A.6.

Filing a Defence

To file a defence under Rule 9, the defendant must simply set out, on a defence form, in numbered paragraphs, in non-technical language, the reasons why the claim is disputed, along with the name, address, and phone number of the defendant's lawyer or paralegal. If there are any parts of the claim that the defendant admits to or has no knowledge of, this should be stated in the defence. A defendant, like a plaintiff, is required to attach to the defence a copy of any document relied upon. An unrepresented defendant should include their address and phone number in the defence. The prescribed Defence form (Figure 10.9) is available online at <http://www.ontariocourtforms.on.ca>, along with other forms used in Small Claims Court and other court proceedings.

The defence must be filed within 20 days of service of the claim, unless service was by mail or courier, in which case service is effective on the fifth day after the document is mailed or verified by courier as delivered. The defendant then has 20 days from the date of service to serve and file a defence. A copy of the defence for the court along with a copy for each party must be filed with the court. The defendant is responsible for service of the defence. The defence does not need to be personally served. It may be served by mail, fax, courier, or any other method permitted under the Rules. Without consent in writing from the plaintiff or an order of the court, there is no provision for the clerk to accept a defence after the time for filing it has passed. When acting for a defendant, it is wise to ask the plaintiff to extend the time for filing the defence, if more time is needed, and to obtain and file the plaintiff's consent with the defence.

Proposals

Rule 9.03 permits a defendant to admit liability for all or part of the plaintiff's claim, including the monetary amount claimed, and to file a defence that proposes terms of payment (Figure 10.10). If the plaintiff does not dispute the proposal within 20 days of service of the defence, the defendant should make payment in accordance with the proposal, as if a court order had been made; if the defendant defaults, the plaintiff shall serve a Notice of Default of Payment (Figure 10.11)[27] on the defendant and file an Affidavit of Default of Payment (Figure 10.12) with the court 15 days after serving the defendant with notice of default if nothing has been paid. The court clerk will then sign judgment for the unpaid balance of the proposal.

If the defendant submits a proposal that the plaintiff wishes to dispute, the plaintiff serves on the defendant and files, with the court, a Request to Clerk form

27 Note that in order to reduce the number of cases used in the example documents in the figures, the *Cape v Feckless* case has been shown with a variety of different outcomes: first, as if it was defended, then as if there was a proposal and the proposal had not been met, then as if a proposal was not accepted, and finally as if the claim was undefended and there was default judgment granted.

requesting a terms of payment hearing (Figure 10.13). The plaintiff must do this within 20 days of being served with the defendant's defence/proposal. If the defendant is an individual, the clerk will serve a Financial Information Form on the defendant, who must complete it and serve it on the plaintiff prior to the terms of payment hearing. On this form the defendant will provide financial information about income, expenses, and assets. This hopefully will provide some hard evidence of the defendant's ability to pay. If the plaintiff fails to dispute the proposal within the time provided for in the Rules, then the plaintiff is deemed to have accepted the proposal.

Once a proposal has been made, the defendant should make payments directly to the plaintiff as proposed, whether the plaintiff objects and whether the proposal has been approved by the court and confirmed in an order. A court is more likely to look favourably on a "cooperative" defendant than on one who is holding off making payment.

In the event that the proposal only admitted partial liability for the claim, the court will schedule the matter for a settlement conference to deal with the part in dispute.

Defendant's Claim

Rule 10 permits a defendant to make a claim against the plaintiff (counterclaim) and anyone else connected with the same event or transaction that gave rise to the plaintiff's claim (third-party claims, cross-claims).

A Defendant's Claim (Figure 10.14) must be filed and issued within 20 days of the defence being filed, unless the court permits a later filing. This reduces the opportunity to stall and delay an action by making a "late" defendant's claim. The content of the defendant's claim is set out in Rule 10.01(4) and is similar to the required contents of a plaintiff's claim. The clerk will issue the defendant's claim; the defendant will file the original and serve a copy on every other person against whom the claim is made in accordance with the requirements in Rule 8 for serving a claim. A party defending a defendant's claim shall serve and file a defence (along with their affidavit of service) within 20 days of service of the defendant's claim. A sample defence to a defendant's claim is found at Figure 10.15.

The defendant's claim will be decided at the trial of the main action unless the court decides that it would be unduly complicated or prolong the trial, in which case the court can order that the defendant's claim be tried separately, usually after the main action. A "third party" may defend not only the defendant's claim against the "defendant," but may defend the main claim as well.

liquidated damages
a specific sum of money that can be easily and objectively calculated; if a debtor borrows $1,000 for a one-year period at 10 percent interest per year, the amount owing —$1,100—would be a liquidated amount because it is precise and specific and the total is easily calculated using an objective standard or formula

Default Proceedings

Rule 11 provides for default proceedings. If the defendant fails to file a defence within the applicable time period, on request, the clerk will note the defendant in default (Figure 10.16). If the claim was for **liquidated damages**, the clerk may sign default judgment on proof by the plaintiff that the defendant has been served properly within the territorial division of the court that issued the claim:

1. If the affidavit of service shows that at least one defendant was served within the territorial division of the issuing court, the clerk will sign judgment on any liquidated claim.[28] A plaintiff seeking judgment on a claim for unliquidated damages may bring a motion in writing for an assessment of damages using a Form 15A Notice of Motion and Supporting Affidavit and completing Part B of the form. For more complex unliquidated damages claims, a Form 9B Request to Clerk should be completed to ask that an assessment hearing be scheduled. The plaintiff and any other witnesses they might have usually take the stand to give oral testimony at the hearing; however, affidavits of witnesses who cannot attend can sometimes be effectively used at a hearing with the legal representative taking the judge through the key affidavit evidence and making submissions.
2. If proof of service shows that no defendant was served in the territorial division, then the plaintiff must prove jurisdiction by filing an Affidavit for Jurisdiction (Figure 10.1) showing that one or more defendants resides or carries on business within the territorial division of the issuing court (although served somewhere else), or that the cause of action arose within the territorial division of the issuing court, or that it is the court nearest to the place where a defendant resides or carries on business, before the clerk can sign default judgment or set the matter down for a written assessment or for a hearing to prove damages. Oral evidence can be given to prove territorial jurisdiction at an assessment of damages hearing, but it is more efficient to do it by affidavit.

The bottom line is that default judgment can be signed provided that the plaintiff can satisfy the clerk of the court or the judge that at least one defendant resides or carries on business within the territorial division of the issuing court, that the court is the nearest court to the place where a defendant resides or carries on business, or that the cause of action arose within that court's territorial division.

If the claim was filed electronically, default judgment may be requested electronically. Proof of service may be filed electronically. The plaintiff must, however, hold on to the hard copy of the affidavit of service for up to three years in case the court requests a copy.[29] For a liquidated claim that has been filed electronically, once

28 When a request is made for a clerk to sign default judgment, the plaintiff should ensure that they have brought the claim in the correct territorial division and that the matter is for liquidated damages. The court fee for a default judgment must be paid up front to the court clerk, and if the clerk finds that the matter has to be put before a judge on a motion or hearing, the court will not refund the money paid for the default judgment and will not apply it to the next court proceeding. It then becomes money thrown away, as the litigant is paying for a review by the clerk and *possible* signing of the default judgment. If in doubt as to whether or not a clerk will sign a judgment, it is better to pay for a motion or a hearing.

29 See Rule 1.05.1(7).

the time is up for a defence to be filed, and provided an affidavit of service has been filed, the plaintiff requests default judgment online. For unliquidated damages claims, the plaintiff who filed electronically may bring a motion in writing for a default judgment or may request an assessment hearing. If a motion in writing is brought, a Form 15A Notice of Motion and Supporting Affidavit may be filed electronically; however, within 14 days of filing the form online the plaintiff must provide the court clerk with a copy of Form 15A in paper format.[30] An assessment hearing is normally booked by filing a Form 9B Request to Clerk with the court; however, Rule 11.03(2.1)(b) states that an assessment hearing request may be made online without having to file Form 9B electronically or in paper format.

When default judgment is signed, it is for the claim, costs, a claim preparation and filing fee (if applicable), and prejudgment interest, provided the claim is for a liquidated amount. Note that prejudgment interest must be requested in the claim if the plaintiff wants it included in the default judgment. Unlike the Superior Court, this court does not require the litigant to prepare all of the documentation. The clerk will prepare a Default Judgment (Figure 10.17) and mail it to the defendant.

If part of the claim was for a liquidated amount and part was not, the clerk may sign default judgment for the part that was for a liquidated amount and set the balance of the claim down for the plaintiff to prove damages on a motion made in writing or at an assessment hearing. If the documentation on a written motion is insufficient to grant judgment, a judge may request additional documentation or instruct the plaintiff to schedule a hearing.[31] Once the clerk has noted the defendant in default, the defendant is barred from filing a defence, although, as in the Superior Court, it is possible for the defendant to move to set aside default judgment using Rule 11.06 on the grounds that

- the defendant has a meritorious defence;
- the defendant has a reasonable explanation for the default; and
- the motion is made as soon as is reasonably possible in all the circumstances.[32]

If the defendant in a defendant's claim (the plaintiff in the main action) defaults in filing a defence, the plaintiff (the defendant in the main action) cannot obtain default judgment.[33] Judgment on the defendant's claim will be given at the trial of the main action.

Amendment of Pleadings

Rule 12 permits parties to amend claims or defences without the court's permission at any time up to 30 days before trial. In accordance with Rule 12, additions to the document should be underlined and any other changes identified. Because there is

30 See Rules 11.03(2.1)(a) and 11.03(2.2).

31 See Rule 11.03(3).

32 See Rule 11.06.

33 See Rule 11.04.

no formal pre-trial discovery, new facts or information that might have surfaced at discovery are now likely to surface later in the process at settlement conferences. This may result in amendments to claims and defences at a relatively late stage in the proceedings. But, to prevent surprises, amended pleadings must be served at least 30 days before the originally scheduled trial date.

Settlement Conferences

Rule 13 provides for settlement conferences. The purposes of a settlement conference are to

- resolve or narrow the issues in an action;
- speed up the disposition of the action;
- encourage settlement of the action;
- assist the parties in effectively preparing and presenting their case at trial; and
- provide full disclosure between the parties with respect to relevant facts and evidence, including documentary and oral evidence.

There is an expectation, explicitly set out in the rule, that the parties will openly and frankly discuss the issues, that the contents of the discussion will remain confidential, and that statements made in the conference will be treated as having been made on a without-prejudice basis. A judge who presides at a settlement conference cannot preside at the trial.

Under Rule 13, a settlement conference is mandatory and must be held on every defended action within 90 days of the filing of the first defence (unless the defence admits liability and sets out a proposal for payment). The clerk will set a time for the settlement conference and serve a notice of settlement conference and a blank form 13A, List of Proposed Witnesses, to every party filing a claim or defence. The rules require that parties serve and file all documents that were not attached to the claim and defence, and that a party seeks to rely on at trial, including an expert report, along with any other documents or evidence they intend to rely on and that a List of Proposed Witnesses (Figure 10.18) be served and filed at least 14 days prior to the settlement conference. Generally, the court encourages and appreciates full disclosure at this stage. If a person who attends the settlement conference fails to adequately prepare for the settlement conference or does not file the required list of proposed witnesses or documents to be relied upon, the court may award costs against that person.

Judges have been quite creative with this rule and have used it to settle and expedite matters. Judges may use the settlement conference to set a schedule for unrepresented litigants to produce necessary documents or to advise the party of procedural barriers they may face and how they may overcome them, among other things. At the conclusion of the settlement conference, the judge completes a settlement conference memorandum for the file to inform the trial judge of the matters upon which the parties agree, the outstanding issues, the evidentiary issues, the number of witnesses, and whether any interpreters are required. Any orders made on consent or under the authority of Rule 13.05 must be recorded by the judge on an endorsement record, a copy of which is usually given to the parties at the conclusion of the settlement conference.

Where settlement conferences are used to facilitate settlement, the practice is to have the parties sign court form 14D, Terms of Settlement (Figure 10.19). If the defendant defaults, the terms provide that judgment may be obtained, based upon the terms, if the plaintiff brings a motion attesting to the default, or the plaintiff can choose to continue the action as if there had not been a settlement. Theoretically, a party could agree to a settlement for an amount less than the amount claimed and have no intention of making any payments. When default occurs, the plaintiff is then limited to judgment for the lower agreed-upon amount, or has to continue on to trial as if there was not a settlement. Continuing on to trial will require a trial set-down fee plus associated trial costs to be paid, with no guarantee of success. Represented parties will often draft their own minutes of settlement (Figure 10.20), which usually contain a provision that, in the event of a default on the terms of the minutes, judgment is consented to for the amount of the original claim.

Settlement conferences may take place before a court referee. A court referee is not a judge. If a referee makes a recommendation that a legal order be made, this must be confirmed by a Small Claims Court judge.

Once a settlement conference has been scheduled, attendance is mandatory for parties and their representatives unless the court orders otherwise. If a party or a representative knows that they will be unable to attend the conference in person, a motion under Rule 1.07(1) for permission to attend by phone or video conference should be brought in advance of the conference. This motion can be brought in writing using Form 1B, Request for Telephone or Video Conference. If a person who attends a settlement conference does not have the authority to agree to a settlement, arrangements must be made for the person who has the authority to be available by phone.[34]

Failure to attend a settlement conference will result in costs penalties and the scheduling of an additional settlement conference.[35] Failure to attend a second settlement conference may result in the striking out of the defence and any defendant's claim, and a judgment on a liquidated claim or an assessment of damages on an unliquidated one. If a plaintiff fails to appear, the claim *may* be dismissed, but that is not mandatory. Up to $100 in costs can be levied against an uncooperative party, along with an order to pay related disbursements. If there are special circumstances, more than $100 may be awarded in costs.

If a claim is for less than $2,500, the parties can consent to the judge giving judgment at the end of the settlement conference, saving the cost of a trial. However, a settlement conference judge cannot be the trial judge even if the parties consent.[36]

34 See Rule 13.02(2).

35 See Rule 13.02(5).

36 See Rule 13.08.

Formal Offers to Settle

As is the case with Rule 49 of the *Rules of Civil Procedure*, Rule 14.07 of the *Rules of the Small Claims Court* sets up a code for offers to settle that contains cost penalties where a party rejects an offer that turns out to be as good as or better than the judgment. Offers that qualify for costs bonuses and penalties under Rule 14 can be made at any stage until seven days before trial; in the absence of a discovery process, offers are likely to be made at the close of a settlement conference. An offer made under Rule 14 must be made, accepted, and withdrawn in writing. An offer may take the form of a letter from a lawyer or paralegal, or it may take the form of an optional court document, Form 14A, that lists the provisions of the offer in consecutively numbered paragraphs (see the Offer to Settle at Figure 10.21). The offer must remain open for acceptance until the trial commences. It is wise to consider making a counteroffer to an unacceptable offer, rather than reject it outright. Where an offer is made that includes the payment of money, either side can insist on the money being paid into court as a condition of the offer. If the other side accepts, and the money is not paid into court, then the party who was to receive the payment may ask the clerk to sign judgment in accordance with the terms of the offer. This rule also applies when a party fails to comply with an accepted offer, even where there is no order for payment into court.

Under Rule 14.07, where the plaintiff makes an offer in writing seven or more days before trial that is not withdrawn and does not expire before trial, and the defendant refuses to accept it, and the plaintiff obtains a judgment *as good as or better* than the offer, the court may award the plaintiff an award of costs that is up to twice the costs of the action that the plaintiff would otherwise be entitled to.

Where the defendant makes an offer in writing seven or more days before trial that is not withdrawn and does not expire before trial, and the plaintiff refuses to accept it, and the plaintiff obtains a judgment *as favourable as or less favourable* than the offer, the court may award the defendant an amount for costs that is up to twice the costs awardable to a successful party *from the date the offer was made.*

Note that offers to settle may be made within the seven-day period prior to trial or during the trial, but they will not have the costs benefits/penalties available under Rule 14.

Motions

Motions can be brought to deal with pre-trial procedural matters. Generally, because of the need to keep court costs down, motions should be used sparingly. In addition to motions, there are two motion-like procedures:

- a request to the clerk to sign a consent order (these are usually minor administrative orders that do not require judicial discretion), and
- a motion to assess damages based on written filings.

A Notice of Motion and Supporting Affidavit form (Figure 10.22) should be used unless the court orders otherwise; for example, the court may permit a motion made at trial to be made orally. The form may be served personally, by regular or registered mail, by courier, or by fax on all parties not in default. Service must allow for at least seven full days before the motion is heard if it is served personally, and 12 days if it is served by mail. It must be filed at least three days before the hearing. A date for a motion must be obtained from the clerk *before* the documents are drafted and served. Costs of up to $100[37] and disbursements of the motion are recoverable by either party. There is a procedure for motions without notice, where appropriate. There is also a procedure to prohibit a party from bringing further motions where the purpose of that is to delay or hinder proceedings.[38] Motions may be heard by phone or video if an order is obtained in advance under Rule 1.07.

Sample Illustration of the Formation of the Theory of a Case

In this debt collection case, the plaintiff's claim is that the debtor did not pay on a running account. The defence is that payments were made in cash. The theory of the case may be that the defendant is trying to evade payment of the debt with a story that is not credible. The strategy will be to discredit the defendant's evidence. Evidence of the accuracy of the plaintiff's accounting records will need to be provided. Details of the debtor's lack of responsiveness to the plaintiff's demands for payment should also be provided. Documentary supportive evidence would include all of the demand letters and overdue notices, as well as the accounting and banking records for the relevant period.

The Trial Process

Once the defence has been filed and the settlement conference completed, the clerk shall give the parties a notice to request a trial date if the action is not disposed of in the next 30 days. The plaintiff usually requests a trial and pays the trial set-down fee. Once the fee is paid, the clerk fixes the date and sends out the notice of trial to all parties who have filed a claim or defence.

Preparing for Trial

By the time that the claim and defence have been exchanged, the legal representatives will have a fairly good idea of what the case is about and should have developed their theories of the case—based on the facts of the case and applicable law—on which their strategies will be based. The theory of a case cannot be developed until clients and witnesses have been interviewed, relevant documents have been examined, and the legal representative has sifted through the evidence and identified the facts that must be proved (see the box above). If the facts change, the theory will need to be changed to fit the facts, not the other way round.

37 See Rule 15.07.

38 See Rule 15.04.

Summons to Witness

When it has been decided which witnesses will need to be called, they should be summonsed to attend at trial, unless the legal representative is certain that the witnesses will show up. A legal representative should know which witnesses they will need at the time the claim and defence are filed, and certainly by the close of the settlement conference. If the legal representative fails to summons a witness and the witness does not appear, the representative may be compelled by the court to proceed without that witness. If a summonsed witness fails to appear, the representative is entitled to an adjournment if they need it; the witness may be apprehended, brought before the court, and held until the witness's presence is no longer required. If the witness is truly unfriendly and refuses to show up for that reason, consider whether it is worth compelling the witness to testify at all, as allowing that person to testify may damage the case. If a witness is antagonistic and is not responding in good faith to questions asked on examination-in-chief, the judge may be asked to declare the witness hostile on the grounds of non-responsiveness, in which case the representative is allowed to cross-examine their own witness and can frame questions to elicit yes or no answers that tie the witness down to precise, responsive answers, rather than rambling, unhelpful discourses.

A witness may be summonsed by serving a Summons to Witness (Figure 10.23). The summons should be for the date of the trial that is set out in the notice of trial sent by the clerk. The summons should also identify any documents in the witness's power, possession, or control that the representative wants the witness to bring to court to be introduced as evidence. The summons must be drafted and a Request to Clerk form prepared asking the court to issue the summons. The representative must attend at the court with the appropriate fee for the summons. The summons must be served personally and must be accompanied by a cheque for the witness fee and mileage allowance, referred to in the Rules as "attendance money." Experts such as doctors and lawyers are entitled to higher witness fees. The actual amounts required are set out in section 3 of the *Small Claims Court—Fees and Allowances* regulation under the *Administration of Justice Act*. Because these change from time to time, they are not reproduced here. Consult a local court office or obtain them online from <http://www.attorneygeneral.jus.gov.on.ca> by searching for "Small Claims Court fees and allowances" at that website. Although the summons will give the first day of trial as the attendance date, the witness is required to attend on all days of trial until the matter is concluded or the witness is no longer required. The legal representative should ask the judge to bind the witnesses over to the next court date if the matter continues past the first day of trial. Proof of service of the summons and attendance money is by affidavit. The affidavit of service should be brought to court to show to the judge in the event that the witness fails to appear. The judge may then issue a warrant for the apprehension of the defaulting witness, requiring that the witness be apprehended and held in custody until the witness's presence is no longer required. If a witness is summonsed needlessly, the court may order the party summoning the witness to pay the witness an amount of money to compensate for inconvenience and expense, above and beyond attendance money already paid.[39]

39 See Rule 18.03(8).

To prevent surprises, copies of a summons to a witness must be served on all parties so that they can prepare for cross-examination and summons their own reply witnesses.

At the commencement of the trial, a party or the court will usually make a verbal motion to exclude non-party witnesses from the courtroom until it is their turn to testify, in order to protect the integrity of each witness's testimony.

Documentary Evidence at Trial

Most debt collection cases are determined on the basis of documentary evidence rather than on oral evidence. The most important thing for a plaintiff to do in a debt action is to have all the original documents required to prove the case organized and ready for use in court. Rule 18.02 allows for service on the other side, at least 30 days before the trial, of a copy of every document the party intends to rely on at trial to prove their case. Unless the trial judge orders otherwise, these documents may be received in evidence without first having to be identified and commented on by a witness (the usual rule is that documents do not "walk" into court on their own—they have to come in as part of a witness's evidence, where the witness can testify as to what they are, identify them, and otherwise prove their reliability and admissibility). It is advisable to prepare a brief of the documents that are going to be introduced under this rule, with an index identifying each document, listing them in the order they will be referred to as part of the case. It is helpful to have a copy for the court reporter. The judge, clerk, and opposite party should already have copies that were served and filed earlier. Having extra copies is a good idea, in case served copies have gone missing. These documents may include witness statements and expert reports that include facts and opinions on which the witness could give oral testimony. The use of this class of documents shortens a trial by eliminating the need to call witnesses. If the other side wishes to cross-examine a witness on their statement, they may, under Rule 18.02(4), summon that person as a witness. Also, be aware that judges are reluctant to admit witness statements that are controversial or lack credibility. A settlement conference is a good place to settle on which documents and statements would be accepted as evidence if presented in this way. All other documents that would normally be admitted at trial can also be presented in advance in this way. These documents include accounting records, cheques, promissory notes, contracts, and medical reports.

All documents (including photos, videos, and sound recordings) that a party intends to rely on at trial must be served on other parties at least 30 days before the trial date so that the other parties can prepare to serve reply evidence. The parties should have all relevant documents attached to their pleadings, or should have served and filed them 14 or more days before the settlement conference. From these documents, a party can select the ones to be used at trial and serve them on the other side 30 or more days before trial. A party should remember to bring affidavits of service for these documents in case they are challenged on them at trial.

Costs

As in other civil courts, costs follow the event. This means that the party that wins is usually reimbursed for some of their legal costs. A party that loses must pay their own costs in full and some of their opponent's costs as well. Remember that the costs provisions in Rule 19 of the *Rules of the Small Claims Court* are subject to the costs consequences under Rule 14 for refusing or accepting offers to settle made at least seven days before trial, which can double the usual costs award, if a Rule 14 offer is made that is equivalent to or better than the trial judgment.

The successful party is entitled to have reasonable disbursements paid by the unsuccessful party unless the court orders otherwise. Disbursements include court fees required to issue various documents, as well as actual, provable out-of-pocket expenses such as costs of serving documents personally (by a process server) or by mail, the costs of attendance money for witnesses, travel expenses, photocopying, and expert reports. Receipts must be provided to prove out-of-pocket expenses.

The court has power to award costs over and above disbursements as follows:

- The court may allow a successful party up to $100 for the preparation and filing of pleadings upon their providing proof that payment of at least $100 was made to a legal representative for claim preparation and filing.
- A representation fee is used to compensate a party who uses a lawyer, articling student, or paralegal. The amount awarded must be reasonable, subject to the limit set out in section 29 of the *Courts of Justice Act*, which is 15 percent of the amount claimed.
- If the successful party is self-represented, the court may award the successful party up to $500 as compensation for inconvenience.

While a party can expect to recover some of the costs of the action if successful, they still need to have the funds to get the case under way. Where the amount of the claim is relatively small, and where a party has a modest income, court filing fees may present a real barrier to using the court. A poor litigant might be discouraged from proceeding with a meritorious case because of filing fees. It was long thought that the Small Claims Court had no authority to waive fees for those pleading poverty. However, in July 2003, in *Polewsky v Home Hardware*,[40] the Ontario Divisional Court ruled that the *Courts of Justice Act* should be read as amended to allow Small Claims Court judges to waive fees for parties who have meritorious cases but are unable to pay the fees. The court gave the government a grace period to rewrite the legislation. The fee waiver program is now in place under O Reg 2/05 under the *Administration of Justice Act*. An application form to apply for a fee waiver can be obtained from any Small Claims Court office. With a fee waiver, the party does not have to pay any fees and can have an interpreter, in any language, paid for by the court, if required.

40 *Polewsky v Home Hardware Stores Ltd*, 2003 CanLII 48473 (Ont Sup Ct J (Div Ct)).

Varying and Setting Aside Judgments

Because parties, particularly defendants, may be unrepresented and not realize the necessity of showing up for trial, Rule 17 spells out consequences for non-attendance. If neither party shows up, the judge may strike the matter off the trial list, in which case one party or the other will have to reschedule the trial. The judge will not, at this point, dismiss the action or grant default judgment. If one party shows up and the other does not, the judge may proceed in the missing party's absence. If the defendant shows up and the plaintiff does not, the judge may dismiss the action. If the defendant does not show up and the plaintiff does, the judge may grant judgment to the plaintiff or allow the plaintiff to prove their damages. However, if the defendant in their defence had raised the issue of territorial jurisdiction, arguing that the plaintiff had sued in the wrong territorial division, the judge shall make a determination on this issue, and if the judge finds that the action should be tried in another territorial division in accordance with the provisions of Rule 6, the judge will make an order directing where the trial should take place. This allows a defendant to have the matter of territorial jurisdiction determined without having to travel a great distance to simply argue that one issue.

Once judgment has been given against a party who has failed to attend trial, it is open to a court to set aside or vary such a judgment. Rule 17 permits motions to set aside default judgments that resulted from inadvertent non-attendance, or because a defendant had no notice of the action because they had not been successfully served. The court in setting aside judgment may do so on terms, often granting to a plaintiff the costs wasted or "thrown away" on the first action. Such a motion must be brought by a party within 30 days of becoming aware of the judgment, or the party can ask the court to extend the 30-day period.

If a judgment has been sent from one court to another for enforcement, a motion may be brought in the first court to set the judgment aside. The first court will then notify the second, which will stay enforcement until the matter has been completed in the first court. The key here is that the first court—that is, the one that gave judgment in the first place—determines the outcome of a motion to set aside the judgment, and the clerk of the second court will take directions from the clerk of the first court.

A court may also, under Rule 17.01(4), on a motion brought within 30 days of the judgment, vary a default judgment after it has been given. Rule 17.04(1) may be used to bring a motion for a new trial if there is relevant evidence that was not available to the party at the time of the original trial and that could not reasonably have been expected to be available at that time. This does provide an alternative to a more costly and formal appeal. Normally, a variation of a judgment occurs when the court discovers that, through an inadvertent error, the judgment is incorrect in terms of some detail. For example, a judgment for an amount of money that has been determined on accounting record evidence might be varied if, subsequent to the judgment being made, it was discovered that there had been a calculation error or a misreading of the account records.

Adjournments

When a case comes to trial, the judge has the power to postpone or adjourn the trial, and may do so on conditions or terms, and may order one side to compensate the other for inconvenience and costs incurred as a result of the adjournment. In the event that a trial is adjourned two or more times, any further adjournments require that a motion be brought to the court.[41] If a further adjournment is granted, the judge will often make the trial **peremptory** on the party that sought the adjournment or in some cases on both parties.

peremptory
an order that absolutely must be followed such that the person the order is peremptory against must be ready for trial on the next scheduled trial date; the court will not tolerate any further excuses from that party

Case Management

Case management to control delay in the progress of a case is in place in the Small Claims Court.

If by the second anniversary of the commencement of a claim the action has not been disposed of by an order and no step has been taken by the plaintiff to obtain a judgment nor has a trial date been requested, the court clerk shall make an order dismissing the action for delay.[42]

Motion for a New Trial and Appeals

Within 30 days of the end of a trial, either party may bring a motion asking for a new trial. The legal representative must obtain a date from the court clerk and serve and file the notice of motion within the time provided for in Rule 17. Proof must be filed that the legal representative requested transcripts of the reasons for judgment. On the motion, the court has jurisdiction to grant a new trial, grant the judgment that should have been granted at trial, or vary the judgment only if:

1. There was a purely arithmetical error in the determination of the amount of damages awarded.
2. There is relevant evidence that was not available to the party at the time of trial and could not reasonably be expected to be available at that time.

Where the amount claimed exceeds $2,500,[43] an appeal goes to the Divisional Court. An appeal is appropriate where the judge has made an error in law. The rules for appeals are set out in Rule 61 of the *Rules of Civil Procedure*, not in the *Rules of the Small Claims Court*. To appeal, a legal representative must, within 30 days of the judgment being handed down, serve and file a notice of appeal and a certificate that lays out the evidence. There are provisions to extend the time for filing a notice of appeal. The cost of an appeal can easily be more than the amount of the judgment. Transcripts alone cost approximately $400 per day of the trial. Appeal preparation fees and counsel fees on the appeal can easily top $10,000. Appeals can only be argued by lawyers. An appeal is simply not economically feasible in most cases, and is beyond the scope of this text.[44]

41 See Rule 17.02(2).

42 See Rule 11.1.01.

43 See s 31 of the *Courts of Justice Act* and O Reg 626/00 as amended.

44 For a detailed discussion of an appeal from a judgment of the Small Claims Court, see Marvin Zuker, *Ontario Small Claims Court Practice* (Toronto: Carswell, 2015) at 261.

CHAPTER SUMMARY

Chapter 10 introduced the Small Claims Court and its culture, noting how it differs in its operations from the Superior Court. Court jurisdiction is based on monetary amount and the place where parties reside or the cause of action arose. Determining the proper parties to sue was discussed, with particular attention paid to suing various business entities and parties under a disability. Preparation, filing, and service of the claim were examined, along with the various modes of service. Once served, the defendant then has the option of filing a defence or a proposal, and may also file a defendant's claim if the defendant has a counterclaim (a claim against the plaintiff), a cross-claim (against another defendant), or a third-party claim (a claim against a person not already a party). How pleadings may be amended was also discussed. Special attention was paid to the mechanics of default proceedings.

The chapter then moved on to settlement conferences, formal offers to settle, and motions, which usually come into play as the case gets closer to trial.

After this, the chapter focused on the trial itself, paying particular attention to trial preparation: summoning witnesses and organizing documentary evidence. Consideration was then given to how costs are awarded, how judgments may be varied or set aside, and how appeals are made after the trial has concluded.

KEY TERMS

Children's Lawyer, 250
declaratory judgment, 246
full legal age and capacity, 249
gazetteer, 247
liquidated damages, 256
litigation guardian, 249
peremptory , 267
Public Guardian and Trustee, 250
specific performance, 246

REVIEW QUESTIONS

1. In what way does the operation of the Small Claims Court assist litigants who are not represented?
2. What advantages does the Small Claims Court offer to litigants that the Superior Court does not offer?
3. What are the Small Claims Court's jurisdictional limits?
4. If you operate in Kenora and have as part of your standard contract a section that says "the parties consent to all disputes being tried in the Small Claims Court at Kenora," does this allow you to sue for breach of contract in the Kenora Small Claims Court no matter where the defendant resides or carries on business?
5. How do you prove to the court that your claim has been brought in the correct territorial division?
6. What choices do you have if you wish to sue a sole proprietorship? A partnership? A corporation?
7. In what circumstances can you electronically file a claim?
8. In what circumstances would a party require a litigation guardian?
9. Suppose you serve a defendant who you know is mentally incapable and no defence has been filed within 20 days of personal service on the defendant. Can you simply ask the clerk to sign default judgment?

10. May the plaintiff personally serve the defendant?
11. Suppose you served a claim and the 20th day after service was effected was Christmas day, which was a Friday. On what day would the defendant be deemed to be in default?
12. If the defendant admits to owing the money claimed by the plaintiff, should the defendant file a defence anyway? What are the advantages in filing a defence? What are the advantages in not filing?
13. Suppose the defendant owes money to the plaintiff, but the plaintiff also owes the defendant a refund on certain purchases, which the plaintiff has not paid yet. How might this situation affect what the defendant includes in a written defence?
14. What are the conditions precedent to having the clerk sign default judgment?
15. If Superior Court discovery is not part of the Small Claims Court procedure, how can disclosure be obtained in order to prepare a case?
16. What are the purposes of the settlement conference?
17. What happens if a settlement conference is called and there is a failure to attend or a party has not prepared their case before attending?
18. Suppose the defendant makes an offer to settle. Explain to the client the consequences of not accepting the offer.
19. If the defendant accepts the plaintiff's offer to settle and later reneges on the payment of money required by the settlement, what may the plaintiff do?
20. How do you present evidence at trial?
21. What do you need to do to be sure that your witnesses show up at trial?
22. Explain what a client can expect to recover for costs if successful on a claim for $1000.
23. Tell your client what their procedural options are if, after trial, you discover that there is new documentary evidence that would have helped their case.

CASE STUDY

MEMO

DATE: September 10, year 0
TO: Collections Clerk
FROM: I.M. Just
RE: Harbour Master v Pretentious

Harbour Master Ltd. at 2133 Princess Street, Kingston, ON K1R 3T4, 613-547-8304 is a vendor of sailing supplies. Harbour Master sold a main sheet rig to Peter Pretentious on August 29, year 0 for $1,500 incl. HST. Interest was set out on the bill of sale at 12 percent per year on overdue accounts, with a $25 charge for NSF cheques. We did some checking: Peter lives at 1 Queen's Quay, Suite 1500, Toronto, ON M2J 1P3. His cheque for $1,500 was dishonoured and returned by the bank marked NSF. Calls and letters have received no response. We have been asked to collect the money. Payment was due on the invoice date, August 29.

1. Prepare a claim. The claim was issued on September 15, year 0.
2. Assume that Peter Pretentious was served at home on September 17, year 0. Draft the affidavit of service.

3. Suppose that Mr. Pretentious finds out he's been sued after judgment is obtained. He says he was ill in September year 0 and forgot about being served, so the matter slipped his mind. Had he remembered, he would have defended. He says that he had asked the plaintiff to hold off on cashing the cheque for two days, which the plaintiff verbally agreed to and then cashed it that same day such that there were insufficient funds in the account to pay it. Draft the notice of motion and supporting affidavit to set aside default judgment. Assume that the judgment was obtained on October 29, year 0 from the Kingston Small Claims Court, and that you have obtained from the court a motion date for November 13, year 0.

4. Suppose that Mr. Pretentious is successful at getting the judgment set aside; he wants to defend on the basis that the rig he was sold was defective. He wishes to have a sailing crew member who saw the rig and the difficulties it caused testify. Her name is Sara Silandro; she lives at 83 Caulfield Street, Oshawa, ON K3B 1X8; the trial will be at the Kingston Small Claims Court on April 23, year 1. Prepare the necessary documents to ensure that she appears at trial.

FIGURE 10.1 Affidavit for Jurisdiction

ONTARIO
Superior Court of Justice

Affidavit for Jurisdiction
Form 11A Ont. Reg. No.: 258/98

Toronto
Small Claims Court

SC-10-00012345-0000
Claim No.

47 Sheppard Ave. E., 3rd Floor
Toronto, ON M2N 3X5
Address

416-326-3554
Phone number

BETWEEN

Cape Credit Corporation Ltd.
Plaintiff(s)

and

Feckless Enterprises
Defendant(s)

My name is Charles Dickens
(Full name)

I live in Toronto, ON
(Municipality & province)

and I swear/affirm that the following is true:

1. In this action, I am the

☐ plaintiff
☒ representative of the plaintiff(s) Cape Credit Corporation Ltd.
(Name of plaintiff(s))

2. I make this affidavit in support of the plaintiff's request to note the defendant(s) in default, where all the defendants have been or will be served outside the court's territorial division [R. 11.01 (3)].

3. The plaintiff is entitled to proceed with this action in this territorial division because this is:

☒ where the event (cause of action) took place.
☐ where the defendant lives or carries on business.
☐ the court nearest to the place where the defendant lives or carries on business [R. 6.01].

Sworn/Affirmed before me at Toronto
(Municipality)

in Ontario
(Province, state or country)

on Oct. 30, year 0 , 20 ____

Commissioner for taking affidavits
(Type or print name below if signature is illegible.)

Signature
(This form is to be signed in front of a lawyer, justice of the peace, notary public or commissioner for taking affidavits.)

WARNING: IT IS AN OFFENCE UNDER THE *CRIMINAL CODE* TO KNOWINGLY SWEAR OR AFFIRM A FALSE AFFIDAVIT.

Les formules des tribunaux sont affichées en anglais et en français sur le site www.ontariocourtforms.on.ca. Visitez ce site pour des renseignements sur des formats accessibles.

SCR 11.01-11A (January 23, 2014) CSD

FIGURE 10.2 Notice to Alleged Partner

ONTARIO
Superior Court of Justice

Notice to Alleged Partner
Form 5A Ont. Reg. No.: 258/98

Toronto
Small Claims Court

SC-10-00012345-0000
Claim No.

47 Sheppard Ave. E., 3rd Floor
Toronto, ON M2N 3X5
Address

416-326-3554
Phone number

BETWEEN

Cape Credit Corporation Ltd.
Plaintiff(s)

and

Feckless Enterprises
Defendant(s)

TO:

Name of alleged partner Henry Feckless
Street and number 108 Elmtree Drive
City, province, postal code Toronto, ON M5W 3A2

YOU ARE ALLEGED TO HAVE BEEN A PARTNER on April 1, year -1 , 20 ____

(or during the period) ______________ , 20 ____ to ______________ , 20 ____

in the partnership/business of ______________________________ ,
(Firm name)

a party named in this proceeding.

IF YOU WISH TO DENY THAT YOU WERE A PARTNER at any material time, you must defend this proceeding separately from the partnership, denying that you were a partner at the material time. If you fail to do so, you will be deemed to have been a partner on the date (or during the period) set out above.

CAUTION:	**AN ORDER AGAINST THE PARTNERSHIP MAY BE ENFORCED AGAINST YOU PERSONALLY** if you are deemed to have been a partner, if you admit that you were, or if the court finds that you were at the material time.

October 30, year 0 , 20 ____

____
(Signature of plaintiff or representative)

Les formules des tribunaux sont affichées en anglais et en français sur le site www.ontariocourtforms.on.ca. Visitez ce site pour des renseignements sur des formats accessibles.

SCR 5.03-5A (January 23, 2014) CSD

FIGURE 10.3 Sample Notice Requiring Disclosure of Individual Partner's Names

Claim no. SC-10-00012345-0000

ONTARIO
Superior Court of Justice

Toronto Small Claims Court
47 Sheppard Avenue E., 3rd Floor
Toronto, ON M2N 2X5
416-326-3554

Plaintiff
Full name
Cape Credit Corporation Ltd.

Address for service (street & number, city, postal code)
c/o Charles Dickens (P02345)
8041 Ryder Street
Mississauga, ON L3R 1Y6

Phone no.
905-381-2620

Plaintiff's legal representative
Charles Dickens

Legal representative's address for service
8041 Ryder Street
Mississauga, ON L2R 1Y6

Legal representative's phone number
905-381-2620

Defendant
Full name
Feckless Enterprises

Address for service (street & number, city, postal code)
c/o Edward Lue (P22331)
365 Bay Street
Toronto, ON M2N 3A8

Phone no.
416-595-1308

Defendant's legal representative
Edward Lue

Legal representative's Address for service
365 Bay Street
Toronto, ON M2N 3A8

Legal representative's phone number
416-595-1308

FIGURE 10.3 Sample Notice Requiring Disclosure of Individual Partner's Names (*continued*)

NOTICE REQUIRING DISCLOSURE OF PARTNERS

Take notice that you are required to disclose and provide to the plaintiff, in writing, the names and addresses of all partners constituting Feckless Enterprises in April, year –1, pursuant to Rule 5.04 of the Rules of the Small Claims Court.

Where the present address is unknown, the partnership will disclose the last-known address of the partner(s).

If you fail to comply with this notice, your claim, if any, may be struck out, proceedings may be stayed, or your defence may be struck out.

Dated at Toronto, Ontario, November 19, year 0

Charles Dickens, Paralegal (P02345)
8041 Ryder Street
Mississauga, ON L2R 1Y6
905-381-2620

FIGURE 10.4 Consent to Act as Litigation Guardian (Plaintiff)

ONTARIO
Superior Court of Justice

Consent to Act as Litigation Guardian
Form 4A Ont. Reg. No.: 258/98

Toronto
Small Claims Court

SC-10-00012346-0000
Claim No.

47 Sheppard Ave. E., 3rd Floor
Toronto, On M2N 3X5
Address

416-326-3554
Phone number

BETWEEN

Sonya Smith
Plaintiff(s)

and

Oliver Twist
Defendant(s)

My name is	Name Alice Smith
And I live at	Street and number 30 Median Way
	City, province, postal code Toronto, ON M3R 1X4
	Phone number and fax number 416-762-1242

1. I consent to act as litigation guardian in this action for the

☒ plaintiff, named Sonya Smith
(Name of plaintiff)

(Check one box only.)

and I acknowledge that I may be personally responsible for any costs awarded against me or against this person.

☐ defendant, named ______________________ .
(Name of defendant)

2. The above-named person is under the following disability:

☒ a minor whose birth date is April 4, year -15 .
(State date of birth of minor)

(Check appropriate box(es).)

☐ mentally incapable within the meaning of Section 6 or Section 45 of the *Substitute Decisions Act, 1992* in respect of an issue in a proceeding.

☐ an absentee within the meaning of the *Absentees Act*.

3. My relationship to the person under disability is:
(State your relationship to the person under disability.)
Mother

Les formules des tribunaux sont affichées en anglais et en français sur le site www.ontariocourtforms.on.ca. Visitez ce site pour des renseignements sur des formats accessibles.

SCR 4.01-4.02-4A (January 23, 2014) CSD

FIGURE 10.4 Consent to Act as Litigation Guardian (Plaintiff) (*continued*)

FORM 4A **PAGE 2** SC-10-00012346-0000
Claim No.

4. I have no interest in this action contrary to that of the person under disability.

5. I am

(Check one box only.)

☒ represented and have given written authority to Emily Dickinson
(Name of representative with authority to act in this proceeding)

of 265 Queen St. E., Toronto, ON M3R 2X4
(Address for service)

416-283-0946
(Phone number and fax number)

to act in this proceeding.

☐ not represented by a representative.

May 8, year 0 , 20 ____

____
(Signature of litigation guardian consenting)

____
(Signature of witness)

Emily Dickinson
(Name of witness)

NOTE:	Within seven (7) calendar days of changing your address for service, notify the court and all other parties in writing.

SCR 4.01-4.02-4A (January 23, 2014) CSD

FIGURE 10.5 Consent to Act as Litigation Guardian (Defendant)

ONTARIO
Superior Court of Justice

Consent to Act as Litigation Guardian
Form 4A Ont. Reg. No.: 258/98

Toronto
Small Claims Court

SC-10-00012346-0000
Claim No.

47 Sheppard Ave. E., 3rd Floor
Toronto, On M2N 3X5
Address

416-326-3554
Phone number

BETWEEN

Sonya Smith
Plaintiff(s)

and

Oliver Twist
Defendant(s)

My name is	Name **Malcolm Twist**
And I live at	Street and number **4905 Yonge St.**
	City, province, postal code **Toronto, ON M3R 2A6**
	Phone number and fax number **416-233-4547**

1. I consent to act as litigation guardian in this action for the

(Check one box only.)

☐ plaintiff, named ______________________
(Name of plaintiff)

and I acknowledge that I may be personally responsible for any costs awarded against me or against this person.

☒ defendant, named **Oliver Twist**.
(Name of defendant)

2. The above-named person is under the following disability:

(Check appropriate box(es).)

☐ a minor whose birth date is ______________________.
(State date of birth of minor)

☒ mentally incapable within the meaning of Section 6 or Section 45 of the *Substitute Decisions Act, 1992* in respect of an issue in a proceeding.

☐ an absentee within the meaning of the *Absentees Act*.

3. My relationship to the person under disability is:
(State your relationship to the person under disability.)
Father

Les formules des tribunaux sont affichées en anglais et en français sur le site www.ontariocourtforms.on.ca. Visitez ce site pour des renseignements sur des formats accessibles.

SCR 4.01-4.02-4A (January 23, 2014) CSD

FIGURE 10.5 Consent to Act as Litigation Guardian (Defendant) (*continued*)

FORM 4A **PAGE 2** SC-10-00012346-0000
Claim No.

4. I have no interest in this action contrary to that of the person under disability.

5. I am

(Check one box only.)

☒ represented and have given written authority to I.M. Horn
(Name of representative with authority to act in this proceeding)

of 805 Avenue Rd., Toronto, ON M2R 1J6
(Address for service)

416-964-3101
(Phone number and fax number)

to act in this proceeding.

☐ not represented by a representative.

June 2, year 0 , 20 ____

____
(Signature of litigation guardian consenting)

____
(Signature of witness)

I.M. Horn
(Name of witness)

NOTE: Within seven (7) calendar days of changing your address for service, notify the court and all other parties in writing.

SCR 4.01-4.02-4A (January 23, 2014) CSD

FIGURE 10.6 Sample Demand Served on Person Under Disability

Claim no. SC-10-00012251-0000

ONTARIO
Superior Court of Justice

Toronto Small Claims Court
47 Sheppard Avenue E., 3rd Floor
Toronto, ON M2N 2X5
416-326-3554

Plaintiff

Full name
O'Hooligan's Bar Ltd.

Address for service (street & number, city, postal code)
c/o I.M. Horn (P03478)
39 Bedford Avenue
Toronto, ON M3T 9V5

Plaintiff's legal representative
I.M. Horn

Legal representative's address for service
39 Bedford Avenue
Toronto, ON M3T 9V5

Legal representative's phone number
416-469-3963

Defendant

Full name
Patrick Bratty

Address for service (street & number, city, postal code)
48 Overreach Boulevard
Toronto, ON M2R 5X3

Defendant's legal representative

Legal representative's Address for service

Legal representative's phone number

FIGURE 10.6 Sample Demand Served on Person Under Disability (*continued*)

DEMAND

TAKE NOTICE that because Patrick Bratty, the above-named defendant, is a party under disability by reason of being a minor under the age of 18 years, he must defend this action by a litigation guardian appointed for this purpose.

AND FURTHER TAKE NOTICE that unless, within 20 days from the receipt of this notice, action is taken to have the defendant's father, mother, or other suitable adult appointed as litigation guardian for the defendant, an application will be made without further notification to you to have the Children's Lawyer appointed litigation guardian for the purpose of this action.

DATED at Toronto, July 28, Year 0

I.M. Horn (P03478)
Legal Representative for the Plaintiff
39 Bedford Avenue
Toronto, ON M3T 9V5
416-369-3963

TO: PATRICK BRATTY, A person under disability
48 Overreach Boulevard
Toronto, ON M2R 5X3

AND TO: MAUREEN BRATTY, mother of Patrick Bratty
48 Overreach Boulevard
Toronto, On M2R 5X3

FIGURE 10.7 Plaintiff's Claim

ONTARIO
Superior Court of Justice

Plaintiff's Claim
Form 7A Ont. Reg. No.: 258/98

Toronto
Small Claims Court

SC-10-000012345-0000
Claim No.

Seal

47 Sheppard Ave. E., 3rd Floor
Toronto, ON M2N 3X5
Address

416-326-3554
Phone number

Plaintiff No. 1 ☐ Additional plaintiff(s) listed on attached Form 1A. ☐ Under 18 years of age.

Last name, or name of company		
Cape Credit Corporation Ltd.		
First name	Second name	Also known as
Address (street number, apt., unit): c/o Charles Dickens 8041 Ryder Street		
City/Town: Mississauga	Province: ON	Phone no.: 905-381-2620
Postal code: L2R 1Y6		Fax no.
Representative: Charles Dickens		LSUC #: P02345
Address (street number, apt., unit): 8041 Ryder Street		
City/Town: Mississauga	Province: ON	Phone no.: 905-381-2620
Postal code: L2R 1Y6		Fax no.

Defendant No. 1 ☐ Additional defendant(s) listed on attached Form 1A. ☐ Under 18 years of age.

Last name, or name of company		
Feckless Enterprises		
First name	Second name	Also known as
Address (street number, apt., unit): 48 Overreach Blvd.		
City/Town: Toronto	Province: ON	Phone no.: 416-223-4569
Postal code: M6X 3L7		Fax no.
Representative		LSUC #
Address (street number, apt., unit)		
City/Town	Province	Phone no.
Postal code		Fax no.

Les formules des tribunaux sont affichées en anglais et en français sur le site www.ontariocourtforms.on.ca. Visitez ce site pour des renseignements sur des formats accessibles.

SCR 7.01-7A (November 1, 2016) CSD

Continued on next page

FIGURE 10.7 Plaintiff's Claim (*continued*)

FORM 7A **PAGE 2** **SC-10-000012345-0000**
Claim No.

REASONS FOR CLAIM AND DETAILS

Explain what happened, including where and when. Then explain how much money you are claiming or what goods you want returned.

If you are relying on any documents, you **MUST** attach copies to the claim. If evidence is lost or unavailable, you **MUST** explain why it is not attached.

What happened? The defendant failed to pay the amount owing to the plaintiff on a promissory note.
Where? The note was signed at Toronto, Ontario.
When? The note was signed on April 1, year -1 and was due on April 1, year 0.

1.The plaintiff, Cape Credit Corporation Ltd. (Cape), is a corporation with its head office in Toronto, Ontario.

2. The defendant, Feckless Enterprises (Feckless), is a partnership located in Toronto, Ontario.

3. Feckless signed a promissory note (note) in favour of Cape on April 1, year -1 at Toronto, Ontario.

4. The note, a true copy of which is attached to this claim as document "A," was in the amount of $3000.00 with interest at 10% per year both before and after maturity. The note was due on April 1, year 0.

5. Feckless received the amount of $3000 in accordance with the note, on April 1, year -1.

6. Feckless has neglected or refused to pay the principal and interest due under the note.

SCR 7.01-7A (November 1, 2016) CSD

Continued on next page

FIGURE 10.7 Plaintiff's Claim (*continued*)

FORM 7A **PAGE 3** SC-10-000012345-0000
Claim No.

How much? $ 3000.00
(Principal amount claimed)

☐ **ADDITIONAL PAGES ARE ATTACHED BECAUSE MORE ROOM WAS NEEDED.**

The plaintiff also claims pre-judgment interest from April 1, year 0 (Date) **under:**

(Check only one box)
☐ **the *Courts of Justice Act***
☒ **an agreement at the rate of** 10 **% per year**

and post-judgment interest, and court costs.

Prepared on: October 30, year 0, 20 ____ ______________________
(Signature of plaintiff or representative)

Issued on: ______________, 20 ____ ______________________
(Signature of clerk)

CAUTION TO DEFENDANT:	**IF YOU DO NOT FILE A DEFENCE** (Form 9A) and an Affidavit of Service (Form 8A) with the court within twenty (20) calendar days after you have been served with this Plaintiff's Claim, judgment may be obtained without notice and enforced against you. Forms and self-help materials are available at the Small Claims Court and on the following website: www.ontariocourtforms.on.ca.
CAUTION TO PARTIES:	Unless the court orders or the rules provide otherwise, **THIS ACTION WILL BE AUTOMATICALLY DISMISSED** if it has not been disposed of by order or otherwise two (2) years after it was commenced and a trial date or assessment under subrule 11.03(2) has not been requested.

For information on accessibility of court services for people with disability-related needs, contact:

Telephone: 416-326-2220 / 1-800-518-7901 TTY: 416-326-4012 / 1-877-425-0575

SCR 7.01-7A (November 1, 2016) CSD

FIGURE 10.8 Affidavit of Service

ONTARIO
Superior Court of Justice

Affidavit of Service
Form 8A Ont. Reg. No.: 258/98

North Bay
Small Claims Court

SC-10-00012350-0000
Claim No.

333 Plouffe Street
North Bay, ON P1B 9L5
Address

705-495-8309
Phone number

BETWEEN

Abdullah Karim
Plaintiff(s)

and

Antonio Salieri
Defendant(s)

My name is Domenico Scarlatti
(Full name)

I live in Kingston, Ontario
(Municipality & province)

and I swear/affirm that the following is true:

1. **I served** Antonio Salieri (Full name of person/corporation served), on May 23, year 0 (Date), 20 ____,

 at 177 Main Street, Kingston, ON K7L 2T2
 (Address (street and number, unit, municipality, province))

 which is
 - ☒ the address of the person's home
 - ☐ the address of the corporation's place of business
 - ☐ the address of the person's or corporation's representative on record with the court
 - ☐ the address on the document most recently filed in court by the party
 - ☐ the address of the corporation's attorney for service in Ontario
 - ☐ other address: ____________ (Specify.)

 with Plaintiff's Claim
 (Name(s) of document(s) served)

2. **I served the document(s) referred to in paragraph one by the following method:**
 (Tell how service took place by checking appropriate box(es).)

Personal service
- ☒ leaving a copy with the person.
- ☐ leaving a copy with the ____________ (Office or position) of the corporation.
- ☐ leaving a copy with: ____________ (Specify person's name and office/position.)
 at the place of business of the corporation who appeared to be in control or management of the place of business.

Les formules des tribunaux sont affichées en anglais et en français sur le site www.ontariocourtforms.on.ca. Visitez ce site pour des renseignements sur des formats accessibles.

SCR 8.06-8A (November 1, 2015) CSD

Continued on next page

FIGURE 10.8 Affidavit of Service (*continued*)

FORM 8A **PAGE 2** SC-10-00012350-0000
Claim No.

Service at place of residence ☐ leaving a copy in a sealed envelope addressed to the person at the person's place of residence with a person who appeared to be an adult member of the same household, and sending another copy of the same document(s) to the person's place of residence on the same day or the following day by:

- ☐ regular lettermail.
- ☐ registered mail.
- ☐ courier.

Service by registered mail ☐ registered mail.
(If a copy of a plaintiff's claim or defendant's claim was served by registered mail, attach a copy of the Canada Post delivery confirmation, showing the signature verifying delivery, to this affidavit.)

Service by courier ☐ courier.
(If a copy of a plaintiff's claim or defendant's claim was served by courier, attach a copy of the courier's delivery confirmation, showing the signature verifying delivery, to this affidavit.)

Service on lawyer or paralegal ☐ leaving a copy with a lawyer or paralegal or an employee in the lawyer's or paralegal's office, who accepted service on the person's behalf.
(Attach a copy of the document endorsed with an acceptance of service.)

Service by regular lettermail ☐ regular lettermail.

Service by fax ☐ fax sent at ____________ (Time) at the following fax number: ____________ (Fax number)

Service to last known address of corporation or attorney for service, and to the directors ☐ mail/courier to corporation or attorney for service at last known address recorded with the Ministry of Government Services, and

mail/courier to each director, as recorded with the Ministry of Government Services, as set out below:

Name of director	Director's address as recorded with the Ministry of Government Services (street & number, unit, municipality, province)

(Attach separate sheet for additional names if necessary.)

Substituted service ☐ substituted service as ordered by the court on ____________ (Date), 20 ____,

as follows: (Give details.)

Sworn/Affirmed before me at Kingston (Municipality)

in Ontario (Province, state, or country)

on May 25, year 0 , 20 ____

____
Commissioner for taking affidavits
(Type or print name below if signature is illegible.)

____
Signature
(This form is to be signed in front of a lawyer, justice of the peace, notary public or commissioner for taking affidavits.)

SCR 8.06-8A (November 1, 2015) CSD

FIGURE 10.9 Defence (to Plaintiff's Claim)

ONTARIO
Superior Court of Justice

Defence
Form 9A Ont. Reg. No.: 258/98

Toronto
Small Claims Court

47 Sheppard Ave. E., 3rd Floor
Toronto, ON M2N 2X5
Address

416-326-3554
Phone number

SC-10-000012345-0000
Claim No.

Plaintiff No. 1 ☐ Additional plaintiff(s) listed on attached Form 1A. ☐ Under 18 years of age.

Last name, or name of company		
Cape Credit Corporation Ltd.		
First name	Second name	Also known as
Address (street number, apt., unit)		
c/o Charles Dickens 8041 Ryder Street		
City/Town	Province	Phone no.
Mississauga	ON	905-381-2620
Postal code		Fax no.
L2R 1Y6		
Representative		LSUC #
Charles Dickens		P02345
Address (street number, apt., unit)		
8041 Ryder Street		
City/Town	Province	Phone no.
Mississauga	ON	905-381-2620
Postal code		Fax no.
L2R 1Y6		

Defendant No. 1 ☐ Additional defendant(s) listed on attached Form 1A. ☐ Under 18 years of age.

Last name, or name of company		
Feckless Enterprises		
First name	Second name	Also known as
Address (street number, apt., unit)		
c/o Edward Lue 365 Bay Street		
City/Town	Province	Phone no.
Toronto	ON	416-595-1308
Postal code		Fax no.
M2N 3A8		
Representative		LSUC #
Edward Lue		P02361
Address (street number, apt., unit)		
365 Bay Street		
City/Town	Province	Phone no.
Toronto	On	416-595-1308
Postal code		Fax no.
M2N 3A8		

Les formules des tribunaux sont affichées en anglais et en français sur le site www.ontariocourtforms.on.ca. Visitez ce site pour des renseignements sur des formats accessibles.

SCR 9.01-10.03-9A (January 23, 2014) CSD

FIGURE 10.9 Defence (to Plaintiff's Claim) (*continued*)

FORM 9A **PAGE 2** SC-10-000012345-0000
Claim No.

THIS DEFENCE IS BEING FILED ON BEHALF OF: (Name(s) of defendant(s))

Feckless Enterprises

and I/we: (Check as many as apply)

☒ Dispute the claim made against me/us.

☐ Admit the full claim and propose the following terms of payment:

$ ________ (Amount) per ________ (Week/month) commencing ________ , 20 ___ .

☐ Admit part of the claim in the amount of $ ________ (Amount) and propose the following terms of payment:

$ ________ (Amount) per ________ (Week/month) commencing ________ , 20 ___ .

REASONS FOR DISPUTING THE CLAIM AND DETAILS:

Explain what happened, including where and when. Explain why you do not agree with the claim made against you.

If you are relying on any documents, you **MUST** attach copies to the Defence. If evidence is lost or unavailable, you **MUST** explain why it is not attached.

What happened?
Where?
When?

The defendant signed a promissory note for $3000 on April 1, year -1 maturing on April 1, year 0 with interest at 10%.

The note was signed at Toronto, ON.

The defendant paid the plaintiff the full amount due on the promissory note, in cash, on April 1, year 0.

The plaintiff's claim should be dismissed with costs to the defendant.

SCR 9.01-10.03-9A (January 23, 2014) CSD

Continued on next page

FIGURE 10.9 Defence (to Plaintiff's Claim) (*continued*)

FORM 9A **PAGE 3** SC-10-000012345-0000
Claim No.

Why I/we disagree with all or part of the claim:

☐ **ADDITIONAL PAGES ARE ATTACHED BECAUSE MORE ROOM WAS NEEDED.**

Prepared on: November 18, year 0 , 20 ____ ______________________
(Signature of defendant or representative)

NOTE:	Within seven (7) calendar days of changing your address for service, notify the court and all other parties in writing.

CAUTION TO PLAINTIFF(S):	If this Defence contains a proposal of terms of payment, you are deemed to have accepted the terms **unless** you file with the clerk and serve on the defendant(s) a Request to Clerk (Form 9B) for a terms of payment hearing **WITHIN TWENTY (20) CALENDAR DAYS** of service of this Defence [R. 9.03(3)].

SCR 9.01-10.03-9A (January 23, 2014) CSD

FIGURE 10.10 Defence (with Proposal to Pay)

ONTARIO
Superior Court of Justice

Defence
Form 9A Ont. Reg. No.: 258/98

Toronto
Small Claims Court

SC-10-000012345-0000
Claim No.

47 Sheppard Ave. E., 3rd Floor
Toronto, ON M2N 2X5
Address

416-326-3554
Phone number

Plaintiff No. 1 ☐ Additional plaintiff(s) listed on attached Form 1A. ☐ Under 18 years of age.

Last name, or name of company		
Cape Credit Corporation Ltd.		
First name	Second name	Also known as
Address (street number, apt., unit)		
c/o Charles Dickens 8041 Ryder Street		
City/Town	Province	Phone no.
Mississauga	ON	905-381-2620
Postal code		Fax no.
L2R 1Y6		
Representative		LSUC #
Charles Dickens		P02345
Address (street number, apt., unit)		
8041 Ryder Street		
City/Town	Province	Phone no.
Mississauga	ON	905-381-2620
Postal code		Fax no.
L2R 1Y6		

Defendant No. 1 ☐ Additional defendant(s) listed on attached Form 1A. ☐ Under 18 years of age.

Last name, or name of company		
Feckless Enterprises		
First name	Second name	Also known as
Address (street number, apt., unit)		
c/o Edward Lue 365 Bay Street		
City/Town	Province	Phone no.
Toronto	ON	416-595-1308
Postal code		Fax no.
M2N 3A8		
Representative		LSUC #
Edward Lue		P02361
Address (street number, apt., unit)		
365 Bay Street		
City/Town	Province	Phone no.
Toronto	On	416-595-1308
Postal code		Fax no.
M2N 3A8		

Les formules des tribunaux sont affichées en anglais et en français sur le site www.ontariocourtforms.on.ca. Visitez ce site pour des renseignements sur des formats accessibles.

SCR 9.01-10.03-9A (January 23, 2014) CSD

FIGURE 10.10 Defence (with Proposal to Pay) (*continued*)

FORM 9A **PAGE 2** SC-10-000012345-0000
Claim No.

THIS DEFENCE IS BEING FILED ON BEHALF OF: (Name(s) of defendant(s))

Feckless Enterprises

and I/we: (Check as many as apply)

☐ Dispute the claim made against me/us.

☒ Admit the full claim and propose the following terms of payment:

$ 40.00 (Amount) per week (Week/month) commencing December 1, year 0 , 20 ____ .

☐ Admit part of the claim in the amount of $ ________ (Amount) and propose the following terms of payment:

$ ________ (Amount) per ________ (Week/month) commencing ________ , 20 ____ .

REASONS FOR DISPUTING THE CLAIM AND DETAILS:

Explain what happened, including where and when. Explain why you do not agree with the claim made against you.

If you are relying on any documents, you **MUST** attach copies to the Defence. If evidence is lost or unavailable, you **MUST** explain why it is not attached.

What happened?
Where?
When?

SCR 9.01-10.03-9A (January 23, 2014) CSD

Continued on next page

FIGURE 10.10 Defence (with Proposal to Pay) (*continued*)

FORM 9A **PAGE 3** **SC-10-000012345-0000**
Claim No.

Why I/we disagree with all or part of the claim:

☐ **ADDITIONAL PAGES ARE ATTACHED BECAUSE MORE ROOM WAS NEEDED.**

Prepared on: **November 18, year 0** , 20 ____ ______________________________
(Signature of defendant or representative)

NOTE:	Within seven (7) calendar days of changing your address for service, notify the court and all other parties in writing.

CAUTION TO PLAINTIFF(S):	If this Defence contains a proposal of terms of payment, you are deemed to have accepted the terms **unless** you file with the clerk and serve on the defendant(s) a Request to Clerk (Form 9B) for a terms of payment hearing **WITHIN TWENTY (20) CALENDAR DAYS** of service of this Defence [R. 9.03(3)].

SCR 9.01-10.03-9A (January 23, 2014) CSD

FIGURE 10.11 Notice of Default of Payment

ONTARIO
Superior Court of Justice

Notice of Default of Payment
Form 20L Ont. Reg. No.: 258/98

Toronto
Small Claims Court

SC-10-00012345-0000
Claim No.

47 Sheppard Ave. E., 3rd Floor
Toronto, On M2N 2X5
Address

416-326-3554
Phone number

BETWEEN

Cape Credit Corporation Ltd.
Plaintiff(s)/Creditor(s)

and

Feckless Enterprises
Defendant(s)/Debtor(s)

TO: Feckless Enterprises
(Name of defendant(s)/debtor(s))

TAKE NOTICE that you defaulted in your payment(s) to
Cape Credit Corporation Ltd.
(Name of plaintiff(s)/creditor(s))

(Check appropriate box.)

☐ under an order for periodic payment, dated ____________, 20 ____.

According to Rule 20.02(4) of the *Rules of the Small Claims Court*, the order for periodic payment terminates on the day that is 15 days after the creditor serves the debtor with this notice, unless before that date, a Consent (Form 13B) is filed in which the creditor waives the default.

☒ under a proposal of terms of payment in the Defence (Form 9A) dated November 18, year 0 , 20 ____.

According to Rule 9.03(2)(c) the clerk may sign judgment for the unpaid balance of the undisputed amount on the day that is 15 days after the plaintiff serves the defendant with this notice.

Les formules des tribunaux sont affichées en anglais et en français sur le site www.ontariocourtforms.on.ca. Visitez ce site pour des renseignements sur des formats accessibles.

SCR 20.02-20L (January 23, 2014) CSD

FIGURE 10.11 Notice of Default of Payment (*continued*)

FORM 20L **PAGE 2** **SC-10-00012345-0000**
Claim No.

You can get forms and self-help materials at the Small Claims Court or online at: www.ontariocourtforms.on.ca.

NOTE TO DEFENDANT/DEBTOR:

If you

- ☐ failed to make payments but intend to do so; or
- ☐ made payments but the payments were not received by the creditor;

contact the plaintiff/creditor to make payment arrangements or correct the reason for non-receipt of payments. You may obtain the plaintiff/creditor's written consent (Form 13B may be used) to waive the default and file it with the court within 15 days of being served with this notice. Failure to do so may result in the following:

- ☐ in the case of default under a proposal of terms of payment in the Defence (Form 9A), the plaintiff may obtain default judgment for the unpaid balance of the undisputed amount; or
- ☐ in the case of default under an order for periodic payment, the order will terminate and the creditor may take other steps to enforce the order.

December 20, year 0 , 20 ____ ______________________________
(Signature of plaintiff/creditor or representative)

____
(Name, address and phone number of plaintiff/creditor or representative)

SCR 20.02-20L (January 23, 2014) CSD

FIGURE 10.12 Affidavit of Default of Payment

ONTARIO
Superior Court of Justice

Affidavit of Default of Payment
Form 20M Ont. Reg. No.: 258/98

Toronto
Small Claims Court

SC-10-000012345-0000
Claim No.

47 Sheppard Ave. E., 3rd Floor
Toronto, ON M2N 2X5
Address

416-326-3554
Phone number

BETWEEN

Cape Credit Corporation Ltd.
Plaintiff(s)/Creditor(s)

and

Feckless Enterprises
Defendant(s)/Debtor(s)

My name is Charles Dickens
(Full name)

I live in Toronto, Ontario
(Municipality & province)

and I swear/affirm that the following is true:

1. In this action, I am the

(Check one box only.)

☐ plaintiff/creditor.
☒ representative of the plaintiff(s)/creditor(s) Cape Credit Corporation Ltd.
(Name of plaintiff(s)/creditor(s))

2. To date, I have received from the defendant(s)/debtor(s) $ 0.00 (Amount), the last payment being made on or about ________, 20 ____ .

3. I make this affidavit in support of a request that:

(Check appropriate box and complete paragraph.)

☒ the clerk of the court issue a Default Judgment (Form 11B) [R. 9.03(2)(c)]. The defendant(s) Feckless Enterprises
(Name(s) of defendant(s))
failed to make payment in accordance with the proposed terms of payment in the Defence (Form 9A) dated November 18, year 0 , 20 ____ and fifteen (15) days have passed since the defendant was served with a Notice of Default of Payment (Form 20L) at the following address(es):
____
(Address(es) of defendant(s))

☐ the clerk of the court issue a Default Judgment (Form 11B) [R. 9.03(7)]. The defendant(s)
____
(Name of defendant(s))
failed to make payment in accordance with the terms of payment order dated ________, 20 ____ .

Les formules des tribunaux sont affichées en anglais et en français sur le site www.ontariocourtforms.on.ca. Visitez ce site pour des renseignements sur des formats accessibles.

SCR 9.03-20M (January 23, 2014) CSD

FIGURE 10.12 Affidavit of Default of Payment (*continued*)

FORM 20M **PAGE 2** SC-10-000012345-0000
Claim No.

☐ I may enforce the judgment [R. 20.02(3)]. The debtor(s)

(Name(s) of debtor(s))

(Check appropriate box and complete paragraph.)

failed to make payment in accordance with the order for periodic payment dated ______, 20 ____, and fifteen (15) days have passed since the debtor(s) has/have been served with a Notice of Default of Payment (Form 20L) at the following address(es):

(Address(es) of debtor(s))

A Consent (Form 13B) in which the creditor waives the default has not been filed.

4. The unpaid balance is calculated as follows:

(A) **DEBT** $ 3000.00

(B) **PRE-JUDGMENT INTEREST** calculated

on the sum of $ 3000.00 at the rate of 10 %

per annum from April 1, year -1, 20 ____ to Dec. 1, year 0, 20 ____,

being 610 days. $ 501.37

NOTE:	Calculation of interest is always on the amount owing from time to time as payments are received. This is true for both pre-judgment and post-judgment interest. Attach a separate sheet setting out how you calculated the total amount of any pre/post-judgment interest.

SUBTOTAL (amount of judgment) **$** 3501.37

(C) **COSTS** to date of judgment $ 95.00

(D) **TOTAL AMOUNT OF PAYMENTS RECEIVED FROM DEBTOR** after judgment (if any) (minus) $ ______

(E) **POST-JUDGMENT INTEREST** to date calculated

on the sum of $ ______ at the rate of ______ %

per annum from ______, 20 ____ to ______, 20 ____,

being ______ days. $ ______

(F) **SUBSEQUENT COSTS** incurred after judgment (including the cost of serving the Notice of Default of Payment (Form 20L)) $ 25.00

TOTAL DUE $ 3621.37

Sworn/Affirmed before me at Toronto
(Municipality)

in Ontario
(Province, state, or country)

on Dec. 1, year 0, 20 ____

Commissioner for taking affidavits
(Type or print name below if signature is illegible.)

Signature
(This form is to be signed in front of a lawyer, justice of the peace, notary public or commissioner for taking affidavits.)

WARNING:	**IT IS AN OFFENCE UNDER THE *CRIMINAL CODE* TO KNOWINGLY SWEAR OR AFFIRM A FALSE AFFIDAVIT.**

SCR 9.03-20M (January 23, 2014) CSD

FIGURE 10.13 Request to Clerk

ONTARIO
Superior Court of Justice

Request to Clerk
Form 9B Ont. Reg. No.: 258/98

Toronto
Small Claims Court

SC-10-00012345-0000
Claim No.

47 Sheppard Ave. E., 3rd Floor
Toronto, ON M2N 2X5
Address

416-326-3554
Phone number

BETWEEN

Cape Credit Corporation Ltd.
Plaintiff(s)

and

Feckless Enterprises
Defendant(s)

TO THE CLERK OF THE Toronto **SMALL CLAIMS COURT:**
(Name of Small Claims Court location)

My name is Charles Dickens **and I request that the clerk of the court:**
(Name of party/representative)

(Check appropriate box(es).)

☐ note defendant(s) ______________________
(Name of defendant(s))
in default for failing to file a Defence (Form 9A) within the prescribed time period [R. 11.01(1)].

☐ schedule an assessment hearing (all defendants have been noted in default) [R. 11.03(2)(b)].

☒ schedule a terms of payment hearing because I dispute the defendant's proposed terms of payment contained in the Defence (Form 9A) [R. 9.03(3)].

☐ schedule a trial [R. 16.01(1)(b)].

☐ accept payment in the amount of $ __________ into court
(Amount)

☐ according to an order of the court, dated __________, 20 ____.

☐ for a person under disability according to an order or settlement dated __________, 20 ____ [R. 4.08(1)].

☐ pursuant to the attached written offer to settle, dated __________, 20 ____ [R. 14.05(2)].

☐ according to the following legislation:
______________________________________.
(Name of statute or regulation and section)

Les formules des tribunaux sont affichées en anglais et en français sur le site www.ontariocourtforms.on.ca. Visitez ce site pour des renseignements sur des formats accessibles.

SCR 4-9-11-14-16-9B (January 23, 2014) CSD

FIGURE 10.13 Request to Clerk (*continued*)

FORM 9B **PAGE 2** **SC-10-00012345-0000**
Claim No.

☐ Other: (Specify.)

Nov. 21, year 0 , 20 ______ ______________________
(Signature of party or representative)

CAUTION:	To obtain an assessment of damages, all defendants must be noted in default. If one or more defendants has filed a defence, the matter must proceed to a settlement conference. To bring a motion in writing for an assessment of damages, file a Notice of Motion and Supporting Affidavit (Form 15A). You can get forms at court offices or online at www.ontariocourtforms.on.ca.

SCR 4-9-11-14-16-9B (January 23, 2014) CSD

FIGURE 10.14 Defendant's Claim

ONTARIO
Superior Court of Justice

Defendant's Claim
Form 10A Ont. Reg. No.: 258/98

Seal

Toronto
Small Claims Court

47 Sheppard Ave. E., 3rd Floor
Toronto, ON M2N 2X5
Address

416-326-3554
Phone number

SC-10-00012349-001
Claim No.

Plaintiff by Defendant's Claim No. 1 ☐ Additional plaintiff(s) listed on attached Form 1A. ☐ Under 18 years of age.

Last name, or name of company		
Feckless Enterprises		
First name	Second name	Also known as
Address (street number, apt., unit): c/o Edward Lue 365 Bay Street		
City/Town: Toronto	Province: ON	Phone no.: 416-595-1308
Postal code: M2N 3A8		Fax no.
Representative: Edward Lue		LSUC #: P02361
Address (street number, apt., unit): 365 Bay Street		
City/Town: Toronto	Province: ON	Phone no.: 416-595-1308
Postal code: M2N 3A8		Fax no.

Defendant by Defendant's Claim No. 1 ☐ Additional defendant(s) listed on attached Form 1A. ☐ Under 18 years of age.

Last name, or name of company		
Slipaway		
First name: Sharon	Second name	Also known as
Address (street number, apt., unit): 33 Gardenia Crescent		
City/Town: Toronto	Province: ON	Phone no.: 416-223-0641
Postal code: M2N 2A8		Fax no.
Representative		LSUC #
Address (street number, apt., unit)		
City/Town	Province	Phone no.
Postal code		Fax no.

Les formules des tribunaux sont affichées en anglais et en français sur le site www.ontariocourtforms.on.ca. Visitez ce site pour des renseignements sur des formats accessibles.

SCR 10.01-10A (January 23, 2014) CSD

FIGURE 10.14 Defendant's Claim (*continued*)

FORM 10A **PAGE 2** SC-10-00012349-001
Claim No.

REASONS FOR CLAIM AND DETAILS

Explain what happened, including where and when. Then explain how much money you are claiming or what goods you want returned.

If you are relying on any documents, you **MUST** attach copies to the claim. If evidence is lost or unavailable, you **MUST** explain why it is not attached.

What happened?
Where?
When?

The plaintiff by defendant's claim, Feckless Enterprises (Feckless) signed a promissory note in favour of Cape Credit Corporation Ltd. (Cape) in the amount of $3000 plus interest at 10%. The note was signed at Toronto, Ontario on April 1, year -1.
The defendant by defendant's claim, Sharon Slipaway (Slipaway), agreed to pay $1000 of this promissory note if Feckless was obliged to honouor its promissory note to Cape.
The agreement between Feckless and Slipaway was entered into at Toronto.

1. Feckless is a business located in Toronto, Ontario. Slipaway is an individual residing in Toronto, Ontario.

2. On April 1, year -1, Feckless signed a promissory note for $3000 plus interest of 10% in favour of Cape. The note was due one year later on April 1, year 0.

3. On April 2, year -1 Slipaway applied for an account with Feckless. As a condition of maintaining an account with Feckless, Slipaway agreed to pay the sum of $1000 toward the promissory note that Feckless had with Cape. The $1000 would bear interest at the rate of 10% per year from the time a demand was made to pay it.

4. Cape called in its note on April 1, year 0.

5. On April 3, year 0, Feckless demanded the sum of $1000 toward the note from Slipaway as agreed.

6. As of the date of the preparation of this claim, Slipaway has refused to pay the amount due.

7. The amount of $1000 plus interest at the rate of 10% per year is due from Slipaway from April 3, year 0 to now.

SCR 10.01-10A (January 23, 2014) CSD

Continued on next sheet

FIGURE 10.14 Defendant's Claim (*continued*)

FORM 10A **PAGE 3** SC-10-00012349-001
Claim No.

How much? $ 1000.00
(Principal amount claimed)

☐ **ADDITIONAL PAGES ARE ATTACHED BECAUSE MORE ROOM WAS NEEDED.**

The plaintiff by defendant's claim also claims pre-judgment interest from April 4, year 0 (Date) **under:**

(Check only one box)
☐ **the *Courts of Justice Act***
☒ **an agreement at the rate of** 10 **% per year**

and post-judgment interest, and court costs.

Prepared on: November 18, year 0 , 20 ______ ______________________
(Signature of plaintiff or representative)

Issued on: November 18, year 0 , 20 ______ ______________________
(Signature of clerk)

CAUTION TO DEFENDANT BY DEFENDANT'S CLAIM:	**IF YOU DO NOT FILE A DEFENCE** (Form 9A) and an Affidavit of Service (Form 8A) with the court within twenty (20) calendar days after you have been served with this Defendant's Claim, judgment may be obtained by Defendant's Claim without notice and enforced against you. Forms and self-help materials are available at the Small Claims Court and on the following website: www.ontariocourtforms.on.ca.

For information on accessibility of court services for people with disability-related needs, contact:

Telephone: 416-326-2220 / 1-800-518-7901 TTY: 416-326-4012 / 1-877-425-0575

SCR 10.01-10A (January 23, 2014) CSD

FIGURE 10.15 Defence (to Defendant's Claim)

ONTARIO
Superior Court of Justice

Defence
Form 9A Ont. Reg. No.: 258/98

Toronto Small Claims Court	SC-10-0012349-0001 Claim No.
47 Sheppard Ave. E., 3rd Floor Toronto, ON M2N 2X5 Address	
416-326-3554 Phone number	

Plaintiff No. 1 ☐ Additional plaintiff(s) listed on attached Form 1A. ☐ Under 18 years of age.

Last name, or name of company		
Feckless Enterprises		
First name	Second name	Also known as
Address (street number, apt., unit)		
c/o Edward Lue 365 Bay Street		
City/Town	Province	Phone no.
Toronto	ON	416-595-1308
Postal code		Fax no.
M2N 3A8		
Representative		LSUC #
Edward Lue		P02361
Address (street number, apt., unit)		
365 Bay Street		
City/Town	Province	Phone no.
Toronto	ON	416-595-1308
Postal code		Fax no.
M2N 3A8		

Defendant No. 1 ☐ Additional defendant(s) listed on attached Form 1A. ☐ Under 18 years of age.

Last name, or name of company		
Slipaway		
First name	Second name	Also known as
Sharon		
Address (street number, apt., unit)		
c/o April Waters 22 Toronto Street		
City/Town	Province	Phone no.
Toronto	ON	416-977-7897
Postal code		Fax no.
M4K 3J2		
Representative		LSUC #
April Waters		P02789
Address (street number, apt., unit)		
22 Toronto Street		
City/Town	Province	Phone no.
Toronto	ON	416-977-7897
Postal code		Fax no.
M4K 3J2		

Les formules des tribunaux sont affichées en anglais et en français sur le site www.ontariocourtforms.on.ca. Visitez ce site pour des renseignements sur des formats accessibles.

SCR 9.01-10.03-9A (January 23, 2014) CSD

FIGURE 10.15 Defence (to Defendant's Claim) (*continued*)

FORM 9A **PAGE 2** **SC-10-0012349-0001**
Claim No.

THIS DEFENCE IS BEING FILED ON BEHALF OF: (Name(s) of defendant(s))

Sharon Slipaway

and I/we: (Check as many as apply)

☒ Dispute the claim made against me/us.

☐ Admit the full claim and propose the following terms of payment:

$ ________ (Amount) per ________ (Week/month) commencing ________ , 20 ___ .

☐ Admit part of the claim in the amount of $ ________ (Amount) and propose the following terms of payment:

$ ________ (Amount) per ________ (Week/month) commencing ________ , 20 ___ .

REASONS FOR DISPUTING THE CLAIM AND DETAILS:

Explain what happened, including where and when. Explain why you do not agree with the claim made against you.

If you are relying on any documents, you **MUST** attach copies to the Defence. If evidence is lost or unavailable, you **MUST** explain why it is not attached.

What happened?
Where?
When?

The defendant Sharon Slipaway (Slipaway) had agreed to honour $1000 on a promissory note for the plaintiff Feckless Enterprises (Feckless) but has discharged the obligation. The parties entered into their agreement on April 2, year -1 at Toronto.

1. The defendant agrees with paragraph 1 of the defendant's claim.

2. The defendant disagrees with paragraphs 2 to 7 of the defendant's claim.

3. Although Slipaway did agree to pay the sum of $1000 toward the promissory note that Feckless had with Cape, Slipaway discharged this obligation when she provided over $1000 in services to Feckless and Feckless agreed that the obligation had been discharged.

4. The defendant seeks the dismissal of the defendant's claim with costs payable to her.

SCR 9.01-10.03-9A (January 23, 2014) CSD

Continued on next page

FIGURE 10.15 **Defence (to Defendant's Claim) (*continued*)**

FORM 9A **PAGE 3** **SC-10-0012349-0001**
Claim No.

Why I/we disagree with all or part of the claim:

☐ **ADDITIONAL PAGES ARE ATTACHED BECAUSE MORE ROOM WAS NEEDED.**

Prepared on: **November 28, year 0** , 20 ____ ______________________________
(Signature of defendant or representative)

NOTE:	Within seven (7) calendar days of changing your address for service, notify the court and all other parties in writing.

CAUTION TO PLAINTIFF(S):	If this Defence contains a proposal of terms of payment, you are deemed to have accepted the terms **unless** you file with the clerk and serve on the defendant(s) a Request to Clerk (Form 9B) for a terms of payment hearing **WITHIN TWENTY (20) CALENDAR DAYS** of service of this Defence [R. 9.03(3)].

SCR 9.01-10.03-9A (January 23, 2014) CSD

FIGURE 10.16 Request to Clerk (to Note Defendant in Default)

ONTARIO
Superior Court of Justice

Request to Clerk
Form 9B Ont. Reg. No.: 258/98

Toronto
Small Claims Court

SC-10-00012345-0000
Claim No.

47 Sheppard Ave. E., 3rd Floor
Toronto, ON M2N 2X5
Address

416-326-3554
Phone number

BETWEEN

Cape Credit Corporation Ltd.
Plaintiff(s)

and

Feckless Enterprises
Defendant(s)

TO THE CLERK OF THE Toronto **SMALL CLAIMS COURT:**
(Name of Small Claims Court location)

My name is Charles Dickens **and I request that the clerk of the court:**
(Name of party/representative)

(Check appropriate box(es).)

☒ note defendant(s) Feckless Enterprises
(Name of defendant(s))
in default for failing to file a Defence (Form 9A) within the prescribed time period [R. 11.01(1)].

☐ schedule an assessment hearing (all defendants have been noted in default) [R. 11.03(2)(b)].

☐ schedule a terms of payment hearing because I dispute the defendant's proposed terms of payment contained in the Defence (Form 9A) [R. 9.03(3)].

☐ schedule a trial [R. 16.01(1)(b)].

☐ accept payment in the amount of $ ____________ into court
(Amount)

- ☐ according to an order of the court, dated ____________, 20 ____ .
- ☐ for a person under disability according to an order or settlement dated ____________, 20 ____ [R. 4.08(1)].
- ☐ pursuant to the attached written offer to settle, dated ____________, 20 ____ [R. 14.05(2)].
- ☐ according to the following legislation:
  ____ .
  (Name of statute or regulation and section)

Les formules des tribunaux sont affichées en anglais et en français sur le site www.ontariocourtforms.on.ca. Visitez ce site pour des renseignements sur des formats accessibles.

SCR 4-9-11-14-16-9B (January 23, 2014) CSD

FIGURE 10.16 Request to Clerk (to Note Defendant in Default) (*continued*)

FORM 9B **PAGE 2** SC-10-00012345-0000
Claim No.

☐ Other: (Specify.)

November 20, year 0 , 20 ____ ______________________
(Signature of party or representative)

CAUTION:	To obtain an assessment of damages, all defendants must be noted in default. If one or more defendants has filed a defence, the matter must proceed to a settlement conference. To bring a motion in writing for an assessment of damages, file a Notice of Motion and Supporting Affidavit (Form 15A). You can get forms at court offices or online at www.ontariocourtforms.on.ca.

SCR 4-9-11-14-16-9B (January 23, 2014) CSD

FIGURE 10.17 Default Judgment

ONTARIO
Superior Court of Justice

Default Judgment
Form 11B Ont. Reg. No.: 258/98

Toronto
Small Claims Court

SC-10-00012345-0000
Claim No.

Seal

47 Sheppard Ave. E., 3rd Floor
Toronto, ON M2N 2X5
Address

416-326-3554
Phone number

Plaintiff No. 1 ☐ Additional plaintiff(s) listed on attached Form 1A.

Last name, or name of company		
Cape Credit Corporation Ltd.		
First name	Second name	Also known as
Address (street number, apt., unit): c/o Charles Dickets 8041 Ryder Street		
City/Town: Mississauga	Province: ON	Phone no.: 905-381-2620
Postal code: L2R 1Y6		Fax no.
Representative: Charles Dickens		LSUC #: P02345
Address (street number, apt., unit): 8041 Ryder Street		
City/Town: Mississauga	Province: ON	Phone no.: 905-381-2620
Postal code: L2R 1Y6		Fax no.

Defendant No. 1 ☐ Additional defendant(s) listed on attached Form 1A.

Last name, or name of company		
Feckless Enterprises		
First name	Second name	Also known as
Address (street number, apt., unit): 48 Overreach Blvd		
City/Town: Toronto	Province: ON	Phone no.: 416-223-4569
Postal code: M6X 3I7		Fax no.
Representative		LSUC #
Address (street number, apt., unit)		
City/Town	Province	Phone no.
Postal code		Fax no.

Les formules des tribunaux sont affichées en anglais et en français sur le site www.ontariocourtforms.on.ca. Visitez ce site pour des renseignements sur des formats accessibles.

SCR 11.02-11B (January 23, 2014) CSD

Continued on next page

FIGURE 10.17 Default Judgment (*continued*)

FORM 11B **PAGE 2** SC-10-00012345-0000
Claim No.

NOTICE TO THE DEFENDANT(S):
(Check one box only.)

☒ You have been noted in default according to Rule 11.01.

☐ You have defaulted in your payment according to Rule 9.03(2)(b), pursuant to

__________ dated __________, 20 ____,
(Name of document)

and 15 days have passed since you were served with a Notice of Default of Payment (Form 20L).

DEFAULT JUDGMENT IS GIVEN against the following defendant(s):

Last name, or name of company		
Feckless Enterprises		
First name	Second name	Also known as

Last name, or name of company		
First name	Second name	Also known as

Last name, or name of company		
First name	Second name	Also known as

☐ Additional defendant(s) listed on attached page (*list in same format*).

THE DEFENDANT(S) MUST PAY to the plaintiff(s) the following sums:

(A) **DEBT** (principal amount claimed minus any payments received since the plaintiff's claim was issued) $ 3000.00

(B) **PRE-JUDGMENT INTEREST** calculated
on the sum of $ 3000.00 at the rate of 10 %
per annum from April 1, year -1, 20 ____, to Nov. 20, year 0, 20 ____,
being 599 days. $ 492.33

(C) **COSTS** to date (including the cost of issuing this judgment) $ 150.00

TOTAL $ 3642.33

This judgment bears post-judgment interest at ______ % per annum commencing this date.

November 20, year 0, 20 ____ ________________
(Signature of clerk)

CAUTION TO DEFENDANT:	**YOU MUST PAY THE AMOUNT OF THIS JUDGMENT DIRECTLY TO THE PLAINTIFF(S) IMMEDIATELY.** Failure to do so may result in additional post-judgment interest and enforcement costs.

SCR 11.02-11B (January 23, 2014) CSD

FIGURE 10.18 List of Proposed Witnesses

ONTARIO
Superior Court of Justice

List of Proposed Witnesses
Form 13A Ont. Reg. No.: 258/98

Toronto
Small Claims Court

SC-10-00012345-0000
Claim No.

47 Sheppard Ave. E., 3rd Floor
Toronto, ON M2N 2X5
Address

416-326-3554
Phone number

BETWEEN

Cape Credit Corporation Ltd.
Plaintiff(s)

and

Feckless Enterprises
Defendant(s)

My name is Edward Lue
(Name of party/representative)

The following is my list of proposed witnesses in this case:

	Name of witness	Address, phone and fax numbers
1.	Henry Snore	35 Morton Avenue Toronto, ON M2K 3J5 416-222-5549
2.		
3.		

Les formules des tribunaux sont affichées en anglais et en français sur le site www.ontariocourtforms.on.ca. Visitez ce site pour des renseignements sur des formats accessibles.

SCR 13.01-13A (January 23, 2014) CSD

FIGURE 10.18 List of Proposed Witnesses (*continued*)

FORM 13A **PAGE 2** **SC-10-00012345-0000**
Claim No.

4. ______________________ ______________________

5. ______________________ ______________________

The following is my list of other persons with knowledge of the matter in dispute in this case:

Name of person	Address, phone and fax numbers
1. ______________________	______________________
2. ______________________	______________________

(Attach a separate sheet in the above format for additional witnesses or other persons.)

Dec. 4, year 0, 20 ____ ______________________
(Signature of party or representative)

____
(Name, address and phone number of party or representative)

NOTE:	**EACH PARTY MUST SERVE THIS LIST** on all other parties and file it with the court at least fourteen (14) days before the settlement conference [R. 13.03(2)(b)].

SCR 13.01-13A (January 23, 2014) CSD

FIGURE 10.19 Terms of Settlement

ONTARIO
Superior Court of Justice

Terms of Settlement
Form 14D Ont. Reg. No.: 258/98

Toronto
Small Claims Court

SC-10-00012345-0000
Claim No.

47 Sheppard Ave. E., 3rd Floor
Toronto, ON M2N 2X5
Address

416-326-3554
Phone number

BETWEEN

Cape Credit Corporation Ltd.
Plaintiff(s)

and

Feckless Enterprises
Defendant(s)

We have agreed to settle this action on the following terms:

1. Feckless Enterprises shall pay to
(Name of party(ies))

Cape Credit Corporation Ltd. the sum of
(Name of party(ies))

$ 3000.00 as follows as full and final settlement of the claim, inclusive of interest and costs:

(Provide terms of payment such as start date, frequency, amount and duration.)

The sum of $1000.00 shall be paid to the plaintiff on each of the 15th days of December year 0, January year 1, and February year 1 for a total of $3000.00 commencing December 1, year 0.

Put a line through any blank space and initial.

Les formules des tribunaux sont affichées en anglais et en français sur le site www.ontariocourtforms.on.ca. Visitez ce site pour des renseignements sur des formats accessibles.

SCR 14D (January 23, 2014) CSD

FIGURE 10.19 Terms of Settlement (*continued*)

FORM 14D **PAGE 2** **SC-10-00012345-0000**
Claim No.

2. This claim (and Defendant's Claim, if any) is withdrawn.

3. If a party to these terms of settlement fails to comply, judgment in the terms of settlement may be obtained against that party on motion to the court or this action may continue as if there has been no settlement.

4. Provided that the terms of settlement are complied with, the parties above fully and finally release one another from all claims related to the facts and issues raised in this action.

The parties do not need to sign terms of settlement on the same day, but each must sign in the presence of his or her witness who signs a moment later. (For additional parties' signatures, attach a separate sheet in the below format.)

Dec. 15, year 0, 20 ____	Dec. 15, year 0, 20 ____
(Signature of party)	(Signature of party)
Cape Credit Corporation Ltd. I have authority to bind the corporation (Name of party)	Feckless Enterprises (Name of party)
(Signature of witness)	(Signature of witness)
(Name of witness)	(Name of witness)
____, 20 ____	____, 20 ____
(Signature of party)	(Signature of party)
(Name of party)	(Name of party)
(Signature of witness)	(Signature of witness)
(Name of witness)	(Name of witness)

SCR 14D (January 23, 2014) CSD

FIGURE 10.20 Sample Minutes of Settlement—Settlement Conference

Claim no. SC-10-00012345-0000

ONTARIO
Superior Court of Justice

Toronto Small Claims Court
47 Sheppard Avenue E., 3rd Floor
Toronto, ON M2N 2X5
416-326-3554

Plaintiff
Full name
Cape Credit Corporation Ltd.

Address for service (street & number, city, postal code)
c/o Charles Dickens (P02345)
8041 Ryder Street
Mississauga, ON L3R 1Y6

Phone no.
905-381-2620

Plaintiff's legal representative
Charles Dickens

Legal representative's address for service
8041 Ryder Street
Mississauga, ON L2R 1Y6

Legal representative's phone number
905-381-2620

Defendant
Full name
Feckless Enterprises

Address for service (street & number, city, postal code)
c/o Edward Lue (P22331)
365 Bay Street
Toronto, ON M2N 3A8

Phone no.
416-595-1308

Defendant's legal representative
Edward Lue

Legal representative's Address for service
365 Bay Street
Toronto, ON M2N 3A8

Legal representative's phone number
416-595-1308

FIGURE 10.20 Sample Minutes of Settlement—Settlement Conference (*continued*)

MINUTES OF SETTLEMENT

The above parties have agreed to settle this action on the following terms:

1. The Defendant shall pay to the Plaintiff the sum of $3000 as follows:

The sum of $1000 shall be paid to the plaintiff on each of the 15th days of December year 0, January year 1, and February year 1, for a total of $3000 commencing December 1, year 0 as a full and final settlement of this claim, inclusive of interest and costs.

2. This claim is dismissed upon payment in full.

3. In the event that the defendant defaults in payment, the plaintiff may ask the clerk of the court to sign judgment, without notice, for $3000 plus interest and costs less any payments made.

4. Once these terms of settlement are complied with the parties each fully and finally release one another from all claims related to the facts and issues raised in this action.

Dated at Toronto, Ontario, this 15th day of December, year 0

Cape Credit Corporation Ltd.	Feckless Enterprises
Plaintiff	Defendant
Per: ____________________	Per: _______________
I have authority to bind the corporation.	
Witness: _________________	Witness: ____________

FIGURE 10.21 Offer to Settle

ONTARIO
Superior Court of Justice

Offer to Settle
Form 14A Ont. Reg. No.: 258/98

Toronto
Small Claims Court

SC-10-00012345-0000
Claim No.

47 Sheppard Ave. E., 3rd Floor
Toronto, ON M2N 3X5
Address

416-326-3554
Phone number

BETWEEN

Cape Credit Corporation Ltd.
Plaintiff(s)

and

Feckless Enterprises
Defendant(s)

My name is Charles Dickens
(Full name)

1. In this action, I am the

- ☐ Plaintiff
- ☐ Defendant
- ☒ representative of Cape Credit Corporation Ltd.
(Name of party(ies))

2. I offer to settle this action against Feckless Enterprises
(Name of party(ies))

on the following terms: *(Set out terms in numbered paragraphs, or on an attached sheet.)*

The defendant shall pay to the plaintiff the sum of $3000.00 with $1000.00 to be paid December 15, year 0, January 15, year 1, and February 15, year 1.

Les formules des tribunaux sont affichées en anglais et en français sur le site www.ontariocourtforms.on.ca. Visitez ce site pour des renseignements sur des formats accessibles.

SCR 14.01.1-14A (January 23, 2014) CSD

FIGURE 10.21 Offer to Settle (*continued*)

FORM 14A **PAGE 2** SC-10-00012345-0000
Claim No.

3. This offer to settle is available for acceptance until December 15, year 0 , 20 ____ .

This offer to settle may be accepted by serving an acceptance of offer to settle (Form 14B may be used) on the party who made it, at any time before it is withdrawn or before the court disposes of the claim to which the offer applies [R. 14.05(1)]. You can get forms at court offices or online at www.ontariocourtforms.on.ca.

December 14, year 0 , 20 ____ ______________________________
(Signature of party or representative making offer)

____
(Name, address and phone number of party or representative)

NOTE:	**IF YOU ACCEPT AN OFFER TO SETTLE, THEN FAIL TO COMPLY WITH ITS TERMS,** judgment in the terms of the accepted offer may be obtained against you on motion to the court, or the action may continue as if there has been no offer to settle [R. 14.06].

NOTE:	**IF THIS OFFER TO SETTLE IS NOT ACCEPTED, IT SHALL NOT BE FILED WITH THE COURT OR DISCLOSED** to the trial judge until all questions of liability and relief (other than costs) have been determined [R. 14.04].

SCR 14.01.1-14A (January 23, 2014) CSD

FIGURE 10.22 Notice of Motion and Supporting Affidavit

ONTARIO
Superior Court of Justice

Notice of Motion and Supporting Affidavit
Form 15A Ont. Reg. No.: 258/98

Toronto
Small Claims Court

SC-10-00012345-0000
Claim No.

47 Sheppard Ave. E., 3rd Floor
Toronto, ON M2N 2X5
Address

416-326-3554
Phone number

Plaintiff No. 1 ☐ Additional plaintiff(s) listed on attached Form 1A.

Last name, or name of company Cape Credit Corporation Ltd.		
First name	Second name	Also known as
Address (street number, apt., unit) c/o Charles Dickens 8041 Ryder Street		
City/Town Mississauga	Province ON	Phone no. 905-381-2620
Postal code M5R 1K3		Fax no.
Representative Charles Dickens		LSUC # P02345
Address (street number, apt., unit) 8041 Ryder Street		
City/Town Mississauga	Province ON	Phone no. 905-381-2620
Postal code L2R 1Y6		Fax no.

Defendant No. 1 ☐ Additional defendant(s) listed on attached Form 1A.

Last name, or name of company Feckless Enterprises		
First name	Second name	Also known as
Address (street number, apt., unit) c/o Edward Lue 365 Bay Street		
City/Town Toronto	Province ON	Phone no. 416-595-1308
Postal code M2N 3A8		Fax no.
Representative Edward Lue		LSUC # P02361
Address (street number, apt., unit) 365 Bay Street		
City/Town Toronto	Province ON	Phone no. 416-595-1308
Postal code M2N 3A8		Fax no.

Les formules des tribunaux sont affichées en anglais et en français sur le site www.ontariocourtforms.on.ca. Visitez ce site pour des renseignements sur des formats accessibles.

SCR 15.01-15A (November 1, 2015) CSD

FIGURE 10.22 Notice of Motion and Supporting Affidavit (*continued*)

FORM 15A **PAGE 2** SC-10-00012345-0000
Claim No.

Complete Part A or Part B below, then complete the affidavit in support of motion on page 3.

A. THIS COURT WILL HEAR A MOTION on December 1, year 0 , 20 ____ , **at** 10:00 a.m. ,
(Time)

or as soon as possible after that time, at 47 Sheppard Ave. E., Toronto, ON Courtroom 4
(Address of court location and courtroom number)

This motion will be made in person by Feckless Enterprises ,
(Name of party)

for the following order:

- ☐ the court's permission to extend time to (Specify) ____________ .
- ☐ set aside default judgment and noting in default.
- ☐ set aside noting in default.
- ☐ permission to file a Defence.
- ☐ permission to file a Defendant's Claim.
- ☐ set aside order dismissing claim as abandoned.
- ☐ terminate garnishment and/or withdraw writ(s).
- ☒ Other:
  For an order requiring the plaintiff to disclose its accounting records.

☐ **ADDITIONAL PAGES ARE ATTACHED BECAUSE MORE ROOM WAS NEEDED.**

☐ **DOCUMENTS ARE ATTACHED.**

NOTE:	**IF YOU FAIL TO ATTEND AN IN-PERSON MOTION,** an order may be made against you, with costs, in your absence. If you want to attend the motion by telephone or video conference, complete and file a Request for Telephone or Video Conference (Form 1B). If the court permits it, the clerk will make the necessary arrangements and notify the parties [R. 1.07(5)].

B. This motion in writing for an assessment of damages is made by

____________ ,
(Name of plaintiff)

who asks the court for an order assessing damages against

____
(Name of defendant(s))

who have/has been noted in default.

SCR 15.01-15A (November 1, 2015) CSD **Continued on next page**

FIGURE 10.22 Notice of Motion and Supporting Affidavit (*continued*)

FORM 15A **PAGE 3** SC-10-00012345-0000
Claim No.

AFFIDAVIT IN SUPPORT OF MOTION

My name is Henry Feckless
(Full name)

I live in Toronto, Ontario
(Municipality & province)

I swear/affirm that the following is true:

Set out the facts in numbered paragraphs. If you learned a fact from someone else, you must give that person's name and state that you believe that fact to be true.

1. I am one of the partners of Feckless Enterprises.

2. The key element of the defence in this matter is that the defendant paid the plaintiff, in cash, the sum that the plaintiff claims is outstanding.

3. The defendant did not keep a record of the cash payment; however, the plaintiff's accounting records should show receipt of the cash payment made in satisfaction of the promissory note between the parties.

4. The defendant's paralegal, Edward Lue, has requested the plaintiff's accounting records for inspection, but to date has not had a response. Attached as Exhibit "A" to this affidavit is a true copy of the letter sent by Mr. Lue requesting the accounting records.

5. The defence would be prejudiced at trial if the accounting records are not provided for their review.

6. I make this affidavit in support of this motion and for no other purpose.

SCR 15.01-15A (November 1, 2015) CSD

Continued on next page

FIGURE 10.22 Notice of Motion and Supporting Affidavit (*continued*)

FORM 15A **PAGE 4** **SC-10-00012345-0000**
Claim No.

AFFIDAVIT IN SUPPORT OF MOTION, continued

If more space is required, attach and initial extra pages.

Sworn/Affirmed before me at Toronto
(Municipality)

in Ontario
(Province, state or country)

on Nov. 20, year 0 , 20 ____
Commissioner for taking affidavits
(Type or print name below if signature is illegible.)

Signature
(This form is to be signed in front of a lawyer, justice of the peace, notary public or commissioner for taking affidavits.)

WARNING: IT IS AN OFFENCE UNDER THE *CRIMINAL CODE* TO KNOWINGLY SWEAR OR AFFIRM A FALSE AFFIDAVIT.

For information on accessibility of court services for people with disability-related needs, contact:

Telephone: 416-326-2220 / 1-800-518-7901 TTY: 416-326-4012 / 1-877-425-0575

SCR 15.01-15A (November 1, 2015) CSD

FIGURE 10.23 Summons to Witness

ONTARIO

Superior Court of Justice

Summons to Witness
Form 18A Ont. Reg. No.: 258/98

Seal

Toronto
Small Claims Court

47 Sheppard Ave. E. 3rd Floor
Toronto, ON M2N 2X5
Address

416-326-3554
Phone number

SC-10-00012345-0000
Claim No.

BETWEEN

Cape Credit Corporation Ltd.
Plaintiff(s)

and

Feckless Enterprises
Defendant(s)

TO: Henry Snore, 35 Morton Avenue, Toronto, ON M2K 3J5
(Name of witness)

YOU ARE REQUIRED TO ATTEND AND TO GIVE EVIDENCE IN COURT at the trial of this action on

February 15, year 1 , 20 ____ **at** 10:00 a.m. (Time) **, at**

47 Sheppard Ave. E., Toronto, ON M2N 2X5
(Address of court location)

and to remain until your attendance is no longer required. You may be required to return to court from time to time.

YOU ARE ALSO REQUIRED TO BRING WITH YOU AND PRODUCE AT THE TRIAL the following documents or other things in your possession, control or power: (Identify and describe particular documents and other things required)

Les formules des tribunaux sont affichées en anglais et en français sur le site www.ontariocourtforms.on.ca. Visitez ce site pour des renseignements sur des formats accessibles.

SCR 18.03-18A (January 23, 2014) CSD

FIGURE 10.23 Summons to Witness (*continued*)

FORM 18A **PAGE 2** SC-10-00012345-0000
Claim No.

and all other documents or other things in your possession, control or power relating to the action.

Feckless Enterprises has requested the clerk to issue this summons.
(Name of party)

Feb. 1, year 1 , 20 ______ ____________________
(Signature of clerk)

NOTE:	**THIS SUMMONS MUST BE SERVED** personally, at least 10 days before the trial date, on the person to be summoned together with attendance money calculated in accordance with the Small Claims Court Schedule of Fees, which is a regulation under the *Administration of Justice Act*. To obtain a copy of the regulation, attend the nearest Small Claims Court or access the following website: www.e-laws.gov.on.ca.

CAUTION:	**IF YOU FAIL TO ATTEND OR REMAIN IN ATTENDANCE AS REQUIRED BY THIS SUMMONS, A WARRANT MAY BE ISSUED FOR YOUR ARREST.**

For information on accessibility of court services for people with disability-related needs, contact:

Telephone: 416-326-2220 / 1-800-518-7901 TTY: 416-326-4012 / 1-877-425-0575

SCR 18.03-18A (January 23, 2014) CSD

Small Claims Court Enforcement Proceedings

11

LEARNING OUTCOMES

After reading this chapter, students will:

- Recognize the most common Small Claims Court enforcement mechanisms.
- Understand how to enforce a judgment in a different territorial division from the one the judgment was granted in.
- Know the procedure for arranging and conducting an examination in aid of execution, including contempt proceedings.
- Understand the procedure for obtaining and enforcing writs of seizure and sale of personal property and land.
- Know how to garnish wages and other funds from third parties.
- Recognize when and how a consolidation order can be obtained by a debtor.
- Know when orders made by boards, tribunals, and courts in other provinces can be filed with and enforced by the Ontario Small Claims Court.
- Recognize when a sheriff may use the *Creditors' Relief Act, 2010* to seize funds held by the Small Claims Court.
- Know what to file with the court once a judgment has been paid in full.

The Enforcement Environment

A high percentage of Small Claims Court cases are undefended. Many of these cases are for small amounts. Many of the defendants are consumer debtors who are in debt for relatively small amounts and who are simply unable—or think they are unable—to pay what they owe. The Small Claims Court enforcement procedures in Rule 20[1] reflect the reality of an environment where debtors owe relatively small amounts. The usual enforcement mechanisms found in the Superior Court are also found here:

- examinations in aid of execution (also known as judgment debtor examinations);
- writs of seizure and sale of land and personal property;
- writs of delivery (for recovery of personal property); and
- garnishment.

However, the usual mechanisms outlined above are not of much use where a debtor is broke and has few assets. In this environment, the *Rules of the Small Claims Court*[2] provide other solutions that allow a debtor to consolidate debts, have payments scheduled over time, have periodic payment amounts fixed, and have other enforcement proceedings stayed while payments are being made. This permits debtors to avoid being hounded by creditors, and it permits creditors to get their money through installment payments over time. This is an advantage for creditors, who might otherwise find the debtor going bankrupt. If the debtor goes bankrupt, creditors would likely recover far less than they would using the small claims enforcement provisions. In fact, it may be better financially for a debtor to go bankrupt than to pay everything owed by way of installment payments in the Small Claims Court over a long period of time.

Rule 20.02 gives the court the general power to stay enforcement proceedings. This means that if such an order is made, enforcement proceedings stop, including payments by garnishees on garnishment orders. Stays can be ordered, for example, on the filing of an appeal or on the making of a consolidation order where small claims creditors of the same debtor receive a portion of periodic installment payments from the debtor, as ordered by the court. Where the court has made an order for payment of a judgment debt by installments, any party may bring a motion to vary the times and proportions in which money is paid if the debtor's circumstances have changed. A debtor whose situation has become worse may apply to have the payments reduced. Where the debtor's situation has improved, a creditor may apply to increase the amounts. Rule 20.02(2) provides that creditors may not take enforcement proceedings while the debtor is subject to an order to pay creditors by installments, except that a creditor may require the clerk to issue a writ of seizure and sale against land and file it with the sheriff.

---

1 References made to Rules in the text of Chapters 10 and 11 refer to the *Rules of the Small Claims Court*, not the *Rules of Civil Procedure*.

2 O Reg 258/98, as amended.

Enforcement in a Different Territorial Division

A debtor may have property in a different territorial division from the one in which the judgment was obtained. If, for example, a judgment was obtained in the court in North Bay, and there has been default in payment and the creditor wishes to enforce the judgment against property in the court in Kingston, the legal representative must direct the court in Kingston to enforce the North Bay order or judgment. In this situation a certificate of judgment must be obtained from the North Bay court. To obtain this certificate, the legal representative must pay a fee and file, with the North Bay Small Claims Court, an Affidavit for Enforcement Request (Figure 11.3) along with a draft Certificate of Judgment (Figure 11.1) that sets out the amount still owing (inclusive of prejudgment interest and costs), the date and the original amount of the order, the rate of postjudgment interest payable, and the name of the court that you are asking enforcement action to be taken in. Once the certificate has been issued, the court sends it to the clerk of the court where the creditor is seeking enforcement—in this example, the Kingston court.

Examination of Judgment Debtors

Although it is wise to file a writ of seizure and sale against personal property and another one against land immediately after obtaining a judgment, unless a lot is known about the debtor's financial circumstances, it is a good idea to schedule an examination of the judgment debtor before embarking on any serious and expensive enforcement efforts.

The procedure for doing this is as follows:

1. Request, in person or by letter, that the clerk of the court where the debtor resides or carries on business set a date for an examination hearing and issue a Notice of Examination (Figure 11.2). If the claim was filed electronically, a hard copy of the claim and the affidavit of service for the claim must be filed with the court when the notice of examination is being issued.[3]
2. Provide an Affidavit for Enforcement Request (Figure 11.3) that sets out the date of the order and amount awarded, the territorial division in which the order was made, the rate of postjudgment interest payable, the total amount of any payments received since judgment was given, and the amount owing, including postjudgment interest. (This affidavit must be filed to support any enforcement remedy requested.) The applicable fee(s) for the enforcement remedies requested must be paid.[4]
3. Enclose a Certificate of Judgment (Figure 11.1) if the judgment was from a different territorial division than the one that is issuing the notice of examination.

---

3 Rule 7.02(5)6.

4 The fees and allowances for Small Claims Court can be found in O Reg. 332/16 made under the *Administration of Justice Act*.

4. The clerk issues the notice and returns it for personal service on the debtor. If the judgment debtor is a partnership or a corporation, some searches may need to be conducted to determine which partner, officer, or director should be served. Chapter 3 has information on conducting searches on partnerships and corporations. If the debtor is an individual, along with the notice, a blank financial information form (see Figure 11.4, Financial Information Form) must also be served, which the debtor must complete and serve on the creditor prior to the examination. The debtor must also bring a copy of the completed financial information form to the examination, along with any documents that support the information in the form. The debtor will need to make the financial information form and the supporting documents available for the judge at the examination to review; however, they will not become part of the court file because court files are usually public records.
5. The notice of examination must be served on the debtor at least 30 days before the hearing. An affidavit of service will need to be filed with the court at least three days before the hearing date.[5]

The rules permit service by alternatives to personal service, but, if it is necessary to bring contempt proceedings for non-attendance, it will be easier to conclusively prove service if the debtor was personally served.

The examination takes place in most territorial divisions under the supervision of a judge or referee. This approach recognizes that where parties are not represented by lawyers or paralegals, the whole business may degenerate into an unseemly and unproductive performance. The judge or referee may take quite an active part in the process. The examination is also private, unless the court orders it to be held in public. At the end of the examination hearing, the court may make an order for payment in full, by installments, and otherwise use its discretion to construct an orderly system for payment. Following an examination, if payments are being made under an order, no other enforcement remedies may be taken, except for filing a writ of seizure and sale against land with the sheriff.

The questions to be asked on an examination are the same as those set out in Chapter 9.

The creditor may also request that witnesses be examined, other than or in addition to the debtor, if they have knowledge concerning the debtor's assets, liabilities, and means of complying with the judgment. The scope of the examination is broad and covers the same ground as an examination in the Superior Court. If the debtor is a corporation, partnership, or sole proprietorship, the creditor has the same right as in the Superior Court to examine officers, directors, partners, and owners of sole proprietorships.

contempt
an act that demonstrates disrespect or defiance of the court and the administration of justice

If the debtor or other person summoned fails to attend the examination, or attends but is obstructive, uncooperative, or refuses to answer questions, the creditor may ask that the court find the person in **contempt**. Rule 20.11(2) provides that a Small Claims Court judge can order a person who has failed to attend an

5 Rule 8.01(12)(b).

examination to attend a contempt hearing. The court sets a date for a contempt hearing and provides the creditor with a notice of contempt hearing form, which the creditor must personally serve on the debtor and file with the court at least seven days before the hearing. A debtor who is served with a notice of contempt hearing may bring a motion to the court to cancel the order for the hearing. The affidavit portion of the notice of motion and supporting affidavit form should set out why the debtor did not attend the examination hearing and establish that the debtor is now willing to attend a hearing. Even if the debtor pays the debt in the meantime, a motion must still be brought by the debtor to cancel the contempt hearing because it concerns their behaviour and not the payment itself. A contempt hearing may be held before a Small Claims Court judge. Section 30(2) of the *Courts of Justice Act*[6] permits a finding of contempt if the court is satisfied that the debtor was required to attend the examination, was personally served with a notice to attend the examination, failed to attend, and that the failure to attend was wilful. The burden of proof is on the debtor to show that they are not in contempt. Under Rule 20.11(7), the court may order the debtor to be apprehended and jailed for up to five days. The Committee of Administrative Judges for the Small Claims Court has directed that Small Claims Court judges do not have the statutory authority to issue warrants for arrest to compel attendance at a contempt hearing. This is based on the fact that the *Rules of the Small Claims Court* lack a process to compel the attendance of a debtor at a contempt hearing. Once the Small Claims Court judge has noted that, despite being personally served, the debtor has failed to attend, an endorsement is made to place the matter before a Superior Court judge for further action.[7] If a finding of contempt is made and a Warrant of Committal (Figure 11.5) is issued, the debtor can file a motion using a notice of motion and supporting affidavit to ask to set aside the contempt order and the warrant. The affidavit must set out the reasons why the contempt order should be set aside.

If an order jailing the person is issued, the clerk issues a Warrant of Committal (Figure 11.5). The warrant directs police in Ontario to apprehend and jail, in the nearest provincial correctional institution, the person found in contempt. The person found in contempt may be discharged at the end of five days, or earlier, if the **contempt is purged** by doing what was originally required (i.e., in this case, attending an examination in aid of execution). In some cases, a warrant is made that states that the debtor, upon making a promise to attend at the Small Claims Court within seven days of their arrest, can be released.

to purge contempt
when an order has been made by the court finding someone in contempt, the person may avoid punishment for contempt by doing what was required; this is referred to as purging contempt—for example, a person who refuses to answer questions on an examination may purge their contempt by re-attending and answering the questions

The Writ of Delivery

The Small Claims Court has jurisdiction to order the return to the plaintiff of property unlawfully taken or held by the defendant, when the property is worth $25,000 or less. A plaintiff seeking the return of property should also, in their plaintiff's

6 RSO 1990, c C.43.

7 Rule 60.11(4) of the *Rules of Civil Procedure* contemplates Superior Court judges issuing warrants for arrest where a person is unlikely to voluntarily appear at a contempt hearing.

claim, request an order that a writ of delivery be issued. If the property is located in a private dwelling, a request should also be made for an order that reasonable force and the services of a locksmith may be used to enter the premises. After obtaining an order for the return of property, the legal representative can write to the defendant, enclosing a copy of the order, and demand that the property be delivered to a specific place on or before a fixed date. The order may be enforced by obtaining a writ of delivery from the court clerk. To obtain a writ, an Affidavit for Enforcement Request (Figure 11.3) must be completed, asking for a writ of delivery and specifying in the affidavit the particulars of the court order and a description of the property to be delivered, including any serial numbers. Which court is to enforce the writ should also be indicated. A draft Writ of Delivery (Figure 11.6) must be prepared and filed along with a fee. The writ will be issued by the clerk. The writ must be filed with the bailiff of the enforcing court for enforcement.[8] Under the *Execution Act*,[9] the bailiff may use reasonable force to enter a location that is not a private dwelling. If the property to be returned is in a private dwelling, a motion may be required (if such an order was not sought in the claim) to request an order that the bailiff be permitted to use reasonable force to enter. In some cases, the creditor may wish to seek an order that the picking of a lock be permitted. Some plaintiffs also seek an order that a representative of the plaintiff be permitted to attend with the bailiff in order to assist in identification of the property that is to be removed. In order to enforce the writ, the original writ along with copies of the affidavit for enforcement request and the order granting the writ must be filed with the enforcement office along with the fee. The bailiff will charge mileage for executing the writ. Prior to setting out on the execution, the enforcement office will ask the plaintiff to arrange for appropriate transportation and any movers required to remove the property. If a locksmith is required to access the property to be removed, the creditor will have to arrange to hire one. If the bailiff is unable to recover the specific property referred to, this will be reported to the clerk, who will advise the creditor or the creditor's legal representative. At this stage, a motion may be brought to the court requesting an order directing the bailiff to seize other personal property of the debtor. If the creditor knows of specific property that could be seized, it should be referred to in the supporting affidavit. In effect, the creditor is going to be permitted to take hostage some of the defendant's personal property until the property that has been wrongfully withheld has been returned. The bailiff, however, does not turn this property over to the creditor; instead, the property is held "hostage" until other orders of the court regarding the property's disposal are made.[10] If the property that is removed must be stored by the bailiff, the creditor is responsible for the storage costs.[11]

8 Bailiffs work under the sheriff and carry out similar functions, particularly with respect to the execution of writs of seizure and sale of personal property. Proposed changes to privatize judgment enforcement will probably cover this court and eliminate bailiffs as court staff.

9 RSO 1990 c E.24, s 20.

10 Rule 20.05(2).

11 Rule 20.05(4).

The Writ of Seizure and Sale of Personal Property

This writ is similar in function to the writ of the same name in the Superior Court, as is the procedure for using it. To obtain a writ, pay the prescribed fee and file an Affidavit for Enforcement Request (Figure 11.3) and a completed Writ of Seizure and Sale of Personal Property (Figure 11.7) with the clerk where the writ is to be issued showing the amount outstanding, including costs and postjudgment interest, less any amount received. Once the writ is issued, it is filed with the bailiff. Enforcement of the writ can be requested by filing a Direction to Enforce Writ of Seizure and Sale of Personal Property (Figure 11.8). The bailiff will enforce the writ for the amount owing plus the bailiff's costs. However, before the bailiff is sent out, instructions must be given in writing about any property that is available for seizure. A judgment debtor examination is a useful way to obtain this information; the legal representative may also have information from earlier investigations and searches. Some of the information can be set out on the Direction to Enforce Writ of Seizure and Sale of Personal Property (Figure 11.8). When a vehicle, boat, or snowmobile is to be seized, the bailiff will need to be provided with copies of up-to-date *Personal Property Security Act*[12] and *Repair and Storage Liens Act*[13] searches, along with a vehicle ownership abstract. The bailiff will review these searches to determine who owns the property and to see whether there are any liens registered against the property and whether there is any equity in the property. For more detail on these searches, see Chapter 3. For vehicles, a used motor vehicle package that is less than one week old is also required. Used motor vehicle packages can be obtained from the Ministry of Transportation. A deposit will need to be paid to the enforcement office toward the expenses to be incurred in the seizure. Such expenses usually include mileage, freight, insurance, a locksmith, storage, and advertising for the sale of the property.

The bailiff is subject to the restrictions on and exemptions from seizure, outlined in Chapter 9. In selling property, the bailiff is subject to the same general requirements as the sheriff concerning an open and fair selling process, obtaining a reasonable price, and so on. Rule 20.06(5) of the *Rules of the Small Claims Court* specifically requires that, on the debtor's request, the bailiff shall deliver to the debtor an inventory of goods seized. The Rules also provide that notice be given to the debtor and the creditor of the time and place of sale at least 30 days before the sale. The sale must be advertised "in a manner that is likely to bring it to the attention of the public." Unlike the sheriff's requirement, there are no specific requirements for advertising. A writ is in force for six years from the date it is issued. Under Rule 20.06(1.1), if more than six years have passed since the judgment was made, a writ may only be issued with leave of the court. The writ must be issued within one year of the order or a further order must be sought for more time to issue the writ. A writ may be

12 RSO 1990, c P.10.

13 RSO 1990, c R.25.

renewed for further periods of six years each.[14] The legal representative should diarize the renewal date and keep track of renewals. A Request to Renew Writ of Seizure and Sale form (Figure 11.9) can be filed, along with an affidavit for enforcement request form, before the writ expires. There is a fee payable for renewing the writ.

The Writ of Seizure and Sale of Land

To enforce a judgment against real property, a Writ of Seizure and Sale of Land should be used (Figure 11.10). An Affidavit for Enforcement Request (Figure 11.3), setting out the amount still owing, must be delivered to the clerk. This is the same procedure that was used to commence the process to obtain a writ for the seizure and sale of personal property. The same affidavit may be used to support the request for both writs. A completed Writ of Seizure and Sale of Land (Figure 11.10) will need to be filed. A request will then need to be made to the clerk to issue a writ of seizure and sale of land to the sheriff (not to the bailiff) in the territorial division where the debtor's real property is or may be located. Thereafter, the writ may be enforced by the sheriff against real property only, and the same procedure will be followed as if the writ had been issued by the Superior Court—Rule 60 of the *Rules of Civil Procedure*[15] applies (see Chapter 9). In general, enforcement of an order by way of the sale of real property by the sheriff is a long, complicated, and costly procedure that is not often used for Small Claims Court orders. However, filing a writ that will hold up the sale or mortgaging of property by the debtor can be an effective tool to enforce payment of an order. As with the writ of seizure and sale of personal property, if more than six years have passed since the order was made, leave of the court will be required in order to file a writ. If the order is granted, the creditor then has one year to file the writ. Writs of seizure and sale of land are effective for six years and may be renewed for further periods of six years in the same manner in which writs of seizure and sale of property are renewed.

E-Filing of Writs of Seizure and Sale of Land

A writ of seizure and sale of land can now be obtained online. Lawyers, paralegals, or other persons who have filed a requisition with the clerk to provide for the electronic filing and issuance of documents in relation to the enforcement of an order, may electronically request a writ of seizure and sale of land.[16] An affidavit for enforcement request does not need to be filed when seeking a writ of seizure and sale of land electronically.[17] A writ that is requested electronically shall be issued electronically.[18] Interestingly, requests for writs of seizure and sale of land are not subject to the provision that any documents filed or issued outside of regular

14 Rule 20.06(2).

15 RRO 1990, Reg 194.

16 Rule 20.07(1.3).

17 *Ibid.*

18 Rule 20.07(1.4).

business hours are deemed to have been filed or issued on the next day that is not a holiday.[19]

Garnishment

If the creditor knows of a third party who owes money to the debtor, the creditor may garnish the third party. This third party will be named as the garnishee on court enforcement documents. Note that if the garnishee is the provincial crown, the *Proceedings Against the Crown Act*[20] must be followed. A garnishment is obtained by filing a Notice of Garnishment (Figure 11.11) and an Affidavit for Enforcement Request (see Figure 11.3) with the court. If the garnishee is located in a different territorial division from the one that granted the judgment, a Certificate of Judgment (Figure 11.1) will be required. The clerk will issue a Notice of Garnishment (Figure 11.11) when these documents have been filed and the fee has been paid.

The rules permit the garnishment of joint debts.[21] A joint debt is one where the garnishee owes a sum of money to the debtor together with another person who co-owns the right to that sum. The general rule is that the creditor may require the garnishee to pay half the amount of a garnished joint debt into court. However, the creditor, debtor, co-owner of the debt, or garnishee may apply for an order increasing or decreasing the amount the creditor may seize by garnishment. This may occur, for example, where a creditor argues that the so-called joint debt is a sham arrangement, which may happen where the debtor is owed money by a garnishee that is a family-run business.

A garnishee must disclose the existence of any co-owner(s) of the debt on the Garnishee's Statement (Figure 11.13). The creditor must then serve the co-owner(s) of the debt with a Notice to Co-owner of Debt (Figure 11.12) and a copy of the garnishee's statement.[22]

The Affidavit for Enforcement Request (Figure 11.3) should be sworn or affirmed by the creditor, and its paragraphs should cover the following by setting out:

- the date of the order and the amount awarded;
- the territorial division in which the order was made;
- the rate of postjudgment interest payable;
- the total amount of any payments received since the order was granted;
- the amount owing, including postjudgment interest to date;
- the name and address of each person to whom a notice of garnishment should be directed;
- a statement to the effect that the creditor believes that those persons are or will become indebted to the debtor and the grounds for that belief; and

19 Rules 20.07(1.5) and 1.05.1(6).

20 RSO 1990, c P.27.

21 Rule 20.08(2).

22 Rule 20.08(14).

- the amount owing by the garnishee to the debtor—if the amount is not known, include a statement to that effect.

If the legal representative is uncertain of the legal name of the garnishee (for example, the name of the debtor's employer), a search of the name should be done to ensure that the notice of garnishment will be effective. Business name and corporate searches are covered in Chapter 3. Upon receipt of the affidavit for enforcement request, the notice of garnishment and the fee payable, the clerk will issue a notice of garnishment. The garnishee should be served first. The garnishee must be served with the notice of garnishment and garnishee's statement. Service may be by mail, courier, personal service, or by an alternative to personal service.[23] Service on a bank or trust company must be to the branch where the debt is payable by the garnishee.[24] The debtor must be served with the notice of garnishment within five days of service of the notice on the garnishee.[25] The notice of garnishment along with the affidavit for enforcement request may be served on the debtor by mail, courier, personal service, or by an alternative to personal service.[26] Affidavits of service proving service upon the garnishee and the debtor must be filed with the court. The garnishment notice takes effect at the time it is served and attaches all funds owing to the debtor as of that time. The garnishee must pay to the clerk any amount owing, up to the total amount shown in the notice, within ten days of service of the notice, or ten days after the debt became payable, whichever is later. For example, if the notice is served on October 1 and the debt is not payable until October 12, then the garnishee need not pay the clerk until October 22. The garnishment notice will stay in effect for six years after it is issued and may be renewed for further periods of six years each.[27] To renew a notice of garnishment, a notice of garnishment renewal must be filed with the court along with an affidavit for enforcement request.[28]

The garnishee who admits the debt owing to the debtor will pay the debt to the clerk in accordance with instructions in the notice of garnishment. If the garnishee is an employer, it will pay out 20 percent of the net wages in accordance with the *Wages Act*.[29]

It may be the case that there are several garnishment notices issued by several creditors of the same debtor. When this happens, those who have filed notices in the territorial division where the funds are being paid share the amount garnished equally (and not on a pro rata basis, as is the case for execution creditors on writs of seizure and sale of land).[30] The first payment to garnishors takes place 30 days after funds are received by the clerk, with subsequent payments being made as the

---

23 Rule 8.01(8)(b).

24 Rule 20.08(6.2).

25 Rule 20.08(6.1).

26 Rule 8.01(8)(a).

27 Rule 20.08(5.1).

28 Rule 20.08(5.2).

29 RSO 1990, c W.1.

30 Rule 20.08(10).

clerk receives funds.[31] For example, if one creditor garnishes a bank account and another garnishes wages, the court receiving the money from both garnishees will divide the total among all creditors who have filed notices in that court. This will, arguably, include creditors whose own notices of garnishment have not yet produced any payment.

If a garnishee wishes to dispute the garnishment because no money is owing to the debtor or because the garnishee will be paying less than the amount in the notice, the garnishee must file with the court a Garnishee's Statement (Figure 11.13) setting out the nature of the dispute or underpayment, as the case may be, along with the facts on which the dispute is based. The statement should be sent to the court that issued the notice within ten days of the notice having been served on the garnishee.

A creditor, debtor, or garnishee may request a hearing to determine any matter concerning the garnishment. This may include, but is not limited to, the following situations:

- the creditor, debtor, or co-owner of a debt questions the position taken by a garnishee in refusing to pay into court the amount requested; or
- the creditor questions a situation where the garnishee's debt to the debtor has been assigned by the debtor to someone else. In such a case, the garnishee would owe nothing to the debtor.

The first step in setting up a garnishment hearing is to obtain a date from the court. A Notice of Garnishment Hearing (Figure 11.14) needs to be completed and served on the debtor, the creditor, the garnishee, any co-owner of a debt, and any other interested person.[32] A copy of the notice along with affidavits of service must be filed with the court. There is no fee payable for a garnishment hearing. If the claim was filed electronically, the plaintiff must file a paper copy of the claim and the affidavit of service at the time that the garnishment hearing[33] is requested. If a party other than the plaintiff requested the garnishment hearing, the documents shall be filed with the court at least three days before the hearing.[34]

As is the case in the Superior Court with garnishment, where the garnishee neither pays nor files a garnishee's statement disputing payment, the creditor may obtain an order requiring the garnishee to pay the clerk the entire amount set out in the notice, as if the garnishee were the principal debtor. Payment of the amount required to another person, other than the clerk, exposes the garnishee to liability to pay the debt again to the clerk.[35] This latter situation can arise in cases where the debtor assigns the right to be paid to someone else, and the garnishee then pays the assignee, rather than the clerk, as described above.

Garnishments are effective for six years and can be renewed for further six-year periods by filing a notice of renewal of garnishment and an affidavit for enforcement

31 Rule 20.08(20.1).

32 Rules 20.08(15.1) and 8.01(9).

33 Rule 7.02(5)5(i).

34 Rule 7.02(5)5(ii).

35 Rule 20.08(18).

request. Once a judgment has been paid in full, the creditor must serve a notice of termination of garnishment on the garnishee and the court clerk. If the creditor does not serve a notice of termination, then the debtor can complete a request for clerk's order on consent form, have the other party sign it, and then file it with the court. If the other party refuses to sign the request form, the debtor can bring a motion to the court for an order to terminate the garnishment.

Consolidation Orders

It is not unusual for consumer debtors to have several small claims judgments filed against them. When this happens, debtors may find themselves in unpleasant situations in which they are badgered by creditors. To solve this problem, a debtor who has two or more unsatisfied judgments can bring a motion for a consolidation order.[36] If the court is satisfied that the debtor is entitled to a consolidation order, it can order the debtor to make installment payments of a specified amount, to be divided equally among participating creditors. The clerk will pay the creditors at least once every six months.[37]

To obtain this order the debtor must file a notice of motion and supporting affidavit for a consolidation order (see Figure 11.15) that sets out:

- the names and addresses of judgment creditors and the amounts outstanding on each judgment;
- the debtor's income from all sources, identifying each source; and
- the debtor's current financial obligations and any other relevant facts.

All judgment creditors mentioned in the affidavit should be served by mail, personal service, or by an alternative to personal service with the notice of motion and supporting affidavit for a consolidation order. Allow at least seven days' notice of the date of the hearing. Be sure to obtain a motion date before serving the documents so that there will be enough time to serve the creditors.

At the hearing, the creditors may all be heard and make submissions on the propriety of making the order. If the court makes an order, it will set out in the order:

- a list of unsatisfied orders, including the date, court, amount, and amount unpaid;
- the amounts to be paid into court by the debtor under this order; and
- the dates on which the payments are to be made.

The total amount paid by the debtor on the order is not to exceed the amount of the debtor's income available for seizure under section 7 of the *Wages Act*. This means that 20 percent of the debtor's net wages are available for payment of the consolidation order. In order not to lose the benefit of a consolidation order, the debtor

36 Rule 20.09.

37 Rule 20.09(13).

must not be sued further for debt. If a judgment is obtained against the debtor *after* the consolidation order was made for a debt incurred *after* the consolidation order was made, the consolidation order is terminated. However, if the judgment obtained *after* the consolidation order was made is for a debt incurred *before* the consolidation order was made, the creditor may, upon obtaining a certified copy of the judgment, have the judgment added to the consolidation order such that the creditor may share equally in the payments made under the order. If the consolidation order is terminated, the clerk will notify the creditors, and no further order may be made for one year from the date the order was terminated. A consolidation order may also terminate if it is in default for 21 days or longer.

Enforcement of Orders from Other Courts or Tribunals

Some orders for $25,000 or less made by some other courts, tribunals, or boards may be enforced by the Small Claims Court. Orders made under the *Residential Tenancies Act, 2006*,[38] the *Employment Standards Act, 2000*,[39] and the *Provincial Offences Act*[40] are routinely filed in and enforced by the Small Claims Court. Under the *Provincial Offences Act*, unpaid fines levied in provincial offences court may be collected in the Small Claims Court.[41] Under the *Statutory Powers Procedure Act*,[42] a certified copy of the tribunal decision or order may be filed in the Small Claims Court. Restitution orders made under Canada's *Criminal Code*[43] can also be filed for enforcement in Small Claims Court. Upon filing, the order is deemed to be an order of the Small Claims Court and is subject to its enforcement. Orders from other courts and tribunals are filed in the Small Claims Court by submitting a completed affidavit for enforcement request (Form 20P, as seen in Figure 11.3) along with a draft certificate of judgment (Form 20A, as seen in Figure 11.1) and paying the applicable fee.

Orders made in other provinces or territories (with the exception of Quebec) in the previous six years for $25,000 or less or for the return of property worth that amount or less may be filed for enforcement in the Ontario Small Claims Court under the *Reciprocal Enforcement of Judgments Act*.[44] If the judgment debtor was not originally personally served with the claim or failed to defend but appeared, the judgment debtor must be given reasonable notice of the application to file judgment in the Ontario Small Claims Court. An extra provincial order is filed in Small Claims Court by bringing a motion to the court and filing a certified copy of the original judgment along with an affidavit that states that the original court was not

38 SO 2006, c 17.

39 SO 2000, c 41.

40 RSO 1990, c P33.

41 *Ibid*, s 68.

42 RSO 1990, c S.22, s 19.

43 RSC 1985, c C-46.

44 RSO 1990, c R.5.

acting without jurisdiction and that there is no appeal pending. An explanation must be provided as to why the creditor wants to file the order with the Ontario court for enforcement. The motion can be done in writing.

Control of Funds Held by the Small Claims Court

The courts receive and disburse money in the following situations when payments have been made into court:

- when garnishees make payments into court;
- when the bailiff is holding funds from a seizure and sale; and
- when funds have been ordered to be paid into court—for example, on a settlement offer.

The sheriff, under the *Creditors' Relief Act, 2010*,[45] has the authority to seize funds paid into the Small Claims Court and distribute them among execution creditors from the Superior Court of Justice.

Section 3(4) of the *Creditors' Relief Act, 2010* states that when money recovered by garnishment is paid to a Small Claims Court clerk, the sheriff may, at the request of an execution creditor, demand and receive the money from the clerk of the court to distribute it to the judgment creditors. Garnishment creditors, however, under section 3(5), are entitled to share in the distribution of the money in respect of their claim against the debtor.

Under sections 10(1) and (2) of the *Creditors' Relief Act, 2010*, if the sheriff does not find property of an execution debtor that is sufficient to satisfy all amounts in respect of executions filed with the sheriff, and the sheriff is advised that the bailiff of the Small Claims Court holds personal property of the debtor or proceeds from the sale of personal property of the debtor, at the request of an execution creditor, the sheriff shall demand the property or proceeds from the bailiff, and the bailiff shall promptly deliver to the sheriff:

1. the property or proceeds;
2. a copy of every execution and attachment against the debtor that has been filed with the bailiff; and
3. a memorandum showing the amount to be paid under each execution, including the bailiff's fees, and the date when each execution and attachment was filed with the bailiff.

For the purposes of determining to whom the proceeds may be distributed, the Small Claims Court execution creditors are treated as if their executions had been filed with the sheriff.

45 SO 2010, c 16, Schedule 4.

CHAPTER SUMMARY

Chapter 11 began with a discussion of the Small Claims Court enforcement environment and noted how, with its various procedures for structuring debt repayment, it differs from that of the Superior Court. The enforcement methods include judgment debtor examinations to obtain enforcement information followed by writs of seizure and sale for personal property and land, writs of delivery of personal property, and garnishment. It was explained that enforcement in a different territorial division requires a certificate of judgment to be filed in the enforcing court and that debtors may ask for debt payments to be structured by the use of consolidation orders. The filing of orders from other courts and tribunals (including courts from other provinces and territories) for enforcement in the Ontario Small Claims Court was examined. Lastly, note was made of how funds that have been seized are distributed. This includes situations where the Small Claims Court may have to pay out seized funds to a sheriff enforcing Superior Court judgments.

KEY TERMS

contempt, 326
to purge contempt, 327

REVIEW QUESTIONS

1. How does the enforcement environment in the Small Claims Court differ from that in the Superior Court? What accounts for these differences?
2. Does the court have any power to alter or stop an order after it is made?
3. If the debtor is sued in Brampton and judgment is obtained there, but the creditor seeks to seize the debtor's boat located in Belleville, what needs to be done before an order can be enforced?
4. What needs to be done in order to bring a judgment debtor before the court for a judgment debtor examination?
5. What needs to be done if the debtor shows up but refuses to answer questions at the examination?
6. Suppose the clerk has been requested to issue a writ of delivery. The bailiff is unable to locate the specific property named in the writ and is getting no cooperation from the debtor. Is there anything else that can be done to recover the property?
7. What must be done to issue a writ of seizure and sale against personal property? Is the process different if a writ of execution is issued against land? What are the differences, if any?
8. Tell a client what would have to be done to garnish funds from someone who owes money to a debtor.
9. How will the money paid by garnishees to the court be divided up if there are several creditors who have filed garnishment notices in respect of the same debtor?
10. What needs to be done that would not otherwise have to be done in the garnishment process if a garnishee owes money to a debtor together with another person as a co-owner?
11. If a garnishee asks whether anything has to be done when the garnishee is served with a garnishment notice and doesn't owe the debtor any money, what do you tell the garnishee?
12. Suppose there are four judgments against a debtor in the Toronto Small Claims Court, and the debtor is constantly being bothered by bailiffs looking for things to seize—is there anything that can be done to prevent creditors from badgering the debtor?

13. Explain what might happen to a consolidation order if the debtor incurs another debt for $500 after the consolidation order is made, and the creditor later obtains a judgment in respect of the $500 debt.

14. A landlord has an order from the Landlord and Tenant Board that states that their former tenant is to pay the sum of $5,000 to the landlord. The landlord has not been paid and wants to know whether the Small Claims Court can help with enforcement of the order.

15. Explain whether an order for the payment of $10,000 made in British Columbia can be enforced in Ontario.

16. If a Superior Court judgment has been obtained and a writ of execution has been filed, is there any useful purpose in having the sheriff attempt to enforce the writ against the debtor by making a demand on the bailiff or clerk of the Small Claims Court?

CASE STUDY

Rhonda Rhodes (45567H)
Lawyer
111 – 392 Bay Street
Toronto, ON M3P 1J8
tel.: 416-383-5679

MEMO

DATE: September 3, year 0
TO: Elsie Clerk
FROM: Rhonda Rhodes
RE: Enforcement of Small Claims Judgment

OUR CLIENT: Adam Shredlu
JUDGMENT DEBTOR: Daryl Tinamou

Our client obtained a judgment against the debtor on June 28, year 0 in the Toronto Small Claims Court, court file no. SC-10-0006875-0000, for the sum of $3,000, prejudgment interest of $24.42, and costs of $329. The judgment was for failure to honour a promissory note due June 1, year 0. The interest on the note was 11 percent per year. The judgment bears post judgment interest at 11 percent per year.

The creditor lives at 123 Anywho St., Toronto, ON M5K 1J6 and the phone number is 416-833-1234.

The debtor lives at 31 Hardcase Road, Toronto, ON M4P 1X3. The house is owned by him alone. He has a car, a 2008 Ford Taurus sedan, licence plate no. BAAL 678, VIN 123456768. It does not appear to be collateral on any loan. Tinamou works as an engraver for Junk Jewel Ltd., 93 Dorfus Road, Toronto, ON M7S 1Y8 and the phone number is 416-667-3101. He earns about $1,400 a week gross, but we are not exactly sure of the amount he actually makes.

Prepare the necessary documentation to enforce the judgment through the use of writs of seizure and sale and garnishment. Also, prepare the necessary documentation to conduct a judgment debtor examination. All documents are to be filed with the court as of September 15, year 0.

FIGURE 11.1 Certificate of Judgment

ONTARIO
Superior Court of Justice

Certificate of Judgment
Form 20A Ont. Reg. No.: 258/98

North Bay
Small Claims Court

SC-10-00012350-0000
Claim No.

Seal

360 Plouffe Street
North Bay, ON P1B 9L5
Address

705-495-8309
Phone number

BETWEEN

Abdullah Karim
Creditor(s)

and

Antonio Salieri
Debtor(s)

A judgment was made in this action on May 8, year 0 **, 20 _____ , in the**

North Bay Small Claims Court
(Name of court where judgment was made)

against

Last name of debtor, or name of company		
Salieri		
First name	Second name	Third name
Antonio		
Address		
177 Main Street, Kingston, ON K7L 2T2		

Last name of debtor, or name of company		
First name	Second name	Third name
Address		

Last name of debtor, or name of company		
First name	Second name	Third name
Address		

☐ Additional debtor(s) and also known as names are listed on attached Form 1A.1.

Les formules des tribunaux sont affichées en anglais et en français sur le site www.ontariocourtforms.on.ca. Visitez ce site pour des renseignements sur des formats accessibles.

SCR 20.04-20A (January 23, 2014) CSD

FIGURE 11.1 Certificate of Judgment (*continued*)

FORM 20A **PAGE 2** SC-10-00012350-0000
Claim No.

Judgment was made for the following sums:

(A) **AMOUNT OF JUDGMENT** (debt and pre-judgment interest) $ 3000.00

(B) **COSTS** to date of judgment $ 265.00

Post-judgment interest continues to accrue at 4 % per annum.
(Interest rate)

May 20, year 0, 20 ____ ______________________
(Signature of clerk)

TO THE CLERK OF THE Kingston **SMALL CLAIMS COURT:**
(Name of court to where the judgment is to be filed)

The person requesting this certificate is Abdullah Karim
(Name of party requesting certificate)

280 Queen Street, North Bay, ON P2P 3A5
(Address of party requesting certificate)

SCR 20.04-20A (January 23, 2014) CSD

FIGURE 11.2 Notice of Examination

ONTARIO

Superior Court of Justice

Notice of Examination
Form 20H Ont. Reg. No.: 258/98

Toronto
Small Claims Court

SC-10-00012345-0000
Claim No.

(Seal)

47 Sheppard Ave. E., 3rd Floor
Toronto, ON M2N 2X5
Address

416-326-3554
Phone number

BETWEEN

Cape Credit Corporation Ltd
Creditor(s)

and

Feckless Enterprises
Debtor(s)

TO: Henry Feckless
(Name of person to be examined)

of 48 Overreach Blvd. Toronto, ON M2R 5X3
(Address of person to be examined)

The creditor Cape Credit Corporation Ltd. (Name of creditor) of 1002-40 College St, Toronto, ON M5G 2J3 (Address of creditor)

has obtained a judgment against Feckless Enterprises (Name of debtor) on Feb. 15, year 1 ,

20 ______ , in the Toronto (Name of court where judgment was made) Small Claims Court.

According to the supporting affidavit filed by the creditor, the total due on the judgment is

$ $3927.94 (Total) . *(This amount must match the total amount identified in the supporting affidavit.)*

This total due takes into account all money received, accrued post-judgment interest and costs to this date: Mar 30, year 1 , 20 ______ . *(This date must match the date of the supporting affidavit.)*

YOU ARE REQUIRED TO ATTEND AN EXAMINATION HEARING to explain how the debtor will pay this judgment and if there are any reasons for not doing so.

Les formules des tribunaux sont affichées en anglais et en français sur le site www.ontariocourtforms.on.ca. Visitez ce site pour des renseignements sur des formats accessibles.

SCR 20.10-20H (January 23, 2014) CSD

Continued on next page

FIGURE 11.2 Notice of Examination (*continued*)

FORM 20H **PAGE 2** SC-10-00012345-0000
Claim No.

THIS COURT WILL HOLD AN EXAMINATION HEARING

on May 10, year 1 **, 20** ____ **, at** ____________ (Time) **or as soon as possible after that time, at**

47 Sheppard Ave. E. Toronto, ON M2N 2X5
(Address of court location)

4
(Courtroom number)

March 30, year 1 , 20 ____ ______________________
(Signature of clerk)

CAUTION TO PERSON BEING EXAMINED:	If you fail to attend the examination hearing or attend and refuse to answer questions or produce documents, you may be ordered to attend a contempt hearing. At the contempt hearing, you may be found in contempt of court and the court may order you to be jailed.

NOTE TO DEBTOR:	A debtor who is an individual must serve on the creditor a completed Financial Information Form (Form 20I) prior to the hearing. This form must **not** be filed with the court. The debtor must provide a completed copy of this form to the judge at the examination hearing. The debtor must also bring to the hearing documents that support the information given in this form.

For information on accessibility of court services for people with disability-related needs, contact:
Telephone: 416-326-2220 / 1-800-518-7901 TTY: 416-326-4012 / 1-877-425-0575

SCR 20.10-20H (January 23, 2014) CSD

FIGURE 11.3 Affidavit for Enforcement Request

ONTARIO
Superior Court of Justice

Affidavit for Enforcement Request
Form 20P Ont. Reg. No.: 258/98

Toronto
Small Claims Court

SC-10-00012345-0000
Claim No.

47 Sheppard Ave. E., 3rd Floor
Toronto, ON M2N 2X5
Address

416-326-3554
Phone number

BETWEEN

Cape Credit Corporation Ltd
Plaintiff(s)/Creditor(s)

and / *et*

Feckless Enterprises
Defendant(s)/Debtor(s)

My name is Charles Dickens
(Full name)

I live in Toronto, Ontario
(Municipality & province)

and I swear/affirm that the following is true:

1. In this action, I am the

(Check one box only.)
☐ plaintiff/creditor.
☒ representative of the plaintiff(s)/creditor(s).

I make this affidavit in support of a request that the clerk of the court issue the following enforcement process(es):

☐ Certificate of Judgment (Form 20A) to the clerk of the ____________________
(Name of court where the judgment is to be filed)
Small Claims Court.

☐ Writ of Seizure and Sale of Personal Property (Form 20C) directed to the bailiff of
____________________ Small Claims Court.
(Name of court location)

☐ Writ of Seizure and Sale of Land (Form 20D) directed to the sheriff of ____________________
(Name of county/region in which the enforcement office is located)

Les formules des tribunaux sont affichées en anglais et en français sur le site www.ontariocourtforms.on.ca. Visitez ce site pour des renseignements sur des formats accessibles.

SCR 20.04-10-20P (January 23, 2014) CSD

FIGURE 11.3 Affidavit for Enforcement Request (*continued*)

FORM 20P **PAGE 2** **SC-10-00012345-0000**
Claim No.

☐ Notice of Garnishment (Form 20E)/Notice of Renewal of Garnishment (Form 20E.1).

I believe that the garnishee ______________________
(Name of garnishee)

at ______________________
(Address of garnishee)

is indebted to the debtor or will become indebted to the debtor for the following reasons:

The Notice will be served on the debtor ______________________
(Name of debtor)

at ______________________
(Address of debtor for service)

within five days of serving it on the garnishee.

☒ Notice of Examination (Form 20H).

☐ Writ of Delivery (Form 20B).

☐ Other *(Set out the nature of your request):*

Complete this section if you are requesting a Writ of Delivery.

2. An order for the delivery of the following personal property:
(According to the court order, set out a description of the property to be delivered. Identify any marks or serial numbers.)

was made in this action against: ______________________
(Name of person against whom the order was made)

on ______________ , 20 ____ , in the ______________________
(Name of court location where order was made)

Small Claims Court. Since the above listed personal property has not been delivered, I make this affidavit in support of a request that the clerk of the court issue a Writ of Delivery (Form 20B) to the bailiff of the

______________________ Small Claims Court.
(Name of court location)

SCR 20.04-10-20P (January 23, 2014) CSD

Continued on next page

FIGURE 11.3 **Affidavit for Enforcement Request (*continued*)**

FORM 20P **PAGE 3** SC-10-00012345-0000
Claim No.

Complete this section if you are requesting a Certificate of Judgment, Writ of Seizure and Sale of Personal Property, Writ of Seizure and Sale of Land, Notice of Garnishment, Notice of Renewal of Garnishment or Notice of Examination.

3. A judgment was made in this action against Feckless Enterprises
(Name of debtor(s))

on Feb. 15, year 1 , 20 ____ in the Toronto
(Name of court where judgment was made)

Small Claims Court for the following sums:

(A) **DEBT** $ 3000.00

(B) **PRE-JUDGMENT INTEREST** calculated

on the sum of $ 3000.00 at the rate of 10 %

per annum from April 1, year -1 , 20 ____ to Feb. 15, year 1 , 20 ____ ,

being 686 days. $ 563.84

SUBTOTAL (Amount of Judgment) $ 3563.84

(C) **COSTS** to date of judgment $ 300.00 (95 issue claim, 145 set down for trial & 60 service)

(D) **TOTAL AMOUNT OF PAYMENTS RECEIVED FROM DEBTOR** after judgment (if any) (minus) $ 0

(E) **POST-JUDGMENT INTEREST** to date calculated

on the sum of $ 3863.84 at the rate of 2 %

per annum from Feb. 16, year 1 , 20 ____ to Mar. 30, year 1 , 20 ____ ,

being 43 days. $ 9.10

NOTE: Calculation of interest is always on the amount owing from time to time as payments are received. This is true for both pre-judgment and post-judgment interest. Attach a separate sheet setting out how you calculated the total amount of any pre/post-judgment interest.

(F) **SUBSEQUENT COSTS** incurred after judgment (including the cost of issuing the requested enforcement(s)) $ 55.00

TOTAL DUE $ 3927.94

Sworn/Affirmed before me at Toronto
(Municipality)

in Ontario
(Province, state or country)

on Mar. 30, year 1 , 20 ____ ____________________
Commissioner for taking affidavits
(Type or print name below if signature is illegible.)

____
Signature
(This form is to be signed in front of a lawyer, justice of the peace, notary public or commissioner for taking affidavits.)

WARNING: IT IS AN OFFENCE UNDER THE *CRIMINAL CODE* TO KNOWINGLY SWEAR OR AFFIRM A FALSE AFFIDAVIT.

SCR 20.04-10-20P (January 23, 2014) CSD

FIGURE 11.4 Financial Information Form

FINANCIAL INFORMATION FORM

Form 20I Ont. Reg. No.: 258/98

This form is to be completed by the debtor and served on the creditor.

This form is not to be filed at the court office. The debtor must provide a completed copy of this form to the judge at the examination hearing. The debtor must also bring to the hearing documents that support the information given in this form.

MONTHLY INCOME		**MONTHLY EXPENSES**	
Employer(s) ______		Rent/Mortgage	$ ______
Employer(s) ______		Maintenance/Support Payments	$ ______
Net salary	$ ______	Property taxes	$ ______
Commissions	$ ______	Utilities (heat, water & light)	$ ______
Tips and gratuities	$ ______	Phone	$ ______
Employment insurance	$ ______	Cable	$ ______
Pension income	$ ______	House/Tenant insurance	$ ______
Investment income	$ ______	Life insurance	$
Rental income	$ ______	Food	$ ______
Business income	$ ______	Childcare/Babysitting	$ ______
Child tax benefit	$ ______	Motor vehicle (lease or loan)	$ ______
Maintenance *(if any)*	$ ______	(licence, insurance, fuel & maintenance)	$ ______
Monthly income of other adult household members	$ ______	Transportation (public)	$ ______
Other	$ ______		
Income assistance	$ ______		
INCOME TOTAL	**$** ______	**EXPENSES TOTAL**	**$** ______

Les formules des tribunaux sont affichées en anglais et en français sur le site www.ontariocourtforms.on.ca. Visitez ce site pour des renseignements sur des formats accessibles.

SCR 9.03-20.10-20I (January 23, 2014) CSD

Continued on next page

FIGURE 11.4 Financial Information Form (*continued*)

FORM 20I **PAGE 2**

MONTHLY DEBTS		**VALUE OF ASSETS**	
Credit card(s) payments *(please specify)*:		Real estate equity	$
	$	Market value $	
	$	Mortgage balance $	
	$	Automobile equity	$
Bank or finance company loan payments *(please specify)*:		Make and year Loan balance $	
	$	Bank or other account balance(s) *(include RRSPs)*	$
	$	Stocks & bonds	$
Department store(s) payments *(please specify)*:		Life insurance (cash value)	$
	$	Money owing to you	$
	$	Name of debtor	
DEBTS TOTAL	**$**	Personal property	$
		Cash	$
		Other	$
		TOTAL VALUE OF ASSETS	$

(Name) (Signature)

SCR 9.03-20.10-20I (January 23, 2014) CSD

FIGURE 11.5 Warrant of Committal

ONTARIO

Superior Court of Justice

Warrant of Committal
Form 20J Ont. Reg. No.: 258/98

Toronto
Small Claims Court

SC-10-00012345-0000
Claim No.

Seal

47 Sheppard Ave. E., 3rd Floor
Toronto, ON M2N 2X5
Address

416-326-3554
Phone number

BETWEEN

Cape Credit Corporation Ltd
Plaintiff(s)

and

Feckless Enterprises
Defendant(s)

TO ALL POLICE OFFICERS IN ONTARIO AND TO THE OFFICERS OF ALL CORRECTIONAL INSTITUTIONS IN ONTARIO:

THIS WARRANT IS FOR THE COMMITTAL OF

Last name Feckless		
First name Henry	Second name	Also known as
Address (street number, apt., unit) 48 Overreach Blvd.		
City/Town Toronto	Province ON	Phone no. 416-223-4569
Postal code M5R 5X3		Fax no.

A Notice of Contempt Hearing was issued from this court which required

Henry Feckless
(Name of person required to attend contempt hearing)

to attend the sittings of this court at Toronto (Time) on May 10, year 1 (Date), 20 ____ .

Les formules des tribunaux sont affichées en anglais et en français sur le site www.ontariocourtforms.on.ca. Visitez ce site pour des renseignements sur des formats accessibles.

SCR 20.11-20J (January 23, 2014) CSD

FIGURE 11.5 Warrant of Committal (*continued*)

FORM 20J **PAGE 2** **SC-10-00012345-0000**
Claim No.

At the contempt hearing, it was duly proven that the Notice of Contempt Hearing was properly served, and this court found this person to be in contempt of court because he/she:

(Check appropriate box.)

☒ wilfully failed to attend an examination hearing as required by a Notice of Examination (Form 20H), which was properly served.

☐ attended the examination hearing, refused to answer questions or produce documents or records, and failed to show cause why he/she should not be held in contempt for refusing to answer questions or produce documents or records.

At the contempt hearing, a judge of this court ordered this person to be committed.

YOU ARE ORDERED to take the person named above to the nearest correctional institution and admit and detain him or her there for 5 days.

This warrant expires twelve (12) months from the date of issue, unless renewed by court order. If renewed, the warrant expires twelve (12) months from the date of the renewal.

May 30, year 1, 20 ______ ____________________
(Signature of clerk)

SCR 20.11-20J (January 23, 2014) CSD

FIGURE 11.6 Writ of Delivery

ONTARIO
Superior Court of Justice

Writ of Delivery
Form 20B Ont. Reg. No.: 258/98

Kingston
Small Claims Court

SC-10-00012350-0000
Claim No.

Seal

5 Court Street
Kingston, ON K7L 2N4
Address

613-548-6811
Phone number

BETWEEN

Abdullah Karim
Plaintiff(s)

and

Antonio Salieri
Defendant(s)

TO THE BAILIFF OF Kingston **SMALL CLAIMS COURT:**
(Name of Small Claims Court location)

Under an order of this court made on May 8, year 0 , 20

YOU ARE DIRECTED to seize from Antonio Salieri
(Name of person against whom the order was made)

and to deliver without delay to

Name of person in whose favour the order was made
Abdullah Karim
Street and number 280 Queen Street
City, province, postal code North Bay, ON P2P 3A5
Phone number and fax number, if any 705-732-4561

possession of the following personal property:
(According to the court order, set out a description of the property to be delivered. Identify any marks or serial numbers. If the order refers to items set out in the issued claim, attach a copy of the issued claim.)

Les formules des tribunaux sont affichées en anglais et en français sur le site www.ontariocourtforms.on.ca. Visitez ce site pour des renseignements sur des formats accessibles.

SCR 20.05-20B (January 23, 2014) CSD

FIGURE 11.6 Writ of Delivery (*continued*)

FORM 20B | **PAGE 2** | **SC-10-00012350-0000**
Claim No.

The above personal property is located at: **Faculty of Music, Queen's University, Kingston, ON K7L 3N6**
(Address)

If the address provided does not clearly identify where the items are located, please attach a detailed map that shows the nearest intersection.

(To be completed by the clerk of the court.) ☐ **THE COURT HAS EXPRESSLY ORDERED** that you are authorized to use reasonable force to enter a private dwelling to execute this writ of delivery, if necessary [*Execution Act*, s. 20(2)]. A copy of the court's order on the endorsement record is attached.

May 23, year 0 , 20 ______ ________________________________
(Signature of clerk)

SCR 20.05-20B (January 23, 2014) CSD

FIGURE 11.7 Writ of Seizure and Sale of Personal Property

ONTARIO
Superior Court of Justice

Writ of Seizure and Sale of Personal Property
Form 20C Ont. Reg. No.: 258/98

Toronto
Small Claims Court

SC-10-00012345-0000
Claim No.

Seal

47 Sheppard Ave. E., 3rd Floor
Toronto, ON M2N 2X5
Address

416-326-3554
Phone number

Creditor No. 1

☐ Additional party(ies) listed on attached Form 1A.

Last name, or name of company		
Cape Credit Corporation Ltd.		
First name	Second name	Also known as
Address (street number, apt., unit) c/o Charles Dickens 8041 Ryder Street		
City/Town Mississauga	Province ON	Phone no. 905-381-2620
Postal code L2R 1Y6		Fax no.
Representative Charles Dickens		LSUC # P02345
Address (street number, apt., unit) 8041 Ryder Street		
City/Town Mississauga	Province ON	Phone no. 905-381-2620
Postal code L2R 1Y6		Fax no.

Debtor No. 1

☐ Additional party(ies) listed on attached Form 1A.

Last name, or name of company		
Feckless Enterprises		
First name	Second name	Also known as
Address (street number, apt., unit) c/o Edward Lue 365 Bay Street		
City/Town Toronto	Province ON	Phone no. 416-595-1308
Postal code M2N 3A8		Fax no.
Representative Edward Lue		LSUC # P02361
Address (street number, apt., unit) 365 Bay Street		
City/Town Toronto	Province ON	Phone no. 416-595-1308
Postal code M2N 3A8		Fax no.

Les formules des tribunaux sont affichées en anglais et en français sur le site www.ontariocourtforms.on.ca. Visitez ce site pour des renseignements sur des formats accessibles.

SCR 20.06-20C (January 23, 2014) CSD

FIGURE 11.7 Writ of Seizure and Sale of Personal Property (*continued*)

FORM 20C **PAGE 2** SC-10-00012345-0000
Claim No.

TO THE BAILIFF OF THE Toronto **SMALL CLAIMS COURT:**
(Small Claims Court location)

Under an order of this court made on Feb 15 Year 1 , 20 ____, in favour of

Cape Credit Corporation Ltd.
(Name of creditor(s))

YOU ARE DIRECTED to seize and sell the personal property of

Last name, or name of company		
Feckless Enterprises		
First name	Second name	Third name

☐ Additional debtor(s) and also known as names listed on attached Form 1A.1.

situated within your jurisdiction and to realize from the seizure and sale the following sums:

(A) **AMOUNT OF JUDGMENT** (debt and pre-judgment interest) $ 3563.84

(B) **COSTS** to date of judgment $ 300.00

(C) **TOTAL AMOUNT OF PAYMENTS RECEIVED FROM DEBTOR** after judgment (if any) $ 0

Post-judgment interest continues to accrue

at the rate of 2 % per annum from Feb. 16, year 1 , 20 ____.

(D) **SUBSEQUENT COSTS** incurred after judgment (including the cost of issuing this writ) $ 110.00

(E) Your fees and expenses in enforcing this writ.

YOU ARE DIRECTED to calculate the amount owing at the time of enforcement and to pay the proceeds over to the clerk of this court for the creditor.

Feb. 25, year 1 , 20 ____ ____________________
(Signature of clerk)

Reasonable disbursements necessarily incurred to enforce this writ (Bailiff (enforcement office) fees and expenses)	$ .... (filled in and initialled by the enforcement office) $

NOTE:	**THIS WRIT REMAINS IN FORCE FOR SIX YEARS** after the date of its issue and for a further six years after each renewal. The writ may be renewed before it expires by filing a Request to Renew a Writ of Seizure and Sale (Form 20N) with the bailiff (enforcement office).

SCR 20.06-20C (January 23, 2014) CSD

FIGURE 11.8 Direction to Enforce Writ of Seizure and Sale of Personal Property

ONTARIO

Superior Court of Justice

Direction to Enforce Writ of Seizure and Sale of Personal Property
Form 20O Ont. Reg. No.: 258/98

Toronto
Small Claims Court

SC-10-00012345-0000
Claim No.

47 Sheppard Ave. E., 3rd Floor
Toronto, ON M2N 2X5
Address

416-326-3554
Phone number

BETWEEN

Cape Credit Corporation Ltd
Creditor(s)

and

Feckless Enterprises
Debtor(s)

My name is Charles Dickens
(Full name)

1. In this action, I am the

(Check one box only.)
☐ creditor.
☒ representative of the creditor(s).

A Writ of Seizure and Sale of Personal Property (Form 20C) directed to the bailiff of the
Toronto Small Claims Court was issued on:
(Small Claims Court location)
Feb. 25, year 1 , 20 ____ , in favour of Capricious Credit Corporation Ltd.
(Name of creditor)

2. I am filing this direction to enforce the Writ of Seizure and Sale of Personal Property, and direct the bailiff to seize and sell (if required) the personal property belonging to the following debtor(s):

Last name, or name of company: Feckless Enterprises		
First name	Second name	Third given name (individual only) (if applicable)

☐ Additional debtor(s) and also known as names are listed on attached Form 1A.1.

Set out a description of the property to be seized. Identify any marks or serial numbers.

Les formules des tribunaux sont affichées en anglais et en français sur le site www.ontariocourtforms.on.ca. Visitez ce site pour des renseignements sur des formats accessibles.

SCR 20.06-20O (January 23, 2014) CSD

FIGURE 11.8 Direction to Enforce Writ of Seizure and Sale of Personal Property (*continued*)

FORM 20O **PAGE 2** SC-10-00012345-0000
Claim No.

3. The above personal property is located at: 48 Overreach Blvd., Toronto, ON M2R 5X3
(Address)

If the address provided does not clearly identify where the property is located, please attach a detailed map showing the nearest intersection.

4. From the date that the Writ of Seizure and Sale of Personal Property was issued, the following payments have been received from the debtor and/or subsequent costs incurred by the creditor:

(A) **PAYMENTS RECEIVED FROM DEBTOR**

Date of Payment	Payment Amount
	$
	$
	$
	$

☐ List of additional payments attached

(B) **SUBSEQUENT COSTS** incurred since issuance of Writ of Seizure and Sale of Personal Property

Reason cost was incurred	Cost Amount
	$
	$
	$
	$

☐ List of additional costs attached

The bailiff will calculate the amount owing based on the information provided within the Writ of Seizure and Sale of Personal Property and the details provided above. This amount will include any reasonable disbursements necessarily incurred to enforce this writ.

March 25, year 0 , 20 ____

(Signature of creditor or representative)

Charles Dickens
8041 Ryder Street
Mississauga, ON L2R 1Y6
905-381-2620
(Name, address and phone number of creditor or representative)

SCR 20.06-20O (January 23, 2014) CSD

FIGURE 11.9 Request to Renew Writ of Seizure and Sale

ONTARIO

Superior Court of Justice

Request to Renew Writ of Seizure and Sale

Form 20N Ont. Reg. No.: 258/98

Toronto
Small Claims Court

SC-10-00012345-0000
Claim No.

47 Sheppard Ave. E., 3rd Floor
Toronto, ON M2N 2X5
Address

416-326-3554
Phone number

BETWEEN

Cape Credit Corporation Ltd
Creditor(s)

and

Feckless Enterprises
Debtor(s)

TO THE SHERIFF/BAILIFF OF Toronto :
(Name of county/region and city/town in which the enforcement office is located)

YOU ARE REQUESTED TO RENEW the

☒ Writ of Seizure and Sale of Personal Property (Form 20C)

☐ Writ of Seizure and Sale of Land (Form 20D)

issued on Feb. 25, year 1, 20 ____, in this proceeding and filed in your office for a period of six years from the date of renewal.

Feb. 1, year 7, 20 ____

____
(Signature of creditor or representative)

Charles Dickens
8041 Ryder Street
Mississauga, ON L2R 1Y6
905-381-2620
(Name, address and phone number of creditor or representative)

NOTE: **A WRIT OF SEIZURE AND SALE OF LAND OR OF PERSONAL PROPERTY** remains in force for six years after the date of its issue and for a further six years after each renewal.

Les formules des tribunaux sont affichées en anglais et en français sur le site www.ontariocourtforms.on.ca. Visitez ce site pour des renseignements sur des formats accessibles.

SCR 20.06-20.07-20N (January 23, 2014) CSD

FIGURE 11.10 Writ of Seizure and Sale of Land

ONTARIO
Superior Court of Justice

Writ of Seizure and Sale of Land
Form 20D Ont. Reg. No.: 258/98

Toronto
Small Claims Court

SC-10-00012345-0000
Claim No.

Seal

47 Sheppard Ave. E., 3rd Floor
Toronto, ON M2N 2X5
Address

416-326-3554
Phone number

Creditor No. 1 ☐ Additional party(ies) listed on attached Form 1A.

Last name, or name of company		
Cape Credit Corporation Ltd.		
First name	Second name	Also known as
Address (street number, apt., unit) c/o Charles Dickens 8041 Ryder St.		
City/Town Mississauga, ON	Province ON	Phone no. 905-381-2620
Postal code L2R 1Y6		Fax no.
Representative Charles Dickens		LSUC # P02345
Address (street number, apt., unit) 8041 Ryder St.		
City/Town Mississauga	Province ON	Phone no. 905-381-2620
Postal code L2R 1Y6		Fax no.

Debtor No. 1 ☐ Additional party(ies) listed on attached Form 1A.

Last name, or name of company		
Feckless Enterprises		
First name	Second name	Also known as
Address (street number, apt., unit) c/o Edward Lue 365 Bay Street		
City/Town Toronto	Province ON	Phone no. 416-595-1308
Postal code M2N 3A8		Fax no.
Representative Edward Lue		LSUC # P02361
Address (street number, apt., unit) 365 Bay Street		
City/Town Toronto	Province ON	Phone no. 416-595-1308
Postal code M2N 3A8		Fax no.

NOTE: **THIS WRIT REMAINS IN FORCE FOR SIX YEARS** after the date of its issue and for a further six years after each renewal. The writ may be renewed before it expires by filing a Request to Renew a Writ of Seizure and Sale (Form 20N) with the sheriff (enforcement office.)

Les formules des tribunaux sont affichées en anglais et en français sur le site www.ontariocourtforms.on.ca. Visitez ce site pour des renseignements sur des formats accessibles.

SCR 20.07-20D (January 23, 2014) CSD

FIGURE 11.10 Writ of Seizure and Sale of Land (*continued*)

FORM 20D **PAGE 2**

SC-10-00012345-0000
Claim No.

TO THE SHERIFF OF Toronto :
(Name of county/region in which the enforcement office is located)

Under an order of this court made on Feb. 15, year 1 , 20 ____ , in favour of
Cape Credit Corporation Ltd.
(Name of creditor(s))

YOU ARE DIRECTED to seize and sell the real property of

Last name, or name of company		
Feckless Enterprises		
First name	Second name	Third name

☐ Additional debtor(s) and also known as names listed on attached Form 1A.1.

situated within your jurisdiction and to realize from the seizure and sale the following sums:

(A) **AMOUNT OF JUDGMENT** (debt and pre-judgment interest) $ 3563.84

(B) **COSTS** to date of judgment $ 300.00

(C) **TOTAL AMOUNT OF PAYMENTS RECEIVED FROM DEBTOR** after judgment (if any) $ 0

Post-judgment interest continues to accrue

at the rate of 2 % per annum from Feb. 16, year 1 , 20 ____ .

(D) **SUBSEQUENT COSTS** incurred after judgment (including the cost of issuing this writ) $ 165.00

(E) Your fees and expenses in enforcing this writ.

YOU ARE DIRECTED to calculate the amount owing at the time of enforcement and pay out the proceeds according to law and to report on the execution of this writ if required by a party who filed this writ.

Feb. 25, year 1 , 20 ____ ______________________
(Signature of clerk)

SCR 20.07-20D (January 23, 2014) CSD

FIGURE 11.11 Notice of Garnishment

ONTARIO
Superior Court of Justice

Notice of Garnishment
Form 20E Ont. Reg. No.: 258/98

Kingston
Small Claims Court

SC-10-00012350-0000
Claim No.

(Seal)

5 Court Street
Kingston, ON K7L 2N4
Address

613-548-6811
Phone number

Creditor

☐ Additional creditor(s) listed on the attached Form 1A.

Last name, or name of company: Karim		
First name: Abdullah	Second name:	Also known as:
Address (street number, apt., unit): 280 Queen Street		
City/Town: North Bay	Province: ON	Phone no.: 705-732-4561
Postal code: P2P 3A5		Fax no.:
Representative:		LSUC #:
Address (street number, apt., unit):		
City/Town:	Province:	Phone no.:
Postal code:		Fax no.:

Debtor

Last name, or name of company: Salieri		
First name: Antonio	Second name:	Also known as:
Address (street number, apt., unit): 177 Main Street		
City/Town: Kingston	Province: ON	Phone no.: 613-223-4564
Postal code: K7L 2T2		Fax no.:

Garnishee

Last name, or name of company: Queen's University		
First name:	Second name:	Also known as:
Address (street number, apt., unit): 99 University Avenue		
City/Town: Kingston	Province: ON	Phone no.: 613-595-2300
Postal code: K7L 3N6		Fax no.:

NOTE: **THE CREDITOR SHALL SERVE THIS NOTICE** on the debtor with an Affidavit for Enforcement Request (Form 20P) and serve on the garnishee this notice with a blank Garnishee's Statement (Form 20F).

Les formules des tribunaux sont affichées en anglais et en français sur le site www.ontariocourtforms.on.ca. Visitez ce site pour des renseignements sur des formats accessibles.

SCR 20.08-20E (January 23, 2014) CSD

FIGURE 11.11 Notice of Garnishment (*continued*)

FORM 20E **PAGE 2** SC-10-00012350-0000
Claim No.

TO THE GARNISHEE:

The creditor has obtained a court order against the debtor. The creditor claims that you owe or will owe the debtor a debt in the form of wages, salary, pension payments, rent, annuity or other debt that you pay out in a lump-sum, periodically or by instalments. (A debt to the debtor includes both a debt payable to the debtor alone and a joint debt payable to the debtor and one or more co-owners.)

YOU ARE REQUIRED TO PAY to the clerk of the Kingston Small Claims Court
(Garnishment issuing court)

(a) all debts now payable by you to the debtor, **within 10 days** after this notice is served on you; **and**

(b) all debts that become payable by you to the debtor after this notice is served on you and **within 6 years** after this notice is issued, **within 10 days** after they become payable.

The total amount of all your payments to the clerk is not to exceed $ 3390.00 .
(Amount unsatisfied)

THIS NOTICE IS LEGALLY BINDING ON YOU until it expires or is changed, renewed, terminated or satisfied. If you do not pay the total amount or such lesser amount as you are liable to pay, you must serve a Garnishee's Statement (Form 20F) on the creditor and debtor, and file it with the clerk within 10 days after this notice is served on you.

EACH PAYMENT, payable to the Minister of Finance, MUST BE SENT with a copy of the attached garnishee's payment notice to the clerk at the above court address.

If your debt is jointly owed to the debtor and to one or more co-owners, you must pay the debtor's appropriate share of the amount now payable, or which becomes payable, or such a percentage as the court may order.

The amounts paid into court shall not exceed the portion of the debtor's wages that are subject to seizure or garnishment under Section 7 of the *Wages Act* (information available at: www.attorneygeneral.jus.gov.on.ca and www.e-laws.gov.on.ca). The portion of wages that can be garnished may be increased or decreased only by order of the court. If such a court order is attached to this notice or is served on you, you must follow the direction in that court order.

May 28, year 0 , 20 ______ ______________________
(Signature of clerk)

CAUTION TO GARNISHEE:	**IF YOU FAIL TO PAY** to the clerk the amount set out in this notice and do not file a Garnishee's Statement (Form 20F) disputing garnishment, **JUDGMENT MAY BE OBTAINED AGAINST YOU BY THE CREDITOR** for payment of the amount set out above, plus costs. If you make a payment to anyone other than the clerk of the court, you may be liable to pay again [R. 20.08(17) and (18)].

NOTE:	Any party or interested person may complete and serve a Notice of Garnishment Hearing (Form 20Q) to determine any matter related to this notice. To obtain forms and self-help materials, attend the nearest Small Claims Court or access the following website: www.ontariocourtforms.on.ca.

SCR 20.08-20E (January 23, 2014) CSD

Continued on next page

FIGURE 11.11 Notice of Garnishment (*continued*)

FORM 20E **PAGE 3** SC-10-00012350-0000
Claim No.

The top portion of the garnishee's payment notice, below, is to be completed by the creditor before the Notice of Garnishment is issued. Where it is anticipated that more than one payment will be made by the garnishee, the creditor should supply extra copies of the garnishee's payment notice. Additional copies of the garnishee's payment notice are available at court offices or online at www.ontariocourtforms.on.ca (see Form 20E or 20E.1).

GARNISHEE'S PAYMENT NOTICE

Make payment by cheque or money order payable to the Minister of Finance and send it, along with this payment notice to the clerk of the court at the following address:

Court address: 5 Court Street Kingston, ON K7L 2N4

Claim No.: SC-10-00012350-0000

Creditor: Abdullah Karim

Debtor: Antonio Salieri

Garnishee: Queen's University

TO BE COMPLETED BY GARNISHEE FOR EACH PAYMENT

Date of payment: ____________________, 20 ____

Amount enclosed: $ ____________________

SCR 20.08-20E (January 23, 2014) CSD

FIGURE 11.12 Notice to Co-owner of Debt

ONTARIO
Superior Court of Justice

Notice to Co-owner of Debt
Form 20G Ont. Reg. No.: 258/98

Kingston
Small Claims Court

5 Court Street
Kingston, ON K7L 2N4
Address

613-548-6811
Phone number

SC-10-00012350-0000
Claim No.

Creditor

☐ Additional creditor(s) listed on the attached Form 1A.

Last name, or name of company		
Karim		
First name Abdullah	**Second name**	**Also known as**
Address (street number, apt., unit) 280 Queen Street		
City/Town North Bay	**Province** ON	**Phone no.** 705-732-4561
Postal code P2P 3A5		**Fax no.**
Representative		**LSUC #**
Address (street number, apt., unit)		
City/Town	**Province**	**Phone no.**
Postal code		**Fax no.**

Debtor

Last name, or name of company		
Salieri		
First name Antonio	**Second name**	**Also known as**
Address (street number, apt., unit) 177 Main Street		
City/Town Kingston	**Province** ON	**Phone no.** 613-223-4564
Postal code K7L 2T2		**Fax no.**

Garnishee

Last name, or name of company		
Queen's University		
First name	**Second name**	**Also known as**
Address (street number, apt., unit) 99 University Avenue		
City/Town Kingston	**Province** ON	**Phone no.** 613-595-2300
Postal code K7L 3N6		**Fax no.**

NOTE: **THIS NOTICE SHALL BE SERVED BY THE CREDITOR** on each co-owner of debt together with a copy of the Garnishee's Statement (Form 20F) received from the garnishee.

Les formules des tribunaux sont affichées en anglais et en français sur le site www.ontariocourtforms.on.ca. Visitez ce site pour des renseignements sur des formats accessibles.

SCR 20.08-20G (January 23, 2014) CSD

FIGURE 11.12 Notice to Co-owner of Debt (*continued*)

FORM 20G **PAGE 2**

SC-10-00012350-0000
Claim No.

TO:

(*Attach a separate sheet, in the same format, for additional co-owners of debt.*)

Name of co-owner(s) of debt **W.A. Mozart**
Street and number **c/o Faculty of Music, Queen's University** **99 University Avenue**
City, province, postal code **Kingston, ON K7I 3N6**

The creditor has obtained a court order against the debtor. The creditor has served a Notice of Garnishment (Form 20E), dated **May 8, year 0** , 20 ____, on **Queen's University** ,
(Name of garnishee)

claiming that the garnishee owes or will owe the debtor a debt in the form of wages, salary, pension payments, rent, annuity, or other debt that the garnishee pays out in a lump-sum, periodically or by instalments. (A debt to the debtor includes both a debt payable to the debtor alone and a joint debt payable to the debtor and one or more co-owners.)

The garnishee has set out in the attached Garnishee's Statement (Form 20F) that you are a co-owner of debt. Under the Notice of Garnishment, the garnishee has paid or will pay to the clerk of the Small Claims Court the appropriate share of the amount payable or such a percentage as the court may order.

IF YOU HAVE A CLAIM to the money being paid to the clerk of the Small Claims Court by the garnishee, you have 30 days from service of this notice to request a garnishment hearing by completing and serving a Notice of Garnishment Hearing (Form 20Q) on the creditor, debtor and garnishee, and filing it with the clerk. If you fail to do so, you are not entitled to dispute the enforcement of the creditor's order for the payment or recovery of money and the funds may be paid out to the creditor unless the court orders otherwise.

To obtain forms and self-help materials, attend the nearest Small Claims Court or access the following website: www.ontariocourtforms.on.ca.

July 30, year 0 , 20 ____ ____________________________
(Signature of creditor or representative)

NOTE:	Within seven (7) calendar days of changing your address for service, notify the court and all other parties in writing.

SCR 20.08-20G (January 23, 2014) CSD

FIGURE 11.13 Garnishee's Statement

ONTARIO
Superior Court of Justice

Garnishee's Statement
Form 20F Ont. Reg. No.: 258/98

Kingston
Small Claims Court

SC-10-00012350-0000
Claim No.

5 Court Street
Kingston, ON K7L 2N4
Address

613-548-6811
Phone number

BETWEEN

Abdullah Karim
Creditor(s)

and

Antonio Salieri
Debtor(s)

Name of Garnishee Queen's University
(Full legal name of garnishee)

A Notice of Garnishment was issued on July 20, year 0 , 20 ____ , naming me/us as garnishee in relation to the debtor ____________________ .
(Name of debtor)

☐ **I/WE DO NOT OWE** and do not expect to owe to the debtor the amount set out in the Notice of Garnishment for the following reason(s):

☒ **I/WE OWE OR WILL OWE** the debtor (or the debtor and one or more co-owners), wages or periodic payments based on the terms explained below:
(State the amount(s) and how often the debtor is paid. If the debtor is paid wages, state the gross amount of the debtor's wages before any deductions required by law and the net amount after those deductions, and attach a copy of a pay slip. If you owe or will owe the debtor a lump sum, state when and how much will be paid.)

Les formules des tribunaux sont affichées en anglais et en français sur le site www.ontariocourtforms.on.ca. Visitez ce site pour des renseignements sur des formats accessibles.

SCR 20.08-20F (January 23, 2014) CSD

Continued on next page

FIGURE 11.13 Garnishee's Statement (*continued*)

FORM 20F **PAGE 2** **SC-10-00012350-0000**
Claim No.

☒ **I/We are making payment of less than** the amount stated because the debt is owed to the debtor and to one or more co-owners, or for another reason explained below:

50% ($250) owing to each of Antonio Salieri and W.A. Mozart
(Identify the amount(s) and percentage owed to the debtor and each co-owner)

Co-owner(s) of the debt: **W.A. Mozart**
(Full legal name(s))

c/o Faculty of Music, Queen's University, 99 University Ave., Kingston, ON K7L 3N6
(Address (street & number, unit, municipality, province))

☐ **I/We are not making a payment at this time or are making a payment of less than the amount stated** because I/we have been served with other notice(s) of garnishment against the debtor. (Provide details below.)

Name of creditor	Name of issuing court	Location of court or Sheriff's Office where payment is currently being made	Date Notice of Garnishment received

☐ **I/We will dispute the garnishment** by completing and serving a Notice of Garnishment Hearing (Form 20Q) on the creditor, debtor and co-owner(s) of the debt (if any) and any other interested person, and filing it with the clerk of the court.

August 11, year 0 , 20 ____

____
(Signature of garnishee or representative)

____
(Address, phone and fax number of garnishee or representative)

NOTE TO GARNISHEE:	The garnishee must serve a copy of the Garnishee's Statement on the creditor and the debtor and file it with the court. You can get an electronic version of this form online at www.ontariocourtforms.on.ca.

NOTE TO CREDITOR:	A creditor who is served with a Garnishee's Statement must send it to the co-owners of the debt, if any, together with a Notice to Co-owner of Debt (Form 20G). You can get forms at court offices or online at www.ontariocourtforms.on.ca.

SCR 20.08-20F (January 23, 2014) CSD

FIGURE 11.14 Notice of Garnishment Hearing

ONTARIO
Superior Court of Justice

Notice of Garnishment Hearing
Form 20Q Ont. Reg. No.: 258/98

Kingston
Small Claims Court

5 Court Street
Kingston, ON K7L 2N4
Address

613-548-6811
Phone number

SC-10-00012350-0000
Claim No.

Creditor

☐ Additional creditor(s) listed on the attached Form 1A.

Last name, or name of company		
Karim		
First name: Abdullah	Second name:	Also known as:
Address (street number, apt., unit): 280 Queen Street		
City/Town: North Bay	Province: ON	Phone no.: 705-732-4561
Postal code: P2P 3A5		Fax no.:
Representative:		LSUC #:
Address (street number, apt., unit):		
City/Town:	Province:	Phone no.:
Postal code:		Fax no.:

Debtor

Last name, or name of company		
Salieri		
First name: Antonio	Second name:	Also known as:
Address (street number, apt., unit): 177 Main Street		
City/Town: Kingston	Province: ON	Phone no.: 613-223-4564
Postal code: K7l 2T2		Fax no.:
Representative:		LSUC #:
Address (street number, apt., unit):		
City/Town:	Province:	Phone no.:
Postal code:		Fax no.:

NOTE: The Notice of Garnishment Hearing must be served by the person requesting the hearing on the creditor, debtor, garnishee, co-owner of debt, if any, and any other interested person [R. 8.01(9)].

Les formules des tribunaux sont affichées en anglais et en français sur le site www.ontariocourtforms.on.ca. Visitez ce site pour des renseignements sur des formats accessibles.

SCR 20.08-20Q (January 23, 2014) CSD

FIGURE 11.14 Notice of Garnishment Hearing (*continued*)

FORM 20Q **PAGE 2** **SC-10-00012350-0000**
Claim No.

Garnishee

Last name, or name of company		
Queen's University		
First name	Second name	Also known as
Address (street number, apt., unit): 99 University Avenue		
City/Town: Kingston	Province: ON	Phone no.: 613-595-2300
Postal code: K7L 3N6		Fax no.
Representative		LSUC #
Address (street number, apt., unit)		
City/Town	Province	Phone no.
Postal code		Fax no.

Co-Owner of Debt (if any) ☐ Additional co-owner(s) listed on attached Form 1A.

Last name, or name of company		
Mozart		
First name: William	Second name: Arthur	Also known as: W.A. Mozart
Address (street number, apt., unit): c/o Faculty of Music, Queen's University 99 University Avenue		
City/Town: Kingston	Province: ON	Phone no.
Postal code: K7l 3N6		Fax no.
Representative		LSUC #
Address (street number, apt., unit)		
City/Town	Province	Phone no.
Postal code		Fax no.

Other Interested Person (if any) ☐ Additional interested person(s) listed on attached Form 1A.

Last name, or name of company		
First name	Second name	Also known as
Address (street number, apt., unit)		
City/Town	Province	Phone no.
Postal code		Fax no.
Representative		LSUC #
Address (street number, apt., unit)		
City/Town	Province	Phone no.
Postal code		Fax no.

SCR 20.08-20Q (January 23, 2014) CSD

Continued on next page

FIGURE 11.14 Notice of Garnishment Hearing (*continued*)

FORM 20Q **PAGE 3** SC-10-00012350-0000
Claim No.

TO THE PARTIES:
(The person requesting this garnishment hearing or the person's representative must contact the clerk of the court to choose a time and date when the court could hold this garnishment hearing.)

THIS COURT WILL HOLD A GARNISHMENT HEARING on August 15, year 0 **, 20** ______ **, at** 9:30 a.m. (Time) **, or as soon as possible after that time, at** (Address of court location and courtroom number)

5 Court Street, Kingston, ON K7L 2N4 Courtroom A

because *(Check the appropriate box.)*

☐ the creditor ☐ the debtor ☐ the garnishee ☒ the co-owner of debt

☐ other interested person: ______________________ (Specify)

states the following: *(In numbered paragraphs, provide details of your dispute and the order(s) requested.)*

1. The fee split between the debtor Antonio Salieri and myself is not 50/50 as set out in the Notice to Co-owner. The fee split is 60/40 with 60% being my share. Therefore, it would be incorrect to take 50% of the funds to pay to the creditor in this case.

2. I seek an order reducing the share that may be garnished to the creditor to 40%.

☐ **Additional pages are attached because more space was needed.**

August 1, year 0 , 20 ______ ______________________
(Signature of party or representative)

NOTE:	**If you fail to attend this garnishment hearing, an order may be made in your absence and enforced against you.**

For information on accessibility of court services for people with disability-related needs, contact:

Telephone: 416-326-2220 / 1-800-518-7901 TTY: 416-326-4012 / 1-877-425-0575

SCR 20.08-20Q (January 23, 2014) CSD

FIGURE 11.15 Notice of Motion and Supporting Affidavit

ONTARIO
Superior Court of Justice

Notice of Motion and Supporting Affidavit
Form 15A Ont. Reg. No.: 258/98

Toronto
Small Claims Court

SC-10-00012345-0000
SC-10-00013789-0000
SC-10-00012344-0000
Claim No.

47 Sheppard Ave. E., 3rd Floor
Toronto, ON M2N 2X5
Address

416-326-3554
Phone number

Plaintiff No. 1 ☐ Additional plaintiff(s) listed on attached Form 1A.

Last name, or name of company		
Feckless Enterprises		
First name	Second name	Also known as
Address (street number, apt., unit) c/o Edward Loquacious 365 Bay Street		
City/Town Toronto	Province ON	Phone no. 416-595-1308
Postal code M2N 3A8		Fax no.
Representative Edward Lue		LSUC # P02361
Address (street number, apt., unit) 365 Bay Street		
City/Town Toronto	Province ON	Phone no. 416-595-1308
Postal code M2N 3A8		Fax no.

Defendant No. 1 ☒ Additional defendant(s) listed on attached Form 1A.

Last name, or name of company		
Cape Credit Corporation Ltd.		
First name	Second name	Also known as
Address (street number, apt., unit) c/o Charles Dickens 8041 Ryder Street		
City/Town Mississauga	Province ON	Phone no. 905-381-2620
Postal code L2R 1Y6		Fax no.
Representative Charles Dickens		LSUC # P02345
Address (street number, apt., unit) 8041 Ryder Street		
City/Town Mississauga	Province ON	Phone no. 905-381-2620
Postal code L2R 1Y6		Fax no.

Les formules des tribunaux sont affichées en anglais et en français sur le site www.ontariocourtforms.on.ca. Visitez ce site pour des renseignements sur des formats accessibles.

SCR 15.01-15A (November 1, 2015) CSD

FIGURE 11.15 Notice of Motion and Supporting Affidavit (*continued*)

ONTARIO

Superior Court of Justice

PAGE 1A

Additional Parties

Form 1A Ont. Reg. No.: 258/98

SC-10-00012345-0000
SC-10-00013789-0000
SC-10-00012344-0000

Claim No.

☐ **Plaintiff No.** ☒ **Defendant No.** ADDITIONAL CREDITOR no. 2

Last name, or name of company Forsythe		
First name Wanda	Second name	Also known as
Address (street number, apt., unit) 800 Any Street		
City/Town Toronto	Province ON	Phone no.
Postal code M3J T8J		Fax no.
Representative		LSUC #
Address (street number, apt., unit)		
City/Town	Province	Phone no.
Postal code		Fax no.

☐ **Plaintiff No.** ☒ **Defendant No.** ADDITONAL CREDITOR no. 3

Last name, or name of company Pasternak		
First name Linda	Second name	Also known as
Address (street number, apt., unit) 932 Anyother Street		
City/Town Toronto	Province ON	Phone no.
Postal code M4R 1Y6		Fax no.
Representative		LSUC #
Address (street number, apt., unit)		
City/Town	Province	Phone no.
Postal code		Fax no.

☐ **Plaintiff No.** ☐ **Defendant No.**

Last name, or name of company		
First name	Second name	Also known as
Address (street number, apt., unit)		
City/Town	Province	Phone no.
Postal code		Fax no.
Representative		LSUC #
Address (street number, apt., unit)		
City/Town	Province	Phone no.
Postal code		Fax no.

SCR 1.05-1A (January 23, 2014) CSD

FIGURE 11.15 Notice of Motion and Supporting Affidavit (*continued*)

FORM 15A **PAGE 2**

SC-10-00012345-0000
SC-10-00013789-0000
SC-10-00012344-0000
Claim No.

Complete Part A or Part B below, then complete the affidavit in support of motion on page 3.

A. THIS COURT WILL HEAR A MOTION on September 30, year 1 , 20 ____ , **at** 9:30 a.m. ,
(Time)

or as soon as possible after that time, at 47 Sheppard Ave E., 3rd Floor, Toronto, ON M2N 2X5 Courtroom 4
(Address of court location and courtroom number)

This motion will be made in person by Feckless Enterprises ,
(Name of party)

for the following order:

- ☐ the court's permission to extend time to (Specify) ____________________.
- ☐ set aside default judgment and noting in default.
- ☐ set aside noting in default.
- ☐ permission to file a Defence.
- ☐ permission to file a Defendant's Claim.
- ☐ set aside order dismissing claim as abandoned.
- ☐ terminate garnishment and/or withdraw writ(s).
- ☒ Other:
  For a consolidation order.

☐ **ADDITIONAL PAGES ARE ATTACHED BECAUSE MORE ROOM WAS NEEDED.**

☐ **DOCUMENTS ARE ATTACHED.**

NOTE:	**IF YOU FAIL TO ATTEND AN IN-PERSON MOTION,** an order may be made against you, with costs, in your absence. If you want to attend the motion by telephone or video conference, complete and file a Request for Telephone or Video Conference (Form 1B). If the court permits it, the clerk will make the necessary arrangements and notify the parties [R. 1.07(5)].

B. This motion in writing for an assessment of damages is made by

____________________ ,
(Name of plaintiff)

who asks the court for an order assessing damages against

____
(Name of defendant(s))

who have/has been noted in default.

SCR 15.01-15A (November 1, 2015) CSD

Continued on next page

FIGURE 11.15 Notice of Motion and Supporting Affidavit (*continued*)

FORM 15A | PAGE 3 | SC-10-00012345-0000
SC-10-00013789-0000
SC-10-00012344-0000
Claim No.

AFFIDAVIT IN SUPPORT OF MOTION

My name is Henry Feckless
(Full name)

I live in Toronto, Ontario
(Municipality & province)

I swear/affirm that the following is true:

Set out the facts in numbered paragraphs. If you learned a fact from someone else, you must give that person's name and state that you believe that fact to be true.

1. I am the owner of Feckless Enterprises, a sole proprietorship.

2. During the past three years, Feckless Enterprises has been financially struggling. During that time three judgments were rendered against this business in this court.

3. Claim No. SC-10-00012345-0000 is a judgment in favour of Cape Credit Corporation Ltd. in the amount of $3863.84 granted Feb. 15, year 1.

4. Claim No. SC-10-00013789-0000 is a judgment in favour of Wanda Forsythe in the amount of $2536.00 granted March 21, year 1.

5. Claim No. SC-10-00012344-0000 is a judgment in favour of Linda Pasternak in the amount of $3741.56 granted April 7, year 1.

6. I have not, to date, been able to make any payments on the above-noted judgments.

7. However, recently I became a vendor of fidget spinners and have been able to increase the profits of the business from $2000 per month to $3000 per month. After my business expenses of rent, utilities, insurance, and office supplies of $2500 per month are paid, this would leave me with $500 to pay in total a month toward the 3 outstanding judgments.

8. I make this affidavit in support of this motion and for no other purpose.

SCR 15.01-15A (November 1, 2015) CSD

Continued on next page

FIGURE 11.15 Notice of Motion and Supporting Affidavit (*continued*)

FORM 15A **PAGE 4**

SC-10-00012345-0000
SC-10-00013789-0000
SC-10-00012344-0000
Claim No.

AFFIDAVIT IN SUPPORT OF MOTION, continued

If more space is required, attach and initial extra pages.

Sworn/Affirmed before me at **Toronto**
(Municipality)

in **Ontario**
(Province, state or country)

on **May 30, year 1** , 20

Commissioner for taking affidavits
(Type or print name below if signature is illegible.)

Signature
(This form is to be signed in front of a lawyer, justice of the peace, notary public or commissioner for taking affidavits.)

WARNING: **IT IS AN OFFENCE UNDER THE *CRIMINAL CODE* TO KNOWINGLY SWEAR OR AFFIRM A FALSE AFFIDAVIT.**

For information on accessibility of court services for people with disability-related needs, contact: 

Telephone: 416-326-2220 / 1-800-518-7901 TTY: 416-326-4012 / 1-877-425-0575

SCR 15.01-15A (November 1, 2015) CSD

PART II

Debt Collection: Selected Topics

Thus far, the process of suing and obtaining a judgment for debt has been examined. This was followed by a look at the enforcement of judgments in both the Superior Court and in the Small Claims Court. The focus has been on the parts of these procedures that law clerks and paralegals are most likely to be involved with. The focus will now turn to an examination of some legal topics about which paralegals and law clerks should have a basic knowledge.

Collections and Deceased Debtors 12

LEARNING OUTCOMES

After reading this chapter, students will:

- Know how to determine who represents the estate of a deceased debtor.
- Know how to conduct a search to determine whether an estate trustee has been appointed.
- Draft a creditor's letter to an estate trustee.
- Understand when and how an estate trustee will advertise for creditors.
- Comprehend the role of an estate trustee during litigation.
- Know how to commence a claim against an estate.
- Understand the abatement of gifts in order that creditors can be paid.
- Appreciate what to do if an estate is insolvent.

When a debtor dies, as a matter of law, the estate becomes the entity that participates in any collections matter in which the deceased debtor was involved. Although the death of a debtor does not usually create problems in a collections case, there are some procedural steps that must be taken to commence, continue, or conclude an action against a debtor.

Who Represents the Estate?

When a debtor dies, the law requires that the estate of the deceased carry on in the deceased's place and that the estate have a representative to act on its behalf. This means that court proceedings against a debtor will stop upon death, and a creditor will be prevented from enforcing a judgment until a legal representative is available to represent the estate. If the deceased had a will, the creditors will have to wait for a legal representative to take control of the estate and its assets; if there is no will, the creditors will have to wait for a representative to apply to the court for authority to administer the estate. In Ontario, the legal name for an estate representative is an estate trustee with a will or an estate trustee without a will, depending on whether or not there is a will. Most financial institutions still refer to the estate trustee as the executor if there is a will.

certificate of appointment of estate trustee without a will
when a person dies without a will, it is necessary for someone, usually a relative, to apply to the court for a certificate of appointment of estate trustee without a will; until the appointment is made, no one has authority to do anything with the deceased's assets; once an appointment is made, the estate trustee may deal with the estate, settling its debts and distributing remaining assets to relatives in accordance with a statutory formula that determines the shares family members get

estate trustee
the deceased's legal representative for estate administration purposes; the estate trustee may be named in the will or appointed by the court

If a person dies without a will, an individual, usually a relative of the deceased, must apply for a **certificate of appointment of estate trustee without a will**. In Ontario, if a person dies without a will, the *Estates Act*[1] sets out who has first right to apply to be the estate trustee.[2] The deceased's spouse (including a common law spouse) has first right to be estate trustee, followed by the next of kin, which would be the deceased's children, then grandchildren, followed by other descendants. If there are no descendants, then the deceased's parents, followed by their siblings, have the right to apply to be the estate trustee. Where there are no living relatives, the Public Guardian and Trustee may be appointed as the estate trustee. A creditor may apply to be the estate trustee. According to the *Rules of Civil Procedure*,[3] if a party with a prior right to be the estate trustee does not want to be appointed, a renunciation of the position must be filed with the court.[4] Sometimes no one steps forward and applies, or relatives disagree about who should do it. In this case, it may be necessary for some other interested party to make an application, or at least have the court appoint someone to represent the estate for the limited purpose of maintaining the estate during legal proceedings. This estate trustee is called an estate trustee during litigation.

If the debtor has a will in which an **estate trustee** has been named, that person has the authority to deal with the estate's assets from the moment of the deceased's death. However, because the contents of a will may not be known to others, a

1 RSO 1990, c E.21.

2 *Ibid*, s 29(1).

3 RRO 1990, Reg 194.

4 *Ibid*, Rule 74.06(1).

creditor does not necessarily know who the estate trustee is. In most cases, particularly where the deceased owned property, the estate trustee will apply to the registrar of the Superior Court at the court office in the county or regional municipality where the deceased resided for a **certificate of appointment of estate trustee with a will** (formerly known as a grant of "letters probate"). The certificate does not create the authority for the estate trustee to act; that authority was given by the testator in the will itself—the certificate merely confirms the power granted by the will and certifies that the will is authentic. A search will be conducted of the records of the court to see if a certificate has been filed. In some cases, a deceased will have made split wills. Split wills consist of two validly co-existing wills executed by the testator. One will deals with assets that require a court certificate in order to have the assets transferred out of the estate. Real estate and publicly traded shares held solely in the deceased's name are examples of such assets. A second will is drafted to deal with assets that do not require a certificate in order to be transferred out of the estate—for example, jewellery and most privately held shares. The advantage of having the second will is that estate administration tax does not have to be paid on the value of the assets dealt with in the second will.[5] If a creditor is trying to determine from the will what assets the estate may have, inquiries should be made of the estate trustee to determine whether there is another will. The searches described in Chapter 3 can also help the creditor determine the deceased's assets. These searches should be done soon after the deceased's death because, in some cases, assets may be moved into estate accounts and liquidated fairly quickly.

certificate of appointment of estate trustee with a will
confirmation from the court that the will is the deceased's last will and that the estate trustee named in the will is the proper estate trustee

If the debtor left a will but did not name an estate trustee, or the estate trustee predeceased the **testator**, or the estate trustee refuses to act or is unable to act because of a disability, someone close to the debtor—usually a relative—will have to come forward and apply for a "certificate of appointment" (formerly called "letters of administration with the will annexed"). Note that anyone with a recognizable interest in the administration of the estate could be appointed. This includes creditors of the deceased. However, anyone with a prior right to apply to be the estate trustee would have to renounce that right, or the court would have to make an order dispensing with a renunciation.

testator
one who makes a will to dispose of assets upon death

Whether there is a will or not, the person who administers the estate has the task of collecting and valuing the estate assets, determining liabilities, paying creditors, taking proceedings or administrative steps to safeguard assets, and distributing the residue of the estate subject to any **testamentary trusts** that are to be administered into the future. Until the court appoints or, in the case of the will, certifies the appointment of someone to do this job, all proceedings for the collection of

testamentary trust
a trust set up in a will to preserve and administer assets for specific purposes—for example, for a child beneficiary, capital is set aside for investment by a trustee and the income is used for the child's benefit until the child reaches an age set by the trust when the capital can be paid out

5 In the 1990s, the NDP government in Ontario tripled the rate of estate administration tax (formerly known as probate fees) for estates valued at over $50,000. The rate for assets above $50,000 went from $5 per $1,000 of value to $15 per $1,000 of value. To reduce estate administration tax, the practice of preparing split wills for large estates was developed. The practice of using split wills was challenged in the courts. In *Granovsky Estate v Ontario*, 1998 CanLII 14913 (Ont (Gen Div)), the court ruled that the practice was a valid one and that the government, having tripled fees, could not bar people from using split wills to minimize fees.

debts against the deceased are stayed. Once an estate trustee has been appointed or certified, the estate trustee can defend or settle any lawsuit against the deceased. Until an estate trustee is appointed, the estate cannot act or respond, because it does not have an authorized representative in place to do so. A lawsuit against the debtor cannot proceed until an estate trustee has been appointed by the court. This may have dire consequences for a creditor of a deceased debtor who may have to stand by while assets diminish in value.

To see whether an estate trustee has been appointed, search the Superior Court of Justice court records in the court office in the county or regional municipality where the deceased resided at the time of death for a certificate appointing or, in the case of a will, certifying an estate trustee. Anyone with a financial interest in the estate, including creditors, can file a request with the court to receive notice of the commencement of any estate proceedings. If someone applies for a certificate of appointment, anyone who has filed a request for notice will be notified of the application. A request for notice is good for three years, after which time another request may be filed.[6]

Once an estate trustee has been appointed, the legal representative for a creditor (including a creditor who has not commenced any proceedings) should write a letter to the trustee that sets out the details of the debt so that the trustee receives notice of the creditor's claim (see the sample letter on the next page). The tone of this letter should be informative rather than demanding—the estate trustee may know nothing about the deceased's debts, and receipt of this letter may be the first time that the trustee learns of them. However, do insist on a reply within two weeks and a promise of payment. If no response to this letter is received within the time allotted and diarized, advise the client to continue this as a collection matter and be prepared to sue the estate, either directly or through the summary procedure in the *Estates Act*, which is discussed later in this chapter.

An estate trustee has no statutory duty to advertise for creditors, although it is common to do so where the deceased debtor was engaged in business or other activities where it was likely that the deceased had creditors. The reason for this is that estate trustees may be held personally liable if they fail to give adequate notice to creditors of their intention to distribute assets to estate beneficiaries and then go on to distribute estate assets without paying creditors. Normally, estate trustees will protect themselves from this type of liability by advertising on at least two separate occasions, at least one week apart, in a major daily newspaper. At least one month's notice from the date of the first publication should be given to creditors to come forward with their claims. There is no special form, but the notice should provide the name of the deceased and the date of death, and advise creditors to submit claims to the estate trustee by a given date, after which the estate will be distributed.

6 *Supra* note 3 at Rules 74.03(1) and (3).

Sample Letter from Creditor to Estate Trustee

FOOEY, ARGENT
Lawyers
43 Cutpurse Road
Toronto, ON M4R 1D6
416-223-4567
fax 416-223-4566

January 31, year 0

Ms. Mary Cashedin
100 Moor Hen Way
Toronto, ON M5Q 1W2

Dear Ms. Cashedin:

RE: The Estate of William Cashedin, Deceased

We are lawyers for Triple Q Finance Ltd. According to court records, we understand that you are the estate trustee of the deceased, having been named executor in his will.

Our client loaned the late Mr. Cashedin $27,000 on January 1, year −1 with interest at 12 percent per annum. Mr. Cashedin provided our client with a promissory note in which he promised to pay the sum of $30,240 on January 1, year 0 to discharge this loan. As of this date, that sum remains outstanding and interest continues to accumulate, since the due date, at $8.88 per day.

To avoid further interest charges, we would appreciate it if you would give this matter your urgent attention and now ask that you pay the sum of $30,595.20, including interest, on or before February 10, year 0, so that this debt can be discharged. Please make your cheque payable to "Fooey, Argent in Trust."

A copy of the promissory note is enclosed.

Yours very truly,

Filbert Fooey

Filbert Fooey

Enclosure

The estate trustee's address (usually in care of the estate trustee's lawyer) must also be included. A sample notice to creditors is provided in the box on this page.

Sample Notice to Creditors

Notice to Creditors and Others

IN THE ESTATE OF [*name of deceased*]

ALL CLAIMS against the Estate of [*name of deceased*], late of the [*City of* _________, *Province of* _________], who died on [*date of death*], must be filed with the undersigned estate trustee on or before the [*give date, which is usually at least one month from date of first publication of ad*], after which date the estate will be distributed having regard only to the claims of which the estate trustee then shall have notice.

DATED at [*city*], this [___] day of [*month*], [*year*].

[*name of estate trustee*]
Estate trustee of the estate of
[*deceased's name*]

[*give firm name and address*]
Lawyer for the Estate trustee

intestate, intestacy when a person dies without having made a valid will, they are said to have died intestate; dying without a will creates an intestacy, which is a situation where the estate has to be administered without a will

Legal representatives involved in a collections practice should get into the habit of reading the legal notices in the business section of their local newspapers to watch for any notice that might be relevant to one of their clients. Once notice has been given, the estate trustee may distribute estate assets if no creditor has made a claim within the time provided for in the notice (usually one month from the time of the first publication of the notice). If the debtor died **intestate**, the estate trustee must advertise for creditors, as described here, or in the alternative, must wait at least one year from the date of the deceased's death to distribute estate assets. While these steps will protect the estate trustee from personal liability, a creditor who has not notified the estate trustee before distribution may still be able to bring an action. If there are assets that can be "traced" from the estate to others, the creditor may be able to enforce a judgment against traceable assets in the hands of beneficiaries or other creditors who made claims against the estate in a timely manner.[7]

Appointing an Estate Trustee During Litigation

If the validity of a will is contested, the certificate of appointment will be held up until the matter is settled and no one will represent the estate, perhaps for years. In

7 An estate trustee who is also the sole beneficiary of the estate will usually not advertise for creditors. Although the ad would absolve the estate trustee from liability to unknown creditors, there would still be liability in the estate trustee's capacity as beneficiary.

this situation, the creditor in an existing action, or on bringing an action, might consider making a motion to the court in which the will is being challenged for advice and directions and to ask that an **estate trustee during litigation** be appointed for the limited purpose of tending to the estate's interests during the litigation. The estate trustee in this situation may well be the named trustee, but, in the absence of a court order, this trustee has no authority to pay anything out of the estate until the validity of the will has been determined by the court. During litigation, an estate trustee generally maintains an estate, attending to such tasks as income tax return filings and maintaining insurance on estate property. At any time, such a trustee can seek direction from the court as to how to proceed in a given situation.

estate trustee during litigation
a person appointed by the court to act for the estate when there is a dispute about the validity of the will or about who should administer the estate; during litigation the estate trustee has control of estate assets but has no authority to make payouts until the court has dealt with the validity of the will or decided who should administer the estate

The procedure for appointing an estate trustee during litigation is as follows: If an action has been commenced to contest the will, bring a motion to the court where the litigation is occurring; if one has not been commenced, the creditor may bring an application in the court location where the deceased debtor resided. Either the motion or the application should be accompanied by an affidavit setting out why the creditor is applying to have an estate trustee during litigation appointed. An estate trustee will be appointed during litigation when no one is administering, or is likely to administer, the estate in a timely manner. In some cases, the named estate trustee may suffer from a disability and be unable to carry out the responsibilities of an estate trustee. In other cases, there may be issues about the validity of the will that require the appointment of a neutral trustee during litigation. The affidavit should describe the assets in the estate and their value, to the extent the affiant knows them. Lastly, the affiant should request that an estate trustee during litigation be appointed. Along with the affidavit, the creditor should also file the written consent of the proposed trustee to act and, if the creditor can get them, the consents of potential beneficiaries to the estate. The consents should be accompanied by sworn or affirmed affidavits of execution that confirm that the consents were validly executed. If the court is satisfied with the application or motion on the merits, it will appoint the estate trustee during litigation.

Types of Estate Trustees

Estate trustee with a will	a person named in a will to act and administer an estate
Estate trustee without a will	usually a relative, appointed and authorized by the court to administer the estate of an individual who died without a will
Estate trustee during litigation	a person appointed and approved by the court to represent the interests of the estate and to protect the estate if there is a dispute about the validity of a will or a dispute about who should act as estate trustee

Procedure for Making a Claim Against the Estate

Under the *Estates Act* there is a procedure that allows a creditor to establish a claim against the deceased's estate or to continue a separate action against the estate that was originally brought against the debtor. To take advantage of this procedure, it is necessary to wait for an estate trustee to be appointed.

Continuing an Existing Proceeding

If the creditor sued the debtor and the debtor died before judgment was obtained, the lawsuit is stayed until an estate trustee is in place. When the estate trustee is in place, the creditor may obtain an order to proceed against the estate by transmission of interest to the estate under Rule 11 of the *Rules of Civil Procedure*,[8] which is obtained by a requisition (see Figure 12.1) in the court where the action was started, requesting that the action be permitted to continue against the estate. The requisition must be supported by an affidavit (see Figure 12.2) that sets out the facts on which transmission of liability from the deceased to the estate is based. On the basis of these documents, an order (see Figure 12.3) will be made permitting the action to continue against "Mary Cashedin, estate trustee of William Cashedin." The plaintiff may now continue the action.

Commencing a Claim Against an Estate

Where a creditor has a claim against a debtor who has died, or a claim against the estate that became due after the debtor died, it is advisable to contact the estate trustee to see about having it paid (see the sample letter on page 381). If the claim is not paid, providing that an estate trustee has been appointed, it is possible to pursue the claim against the estate using a summary procedure under section 44 of the *Estates Act* in the estates office of the Superior Court.

If a claim is presented to an estate trustee who declines to pay it and also declines to contest it, the creditor must proceed in the ordinary way by suing the estate in the Superior Court. If the estate trustee declines to pay, a notice of contestation may be issued, which brings the summary procedure in the *Estates Act* into play. The creditor now has 30 days from receipt of the notice of contestation to file a statement of claim, although the creditor can apply for leave to the court for a further three months to file. An affidavit must be filed with the statement of claim, verifying the claim, as well as a copy of the notice of contestation. When this is done, the matter is set down for trial without any further pre-trial proceedings. At trial, the court may require all those with an interest in the outcome to be given notice of proceedings. This order will usually affect estate beneficiaries. If the beneficiaries are minors, in order to protect their interests, notice must be given to the Children's Lawyer.

---

8 *Supra* note 3.

Payment of Creditors

The estate trustee, once satisfied that a debt is legitimate, must usually pay the creditor. With the exception of some family law claims, creditors have priority over most beneficiaries. The creditor will usually be required to sign a release of any further interest in the estate before the funds are released. In some cases, the estate may not have enough assets to pay all of its debts. If this is the case, the estate trustee must abate (reduce) inheritances to free up money to pay the creditors. Inheritances are usually abated in the following order:

1. The residue of the estate is abated. Residue is that part of the estate left over after all gifts have been paid.
2. General legacies are then abated. General legacies are non-specific gifts to a beneficiary; for example, "I give my spouse $25,000."
3. Demonstrative legacies abate next. Demonstrative legacies are gifts where the source of a gift is set out in the will; for example, if someone leaves $10,000 from a certain account to their spouse.
4. Specific legacies abate last. A specific legacy is a particular gift to a beneficiary, such as a car.

If there is no estate trustee, a creditor may file a notice of the claim, verified by an affidavit, in the estates office in the jurisdiction where the deceased resided. This will serve to give public notice to others of a claim against the estate.

An estate trustee has a choice about using the *Estates Act* summary procedure. If the claim is within the jurisdiction of the Small Claims Court, it should proceed in that court in the ordinary way. The estate trustee may object, in which case the claim could proceed under the *Estates Act* procedure. However, any claim for more than $800[9] may, at the estate trustee's request, be brought in the Superior Court in the ordinary way, which would bring it under the Rule 76 simplified procedure. There seems very little use in doing this because Rule 76 also provides for a summary procedure—unless there is a reason to opt out of the simplified procedure too.

If the creditor establishes a claim, leave of the court is required to enforce the order against the estate. This can be done during or at the conclusion of the hearing so that leave to enforce can be included in the judgment. The judgment can then be filed in the court office in the county or regional municipality where the deceased resided or had property, to be enforced in the usual ways.

Insolvent Estates

If an estate's liabilities exceed its assets, the estate trustee should request leave of the court to file an assignment in bankruptcy. If not, all debtors share on a pro rata basis, regardless of the nature of the debt. Bankruptcy is likely to give the beneficiaries more protection from creditors than they would otherwise have if the estate is insolvent. A creditor may also petition an insolvent estate into bankruptcy. A debtor who owes between $5,000 and $250,000 may make a consumer proposal to deal with the debts. Leave of the court to have the proposal approved is required. However, if a creditor's claim is small and the estate is insolvent, it may be best to write the debt off.

9 *Supra* note 1, section 44(6).

CHAPTER SUMMARY

When a debtor dies, steps must be taken by a creditor to continue to try to collect the debt. The estate of the debtor is responsible for carrying out the obligations of the debtor. Court proceedings against the debtor must stop until an estate trustee takes charge of the estate. When that happens, the litigation can continue, naming the estate and its trustee, because the debtor is no longer personally a party to the proceeding. Who the estate trustee is depends on whether or not the debtor made a will. In some cases no representative comes forward. When this happens, someone with an interest in the estate must apply to represent it. In some cases, a creditor may also apply to have a representative appointed for the sole purpose of completing litigation already under way against the debtor. In other cases, a claim made against an estate may be the continuation of an existing proceeding. In such a case, steps must be taken to replace the name of the debtor with that of the estate trustee. This chapter also set out other matters to consider when commencing proceedings against an estate. The chapter concluded with an examination of whether litigation against an estate is either worthwhile or possible.

KEY TERMS

certificate of appointment of estate trustee with a will, 379
certificate of appointment of estate trustee without a will, 378
estate trustee, 378
estate trustee during litigation, 383
intestate, intestacy, 382
testamentary trust, 379
testator, 379

REVIEW QUESTIONS

1. Your client has come to you with the news that a debtor who owes her money has just died. Your client wonders whether this will cause any problems. Explain what the consequences of the debtor's death might be.
2. Explain what needs to be done before an estate trustee can act where
   a. the debtor died without leaving a will;
   b. the debtor died leaving a will; and
   c. the debtor died leaving a will, but there is a dispute about its validity.
3. How do you know if an estate has an estate trustee?
4. What are the duties of an estate trustee?
5. How does an estate trustee obtain protection from personal liability on claims from creditors of the estate?
6. In what circumstances is an estate trustee during litigation appointed?
7. Explain how an order for transmission of interest to an estate is obtained.
8. If your client has a claim against an estate but has not commenced proceedings, what options does the client have in pursuing the claim?
9. What options does your client have as creditor of an estate in which the liabilities are greater than the assets?

CASE STUDY

MEMO

DATE: April 15, year 0
TO: Litigation Clerk
FROM: U.R. Ruffled
RE: Snorkelpus Investments Ltd v Deer-Lee Departed

Our client Snorkelpus started an action against Deer-Lee Departed for failure to repay a personal loan in the amount of $33,000. The loan was due on August 4, year −1 and has not been paid off. We commenced proceedings in the Superior Court on September 3, year −1. Deer-Lee Departed died on November 3, year −1, having filed a statement of defence. We have determined that the deceased did not have a will and that Deer-Lee's husband, Dogpart Departed, applied for and obtained a certificate of appointment of estate trustee without a will, on December 3, year −1, from the Superior Court offices at Toronto.

Draft the necessary documents to obtain an order of transmission of interest to the estate.

FIGURE 12.1 Requisition

Court file no. 4567

ONTARIO

SUPERIOR COURT OF JUSTICE

BETWEEN:

TRIPLE Q FINANCE LTD.

Plaintiff

and

WILLIAM CASHEDIN

Defendant

REQUISITION

TO THE LOCAL REGISTRAR at Toronto

I REQUIRE

An order to continue this proceeding originally commenced in this court, amending the title of proceedings to "Triple Q Finance Ltd." as plaintiff and "Mary Cashedin, estate trustee of the Estate of William Cashedin," as defendant.

THE GROUNDS FOR THIS REQUISITION ARE:

1. The affidavit of Filbert Fooey, sworn February 25, year 0.
2. The certificate of appointment of estate trustee with a will issued by the registrar of this court on December 10, year –1 appointing Mary Cashedin as the estate trustee with a will of the estate of William Cashedin.
3. Rule 11.02 of the *Rules of Civil Procedure*.

February 27, year 0

FOOEY, ARGENT
Lawyers
43 Cutpurse Road
Toronto, ON M4R 1D6

Filbert Fooey (66591F)

ffooey@fooeyargent.ca

416-223-4567
fax 416-223-4566

Lawyers for the Plaintiff

RCP-E 4E (July 1, 2007)

FIGURE 12.2 Affidavit

Court file no. 4567

ONTARIO

SUPERIOR COURT OF JUSTICE

BETWEEN:

TRIPLE Q FINANCE LTD.

Plaintiff

and

WILLIAM CASHEDIN

Defendant

AFFIDAVIT

I, Filbert Fooey, of the City of Toronto, MAKE OATH AND SAY:

1. I am a partner in the law firm of Fooey, Argent, lawyers for the plaintiff in this action, and have knowledge of the matters set out in this affidavit.
2. On November 3, year –1, on the instructions of the plaintiff, our firm commenced proceedings against the defendant, now deceased, for payment on a promissory note.
3. On November 15, year –1 the defendant died.
4. On December 10, year –1, the certificate of appointment of estate trustee with a will was issued by the registrar of this court confirming Mary Cashedin as the estate trustee of the Estate of William Cashedin. Attached to this affidavit and marked exhibit "A" is a true copy of the certificate issued by the court.
5. The lawyers for the plaintiff now request that the local registrar grant an order permitting this proceeding to continue and naming Mary Cashedin, estate trustee of the estate of William Cashedin, as defendant.

SWORN before me at the	)	
	)	
City of Toronto,	)	
	)	______________________
this 25th day of February, year 0	)	Filbert Fooey
	)	
	)	
A commissioner, etc.	)	

RCP-E 4D (July 1, 2007)

FIGURE 12.3 Order to Continue (Transfer or Transmission of Interest)

Court file no. 4567

ONTARIO

SUPERIOR COURT OF JUSTICE

B E T W E E N:

TRIPLE Q FINANCE LTD.

Plaintiff

and

WILLIAM CASHEDIN

Defendant

ORDER

ON THE REQUISITION of the plaintiff and on reading the affidavit of Filbert Fooey, sworn February 25, year 0, filed, and on reading the certificate appointing Mary Cashedin as estate trustee with a will, dated December 10, year –1,

IT IS ORDERED that this proceeding continue with Triple Q Finance as plaintiff and Mary Cashedin, estate trustee of William Cashedin, as defendant, and that the title of proceeding be amended as noted in this order on all documents issued, served, or filed after the date of this order.

Dated: February 27, year 0.

____

Local Registrar

RCP-E 11A (November 1, 2005)

Construction Liens 13

LEARNING OUTCOMES

After reading this chapter, students will:

- Understand the basic problems that construction lien legislation was designed to solve.
- Understand what the construction pyramid is and how it works to funnel payments from the owner to those who improved the property.
- Understand how the holdback system works to ensure payment to those who do not have privity of contract with the payer.
- Understand the nature and function of a trust under the Act.
- Understand how the lien system works to ensure payment for those who improve a property.
- Understand the purpose of the prompt payment system and how it works to ensure that those who improve a property are paid.
- Know how to determine which court will hear a construction lien dispute.
- Be familiar with the procedural requirements for starting and proceeding with a lien claim.
- Know how to prepare and register a lien in order to preserve it for a client.
- Know when and how to perfect a lien by drafting and issuing a statement of claim.
- Know how to vacate a claim for lien.

Rationale and Basic Principles

Construction lien legislation has existed in Ontario since 1875. The rationale behind such legislation dealt with the fact that, prior to its implementation, trades persons, labourers, and material suppliers, if they were not paid for the work done or the materials supplied, normally only had the right to sue the person they contracted with for breach of contract. In other words, there was no special right to attach the claim for payment to the increased value of the real property that their efforts had improved and make the owner of the property, who benefitted from the work, at least partly responsible for payment. Other creditors who had priority rights—such as mortgagees—would have the right to seize the property to satisfy the debts owing to them, while those who had improved the value of the property but who had not received payment would have to wait in line with other ordinary judgment creditors, often recovering little or nothing of what was owed to them. By giving **lien** rights to those who improved the property, the legislation ensured that they would be able to attach their claim to the value of the property and secure payment by being able to claim directly on the value of the property they improved. In effect, this meant that if a labourer or supplier was not paid by the construction contractor with whom they were dealing, they could ultimately make a claim against the owner of the property that had been improved, even though there was no contract between the property owner and the supplier or labourer. But for construction lien legislation, the **privity of contract** rule would have restricted the unpaid worker or supplier to a claim against the party they contracted with, and the owner would have been free of any claim even though the owner benefitted financially from the work done.

lien
a claim to a right to sell or seize property, either real or personal, on the fulfillment of certain conditions

privity of contract
a rule that only parties to a contract can enforce contract rights

In addition to creating lien rights, legislation also provided for a summary construction lien trial process that was designed to be quick and inexpensive to save workers and small trades persons the cost and delay of more formal and complicated legal proceedings.

Although the original legislation was designed to benefit small trades persons and labourers, it also applied to large projects where the players included large construction companies and contractors, large property owners, complex ownership arrangements, and large financial institutions as lenders. The result was that, when a large project got into trouble, hundreds of lien claims were filed, and the banks and lien claimants would make conflicting claims about which parties' claims had priority. Scores of lawyers would become involved, and a construction lien action became horrendously complicated and expensive. What was originally designed to be a simple, non-technical, summary process became more complicated and difficult to manage than an ordinary civil action in the Superior Court.

Construction Lien Legislation

While the original legislation worked well for small construction projects, it was dysfunctional and procedurally inadequate when it came to dealing with modern, complex construction projects. The original *Construction Lien Act*[1] was amended on

1 *Construction Lien Act*, RSO 1990, c C.30, as amended.

a number of occasions and given a major overhaul in 1983. But it became increasingly obvious that disputes involving large projects were too costly and very time consuming to resolve; the process needed procedural changes that would simplify the payment system and resolve disputes more quickly. Smaller projects were also facing challenges given the short time period provided in which to put a lien on a property and the need to follow through with a Superior Court claim.

As a result of the foregoing, the Ontario government introduced a bill called the *Construction Lien Amendment Act, 2017* (CLAA 2017),[2] which changed the name of the *Construction Lien Act* to the *Construction Act* (the Act).[3] As it did before, the Act still gives those persons whose work results in an improvement to real property a right to place a lien on that property for the value of the work done. If those doing work or furnishing materials are not paid, they can exercise their lien rights by forcing the sale of the property and obtaining their money from the sale proceeds. The Act provides a holdback system to ensure that there is a pool of funds from which to pay subcontractors, suppliers, and tradespeople. Further, the Act provides a remedy for a breach of trust action. A breach of trust action does not require a registered lien and may be brought directly in Small Claims Court if the remedy is within the monetary jurisdiction of the Small Claims Court.[4]

In addition, the Act, as amended, will include some changes that reflect and support current construction industry practices and will address concerns that have been voiced by many parties involved in the construction industry. These include changes to rules with regard to invoicing and payment deadlines, a new expedited adjudication system, and new rules related to record keeping and trust payments.

The Prompt Payment System

The new legislation features a prompt payment system to ensure that all of the parties involved make scheduled payments, with the owner and general contractor agreeing on a payment schedule governing payments between themselves, between the contractor and subcontractors, and between subcontractors and other subcontractors. The prompt payment system is triggered by the delivery of a proper invoice.[5] (See the Proposed Prompt Payment Timeline illustration that follows.) The owner and contractor first agree on dates by which invoices to the owner will be delivered. If they cannot agree on dates, then invoices will be submitted on a monthly basis (assuming that work is ongoing over months, as is the case on large construction projects). After receiving an invoice, the owner is responsible for paying the general contractor within 28 days. Then, the general contractor is responsible for paying the subcontractors

2 The *Construction Lien Amendment Act, 2017* passed third reading on December 5, 2017, and received royal assent on December 12, 2017. Bill 142 updated the *Construction Lien Act*. The Act has been renamed the *Construction Act*. Note that attention should be paid to s 87.3, as it sets out when some of the changes set out in the amending act come into force.

3 *Supra* note 2, s 1, as amended.

4 The Ontario government is considering increasing the monetary jurisdiction of the Small Claims Court to $50,000, but there has been no official announcement as of the date of publication.

5 *Supra* note 2, new s 6.1.

Proposed Prompt Payment Timeline

Ontario is proposing new rules to prevent late payments on construction projects. The following deadlines would come into effect as soon as an invoice is submitted to the owner of the project.

1. Owner receives invoice

The invoice is submitted by the contractor to the owner.

28 DAYS

2. Owner pays invoice

The owner is required to pay the general contractor within 28 days of receiving the invoice.

7 DAYS

3. Contractor pays subcontractor

The general contractor is required to pay the subcontractor within 7 days after receiving payment from the owner.

7 DAYS

4. Subcontractor pays other subcontractors

The subcontractor is required to pay other subcontractors within 7 days. The 7 day period continues until all parties involved in supplying services or materials for the project are paid.

Note: This illustration was made prior to enactment of the new *Construction Act* but the procedure shown has been legislated into place.

within 7 days. The subcontractors have to pay their subcontractors within 7 days, and so on through the layers of subcontracts, until everyone has been paid.[6]

If there is a dispute about the amount owing or about the quality of the work done, an owner may deliver a notice of nonpayment within 14 days of receiving the invoice from the general contractor. Because the flow of funds from the general contractor to subcontractors will dry up as a result of the nonpayment, successive subcontractors down the line, who might not be able to pay their subcontractors, will be able to deliver a notice of nonpayment to those below them within 7 days of having received a notice of nonpayment from a contractor from whom payment had been expected.

Because payments will be delayed until resolution of the matter, the Act provides for mandatory interest on late payments. Any party to the construction contract, including an unsatisfied property owner or a party who has not been paid, can now refer the matter for adjudication under the new dispute resolution process (discussed below). If an adjudication order is not obeyed by the property owner, the contractor may suspend further work on the project. The matter will then have to be sorted out under the Act with liens being registered and regular court proceedings commenced.

Interim Adjudication System

The Act includes an interim adjudication system to prevent or quickly sort out payment disputes when a party raises an objection related to the work done, the amount charged, the amount paid or not paid, or the timelines for payment. The process is designed to be quick and inexpensive with the goal of resolving contract disputes, where possible, in a manner that speeds up payments and minimizes any delays in construction work. Under the previous legislation, a payment dispute could stop the flow of funds from owners to contractors and subcontractors, with liens being filed, bringing a project to a halt and generating a complicated and very costly construction lien action in Superior Court that might take months, if not years, to resolve.

Here is how the interim adjudication system works. (See the Prompt Payment, Dispute & Adjudication Process illustration that follows.) Any party to a payment dispute may ask for an adjudication. If, for example, an owner receives an invoice from the contractor and disputes the amount charged and/or the quality of the work, the owner can, instead of paying the invoice, send a notice of nonpayment to the contractor within 14 days of receiving the invoice. The notice must set out

6 *Ibid*, ss 6(1), (2), as amended.

the amount that is not being paid and give reasons why payment is not being made.[7] This triggers an informal dispute resolution process in the form of an inquiry to be carried out by a person with dispute resolution training and construction knowledge and experience. The parties can establish their own procedure, or use the procedure set out in the Act. After adjudication, if the parties agree on the amount owing, the payer pays, and if the parties accept the decision as final, that ends the matter. If the payer refuses to pay, the party deemed to be eligible for payment by the adjudicator may stop work under the contract. The adjudicator's decision is not appealable, but may be challenged by way of judicial review in the Superior Court later if it is alleged that the adjudicator was biased or if it is alleged that the adjudicator made a decision on the basis of something that was not relevant, or otherwise misapplied the law.

If the payer fails to pay some or all of the amount ordered or another party disputes the decision, the parties may continue to use ordinary legal remedies with respect to what is in dispute between them. The aim here is to quickly resolve a dispute about payment so that funds begin to flow, and the construction project can continue while any dispute between contracting parties is sorted out later, between the contracting parties, without stopping the flow of funds to contractors and imperiling the whole project.[8]

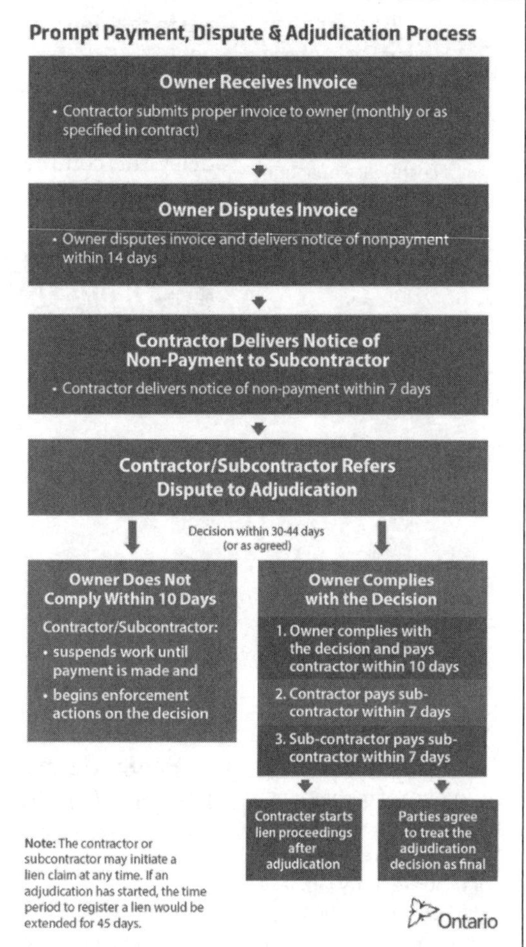

Liens and Holdbacks

The definition of "owner" under the Act has been broadened considerably to cover various kinds of joint ventures, where there are multiple owners, and in particular, leasehold improvements, so that both the leaseholder and the landlord may be considered owners under the Act. The Crown is not subject to liens, but protection has now been extended to subcontractors if the general contractor files for bankruptcy on projects to which the Crown is a party, by requiring the general contractor to secure payment on public sector projects by posting a surety bond. Like Crown property, municipal property is now clearly not subject to liens.[9]

preserve a lien
a right to lien is preserved by registering a claim for lien on title within 60 days of the last work done on the property

The time period for a contractor to **preserve a lien** has increased from 45 to 60 days from the last day that work was done or materials were supplied. The time to

7 *Ibid*, new s 6.3(2).

8 *Ibid*, s 11(1).

9 *Ibid*, ss 16, ss 17(4), and 31 as amended; new Part XI.1 and s 85.2.

perfect a lien
a lien that has been preserved is perfected by commencing legal proceedings and filing a certificate of action within 90 days of preserving the lien

perfect a lien changed from a period of 45 days after preservation to a period of 90 days. The purpose of the extensions is to allow more time to resolve disputes outside of court. In order to perfect a lien, a court action must be commenced. Increasing the time to preserve and perfect from 90 days overall to 150 days will, hopefully, delay the commencement of proceedings and facilitate settlement discussions.[10] During an adjudication, the time periods are put on hold.

Timeline for Perfecting and Preserving a Lien

Last work done or materials furnished

↓

60 days

↓

Preserve the lien

↓

90 days

↓

Pefect the lien

holdback
an amount of money (note that under the CLAA 2017, a letter of credit, a bond, or other security can take the place of money) kept back from the amount due to the contractor that is not paid but is held in trust by the owner until the dispute is resolved, the time for filing a lien has expired, or a registered lien has been discharged or satisfied

Holdbacks must now be paid if the timeline for filing a lien has passed without a lien being filed. The purpose of this change is to create greater certainty about when contractors and subcontractors will be paid out of a holdback so that they can better control the finances of their own operations.[11]

Any lien claim for an amount within the monetary jurisdiction of the Small Claims Court may be heard in the Small Claims Court, if referred there by a Superior Court judge after an action has been started in Superior Court. Proceedings in the Small Claims Court will follow the procedures of the Small Claims Court to the extent they do not conflict with procedural requirements set out in the *Construction Act* or in its regulations. Because the amended Act eliminates some of the court procedures specified in the previous version of the Act in favour of reliance on rules of procedure under the *Courts of Justice Act*[12] (for both the Superior and Small Claims Court), it can be expected that a construction lien claim will proceed like other claims. Another result of this shift to the Small Claims Court is that paralegals may take on lien cases in this court. In the past, lien actions could only be heard in the Superior Court. Holdback matters that fall within the monetary jurisdiction of the Small Claims Court will continue to be heard in the Small Claims Court.[13] Construction lien litigation is specialized work. Most lawyers refer complex construction lien cases to firms that specialize in this type of work. New procedures with the

10 *Ibid*, s 31, as amended.

11 *Ibid*, ss 26, 27; new ss 22(4), 26.1, 26.2.

12 RSO 1900, c C-43.

13 *Supra* note 2, s 58, as amended.

2017 amendments are designed to reduce cost and delay, but they do not simplify the Act's procedural requirements.

The Construction Pyramid

There may be a succession of contractors and subcontractors involved in a construction project, with various linked contracts. The operation of the Act can best be understood by thinking of a construction project as a pyramid, with the owner at the top, the general contractor with whom there is a building contract under the owner, the subcontractors under the general contractor, and subcontractors of subcontractors further down, and so on. Each level of contractual relations represents a class of claimants. Moving further down the contractual chain from the owner, there are more and more class members as the classes become larger, which gives the contractual linkages and relationships a pyramid shape, as in the diagram below.

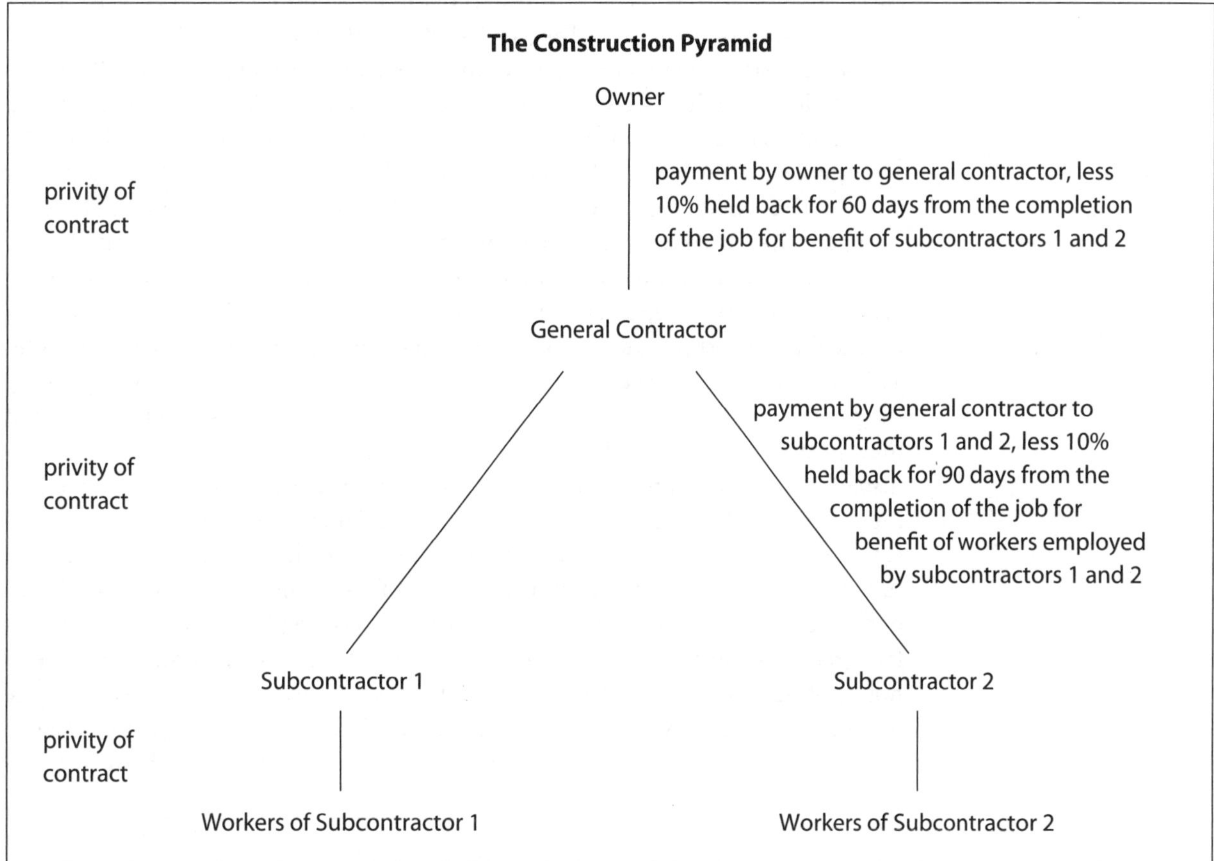

There are some other things in the construction pyramid that require explanation. First, notice that each class, or layer, shares the same class of payers—in the diagram above, the class of subcontractors is paying the class of workers.

Subcontractors include persons who supply services or materials to improve the property. Improvement is defined in the Act to mean:

> (a) any alteration, addition or repair to the land,
> (b) any construction, erection or installation on the land, including the installation of industrial, mechanical, electrical or other equipment on the land or on any building, structure, or works on the land that is essential to the normal or intended use of the land, building, structure or works, or
> (c) the complete or partial demolition or removal of any building, structure, or works on the land.[14]

What defines the class relationship is that there is privity of contract between the classes. Also notice that another relationship is illustrated—that is, the general contractor, in paying the subcontractor class, holds back 10 percent of the amount due until all liens that may be claimed have expired, or have been satisfied, discharged, or vacated (see s 26 of the Act). Lien claimants generally have 60 days from the date that they completed their work or last supplied materials to make a claim for lien. A payer holds back 10 percent for those who are two steps or classes below the payer on the construction pyramid. This is illustrated in the box on page 397.

The holdback is mandatory; parties to construction contracts are not allowed to waive holdback rights (see s 22(1) of the Act, as amended). Any agreement to waive such rights is illegal and unenforceable in the courts. The box on page 399 provides an example to show how the holdback works. When the owner pays the $10,000 that is due to the general contractor, 10 percent of the total, being the amount of $1,000 (or under the CLAA 2017, provision of security, a bond, or a letter of credit in that amount), must be held back from the payment. This money is held in trust for the subcontractors two steps below the general contractor. If subcontractors are not paid within a short period of time (now defined by the new prompt payment rules as 7 days from the day the general contractor or contractor above them is paid) by the general contractor, they may register a claim for lien against the property, and they must do so within 60 days of the last day work was done or materials were furnished. If no claim is made within the 60-day period, then the holdback moneys must be released, in this case by the owner to the general contractor. In a large project, a contract supervisor, usually an engineering firm, is required by the Act to function as a payment certifier and give notice of the payment in the form and manner prescribed by the regulations,[15] in which case those with lien rights have 60 days from receiving notice of payment to register their liens. When an owner receives a notice of lien, either by searching the property's title or by receiving notice of the lien directly, the owner must make the holdback available to the lien claimants. Once this is done, the lien claimants must take their claim out of the holdback. The

---

14 *Ibid*, s 1(1).

15 *Supra* note 2, s 2(1), as amended. Publication in a "construction trade newspaper" is no longer a requirement.

owner is then discharged from any further obligation, and the liens are vacated and cease to be a claim on the land. If the holdback is insufficient to fully compensate the lien claimant, the court action may be continued for the shortfall against the person with whom there is a contract.

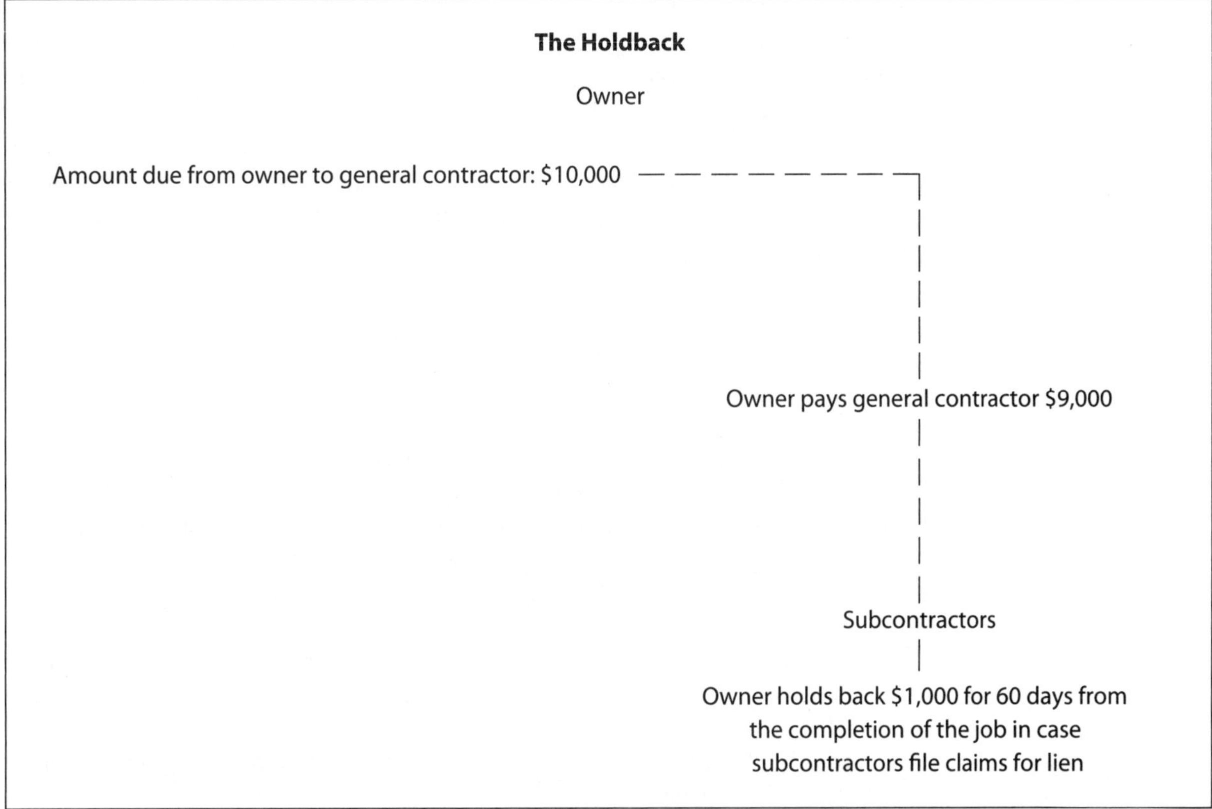

If the owner failed to retain the holdback, or retained it but did not observe the trust requirements and spent the holdback on something else, then the lien holders may enforce their lien rights against the property and force its sale. On both large and small projects, the failure to retain a holdback or make payments on the principal contract occurs from time to time. Many construction projects, particularly large ones, are financed by banks and other financial institutions. On a large project, the lender will approve a building mortgage where the amount loaned is paid out in installments as stages of the construction are completed rather than in one payment of the total amount. When the owner receives an installment at the completion of a stage of the project (called a progress draw), the owner pays the general contractor, in accordance with the prompt payment timetable set out in the parties' contract or by default with the government-set payment schedule. The general contactor in turn uses the money to pay subcontractors, and so on down the pyramid. In effect, everyone is relying on the bank to provide the cash to keep the project going. If one contractor in the chain of contracts defaults on payments, there may be interim adjudication to sort the matter out, or a flurry of liens may be registered. This, in turn, may cause the bank to suspend further payments, triggering yet more liens from other classes of lien claimants and bringing the project to a halt. Disputes may also arise about who among claimants and the bank has priority for eventual payout if the building is sold in a lien action, further complicating matters. On smaller projects, a payer with a cash flow problem who is late or who defaults on paying workers may trigger lien claims and bring the project to a halt.

Because the Act is intended to create a simple and quick remedy for tradespeople and construction workers, it permits a Superior Court judge, where the monetary value of the claim is within the monetary jurisdiction of the Small Claims Court, to refer the matter to the Small Claims Court to be heard there. Otherwise the matter will proceed in the Superior Court. Holdback disputes within the monetary jurisdiction of the Small Claims Court may continue to be brought in that court without the need for a referral from a Superior Court judge.

A Simple Construction Claim

The Scenario

Hi Volt Electrical Ltd. (Hi Volt) is an electrical contractor. Hi Volt was retained by Nicholas Construction Ltd. (Nicholas) to do the electrical work on a small office building owned by Real Land Inc. (Real Land). The building is located at 328 Banburn Drive, Toronto, ON M6R 3Y6. On May 5, year 0, Hi Volt entered into a contract with Nicholas to do the electrical work. The contract price was $180,000. The contract set out that payments were to be made in installments of $60,000 each on August 1, September 1, and October 1, year 0. Hi Volt began work, supplying materials and labour from June 1, year 0 to August 31, year 0. When Hi Volt was not paid on August 1, it decided to stop work on August 31. On September 22, Hi Volt made a written demand to Real Land for payment from the holdback. On September 30, Hi Volt registered a claim for lien. Having received no reply from either Real Land or Nicholas, Hi Volt wishes to exercise its lien rights and sell the land. Under the Act, an owner with a dispute as to the amount owed or the quality of the work can deliver a notice of non-payment to the general contractor within 14 days of the last day worked. The general contractor then has 7 days to respond.[16]

Description of the Lien

Because Hi Volt has supplied materials and labour to improve the property, it is entitled to claim a lien against the property for the value of the work done. It is also entitled to claim all of its contract remedies against Nicholas with whom it has privity of contract. If Real Land had kept a holdback on payments to Nicholas, Hi Volt would share in the holdback on a pro rata basis with other lien claimants who also had Nicholas as a payer and who had privity of contract with Nicholas. If the owner

16 *Supra* note 2, new Part I.1 and ss 7, 8.

failed to hold back the legally required 10 percent of the payment, the owner can be sued for the shortfall.

Who May File a Lien?

Anyone who furnishes materials, services, or labour to improve a particular property may file a lien. This includes contractors, subcontractors, employees of contractors and subcontractors, material suppliers, equipment renters, engineers, and design professionals, including architects. Thus, Hi Volt can file a lien as a supplier of materials and services, and Hi Volt's employees, suppliers, and equipment renters on this job could file liens if Hi Volt failed to pay them.

What May Be Liened?

If a supplier of materials or services supplies them for use on an identifiable property and can prove their incorporation or use on that property, then a lien may attach to the owner's interest. In this scenario, Hi Volt, as a supplier of electrical contracting services that improved the value of the building, can lien the owner's interest in the property. Note that if the lien arises after a mortgage, the mortgagee has priority and the lien claim may be made only against the **owner's equity** that remains after the mortgage loan has been paid off. Also, the lien claim is limited to the value of the improvements, not the price of the contract. Hi Volt, for example, has a $180,000 contract, but if they had only done $60,000 worth of work before they abandoned the contract because of nonpayment, their lien claim would be limited to $60,000 against the property. Real Land may argue that Hi Volt did far less than $60,000 worth of work (or that the work was defective). Hi Volt's dispute with Nicholas, however, may well be for more than the $60,000 that was due—there is the loss to Hi Volt of the profit had the contract been completed and other losses associated with the breach of contract that would be available to Hi Volt in its claim against Nicholas.

owner's equity
refers to how much of a property's value is actually that of the owner's—for example, if a house is worth $500,000 and is mortgaged for $250,000, the mortgagee is entitled to $250,000 to cover what is owing by the owner on the mortgage loan; the remaining $250,000 is free and clear of the mortgage claim and is the owner's equity in the house

Holdbacks

As noted, the owner, and any other payer in the pyramid, must hold back 10 percent of any payment made for the benefit of those who have privity of contract with the recipient of the payment. The holdback should only be released if there are no lien claims on title and the time for any other lien claims to be made has passed. The time period for the holdback is generally 60 days after the work has been completed or the materials have been supplied. The person maintaining the holdback is only liable up to the amount of the holdback, and all those claiming against the holdback can claim on a pro rata basis from the holdback amount. In this scenario, Real Land was obliged to hold back 10 percent of any payment it made to Nicholas, and Hi Volt has a right to claim against the holdback by making a written demand for payment on the holdback within the 60-day period that it has to register a claim for lien. In effect, the lien claimant who has privity with the owner actually claims against the property; the others, who do not have privity with the owner, such as subcontractors, claim against the holdback. Note that if the defaulting party is a subcontractor, the owner is only personally liable to those below the subcontractor for an amount equal to the lesser of their own holdback or the defaulter's holdback amount.[17]

Breach of Trust

Under section 13 of the Act, a director, officer, employee, or agent of a corporation who assents to or acquiesces in conduct that they know or reasonably ought to know amounts to breach of trust by the corporation, may be liable for the breach of trust. Under the CLAA 2017 amendments, section 8.1 sets out duties of trustees regarding how and where trust funds are to be deposited, and what sort of records must be kept. If, for example, a subcontractor is paid funds by the general contractor for work done and fails to set up the required holdback in the manner established by section 8.1 and regulations under the Act, or fails to pass on payment to a materials supplier, the supplier can argue breach of trust for a misappropriation of funds by the subcontractor while acting in a fiduciary capacity. Breach of trust cases that fall within the monetary jurisdiction of the Small Claims Court may be brought in that court.

Because a lien is not required as a prerequisite for a breach of trust claim, such a claim is often brought when the time to register a lien has been missed.

Registration of a Claim for Lien

When Hi Volt decides to enforce its lien, the following steps should be taken:

1. *Interview the client:* Hi Volt's lawyer should interview the manager or a designated employee from Hi Volt to obtain the facts to support a lien claim as soon as possible. Remember, there is a time limit. Potential lien claimants are often reluctant to register lien claims because they may want to maintain a working business relationship for the future and do not want to jeopardize it by appearing to be adversarial. Consequently, they may not give instructions until the 60-day period is almost up. Hopefully, the prompt payment and interim adjudication procedures that are major features of the 2017 amendments will reduce last-minute registrations. New section 34(10) of the amended Act extends the time for preserving and perfecting a lien where a matter has been referred for adjudication. The 60-day period is suspended until the adjudicator has rendered a decision. At that point, the matter is either settled or the time period continues to run, allowing for a lien to be filed and registered, hopefully without a last-minute rush.[18]
2. *Obtain information for the lien claim:* The following information should be obtained in order to draft the claim:
   - the name, address, occupation, and phone number of the client—this information should be verified by the provision of photo identification

17 *Supra* note 2, s 23(3).

18 *Ibid*, new s 29(11).

from the client; if the client is a corporation, the proper corporate name should be obtained and a corporate search carried out to ensure that the corporation has not been dissolved;

- the name, address, and phone number of the party with whom the client is contracting;
- the name, address, and phone number of the property owner;
- the name, address, and phone number of the general contractor;
- the name, address, and phone number of the architect/payment certifier (if any);
- the name, address, and phone number of the lender/bank;
- the name, address, and phone number of subcontractors and others in the client's class;
- a description of work done and/or materials furnished;
- the time period in which the work was done and the date of the last work/materials supplied;
- the contract and the payment particulars—invoices, statement of accounts (including information on receivables), and calculation of amount due and owing, including interest;
- the location and the legal description of the property, including lot and plan number, property identification number assigned, municipal address, identification of owners, and type of interest being liened (leasehold, joint tenancy, tenancy in common, or freehold);
- a title subsearch to verify the legal description and address of the property, owner, mortgagees, and other lien holders;
- a name search to verify the owner's name and, if it is a corporation, a corporate search should be conducted to ensure that the correct party is being named in the action (for more information on searches, see Chapter 3); and
- an execution search against the registered owner to discover any competing claims for the property (for details on how to conduct an execution search, see Chapter 3).

Note that the Act itself acknowledges that in some cases information is needed from the defendant in order to complete a claim. The plaintiff may use section 39 of the Act to request information from the defendant. The 2017 amendments have expanded the right to information, including the details of a contract and information from landlords (in the case of leasehold improvements) and mortgagees.[19] Once a request is made, the information must be provided within 21 days of the request.

3. *Draft the claim for lien:* Prepare a claim for lien[20] (Figure 13.1) suitable for registration.[21] (In order to determine where to register the land, determine

19 *Ibid*, new s 32.

20 Under CLAA 2017, forms including written notices of lien will be standardized. As of the time of publication the new forms had not been released.

21 The forms to use to obtain a lien will be revised once the legislation has been passed. The new forms were not yet available at the time of publication.

the municipality. As creditors often will not know the lot and plan numbers, this may be ascertained by inputting the street address into the Teraview electronic search and registration software system.) Lot and plan numbers are required for registration of the lien, although a property identification number may be used if one has been given. If a building does not yet have a street address (as in a new subdivision), it may be necessary to check the **white prints** in the relevant registry office, which will show plans of new subdivisions. It is very important to have the legal description for registration accurately identified because if the claim for lien on the right property is not registered before the 60-day period is up, the lien rights will be lost, and the debtor will have to be sued in the ordinary course.

white prints
large maps of subdivisions that are kept in a file of subdivisions and that show all of the lots in the subdivision; the white print will usually show an existing street or other identifiable landmark at the edge of the subdivision that will allow one to identify and locate a particular property, identified as a lot on the plan

4. *Include in the claim for lien:*
   - the name and address of the owner and, if they are different, the person for whom the materials or services were supplied—if the owner or recipient is a corporation, a search should be conducted for the proper corporate name to use (information on conducting corporate searches can be found in Chapter 3);
   - the name and address of the lien claimant;
   - a brief description of the work done or materials furnished;
   - the contract price;
   - the amount claimed (be careful not to exaggerate the amount to be claimed because there are cost consequences for exaggerating the size of a claim. In addition to cost consequences, where a claim is an abuse of process, frivolous, or vexatious, the 2017 amendments have given the court the explicit power to discharge a lien);[22] and
   - a description of the property that includes the municipal or street address, lot and plan numbers, and/or property identification number, if any.
5. *Preserve the lien:* Once the claim for lien has been completed, it must be preserved. In most cases, the lien is preserved by registering it on title to the property. A lien that does not attach to the property, such as a lien on a municipal road, is preserved by service of the claim for lien on the defendant. For the majority of liens that are registered on title, registration can be done electronically using Teraview. In order to preserve the lien, registration must take place within 60 days after the work was completed or materials were last supplied. In our example, provided that the claim for lien was registered on the right property and this was done within the 60-day period, then Hi Volt's lien will have been preserved.
6. *Perfect the lien:* Once the lien has been preserved, it must then be perfected. To do this, a court action should be commenced in the Superior Court office for the region or county where the property is located. The lien claimant

22 *Supra* note 2, new s 13.17.

must draft, issue, and serve an ordinary Statement of Claim (Figure 13.2), together with Form 14F, Information for Court Use (an example of Form 14F can be found in Chapter 5 on pages 117 and 118). The defendants will be Real Land Inc, as landowner, and Nicholas Construction Ltd, as the party directly liable on the contract for payment. The statement of claim must be issued prior to the end of the 90-day period following the last day for preservation.[23] Many lawyers make it a practice to issue the claim as soon as possible, even if they preserved the lien on a date less than 60 days after the completion of the work. In some cases a lien can be perfected by sheltering under a certificate of action registered by another lien claimant. Sheltering is a complex matter beyond the scope of this text. A text on construction liens procedure should be consulted for more information. Because a missed deadline can be fatal to the lien claim, it is better to err on the side of caution when preserving and perfecting a lien. After the claim has been issued, a Certificate of Action (Figure 13.3) must be obtained from the registrar of the court. The certificate is proof that the claim has been issued. The certificate of action must then be registered on title. Again, this can usually be filed electronically using Teraview. This provides notice to the public that the lien claim has been perfected. The claim should be issued and served within the times provided for by the *Rules of Civil Procedure*.[24]

7. *Follow pre-trial procedures:* Once an action is commenced, refer to Part VIII of the Act, as amended. Most of the provisions governing procedures on lien claims have been repealed, and procedure is now governed only in part by the Act, and otherwise by the court rules of procedure, as noted above.
8. *Set the lien claim down for trial within the time required by the rules of the court:* If the lien matter is in the Superior Court, it must be set down for trial within the time specified by Rule 48.14 of the *Rules of Civil Procedure*. If the lien matter is in the Small Claims Court, it must be set down for trial within the time specified by Rule 11.1 of the *Small Claims Court Rules*.[25] If the matter is not set down for trial within this time, the action may be dismissed and the claim for lien expires.[26] The action will be tried by a judge in the Superior Court (or by a deputy judge in the Small Claims Court if the case is within the monetary jurisdiction of the Small Claims Court and a Superior Court judge agrees to refer it down). In Toronto, the plaintiff may bring a motion directing a reference for trial under section 58 of the Act to have the action heard by a master who will conduct the trial and give judgment in the form of a report to be confirmed by a judge. A sample Judgment

23 *Ibid*, s 36(2), as amended.

24 RRO 1990, Reg 194.

25 O Reg 258/98.

26 *Supra* note 2, s 37(1). CLAA 2017 does not propose any changes to this subsection.

Directing a Reference for Trial can be found in Figure 13.4. In either case, the first day of a complex matter will be devoted to settlement discussions and sorting out and proving claims. In a straightforward case, the matter will simply be tried like any other civil case. As with other types of cases (even where mandatory interim adjudication was held earlier), the parties may agree to mediation or arbitration to resolve their case. There are mediators and arbitrators who specialize in construction lien litigation. The website of the Canadian College of Construction Lawyers at <http://www.cccl.org> maintains a list of experienced mediators and arbitrators. With a settlement in the plaintiff's favour, the plaintiff will want to ensure that the settlement moneys are paid. The defendant will want to ensure that the lien is discharged, the registration of the claim for lien and the certificate of action are vacated, and the court action is dismissed.

Vacating, Postponing, or Discharging Liens

In response to a lien claim, a defendant can serve and file a statement of defence, leaving the lien in place until the matter is resolved. However, in some circumstances, a defendant will need to have the lien vacated from title in order to deal with the property. If, for example, the defendant is trying to sell a property and a claim for lien is registered on title, the claim must be removed from the title before the property can be transferred. The Act provides that any lien can be vacated by court order, made without notice to the plaintiff, if the defendant pays into court a sum equal to the amount of the lien claim plus a percentage, as specified in the amended Act, of the amount of the lien claimed in order to secure costs (see Part VII of the Act). The plaintiff shall provide the court with a motion record including an affidavit that sets out the details on how the amount of security to be paid into court has been determined. A draft order should be given to the court along with a certified copy of the lien. A sample draft order to vacate a lien upon posting security with the court can be found in Figure 13.5. In some areas, the local court also requires a copy of a title subsearch. The practitioner should consult with the local court office to determine local practice.[27] Payment can be made by certified cheque payable to the Accountant of the Superior Court of Justice[28] or by posting security, such as a letter of credit, with the court. A motion may be brought to reduce the amount of security to be posted. When a lien is vacated, the lien claim is still preserved, and the matter will continue to be before the courts.

---

27 For Toronto court procedures on construction liens, Duncan W Glaholt's book, *Conduct of a Lien Action* (Toronto: Thomson Carswell, 2017) is an excellent reference, although it must be used with care, given the changes introduced in the CLAA 2017. Further, some of the details described here may change in both the Act and the regulations. The publisher of this text will provide any necessary updates to this chapter via their website at https://emond.ca/dclp5 once the legislation has been implemented.

28 Payment in the Small Claims Court is governed by the *Rules of the Small Claims Court*, *supra* note 25, Rule 22. As the CLAA 2017 may change procedures, consult the clerk of the Small Claims Court where the case has been filed.

In some cases, both parties will agree to postpone a lien claim. For example, if a mortgage advance cannot be made with the lien on title, the parties may agree to postpone the lien claim so that funds can be advanced, with the lien claim being restored after the funds have been advanced.

If a lien claim has expired because it was not preserved or perfected in time, a declaration can be sought from the court that the lien has expired. A sample order declaring that a lien has expired can be found in Figure 13.6.

If the claim for lien is settled on consent, the plaintiff or the defendant may make a motion to the court for an order to have the lien discharged from title. In addition to the discharge of the claim for lien from title, the minutes and the court order should also deal with the discharge of the registration of the certificate of action and dismissal of the action itself. A sample order discharging a lien on consent can be found in Figure 13.7.

CHAPTER SUMMARY

Chapter 13 introduced the principles underlying the *Construction Act*. Those who provide improvements to property are entitled to file a lien claim against an owner for the value of the improvement if they are not paid for work done or materials furnished, even when they have no privity of contract with the owner. The chapter went on to examine the "construction pyramid" and the requirements for holdback on payments. A typical simple lien claim was then presented. The chapter examined who may file a lien, what the lien may be filed on, how the holdback system works, how a claim for lien is drafted and registered on title, how a statement of claim is prepared and filed, and how a certificate of action is registered on title. Changes to the Act as a result of the *Construction Lien Amendment Act, 2017* have been noted, including the prompt payment system, the interim adjudication system, the expanded time periods for preserving and perfecting liens, and the new record keeping requirements for holdbacks. The chapter concluded with a discussion of situations where a lien may be vacated, postponed, or discharged.

KEY TERMS

holdback, 396
lien, 392
owner's equity, 401
perfect a lien, 396
preserve a lien, 395
privity of contract, 392
white prints, 404

REVIEW QUESTIONS

1. What are the principal features of the *Construction Lien Act* that are beneficial to suppliers of materials and services that improve property?
2. What are the principal changes affecting payments that resulted from the 2017 amendments to construction lien legislation?
3. How have amendments to the construction lien legislation attempted to reduce cost and delay with respect to disputes?
4. Describe the construction pyramid in terms of the relationships, rights, and remedies among those who make up the pyramid.
5. What defines a class of claimants under the Act?
6. Describe what a holdback is and how it works.
7. When might it be useful to bring a breach of trust claim?
8. Under what circumstances may a paralegal represent a lien claimant?
9. Who may file a lien?
10. On what property can a lien be filed?
11. Will the amount in the claim for a lien against the owner be the same as the amount claimed against the payer with whom the lienor had privity of contract? Explain.
12. When registering a claim for lien, speed is important. Explain why that is the case.
13. What information about the property is required in order to register a claim for a lien?
14. How is a lien preserved and perfected?
15. How does the trial process on lien claims in Toronto differ from the lien claim trial process in other parts of the province?
16. What is the time limit for setting a lien claim down for trial?
17. Explain how a defendant in a lien claim can have a lien claim removed from title prior to trial.

CASE STUDY

Belsize Nappy
Lawyer
504 – 365 Bay Street
Toronto, ON M6W 13Y
tel.: 416-557-1234

MEMO

DATE: January 6, year 0
TO: Morris Clerk
FROM: Belsize Nappy
RE: Construction Lien Claim—Bumble Construction

Our client, Bumble Construction Ltd., had a contract to renovate the kitchen and bathroom of a house owned by Peter Pugnani at 345 Scarlatti Street, Toronto, ON M4R 1D3. The contract was entered into on May 1, year −1 for the amount of $65,500. Our client started work on May 15, year −1. The work was finally completed on December 20, year −1. Pugnani had paid $10,000 when work started but has paid nothing since. Our client's foreman came by on December 22 to pick up the balance and was told to come back after the holidays. Our client doesn't like the smell of this and wants us to lien the property. The results of a title search show that the property is located on part of Lot 68, Plan M-53, city of Toronto, and is registered in the Land Titles Division of Toronto (no. 66).

Prepare the necessary documents to preserve and perfect the lien.

FIGURE 13.1 Claim for Lien (Form 8)

FORM 8
CLAIM FOR LIEN UNDER SECTION 34 OF THE ACT

Construction Lien Act

Name of lien claimant: Hi Volt Electrical Ltd.

Address for service: c/o James Snorglepus, 1234 Bay Street, Toronto, ON M6P 1R2

Name of owner: Real Land Inc.

Address: c/o Banburn Drive, Toronto, ON M6R 1Y6

Name of person to whom lien claimant supplied services or materials: Nicholas Construction Ltd.

Address: 2801 Western Road, Brantford ON N7A 3C2

Time within which services or materials were supplied:

from June 1, year 0 (date supply commenced) to August 31, year 0 (date of most recent supply)

Short description of services or materials that have been supplied:
electrical services and materials at 328 Banburn Drive, Toronto, ON M6R 1Y6

Contract price or subcontract price: $ 180,000.00

Amount claimed as owing in respect of services or materials that have been supplied: $ 60,000.00

(Use A where the lien attaches to the premises; use B where the lien does not attach to the premises)

☒ A. The lien claimant (if claimant is personal representative or assignee, this must be stated) claims a lien against the interest of every person identified above as an owner of the premises described in Schedule A to this claim for lien.

☐ B. The lien claimant (if claimant is personal representative or assignee, this must be stated) claims a charge against the holdbacks required to be retained under the Act and any additional amount owed by a payer to the contractor or any subcontractor whose contract or subcontract was in whole or in part performed by the services or materials that have been supplied by the lien claimant in relation to the premises at:

____
(address or other identification of the location of the premises)

Date: September 30, year 0

Hi Volt Electrical Ltd.
(signature of claimant or agent)
per H. Ampere, President

FIGURE 13.1 Claim for Lien (Form 8) (*continued*)

SCHEDULE A

To the claim for lien of **Hi Volt Electrical Ltd.**

Description of premises:

parts of lot 68, plan M-59 in the Land Titles Division of the City of Toronto, no. 66

(Where the lien attaches to the premises, provide a description of the premises sufficient for registration under the *Land Titles Act* or the *Registry Act*, as the case may be.)

CLA-8 (March 17, 2014) CSD

R.R.O. 1990, Reg. 175, Form 8.

FIGURE 13.1 Claim for Lien (Form 8) (*continued*)

HI VOLT ELECTRICAL LTD.

v

REAL LAND INC.

and

NICHOLAS CONSTRUCTION LTD.

Construction Lien Act

CLAIM FOR LIEN

JAMES Q. SNORGLEPUS (81021S)
1234 Bay Street
Toronto, ON M6P 1R2

jamesq@snorglepus.com
416-456-7890
FAX 416-456-7891

Lawyer for the lien claimant

FIGURE 13.2 Statement of Claim

Court file no. 1831

ONTARIO

SUPERIOR COURT OF JUSTICE

B E T W E E N:

HI VOLT ELECTRICAL LTD

Plaintiff

and

NICHOLAS CONSTRUCTION LTD and REAL LAND INC

Defendants

STATEMENT OF CLAIM

TO THE DEFENDANTS

A LEGAL PROCEEDING HAS BEEN COMMENCED AGAINST YOU by the plaintiff. The claim made against you is set out in the following pages.

IF YOU WISH TO DEFEND THIS PROCEEDING, you or an Ontario lawyer acting for you must prepare a statement of defence in Form 18A prescribed by the Rules of Civil Procedure, serve it on the plaintiff's lawyer or, where the plaintiff does not have a lawyer, serve it on the plaintiff, and file it, with proof of service, in this court office, WITHIN TWENTY DAYS after this statement of claim is served on you, if you are served in Ontario.

If you are served in another province or territory of Canada or in the United States of America, the period for serving and filing your statement of defence is forty days. If you are served outside Canada and the United States of America, the period is sixty days.

Instead of serving and filing a statement of defence, you may serve and file a notice of intent to defend in Form 18B prescribed by the Rules of Civil Procedure. This will entitle you to ten more days within which to serve and file your statement of defence.

IF YOU FAIL TO DEFEND THIS PROCEEDING, JUDGMENT MAY BE GIVEN AGAINST YOU IN YOUR ABSENCE AND WITHOUT FURTHER NOTICE TO YOU. IF YOU WISH TO DEFEND THIS PROCEEDING BUT ARE UNABLE TO PAY LEGAL FEES, LEGAL AID MAY BE AVAILABLE TO YOU BY CONTACTING A LOCAL LEGAL AID OFFICE.

IF YOU PAY THE PLAINTIFF'S CLAIM, and $500.00 for costs, within the time for serving and filing your statement of defence, you may move to have this proceeding dismissed by the court. If you believe the amount claimed for costs is excessive, you may pay the plaintiff's claim and $400 for costs and have the costs assessed by the court.

TAKE NOTICE: THIS ACTION WILL AUTOMATICALLY BE DISMISSED if it has not been set down for trial or terminated by any means within five years after the action was commenced unless otherwise ordered by the court.

Date October 3, year 0 Issued by ....
Local registrar

Address of court office: 393 University Ave.
Toronto, ON M5G 1T4

TO: Nicholas Construction
2801 Western Road
Brantford, ON N7A 3C2

AND

TO: Real Land Inc.
328 Banburn Drive
Toronto, ON M6R 1Y6

FIGURE 13.2 Statement of Claim (*continued*)

~~THIS ACTION IS BROUGHT AGAINST YOU UNDER THE SIMPLIFIED PROCEDURE PROVIDED IN RULE 76 OF THE RULES OF CIVIL PROCEDURE.~~

CLAIM

1. The plaintiff claims:
   a. payment in the amount of $60,000 by the defendants for services and materials supplied under a building construction contract;
   b. payment by the defendant, Nicholas Construction Ltd., for general damages for loss of profit in the amount of $30,000;
   c. in the alternative, payments of the amount owing to the plaintiff in paragraph 1(a) from the holdback required to be maintained by the defendant Real Land Inc. pursuant to the *Construction Lien Act*, RSO 1990, c. C.30 as amended;
   d. in default of payment, that the interest of the defendant Real Land Inc., in the lands and premises located at 328 Banburn Drive in the City of Toronto, be sold pursuant to the provisions of the *Construction Lien Act*, and that amounts owing to the plaintiff be paid out of the proceeds of sale in accordance with the provisions of the *Construction Lien Act*;
   e. prejudgment and postjudgment interest;
   f. cost of the action; and
   g. such further relief as to this honourable court seems appropriate.
2. The plaintiff is a limited company, incorporated pursuant to the laws of Ontario, with its head office located in the City of Toronto. The plaintiff carries on business as an electrical contractor.
3. The defendant Nicholas Construction Ltd. (hereinafter referred to as "Nicholas") is a limited company, incorporated pursuant to the law of Ontario, with its head office located at Brantford, Ontario. Nicholas carries on business as a building contractor.
4. The defendant Real Land Inc. (hereinafter referred to as "Real Land") is a limited company, incorporated pursuant to the law of Quebec, and at all relevant times was the owner of lands and premises located at 328 Banburn Drive in the city of Toronto.
5. At times and places and on terms unknown to the plaintiff at the time of pleading, Real Land entered into an agreement with Nicholas to construct a building at 328 Banburn Drive. Full particulars of this agreement are not within the knowledge of the plaintiff but are within the knowledge of both defendants.
6. In furtherance of its obligations under the contract referred to in paragraph 5, Nicholas, on or about May 5, year 0, entered into a contract with the plaintiff whereby the plaintiff undertook to provide electrician services and materials for the building being constructed at 328 Banburn Rd. The contract price was $180,000 and payments were to be made in installments of $60,000 each on August 1, September 1, year 0, and October 1, year 0

FIGURE 13.2 Statement of Claim (*continued*)

7. In accordance with this contract, the plaintiff provided materials and services from June 1, year 0 to August 31, year 0.

8. Nicholas failed to make the $60,000 payment due on August 1, year 0. As a result, the plaintiff ceased work under the contract on August 31 year 0.

9. The plaintiff has not been paid the amount due to it under the provisions of the contract and, as a result of Nicholas's breach, regards the contract as at an end. As a result of its performance of the contract, the plaintiff became entitled to a lien on the interest of Real Land in the lands and premises at 328 Banburn Drive.

10. On September 30, year 0, the plaintiff registered a claim for lien against the interest of Real Land in the lands and premises located at 328 Banburn Drive, as instrument number 60231 CT in the Land Titles Division of Toronto (no. 66). On September 22, year 0, the plaintiff, by notice in writing, demanded of Real Land that it make the contract payments owing to it by Nicholas out of the holdback required to be maintained under the provisions of the *Construction Lien Act*.

11. Real Land has refused or neglected to make such payments as required.

12. The plaintiff pleads and relies on the provisions of the *Construction Lien Act*, RSO 1990, c. C.30, as amended.

13. Because of the refusal or failure of Real Land to make such payments as are required under the Act, the plaintiff requests that Real Land's interest in the premises at 328 Banburn Drive be sold and that the proceeds of sale be used to satisfy the claim of the plaintiff in this action.

The Plaintiff proposes that this action be tried at: Toronto

DATED at Toronto Oct. 2, year 0	JAMES Q. SNORGLEPUS (81021S) 1234 Bay Street, Toronto, ON M6P 1R2 jamesq@snorglepus.com 416-456-7890 FAX 416-456-7891 Lawyer for the Plaintiff

RCP-E 14A (June 9, 2014)

Note: On passage of the *Construction Act*, references to the *Construction Lien Act* should be updated.

FIGURE 13.2 Statement of Claim (*continued*)

HI VOLT ELECTRICAL LTD Plaintiff	and	NICHOLAS CONSTRUCTION LTD, et al Defendants

Court file no. 1831

ONTARIO

SUPERIOR COURT OF JUSTICE

PROCEEDING COMMENCED AT Toronto

STATEMENT OF CLAIM

JAMES Q. SNORGLEPUS (81021S)
1234 Bay Street
Toronto, ON M6P 1R2
jamesq@snorglepus.com
416-456-7890
FAX 416-456-7891

Lawyer for the Plaintiff

RCP-E 4C (June 9, 2014)

FIGURE 13.3 Certificate of Action (Form 10)

FORM 10
CERTIFICATE OF ACTION UNDER SECTION 36 OF THE ACT

Construction Lien Act

1831
Court File No.

SUPERIOR COURT OF JUSTICE

BETWEEN HI VOLT ELECTRICAL LTD Plaintiff(s)

and

(court seal)

NICHOLAS CONSTRUCTION LTD AND REAL LAND INC Defendant(s)

CERTIFICATE OF ACTION

I certify that an action has been commenced in the Superior Court of Justice under the *Construction Lien Act* between the above parties in respect of the premises described in Schedule A to this certificate, and relating to the claim(s) for lien bearing the following registration numbers:

Date: ______________________ ______________________________

(registrar or local registrar)

FIGURE 13.3 Certificate of Action (Form 10) (*continued*)

SCHEDULE A

Description of premises:

Part of lot 68, Plan M-59 in the Land Titles Division of the City of Toronto, no. 66

(The description of the premises must be the same as in the statement of claim, and must be sufficient for registration under the *Land Titles Act* or the *Registry Act*, as the case may be.)

FIGURE 13.4 Judgment Directing Reference for Trial Under Section 58 of the Act (Form 16)

FORM 16
JUDGMENT DIRECTING A REFERENCE FOR TRIAL UNDER SECTION 58 OF THE ACT

Construction Lien Act

1831
Court File No.

SUPERIOR COURT OF JUSTICE

(name of judge) (day and date)

BETWEEN HI VOLT ELECTRICAL LTD Plaintiff(s)

and

(court seal) NICHOLAS CONSTRUCTION LTD and REAL LAND INC Defendant(s)

JUDGMENT

On motion of the plaintiff made under subsection 58(1) of the *Construction Lien Act* in the presence of counsel for the plaintiff(s) and defendant(s), and on reading the pleadings in this action and on hearing what was alleged by counsel for the parties (or the parties by their counsel consenting to judgment, or as the case may be),

1. THIS COURT ORDERS AND ADJUDGES that this action be referred to the master at Toronto (~~or other place~~) for trial.

2. AND THIS COURT ORDERS AND ADJUDGES that the parties found liable forthwith after confirmation of the report of the master pay to the parties the respective amounts due them.

3. AND THIS COURT ORDERS AND ADJUDGES that the master determine all questions arising in this action and on the reference and all questions arising under the *Construction Lien Act* and that the findings of the master be effective on the confirmation of the report.

4. AND THIS COURT ORDERS AND ADJUDGES that the master determine the question of costs in this action and of the reference, and the costs be taxed and paid as the master shall direct.

Date: ______________ Signed by: ______________
(judge)
(registrar or local registrar)

FIGURE 13.5 Order to Vacate Lien by Posting Security

Court File No. 1831

ONTARIO

SUPERIOR COURT OF JUSTICE

JUSTICE ____________ _____day the ___ day of __________, year 0

BETWEEN

HI VOLT ELECTRICAL LTD Plaintiff(s)

(court seal) and

NICHOLAS CONSTRUCTION LTD and REAL LAND INC Defendant(s)

JUDGMENT

THIS MOTION made by the general contractor Nicholas Construction Ltd., without notice, pursuant to section 44(1) of the *Construction Lien Act*, RSO 1990, c. C.30, as amended, vacating the registration of the Claim for Lien of Hi Volt Electrical Ltd., registered against the title to the lands and premises described in Schedule "A" attached hereto, was heard this day at the Court House, 393 University Avenue, Toronto, Ontario.

ON READING a copy of the Claim for Lien of Hi Volt Electrical Ltd., the Parcel Register (Abbreviated) for Property Identifier 12345-6789 (LT), filed, and upon hearing submissions of counsel on behalf of the General Contractor, Nicholas Construction Ltd., and upon it appearing that the General Contractor, Nicholas Construction Ltd. having posted cash security in the amount of $75,000 with the Accountant of the *Ontario* Superior Court of Justice,

1. THIS COURT ORDERS that the amount of the security to be posted with the Accountant of the Ontario Superior Court of Justice by the General Contractor, Nicholas Construction Ltd., to vacate the registration of the Claim for Lien of Hi Volt Electrical Ltd., described in paragraph 2 herein, be the sum of $60,000, together with the sum of $15,000 as security for costs, for a total of $75,000.
2. THIS COURT ORDERS that the registration of the Claim for Lien of Hi Volt Electrical Ltd. dated September 30, year 0, in the amount of $75,000 and registered on September 30, year 0, as Instrument No. 987654, in the Land Registry Office for the Land Titles Division of the City of Toronto, against the title to the lands and premises described in Schedule "A" attached hereto be vacated.
3. THIS COURT ORDERS that this Order be entered forthwith.
4. THIS COURT ORDERS that a copy of this Order shall be served upon counsel for the Lien Claimant, Hi Volt Electrical Ltd., forthwith after entry.

Date: .... Signed by: ....

(judge)

(registrar or local registrar)

FIGURE 13.5 Order to Vacate Lien by Posting Security (*continued*)

SCHEDULE A

Description of Premises:

Parts of lot 68, Plan M-59 in the Land Titles Division of the City of Toronto Land Registry No. 66.

FIGURE 13.6 Order Declaring Lien Expired

Court File No. 1831

ONTARIO
SUPERIOR COURT OF JUSTICE

JUSTICE ____________ _____day the ___ day of __________, year 0

BETWEEN

HI VOLT ELECTRICAL LTD — Plaintiff(s)

(court seal)

and

NICHOLAS CONSTRUCTION LTD and REAL LAND INC — Defendant(s)

ORDER

THIS MOTION made by the Defendant, Nicholas Construction Ltd., without notice, for an Order, declaring expired the Claim for Lien of the Plaintiff, Hi Volt Electrical Ltd. (the Plaintiff), vacating the registration of the Claim for Lien of the Plaintiff, vacating the registration of the Certificate of the Plaintiff, and dismissing the within action, without costs, was heard this day at the Court House, 393 University Avenue, Toronto, Ontario.

ON READING the Notice of Motion, filed, the Affidavit of Brian Nicholas sworn November 30, year 0, and Exhibits thereto, filed, being *inter alia*, certified copies of the Claim for Lien of the Plaintiff, a certified copy of the Certificate for Action of the Plaintiff, a certified copy of the Abstract Index (Abbreviated for Property Identifier 12345-6789), and an Abstract of Title, all filed, and upon hearing submissions of counsel for the Defendant, Nicholas Construction Ltd.,

1. **THIS COURT DECLARES** that the lien of the Plaintiff, Hi Volt Electrical Ltd., dated September 30, year 0, in the amount of $2,500.00 and registered in the Land Registry Office for the Land Titles Division of the City of Toronto, against the title to the lands and premises described in Schedule "A" attached hereto is expired;
2. **THIS COURT ORDERS** that the registration of the Claim for Lien of the Plaintiff, Hi Volt Electrical Ltd., dated September 30, year 0, in the amount of $60,000 and registered on September 30, year 0, as Instrument No. 987654, in the Land Registry Office for the Land Titles Division of the City of Toronto, against the title to the lands and premises described in Schedule "A" attached hereto be vacated;
3. **THIS COURT ORDERS** that the registration of the Certificate of Action of the Plaintiff, Hi Volt Electrical Ltd., dated September 30, year 0, and registered on dated September 30, year 0 as Instrument No. 987654, in the Land Registry Office for the Land Titles Division of the City of Toronto, against the title to the lands and premises described in Schedule "A" attached hereto be vacated;
4. **THIS COURT ORDERS** that the within action be dismissed, without costs.

Date: .... Signed by: ....
(judge)
(registrar or local registrar)

FIGURE 13.6 Order Declaring Lien Expired (*continued*)

SCHEDULE A

Description of Premises:

Parts of lot 68, Plan M-59 in the Land Titles Division of the City of Toronto Land Registry No. 66.

FIGURE 13.7 Order Vacating Claim for Lien and Discharging Construction Lien

Court File No. 1831

ONTARIO

SUPERIOR COURT OF JUSTICE

JUSTICE ____________ _____day the ___ day of __________, year 0

BETWEEN

HI VOLT ELECTRICAL LTD

Plaintiff(s)

(*court seal*)

and

NICHOLAS CONSTRUCTION LTD and REAL LAND INC

Defendant(s)

ORDER

THIS MOTION, made by the Plaintiff Hi Volt Electrical Ltd., for an Order vacating and discharging its Claim for Lien, vacating the registration of its Certificate of Action and dismissing the within action without costs, was heard this day at the Court House, 393 University Avenue, Toronto, Ontario.

ON READING the Notice of Motion, filed, the Affidavit of Henry Ampere sworn October 30, year 0, and Exhibits attached thereto, filed, and upon hearing the consent of the Plaintiff and the Consent of the Defendants, Nicholas Construction Ltd., filed, and upon being advised that the within action was discontinued as against the defendant, Nicholas Construction Ltd., on October 30, year 0 and upon hearing submissions of counsel for the Plaintiff, Hi Volt Electrical Ltd.,

1. **THIS COURT ORDERS** that the claim for lien of Hi Volt Electrical Ltd. in the amount of $60,000, registered on September 30, year 0 as Instrument No. 987654, in the Land Registry Office for the Land Titles Division of the City of Toronto, Ontario, against the title to the lands and premises described in Schedule "A" hereto, be vacated and the lien be discharged.
2. **THIS COURT ORDERS** that the Certificate of Action of Hi Volt Electrical Ltd., registered on September 30, year 0 as Instrument No. 987654, in the Land Registry Office for the Land Titles Division of the City of Toronto, Ontario, against the lands and premises set out in Schedule "A" hereto be vacated.
3. **THIS COURT ORDERS** that the within action be dismissed without costs.

Date: .... Signed by: ....

(*judge*)
(*registrar or local registrar*)

FIGURE 13.7 Order Vacating Claim for Lien and Discharging Construction Lien (*continued*)

SCHEDULE A

Description of Premises:

Parts of lot 68, Plan M-59 in the Land Titles Division of the City of Toronto Land Registry No. 66.

Bankruptcy and Safeguards Against Fraud

14

LEARNING OUTCOMES

After reading this chapter, students will:

- Have an understanding of how the *Bankruptcy and Insolvency Act* (BIA) affects creditors and debtors, and how it deals with an insolvent debtor's debts.
- Know the definition of bankruptcy.
- Distinguish between the three options a debtor has under the BIA to deal with potential insolvency.
- Understand why a creditor may recover less under bankruptcy procedures than the total amount owing.
- Distinguish between secured and unsecured creditors in terms of how they are treated under the BIA.
- Know how a consumer proposal works, when it may be used, and what advantages it may give an insolvent consumer debtor.
- Describe how a debtor can make a voluntary assignment in bankruptcy.
- Describe how a creditor may petition a debtor into bankruptcy.
- Describe the steps to be taken in an ordinary bankruptcy.
- Understand the role of the trustee in bankruptcy.
- Identify debts that survive bankruptcy.
- Identify the different types of discharge from bankruptcy, and indicate the circumstances in which different types of discharge may be used.
- Recognize debtor actions that may indicate fraud and understand how the BIA controls debtor fraud.
- Understand when insolvent debtors may or may not use assignments and preferences.
- Describe provincial legislation available to control debtor fraud in situations where a debtor is not insolvent or otherwise under control of the BIA.

Chapter 14 gives an overview of the rights and remedies available under the federal *Bankruptcy and Insolvency Act*[1] (BIA). Provincial legislation to control fraudulent activity by debtors is examined.

What Is Bankruptcy?

Bankruptcy is a legal process carried out under the provisions of the BIA. The process involves disclosure by the debtor of all assets and liabilities, along with a surrender of all non-exempt property to a **trustee in bankruptcy**. The debtor, if an individual, must also undergo debt counselling and, in some cases, make a series of monthly payments to a trustee. Bankruptcy relieves debtors of responsibility for their debts, subject to some exclusions.

trustee in bankruptcy an individual, usually an accountant, who is licensed to act as a trustee under the *Bankruptcy and Insolvency Act*; the trustee assists individuals and corporations making proposals or assignments into bankruptcy and creditors who want to petition a debtor into bankruptcy

Who Should Go Bankrupt?

A Canadian resident, or someone who carries on business in Canada, who owes a minimum of $1,000 and has committed an "act of bankruptcy" within the preceding six months is eligible to make an assignment into bankruptcy or be petitioned into bankruptcy by a creditor. There are various "acts of bankruptcy" set out in section 42 of the BIA. The most common "act of bankruptcy" is insolvency. Individuals who are unable to meet their obligations to creditors as they come due or who have ceased paying debts in the ordinary course of business are insolvent persons. Note that those whose liabilities are greater than their assets are not necessarily bankrupt. Many individuals, particularly when they are buying homes, have large mortgages that make their liabilities (debts) greater than their assets. The key is whether they can pay their monthly bills. A temporary shortfall does not mean bankruptcy, nor does a situation where credit counselling or a small claims consolidation order results in a debt restructuring so that the debtor can make payments.

Property Exempt from Seizure

Under Federal Legislation

Registered Retirement Savings Plans

Registered Retirement Savings Plans (RRSPs), Registered Retirement Income Funds (RRIFs), and Deferred Profit Sharing Plans (DPSPs) are exempt from seizure in a bankruptcy, provided that the contributions were made at least one year prior to the assignment of bankruptcy.

Indian Act Property

There are provisions in the *Indian Act*[2] that exempt certain property of status Indians from ordinary seizure in a bankruptcy.

Federal Benefits

Benefits paid under the Canada Pension Plan, Old Age Security, and Employment Insurance, as well as

1 RSC 1985, c B-3, as amended.

2 RSC 1985, c I-5.

financial benefits from Veterans Affairs Canada are exempt from seizure in a bankruptcy but are included in the bankrupt's income to determine whether there is surplus income that should be paid to the trustee for the benefit of the creditors.

Under Provincial Legislation

Insurance Act

Under some provincial insurance acts, including the Ontario *Insurance Act*,[3] the cash value portion of a whole life or universal life insurance policy where a close family member is named as the beneficiary is exempt from seizure. A close family member is defined as being a spouse, child, grandchild, or parent. RRSPs in which there is an insurance component with a close family member named as beneficiary are also exempt from seizure. Insurance products such as segregated funds, held inside or outside of an RRSP, with a close family member listed as beneficiary are eligible for exemption from seizure in a bankruptcy.

Execution Act

Under provincial execution acts, there are exemptions from seizure for the following items. In Ontario, under the *Execution Act*[4] (s 35), the exemptions are adjusted periodically due to changes in the cost of living:

- household furnishings up to $13,150 in value,
- ordinary and necessary clothing (no set monetary limit),
- tools of the trade up to $11,300 in value,
- farm equipment up to $29,100 in value,
- vehicles up to $ $6,600 in value,
- aids and devices used to assist with a disability or a medical or dental condition, and
- a principal residence if the equity in the property is no higher than $10,000.[5]

Other Reasons Property Can Be Exempt from Seizure

Property held in trust by the bankrupt for the benefit of another person is exempt from seizure in the bankruptcy as is property that is the subject of a secured interest. Secured creditors have the option under the BIA of seizing their security. Most do so, because they are likely to recover far more that way than they ever would if they abandoned their security rights and chose to participate in bankruptcy proceedings. A secured creditor may also wish to avoid joining in a bankruptcy in order to avoid the tariff payable to the **Superintendent of Bankruptcy** on any distribution of estate proceeds made by the trustee. At the time of writing, the tariff was 5 percent on the first $1 million of payments to creditors, 1.25 percent on the next million dollars, and 0.25 percent on any payments over $2 million.

If the bankrupt has property that would be of no financial benefit to the bankrupt's estate, it will not be seized. Such property might consist of items that would cost the trustee more to seize and sell than the value of the item itself. In some cases, the courts may order certain assets exempt from seizure.

The effect of bankruptcy is that most of an individual's assets (referred to as their estate) are turned over to a trustee in bankruptcy who is licensed under the BIA, who will then liquidate the assets and distribute funds to creditors. In bankruptcy, creditors rarely recover the full amount they are owed; however, at the end of the process, with a few exceptions, the bankrupt is stripped of most assets, save those exempt from seizure, and the debts are wiped out, with a few exceptions. If a first-time bankrupt completing the Monthly Income and Expense Statement shown in Figure 14.1 has surplus income, then a portion of this surplus, based on income and

Superintendent of Bankruptcy
a government official in Ottawa who supervises and oversees the administration of the *Bankruptcy and Insolvency Act*

3 RSO 1990, c I.8.

4 RSO 1990, c E.24 and O Reg 657/05.

5 For current exemptions, see O Reg 657/05, as amended.

family size, must be paid to the trustee for a period of 21 months. The trustee handles the bankrupt's income tax returns for the bankruptcy period and receives any refunds for the benefit of the creditors. Generally, if the bankrupt has not engaged in fraudulent activity, a discharge from bankruptcy will be ordered when the estate is fully administered. Because the debts have been discharged by the bankruptcy process, the bankrupt will not be sued for those debts, nor can judgments in respect of them be enforced. Discharged bankrupts are free to go their own way. Contrary to what is often assumed, a bankrupt can rebuild a credit rating and borrow money. However, someone who repeatedly goes bankrupt will have great difficulty re-establishing a credit rating.

Bankruptcy Options

Under the BIA, there are three options available.

Consumer Proposals

A consumer proposal is a plan to repay unsecured creditors put forward by an insolvent natural person (an individual as opposed to an artificial corporation such as a limited company) through a trustee or an administrator under the *Bankruptcy and Insolvency Act*. A sample Form 47 Consumer Proposal can be found in Figure 14.2. The proposal may request that unsecured creditors accept a reduction in the amount of the debt to be repaid or extend the overall period in which to pay the debt, or both. Under the BIA, proposals, once made, must be completed in five years or less.[6] A debtor whose debts do not exceed $250,000 exclusive of a home mortgage can use the proposal process.[7] Spouses or others who share a debt load under $250,000 may make a joint proposal. A trustee in bankruptcy or proposal administrator approved by the Superintendent of Bankruptcy must review the debtor's financial and property affairs and provide counselling to the debtor. The administrator will help draft a proposal to pay unsecured creditors of the debtor on terms that the debtor can meet. A proposal will not be possible unless the debtor has sufficient monthly income to make payments on the proposal. The proposal is filed with the **Official Receiver**. Within 10 days of filing, the administrator must send the Official Receiver a report of the investigation of the debtor's property and financial affairs; a statement of the debtor's assets, liabilities, income, and expenses; a list of creditors over $250; and an opinion as to whether the proposal is reasonable and fair and whether the debtor

Official Receiver
a government official in the Office of the Superintendent of Bankruptcy who receives proposals, examines bankrupts under oath, and chairs meetings of creditors

6 *Supra* note 1, s 66.12(5).

7 If the debtor's debt exceeds $250,000, the debtor cannot make a consumer proposal; however, a debtor in that position can make a Division I proposal for which there is no limit on the amount of debt, but the period for creditors to accept the proposal is short—only 21 days. It is also more difficult to get creditor approval for a Division I proposal because a majority of creditors holding at least two-thirds of the value of the debt must accept the Division I proposal. If the proposal is not accepted, the debtor automatically goes into bankruptcy.

will be able to perform it. A copy of the proposal and the report is also sent by the trustee or proposal administrator to all creditors along with a proof of claim form and a statement setting out that a meeting of creditors will not be called unless one is requested, and also that a court review of the proposal will not be made unless requested. A meeting will be held if the Official Receiver directs one to be called or in the event that creditors, having in the aggregate at least 25 percent in value of the proven claims, request one.[8] If no meeting is held, the proposal is deemed to be accepted 45 days after its filing.[9] If a meeting is held, a simple majority of unsecured creditors carries the vote. If the creditors accept the proposal, it is binding on the debtor and on all unsecured creditors. A proposal is deemed to have been approved by the court 15 days after the creditors' acceptance or deemed acceptance. The debtor makes payments to the trustee or administrator, who will distribute payments to unsecured creditors every three months. A consumer proposal stays all court and collection actions against the debtor, subject to any exceptions such as an action concerning fraud against the debtor.

If the proposal is rejected, the debtor may decide to make an assignment into bankruptcy, may be petitioned into bankruptcy by a creditor, or may return to the situation the debtor was in prior to making the proposal. Without a proposal in place, if the debtor does not enter into bankruptcy, the creditors may initiate or continue all lawsuits and judgment enforcements against the debtor. Note that if a proposal is accepted, the debtor is not bankrupt and does not acquire the legal status of a bankrupt. The major advantage of a consumer proposal is that the debtor keeps property and assets. Another advantage is that the fee paid to a trustee or an administrator for a consumer proposal is less than the fee for a bankruptcy.

Voluntary Assignment into Bankruptcy

Where a debtor cannot or chooses not to make a proposal, or where a proposal is rejected, the debtor can voluntarily seek the status of a bankrupt and go through bankruptcy proceedings. If the debtor has realizable assets worth $10,000 or less, the bankruptcy can proceed in a summary manner.[10] With a summary administration of bankruptcy, the trustee is not required to post security, the bankruptcy is not advertised in a newspaper, inspectors are usually not appointed, and a meeting of creditors is not held unless requested by the creditors. If the debtor has realizable assets valued at over $10,000, the bankruptcy proceeds in the ordinary fashion with a meeting of creditors being held within 21 days of the trustee's appointment. The duties of the bankrupt and the steps involved in an ordinary bankruptcy are set out on the following page.

8 *Supra* note 1, s 66.15.

9 *Ibid*, s 66.18.

10 *Ibid*, s 155.

Duties of the Bankrupt

Section 158 of the *Bankruptcy and Insolvency Act* provides that the bankrupt must do the following:

1. Provide disclosure of all assets and liabilities to the trustee and deliver all property, subject to exemptions, to the trustee.
2. Advise the trustee of any property disposed of in the past year.
3. Deliver all books, records, and documents concerning property and income tax records to the trustee.
4. Within five days of making an assignment into bankruptcy, provide the trustee with a Statement of Affairs.
5. Advise the trustee of any gifts of property made in the last five years.
6. Surrender all credit cards to the trustee for cancellation.
7. Attend for an oral examination under oath with the Official Receiver if requested to do so.
8. Attend any meetings of creditors.
9. Advise the trustee of any change in address.
10. Assist the trustee in making an inventory of assets.
11. Sign any required documents.
12. Examine the correctness of any Proofs of Claim.
13. Aid in the distribution of the proceeds.

Steps Involved in an Ordinary Bankruptcy

1. *Initial meeting with trustee:* The debtor will meet with a trustee in bankruptcy to review the debtor's financial situation and available options. The trustee will obtain information on the debtor's assets, income, liabilities, and details of property gifted or otherwise disposed of in the last five years. The trustee will use this information to prepare a Form 79 Statement of Affairs for the debtor. Form 79 is set out in Figure 14.3. The bankrupt then attends the first counselling session. In order to be discharged from bankruptcy, the bankrupt must attend at least two counselling sessions. Counselling is provided concerning financial management and prudent use of credit. The trustee may also make referrals for the bankrupt to receive counselling on non-financial matters such as addictions or familial problems. The trustee will review the debtor's household income and expenses and determine whether the bankrupt has surplus income available to be paid to the trustee each month for distribution to the creditors until the discharge.[11] The Superintendent of Bankruptcy has established guidelines, which are revised periodically, to determine the surplus amount for household income. The surplus income guidelines are contained in Directive No. 11R, which can be found online at <http://strategis.ic.gc.ca/epic/site/bsf-osb.nsf/en/br01055e.html#appA>. The trustee will also have the bankrupt sign a credit bureau authorization and an authorization letter for the Canada Revenue Agency

11 Bankrupt persons with surplus income are not eligible for an automatic discharge for nine months after their assignments. They remain in bankruptcy for a further 12 months and must continue to make surplus income payments to the trustee. With a second bankruptcy, a bankrupt person must remain in bankruptcy for a further three years or longer, and make surplus income payments during that time.

that permits the trustee to represent the bankrupt. The trustee will also review the bankrupt's duties under the BIA. Failure to abide by these duties can result in a negative discharge report, a fine, or, in some cases, a jail sentence. The bankrupt's duties are set out in the box on the previous page.

2. *Assignment into bankruptcy:* The trustee files the assignment into bankruptcy with the Official Receiver. The bankrupt's property then vests in the trustee, subject to any exemptions under the *Execution Act* or as set out in the box on page 428. Most legal and collection actions (such as garnishments and the execution of writs) against the bankrupt are stayed. The court may permit cases involving fraud to continue. Claims against the bankrupt that are insured may also be allowed to continue so that the proceeds from an insurance policy payment can be made available to creditors of the estate of the bankrupt.
3. *Notice given to creditors:* The trustee, within five days of the assignment into bankruptcy, will notify the creditors of the bankruptcy by sending them a notice of first meeting, or in the case of a summary administration of bankruptcy, a notice that there will not be a meeting unless one is requested. The trustee will also include a list of creditors, a blank proof of claim form, and a proxy form to be used in the event that the creditor cannot attend the first meeting.
4. *Examination by the Official Receiver:* The bankrupt may be required to attend before an Official Receiver to answer questions under oath concerning the bankrupt's financial situation. A sample of the questions used in an examination of a non-business bankrupt are set out in Form 27, Examination of Bankrupt by Official Receiver, which is shown in Figure 14.4.
5. *First meeting of creditors:* In an ordinary bankruptcy or in a bankruptcy proceeding by summary administration where a meeting has been requested, a meeting of creditors will be held within 21 days of the assignment into bankruptcy. The bankrupt must attend the meeting. The trustee's appointment will be confirmed, and inspectors may be appointed.
6. *Second counselling session:* A second counselling session for the bankrupt is held between the date set for the first meeting of creditors and 90 days after the assignment into bankruptcy.
7. *Trustee's report on the bankruptcy and request for discharge:* The trustee must prepare a report on the bankruptcy for the creditors (those who requested a copy of the report will receive one) and the court. This report must be filed with the court along with a requisition for a discharge from bankruptcy. A sample of Form 82, Report of Trustee on Bankrupt's Application for Discharge, can be found in Figure 14.5.
8. *Realization of assets:* The trustee will sell the assets and provide an accounting of the proceeds.
9. *Distribution of assets:* The trustee must distribute the assets in accordance with the BIA. The costs of administering the estate will be paid first. The trustee is paid a fee equivalent to a percentage of the estate set under the

BIA. Preferred creditors will then be paid, followed by ordinary unsecured creditors, on a pro rata basis. Preferred creditors include the Canada Revenue Agency,[12] employees (for unpaid wages), and landlords (for unpaid past and future rent of three months duration).

10. *Application for discharge from bankruptcy:* The court will consider the discharge application and usually discharge the bankrupt. Trustees must also apply to be discharged from their duties. When the bankrupt's application for discharge comes before the court, the judge will usually make one of the following decisions:
    - *Absolute discharge:* The debtor is relieved of all debts before bankruptcy, except those that are not dischargeable, such as family support order obligations. The judge, in considering the application for discharge, will take into account the performance of duties carried out by the bankrupt and the bankrupt's rehabilitation.
    - *Conditional discharge:* The debtor will be discharged upon meeting certain conditions, such as providing additional funds to distribute to creditors. The period in which the bankrupt is an undischarged bankrupt is extended to allow payments to be made. This punishes the debtor by extending the period of time before discharge and preventing the rebuilding of the debtor's financial situation. A conditional discharge will often call for additional payments to be made over a period of time ranging from 1 to 12 additional months.
    - *Suspended discharge:* The debtor's discharge is delayed due to such things as an ongoing criminal investigation or an objection by a creditor, a trustee, or the Superintendent of Bankruptcy. Common objections include situations where a debtor failed to account for the disposal of an asset, or continued to get credit while unable to pay.
    - *Refusal to grant a discharge:* In some cases, a discharge will not be granted. This may occur if the bankrupt has gone through more than two bankruptcies in the past, has committed fraud, or has falsified records.

Debts That Survive a Bankruptcy

A discharge from bankruptcy terminates most of the bankrupt's debts; however, there are some debts that survive a bankruptcy. The most common ones are:

- Spousal and child support debts.
- Damages owed by the bankrupt in respect of an assault or an order of restitution made in a criminal case.
- Court fines.
- Debt arising from fraud. Creditors that have been defrauded by the bankrupt should plead fraud in their statements of claim and request a finding of fraud in their court orders in order to have proof of the fraud for the trustee and the Bankruptcy Court.

12 Individuals who owe more than $200,000 in personal income taxes representing 75 percent or more of their unsecured debt are not eligible for an automatic discharge. A court order for a discharge must be sought.

- Student loans survive a bankruptcy and are non-dischargeable for a period of seven years after a student ceases to be a full-time or part-time student. In cases where maintaining liability for all or some of their student debt causes undue hardship and the student acted in good faith in respect of the loan (that is, they used it to pay for their education), the student may apply for a discharge of the loan after five years. Students or former students experiencing financial hardship should consider contacting the student loan Repayment Assistance Plan to discuss restructuring their loan payments. More information on student loan repayment management can be found at <https://www.canada.ca/en/employment-social-development/services/student-financial-aid/student-loan/student-loans/student-loans-repayment-assistance-plan.html>.
- If there is a debt with a co-signor or a guarantor who did not go bankrupt, the creditor may pursue payment from the co-signor/guarantor.

A Creditor Petitions the Debtor into Bankruptcy

Where the debtor is unable to or does not make a proposal or is unwilling to make a voluntary assignment in bankruptcy, a creditor may petition the debtor into bankruptcy. The debt due to the petitioner must be at least $1,000 after deduction of any secured debt, and the petitioner must prove that the debtor has committed an act of bankruptcy within the preceding six months, the most common of which is being unable to meet debts as they fall due. If the petitioner can meet these preconditions, a petition for a receiving order is filed with the registrar of the **Bankruptcy Court** (in Ontario, a branch of the Superior Court) in the place of the court's sitting nearest to where the debtor resides or carries on business. If the petition is filed in Toronto, it goes onto the Commercial List, which is regulated by various practice directions available from the Superior Court office at Toronto or online at <http://www.ontariocourts.ca/scj/civil/commercial-list>. The petition must be served on the debtor personally or in accordance with an order for substituted service. On the day fixed for the hearing, if the debtor does not show up, the bankruptcy judge will grant a receiving order. The order appoints a trustee to act as receiver of the assets of the bankrupt, to investigate the assets and liabilities, and to liquidate them for the benefit of creditors.

Bankruptcy Court
in Ontario, several judges of the Superior Court, with expertise in bankruptcy law, have been assigned to sit in what is called Bankruptcy Court, which is not a formal statutory part of the Superior Court; its judges sit in Toronto, Ottawa, and London

As this process can take some time, a petition may also request the appointment of an interim receiver; such an order may be granted if assets are subject to rapid waste or there is evidence of fraud. An interim receiver does not have the broad powers of the trustee—the interim receiver can only conserve assets, oversee the debtor's operations, and ensure compliance with the law until the trustee is appointed. Should the petition for a receiving order fail, the petitioning creditors may find themselves liable for any acts of the interim receiver that caused the debtor damage.

A debtor may dispute the petition by arguing that no act of bankruptcy has been committed or that the debtor does not owe the debt the petitioner claims is owed.

A creditor should be aware that a petition could be both risky and expensive; however, there are some sound reasons for taking this route. One reason is that if a debtor is truly insolvent, the sooner the debtor goes bankrupt the better for creditors, because assets may rapidly waste or disappear, leaving very little for creditors. A bankruptcy petition, particularly with a request for an interim receiver, can stabilize the assets of the debtor until the trustee can take over.

A second reason is that the BIA gives the creditor some means of investigating and controlling fraudulent preferences and activity by the debtor. Where this is taking place, a petition, with an interim receiver in place, can stop the misconduct. As well, once a trustee is in place, the trustee has broad powers to investigate, as has the Official Receiver, and there are remedies available under the BIA and under provincial insolvency law that the trustee can use. In some cases the interim receiver or trustee may apply to the court for a search warrant of any property that may contain estate assets. The trustee may sue creditors who are given a fraudulent preference and attack transfers for less than fair market value or transfers to relatives and business associates if the debtor has:

- paid some creditors within three months of bankruptcy, but not others, while insolvent;
- transferred property for less than fair market value or in suspicious circumstances; or
- transferred property to a blood relation or to someone who shares control of a business within one year of bankruptcy.

In addition to getting the assets back into the estate, the trustee will also be able to hold up the discharge of an individual (companies are usually liquidated as a result of bankruptcy and do not emerge from it because they cease to exist).

Controlling Debtor Fraud, Assignments, and Preferences Under the Bankruptcy and Insolvency Act

A debtor may attempt to defraud creditors by transferring property to friends or family members for little or no consideration. There may be an agreement between the parties that the property is actually to be held in trust for the debtor and returned after the debtor has been discharged from bankruptcy. In order to return such property to the bankrupt's estate, for the benefit of the creditors, the BIA has certain provisions that give the trustee the power to review and, in some cases, void such transactions.

Section 96 of the BIA provides that any transfer of property made at less than fair market value within the one-year period prior to the bankruptcy to a non-related party or within the five-year period before bankruptcy to a related party may be void as against the trustee. A valid defence might be that the consideration paid was reasonable for the property.

Section 95 of the BIA gives the trustee the power to recover preferential payments made by the bankrupt to a creditor, as well as property that is fraudulently conveyed or mortgaged to a creditor by the bankrupt. To establish a fraudulent preference, the trustee must prove that the transfer, charge, or payment was made within three months of the bankruptcy in the case of unrelated persons, and within the last 12 months if the parties are related. The trustee must also prove that the bankrupt was an insolvent person at the date of the alleged preference and, furthermore, must show that as a result of the transfer, charge, or payment the creditor received a preference. Once these three factors are proven, the onus is on the creditor to prove to the court that there was no intention to prefer this creditor.

Provincial Legislation Controlling Debtor Fraud

Although the BIA has some powerful remedies against a debtor's fraudulent activities in hiding or transferring assets, as a prerequisite for using the remedies, the debtor must be bankrupt. Where the debtor is not bankrupt but is hiding assets and hindering the execution of a judgment, there is provincial legislation that can be of some assistance.

The Fraudulent Conveyances Act

The *Fraudulent Conveyances Act*[13] (FCA) is designed to nullify transfers of assets by the debtor to third parties where the intent of the transfer is to defraud creditors. Where, for example, a debtor who has been sued transfers title to their house to a spouse for little or no payment, a creditor may attack this transaction and obtain an order that sets the transaction aside and vests title with the debtor so that the creditor can seize the property to satisfy a judgment. It is interesting to note that there is no limitation period under the FCA. An action can be brought at any time within the *Limitations Act, 2002*[14] limitation period of two years from the date the fraud was or ought to have been discovered up to a maximum of 15 years from the date of the fraudulent transaction.

To obtain an order, it is necessary to sue the debtor and the transferee in an ordinary lawsuit in the Superior Court. This can be expensive and time consuming. In such an action, the focus is on the intention of the debtor and others involved. The intention is derived from an examination of the facts surrounding a transaction. Although there is rarely a "smoking gun," reasonable inferences may be drawn from the factual circumstances. Over time, the case law has identified "badges of fraud" that, when present, lead to an inference on a balance of probabilities that the transaction is tainted.[15] Once an inference is made, the evidentiary burden is then placed on the debtor to prove that a fraud was not committed.

The usual badges of fraud to watch for are:

1. the debtor was insolvent when the transfers were made or became insolvent as a result of the transfers;

13 RSO 1990, c F.29.

14 SO 2002, c 24.

15 For a discussion of the *Fraudulent Conveyances Act*, badges of fraud, and the role of debtor's intent, see *Abakhan & Associates Inc v Braydon Investments Ltd*, 2009 BCCA 521 and *DBCD Spadina Ltd v Norma Walton*, 2013 ONSC 6833.

2. the debtor was disposing of nearly all assets on the eve of litigation or on the execution of a judgment;
3. the price paid for the asset was clearly inadequate given its value;
4. the transferee was a close relative, business associate, or friend;
5. there was unusual haste in closing the transaction;
6. there was secrecy surrounding the transaction;
7. there was continued possession of, use of, or benefit from the asset by the debtor after transfer; and
8. the debtor had disposed of or was disposing of most other assets at the same time.

In addition to the common law badges of fraud, there are some presumptions in the FCA from which unlawful intent can be presumed. Where the transferee receives no money, there is a presumption of fraud, as there is if the transferee is a close relative. However, a debtor is free to advance evidence that will rebut the presumptions and show that the transaction is innocent. Similarly, a transferee may be able to show that the transaction was a bona fide purchase for value without notice of any defect in the title. To do this, the purchaser must show that a fair market price was paid and that there were no grounds to suspect fraudulent intent by the debtor. If the transferee cannot mount a defence and has sold the property to someone else, the transferee may be ordered to pay an amount equal to the value of the asset. In this situation, where the transferee has conveyed the property to a stranger, the stranger might very well succeed with the defence of being a bona fide purchaser, but the vendor may be obliged to pay an amount equal to the value of the asset.

In addition to the FCA, there are some other ways to curtail the fraudulent debtor. If the creditor has an interest in the land of a debtor, a caution or a notice of pending litigation can be registered on title, which will warn potential purchasers that they buy subject to the rights of the creditor. A Mareva injunction or a writ of sequestration, discussed in Chapter 9, may also be useful here.

The Assignments and Preferences Act

The *Assignments and Preferences Act*[16] (APA) is provincial legislation that was enacted prior to the BIA. The APA allows insolvent persons to turn over assets to an assignee for distribution to creditors. The APA is especially useful in zeroing in on an unjust preference. This happens when a debtor in financial difficulties pays one creditor but not others, conferring a preference on the creditor who was paid. Other creditors may move to set aside the transaction to obtain the return of money or goods to the debtor where these assets will become available to other creditors to satisfy debts owing to them. For example, if a debtor gives security to one creditor for a past debt, but not to others, that is arguably an unjust preference, as would be a transaction where one creditor is paid in full while others receive nothing. Another

16 RSO 1990, c A.33.

example of a situation that under the APA would be void against the debtor's creditors is where a debtor consents to a judgment with the intention of preferring one creditor over others or of defeating or delaying other creditors. In these circumstances the transactions might be set aside. As with the FCA, the intention of the parties, inferred from surrounding circumstances, is important in determining the validity of the transaction.

When seeking remedies under the APA, it is important to note that only unjust preferences can be set aside. In some circumstances, the preference of one creditor over another may be permissible. For example, any payment made by the debtor in the ordinary course of business or on a regular periodic basis is permitted. This includes wages and some monthly bills. Payment to a secured creditor to the value of the security is permitted because the secured creditor could seize the collateral ahead of other creditors anyway. Giving security to a creditor where there is an advance of funds or something of value at the time security is given is permissible if there is evidence that the advance will assist the debtor to stay in business and become solvent. Lastly, if there is pressure on a debtor to pay—for example, from a threat of legal action—and there is evidence that the debtor will be able to continue in business and remain solvent if the debtor responds to the pressure to pay, that may be permitted. However, if the transaction resulted from pressure by a creditor, and it is challenged within 60 days of its occurrence, there is a presumption that the intention was to unjustly prefer a payment, and pressure will not provide the debtor or the transferee with a defence. The statutory presumption arising under the "60-day rule" is, however, rebuttable.

CHAPTER SUMMARY

A bankrupt is defined as a person who is unable to meet financial obligations as they come due. There are three routes that a debtor may pursue through a trustee in bankruptcy. First, a debtor may make a proposal to restructure payment on unsecured debt in certain circumstances. Second, a debtor may make an assignment in bankruptcy by voluntarily filing for bankruptcy. Lastly, a creditor may petition a debtor into bankruptcy. The effect of bankruptcy is that a debtor is stripped of assets, less those exempt from seizure. Once the bankrupt is discharged, the bankrupt cannot be sued for prior debts, with some exceptions. Bankruptcy legislation has a number of safeguards that are meant to protect creditors from fraud by the bankrupt. In addition to bankruptcy legislation, there are provincial statutes that can be used to control debtor fraud when a debtor is not bankrupt. The *Fraudulent Conveyances Act* is designed to set aside transactions where the debtor has tried to transfer assets to others to prevent creditors from seizing them. The *Assignments and Preferences Act* permits creditors to trace proceeds of sale of property by debtors to others where an unjust preference may have been given to one creditor over another.

KEY TERMS

Bankruptcy Court, 435
Official Receiver, 430
Superintendent of Bankruptcy, 429
trustee in bankruptcy, 428

REVIEW QUESTIONS

1. Under what circumstances could a debtor be said to be bankrupt?
2. Why are only unsecured creditors involved in bankruptcy proceedings?
3. What are the options in respect of bankruptcy available to potential bankrupts?
4. What remedies does the *Bankruptcy and Insolvency Act* (BIA) provide to control fraudulent activity by bankrupts?
5. What are the advantages and disadvantages for a creditor in petitioning a debtor into bankruptcy?
6. In what circumstances is it useful to use the *Fraudulent Conveyances Act* (FCA)?
7. For a creditor, what advantages does the FCA have over the bankruptcy legislation?
8. What are the badges of fraud that can assist a creditor under the FCA?
9. What are the statutory presumptions that can assist a creditor under the FCA?
10. How is the *Assignments and Preferences Act* (APA) similar to the FCA? How is it different?

FIGURE 14.1 Monthly Income and Expense Statement (Form 65)

FORM 65

Monthly Income and Expense Statement of the Bankrupt/Debtor and the Family Unit and Information (*or* Amended Information) Concerning the Financial Situation of the Individual Bankrupt (Section 68 and Subsection 102(3) of the Act; Rule 105(4))

(*Title Form 1*)

☐ **Original** ☐ **Amended**

Information concerning the monthly income and expense statement of the bankrupt/debtor and the family unit, financial situation of the bankrupt/debtor and bankrupt's obligation to make payments required under section 68 of the Act to the estate of the bankrupt are as follows:

MONTHLY INCOME	Bankrupt/Debtor	Other members of the family unit	Total
Net employment income	___________		
Net pension/annuities	___________		
Net child support	___________		
Net spousal support	___________		
Net employment insurance benefits	___________		
Net social assistance	___________		
Self-employment income Gross __________ Net	___________		
Other net income	___________		
(*Such as amounts received as damages for wrongful dismissal, as pay equity settlement, or that relate to workers' compensation*) (*Provide details* ____________)			
TOTAL MONTHLY INCOME	$__________ (1)	$__________ (2)[1]	
TOTAL MONTHLY INCOME OF THE FAMILY UNIT ((1) + (2))			►$__________ (3)
MONTHLY NON-DISCRETIONARY EXPENSES			
Child support payments	___________		
Spousal support payments	___________		
Child care	___________		
Health condition expenses	___________		
Fines/penalties imposed by the Court	___________		
Expenses as a condition of employment	___________		
Debts where stay has been lifted	___________		
Other expenses	___________		
(*Provide details*)			
TOTAL MONTHLY NON-DISCRETIONARY EXPENSES		$__________ (4)	$__________ (5)
TOTAL MONTHLY NON-DISCRETIONARY EXPENSES OF THE FAMILY UNIT ((4) + (5))			►$__________ (6)
AVAILABLE MONTHLY INCOME OF THE BANKRUPT/DEBTOR ((1) - (4))	$__________ (7)		
AVAILABLE MONTHLY INCOME OF THE FAMILY UNIT ((3) - (6))			►$__________ (8)
BANKRUPT'S/DEBTOR'S PORTION OF THE AVAILABLE MONTHLY INCOME OF THE FAMILY UNIT ((7) / (8) X 100)			►%__________ (9)

[1] If one of more members of the bankrupt's/debtor's family unit have refused to divulge this information, please provide details as required by paragraph 6(3) of Directive No. 11R2.

FIGURE 14.1 Monthly Income and Expense Statement (Form 65) (*continued*)

FORM 65 – *Concluded*

MONTHLY DISCRETIONARY EXPENSES: (*Family unit*)

Housing expenses
- Rent/mortgage/hypothec .... ______
- Property taxes/condo fees .... ______
- Heating/gas/oil .... ______
- Telephone .... ______
- Cable .... ______
- Hydro .... ______
- Water .... ______
- Furniture .... ______
- Other .... ______

Personal expenses
- Smoking .... ______
- Alcohol .... ______
- Dining/lunches/restaurants .... ______
- Entertainment/sports .... ______
- Gifts/charitable donations .... ______
- Allowances .... ______
- Other .... ______

Non-recoverable medical expenses
- Prescriptions .... ______
- Dental .... ______
- Other .... ______

Living expenses
- Food/grocery .... ______
- Laundry/dry cleaning .... ______
- Grooming/toiletries .... ______
- Clothing .... ______
- Other .... ______

Transportation expenses
- Car lease/payments .... ______
- Repair/maintenance/gas .... ______
- Public transportation .... ______
- Other .... ______

Insurance expenses
- Vehicle .... ______
- House .... ______
- Furniture/contents .... ______
- Life insurance .... ______
- Other .... ______

Payments
- To the estate .... ______
- To secured creditor .... ______
- (*Other than mortgage and vehicle*) .... ______
- Other .... ______

TOTAL MONTHLY DISCRETIONARY EXPENSES (FAMILY UNIT) .... - $ (10)______

MONTHLY SURPLUS OR (DEFICIT) FAMILY UNIT ((8) - (10)) .... = $ (11)______

INFORMATION (*OR* AMENDED INFORMATION) CONCERNING THE FINANCIAL SITUATION OF THE INDIVIDUAL BANKRUPT

Payments to the estate as per agreement

Number of persons in household family unit, including bankrupt: ______

Total amount bankrupt has agreed to pay monthly .... ______ (12)

Amount bankrupt has agreed to pay monthly to repurchase assets

(*Provide details*)______ .... ______ (13)

Residual amount paid into the estate ((12) - (13)) .... ______ (14)

Payments required by Directive No. 11R2 (Surplus Income)

Monthly amount required by Directive No. 11R2 (Surplus Income) based on percentage established on line (9) ... ______ (15)

Difference between (14) and (15) .... ______ (16)

Other applicable comments (*If amount on line (14) is less than amount on line (15), explain why the required payments are not being made:* ______)

Amendment or material change (*If the information relates to a material change or an amendment, provide details:* ______)

Dated at ______, this ______ day of ______ ______.

______
Licensed Insolvency Trustee

______
Bankrupt/Debtor

Notes: In a joint assignment, only one form is required and each debtor's monthly income and non-discretionary expenses have to be explained in detail.

If a copy of this Form is sent electronically by means such as email, the name and contact information of the sender, prescribed in Form 1.1, must be added at the end of the document.

FIGURE 14.2 Consumer Proposal (Form 47)

FORM 47

Consumer Proposal
(Paragraph 66.13(2)(c) of the Act)

(*Title Form 1*)

I, ______________________, a consumer debtor, hereby make the following consumer proposal under the Act:

1. That payment of the claims of secured creditors be made in the following manner:

(*Set out the terms of the proposal in respect of secured claims.*)

2. That payment of all claims directed by the Act to be paid in priority to other claims in the distribution of my property be made in the following manner:

(*Set out the terms of the proposal in respect of preferred claims.*)

3. That payment of the fees and expenses of the administrator of the consumer proposal and payment of the fees and expenses of any person in respect of counselling given by this person pursuant to the Act be made in the following manner:

(*Set out the terms of the proposal in respect of these fees and expenses.*)

4. That the following payments be made to ____________________, the administrator of the consumer proposal, for the benefit of the unsecured creditors:

(*Set out the schedule of payments and the total amount to be paid in respect of unsecured claims.*)

5. That the administrator of the consumer proposal distribute the moneys received to the unsecured creditors in accordance with the following schedule:

(*Describe the manner for distributing dividends.*)

6. That the proposal may include the following additional terms:

(*Set out the additional terms as proposed.*)

Dated at ____________________, this ______ day of __________ ______.

______________________________ Witness

______________________________ Consumer Debtor

NOTE: If a copy of this Form is sent electronically by means such as email, the name and contact information of the sender, prescribed in Form 1.1, must be added at the end of the document.

FIGURE 14.3 Statement of Affairs (Form 79)

FORM 79

Statement of Affairs (Non-Business Bankruptcy/Proposal)
(Subsections 49(2) and 158(*d*) of the Act / Subsections 50(2) and 62(1) and Paragraph 66.13(2)(*d*) of the Act)

(*Title Form 1*)

□ **Original** □ **Amended**

ASSETS							
Type of assets		Description (*provide details*)	Estimate dollar value	Exempt property		Secured amount/ liens	Estimated net realizable dollar value*
				Yes	No		
1. Cash on hand							
2. Furniture							
3. Personal effects							
4. Cash-surrender value of life insurance policies, RRSPs, etc.							
5. Securities							
6. Real property or immovables	House						
	Cottage						
	Land						
7. Motor vehicle	Automobile						
	Motorcycle						
	Snowmobile						
	Other						
8. Recreational equipment							
9. Estimated tax refund							
10. Other assets							
TOTAL							

Date

Bankrupt/Debtor

*For a summary administration, indicate value net of the direct realization costs referred to in Rule 128(1) of the *Bankruptcy and Insolvency Act*.

FIGURE 14.3 Statement of Affairs (Form 79) (*continued*)

FORM 79 -- *Continued*

LIABILITIES						
			Liabilities type code (LTC) 1 Real property or immovable mortgage or hypothec 2 Bank loans (except real property mortgage) 3 Finance company loans 4 Credit cards - bank/trust company issuers 5 Credit cards - other issuers 6 Taxes - federal/provincial/municipal 7 Student loans 8 Loans from individuals 9 Other			
Creditor	Address, including postal code	Account No.	Amount of debt			Enter LTC
			Unsecured	Secured	Preferred	
1						
2						
3						
4						
5						
6						
7						
8						
9						
10						
11						
12						
13						
14						
15						
16						
17						
18						
19						
20						
	TOTAL	Unsecured				
	TOTAL	Secured				
	TOTAL	Preferred				

Date

Bankrupt/Debtor

FIGURE 14.3 Statement of Affairs (Form 79) (*continued*)

FORM 79 -- *Continued*

A. INFORMATION RELATING TO THE AFFAIRS OF THE BANKRUPT/DEBTOR			
1. Family name:	Given names: Gender: F □ M □		Date of birth: _____/___/___ YYYY/ MM / DD
2. Also known as:			
3. Complete address, including postal code:			
4. Marital status: (*specify month and year of event if it occurred in the last five years*)	_____ _____ Married		_____ _____ Single
	_____ _____ Widowed		_____ _____ Separated
	_____ _____ Divorced		_____ _____ Common-law partner
5. Full name of spouse or common-law partner:			
6. Name of present employer:			Occupation (bankrupt/debtor):
7A. Number of persons in household family unit, including bankrupt/debtor:			
7B. Number of persons 17 years of age or younger:			
8. Have you operated a business within the last five years?	Yes	No	(If yes) Name, type and period of operation:

B. WITHIN 12 MONTHS PRIOR TO THE DATE OF THE INITIAL BANKRUPTCY EVENT, HAVE YOU, EITHER IN CANADA OR ELSEWHERE:		
9A. Sold or disposed of any of your property?	Yes	No
9B. Made payments in excess of the regular payments to creditors?	Yes	No
9C. Had any property seized by a creditor?	Yes	No
C. WITHIN FIVE YEARS PRIOR TO THE DATE OF THE INITIAL BANKRUPTCY EVENT, HAVE YOU, EITHER IN CANADA OR ELSEWHERE:		
10A. Sold or disposed of any property?	Yes	No
10B. Made any gifts to relatives or others in excess of $500?	Yes	No

____________________ Date

____________________ Bankrupt/Debtor

FIGURE 14.3 Statement of Affairs (Form 79) (*continued*)

FORM 79 -- *Concluded*

D. BUDGET INFORMATION: ***Attach Form 65 to this form***
11A. Have you ever made a proposal under the *Bankruptcy and Insolvency Act*? Yes ___ No ___
11B. Have you been bankrupt before in Canada? Yes ___ No ___
(If yes, provide the following details for all insolvency proceedings: (a) filing date and location of the proceedings; (b) name of trustee or administrator; (c) if applicable, was the proposal successful; (d) date on which Certificate of Full Performance or Discharge was obtained.) ______________________
12. Do you expect to receive any sums of money that are not related to your normal income, or any other property within the next 12 months? Yes ___ No ___
13. If you answered Yes to any of questions 8, 9 or 11, provide details: ______________________
14. Give reasons for your financial difficulties: ______________________ ______________________ ______________________

I, _______________, of the __________ of ___________________ in the Province of _______________,do swear (*or* solemnly declare) that this statement is, to the best of my knowledge, a full, true and complete statement of my affairs on the ______ day of _________ ______ and fully discloses all property and transactions of every description that is or was in my possession or that may devolve on me in accordance with the *Bankruptcy and Insolvency Act.*

SWORN (*or* SOLEMNLY DECLARED)
before me at ____________________________ (*city, town or village*),
in the Province of _________________________,
on this ____ day of _______________ _________.

_________________________ _________________________

Commissioner of Oaths Bankrupt/Debtor
for the Province of _______________________

NOTE: If a copy of this Form is sent electronically by means such as email, the name and contact information of the sender, prescribed in Form 1.1, must be added at the end of the document.

FIGURE 14.4 Questions for Examination of Non-Business Bankrupt (Form 27)

FORM 27

Examination of Bankrupt by Official Receiver
(Non-Business)
(Section 161 of the Act)

Instructions to Official Receiver

The following questions, or questions to a like effect, are to be put to the person examined under section 161 by the official receiver. The questions should be expanded or supplemented by the official receiver in an endeavour to extract from the examination the maximum of essential information and to determine as nearly as possible the true cause of the bankruptcy, the disposition of the property and the conduct of the bankrupt.

OFFICIAL RECEIVER'S NOTES (*To be completed by Official Receiver*)

Previous Bankruptcy(ies):

Reviewable Transactions:

Undisclosed Assets:

Undisclosed Debts:

Preferential Payments:

Excessive Credit Use:

Settlements:

Other Matters or Concerns:

____

Official Receiver

FIGURE 14.4 Questions for Examination of Non-Business Bankrupt (Form 27) (*continued*)

FORM 27 -- *Continued*

1. Give your full legal name (and aliases) and your birthday.
2. What is your current address?
3. Have you ever been the owner, or are the current owner of the residence that you live in, or does a family member own it?
4. How much is your rent, or your mortgage payments?
5. Have you been informed of your duties, according to the *Bankruptcy & Insolvency Act*?
6. Approximately on what date did you become aware that you were unable to meet your debts as they became due and what made you aware of this fact?
7. Did you use or obtain credit after this date? If yes, from whom did you obtain credit?
8. Have you ever been bankrupt before, or made a proposal to your creditors? If yes, when?
9. Do you have any credit cards in your possession at this time?
10. Who is your present employer, and how much is your monthly "Take Home" pay?
11. Do you have any other source of income, other than your job? If yes, what is the source and amount of the income?
12. What bank or banks do you have accounts at, and what is your present balance?
13. Do you have any other debts that you have not disclosed on your Statement of Affairs? If yes, give details.
14. Do you have any other assets that you have not disclosed on your Statement of Affairs? If yes, give details.
15. Explain the following debts, giving the date they were started, and the reason or cause of the debt.
16. Have you sold, given away or disposed of any assets in the 12 months prior to the date of the initial bankruptcy event? If so, give details.
17. From the sale of the above assets, how much money did you receive, and what did you do with the money?
18. Did you sell or give away anything that you bought on credit before it was fully paid for? If so, give details.

FIGURE 14.4 Questions for Examination of Non-Business Bankrupt (Form 27) (*continued*)

FORM 27 -- *Continued*

19. Have you paid back any debts to family members in the 12 months prior to the date of the initial bankruptcy event? If so, give details.

20. Did you pay your trustee at the time of signing your papers? If so, how much?

21. Are you presently making payments to your trustee? If so, how much?

22. Did you consider any other formal insolvency options before you filed your bankruptcy?

23. What creditors did you make payments to in the 3 months prior to filing bankruptcy? Did you pay any of these creditors in full, or give them larger than normal payments?

24. Are you aware of anyone holding any assets in trust? If so, give details.

25. Are you preparing monthly income and expense statements for your trustee?

26. List all monthly income, including that of your spouse (including common-law), and the source of the income.

27. List all monthly expenses, with the dollar amounts beside them.

28. If your expenses are more than your income, please explain what expenses you are not paying, and what you are doing to correct this problem.

29. Who advised you in regard to your financial problems?

30. Do you own or lease a motor vehicle? If yes, give details (are you paying the trustee to keep the vehicle, or who are paying to keep it, and what amount is being paid).

31. Are you presently borrowing a motor vehicle? If yes, give details.

32. Did you obtain any cash advances on any credit cards in the 12 months prior to the date of the initial bankruptcy event? If so, list them giving cash amounts and the last date an advance was taken.

33. Did you pay for any trips with your credit cards in the 12 months prior to the date of the initial bankruptcy event? If yes, what trips did you take, and how much money was charged on the cards?

34. Please explain why and how you ran up a total credit card debt of over $x.xx on your credit cards. I.e., what type of purchases were made and over what period of time?

35. What do you believe are the causes of your bankruptcy? Please give a brief explanation.

FIGURE 14.4 Questions for Examination of Non-Business Bankrupt (Form 27) (*continued*)

FORM 27 -- *Concluded*

36. Do you feel you are directly or partially responsible for your bankruptcy? Please explain your answer.

NOTE TO OFFICIAL RECEIVER

Any additional questions put by the official receiver and the answers to them should be entered in the space provided below or on a sheet to be attached to this form.

I, ____________________________, of the ______________ of __________, in the Province of____________________________, do swear (*or* solemnly declare) that to the best of my knowledge the above answers are true in every respect. I understand that this examination is being adjourned *sine die* and may be continued at a later date if necessary.

SWORN (*or* SOLEMNLY DECLARED)
before me at the ________________
__________ of ________ in the Province
of ____________________, this ____ day
of __________ ____.

____
Official Receiver for Bankruptcy
Division No__________ of the
Bankruptcy District of
____

____
Bankrupt

FIGURE 14.5 Report of Trustee on Bankrupt's Application for Discharge (Form 82)

FORM 82

Report of Trustee on Bankrupt's
Application for Discharge
(Subsection 170(1) of the Act)

(Title Form 1)

Date of bankruptcy:		Date of initial bankruptcy event:	
Marital status:			
Type of employment:	Number of persons in household family unit, including bankrupt:		
LIABILITIES			
	Secured	Preferred	Unsecured
Declared	$	$	$
Proven	$	$	$
ASSETS			
Description	Value as per Statement of Affairs	Amount realized	Estimate of assets to be realized
	$	$	$
TOTAL			
ANTICIPATED RATE OF DIVIDENDS			
Preferred creditors:		Unsecured creditors	

A. CAUSES OF BANKRUPTCY

1. Provide details of the causes of bankruptcy:

____

____

____

B. INFORMATION CONCERNING THE FINANCIAL SITUATION (*The same method of calculation must be used to establish the available monthly income of the bankrupt and the family unit at date of bankruptcy and at date of this report. Explain any material changes.*)

2. a) Available monthly income of the bankrupt at date of bankruptcy (*Same amount as line (7) on Form* 65) . . . . $__________

   b) Available monthly income of the bankrupt at date of this report . . . . $__________

3. a) Available monthly income of the family unit at date of bankruptcy (*Same amount as line (8) on Form* 65) . . . . $__________

   b) Available monthly income of the family unit at date of this report . . . . $__________

FIGURE 14.5 Report of Trustee on Bankrupt's Application for Discharge (Form 82) (*continued*)

FORM 82 - *Continued*

C. CONDUCT OF THE BANKRUPT

4. a) Was the bankrupt required to pay to the estate an amount established by Directive No. 11R2 (Surplus Income)? (*If yes, attach Appendix A*) □Yes □ No

   b) Could the bankrupt have made a viable proposal rather than proceeding with bankruptcy? (*If yes, attach Appendix A*) □Yes □ No

5. Did the bankrupt have high income tax debts pursuant to section 172.1 of the Act? □Yes □ No

6. a) Did the bankrupt fail to perform any of the duties imposed on him/her under the Act? (*If yes, provide details*) □Yes □ No

   b) Can the bankrupt be justly held responsible for any of the facts referred pursuant to section 173 of the Act? (*If yes, provide details*) □Yes □ No

   c) Did the bankrupt commit any offence in connection with the bankruptcy? (*If yes, provide details*) □Yes □ No

7. a) Did the bankrupt ever make a proposal under the *Bankruptcy and Insolvency Act*? (*If yes, provide details*) □Yes □ No

   b) Has the bankrupt been bankrupt before either in Canada or elsewhere? (*If yes, provide details*) □Yes □ No

8. Were inspectors appointed in this estate? □Yes □ No
   (*Provide details if the trustee has reasonable grounds to believe that the inspectors will not approve this report. Attach a copy of the resolution.*)

D. DISCHARGE OF THE BANKRUPT

9. a) Is it the intention of the trustee to oppose the bankrupt's discharge? (*If yes, provide details*) □Yes □ No

   b) Does the trustee have reasonable grounds to believe that a creditor or the Superintendent will oppose the bankrupt's discharge for a reason other than those set out in section 173(1)(*m*) or (*n*) of the Act? (*If yes, provide details*) □Yes □ No

10. Did the bankrupt refuse or neglect to receive counselling pursuant to Directive No. 1R3 (Counselling in Insolvency Matters)? (*If yes, provide details*) □Yes □ No

11. Are there other facts, matters or circumstances that would justify the Court in refusing an absolute order of discharge? (*If yes, provide details*) □Yes □ No

12. Other pertinent information (e.g. exceptional personal circumstances, preferential payments, etc.). (*If yes, provide details*) □Yes □ No

Additional details as required

Number   Additional information

____

____

____

Dated at ____________________, this ____________ day of ________________ ______.

____

Licensed Insolvency Trustee

FIGURE 14.5 Report of Trustee on Bankrupt's Application for Discharge (Form 82) (*continued*)

FORM 82 – *Concluded*

APPENDIX A

A. AMOUNT REQUIRED TO BE PAID MONTHLY BY THE BANKRUPT

Monthly amount required by Directive No. 11R2 (Surplus Income)
(*Same amount as line (15) on Form 65*) .... $__________(1)
Amount bankrupt has agreed to pay monthly (*Same amount as line (12) on Form 65*) ...... $__________(2)
Difference between lines (1) and (2) .... $__________
Amount bankrupt has agreed to pay monthly to repurchase assets
(*Same amount as line (13) on Form 65, provide details*) .... $__________(3)
Total anticipated payments, lines (2) + (3): .... $__________

B. SURPLUS INCOME

1. Did the bankrupt make all required payments pursuant to section 68 of the Act? (*If no, provide details*) ☐Yes ☐ No
2. Does amount established to be paid correspond with Directive No. 11R2 (Surplus Income)? (*If no, provide details of any extenuating circumstances that would affect amount to be paid as per Directive*) ☐Yes ☐ No
3. Was the bankrupt made aware of the possibility of requesting mediation? ☐Yes ☐ No
4. Were there any amendments or material changes during the period of bankruptcy? (*If yes, provide details*) ☐Yes ☐ No
5. Was mediation necessary under subsections 68(6) or 68(7) of the Act to determine the amount to be paid by the bankrupt? ☐Yes ☐ No

Dated at ____________________, this ____________ day of ________________.

____
Licensed Insolvency Trustee

NOTE: If a copy of this Form is sent electronically by means such as email, the name and contact information of the sender, prescribed in Form 1.1, must be added at the end of the document.

PART III

Debtors' Remedies

In previous chapters, debtors were primarily dealt with in the context of a creditor's collection action. With the exception of the chapter on bankruptcy, the focus has been on the creditor, with some mention, from time to time, of possible actions that a debtor might take.

In this final chapter we bring together a range of strategies that a debtor might be able to exercise proactively or in response to a creditor's action taken against the debtor. Additional information, not available elsewhere in the text, on debt management, credit counselling, and credit report rectification is included in this part.

Debtors' Remedies 15

LEARNING OUTCOMES

After reading this chapter, the student will:

- Be able to identify and recognize strategies available to debtors to deal with and respond to debt enforcement.
- Know how to review a debt contract to determine payment terms and other provisions affecting creditors and debtors.
- Be able to determine if debts can be consolidated and whether terms of payment can be renegotiated.
- Know how to respond to collection agents.
- Know what steps a debtor should consider and take if sued in Superior Court or Small Claims Court.
- Know the steps a debtor must take and the strategies they may use if summoned for an examination in aid of execution.
- Know how garnishment works, and know what limits there are when garnishment is used.
- Know how a debtor is affected by filing and enforcement of a writ of seizure and sale, and know what rights they may have when a writ has been executed.
- Understand when and how a debtor should seek help from a credit counselling agency or seek other help with debt management.
- Recognize when bankruptcy may be an option for a debtor or when a debtor can make a consumer proposal and assess which of these options would be most effective.
- Know the steps a debtor must take and the protections afforded to the debtor if the debtor is petitioned into bankruptcy.
- Know how to read, understand, and interpret credit reports and correct errors in those reports.
- Know how to improve credit ratings and scores.

Dealt with in this chapter are various strategies that a debtor might use to

- renegotiate debt,
- defend debt actions,
- bring court motions for installment payments and consolidation orders,
- enter into credit counselling and a debt management plan, and
- file a consumer proposal or bankruptcy.

Information is also included on how to make proposals to pay debts in the Small Claims Court and to effectively participate in a judgment-debtor examination.

Paying the Debt

An agreement between a debtor and a creditor is a contract. The debtor should review the contractual terms of the agreement, whether it is a credit card agreement, loan agreement, or security agreement, to determine what the consequences are for missing a payment or making a late payment. Some agreements contain a clause permitting a debtor to make a late payment or miss one payment, but make up the payment later before the contract ends, with minimal or no penalty. If a debtor intends to rely on such a clause to get over a short-term cash-flow problem, it is a good idea for the debtor to contact the creditor so the creditor will be aware of the debtor's intention to rely on that clause for that particular payment.

acceleration clause provides that if the debtor misses a payment, the entire debt is accelerated and becomes immediately due and payable

Most agreements contain an **acceleration clause**, which states that if one payment is missed, the entire debt, at the creditor's option, becomes due. In that case, instead of facing one catch-up payment, the debtor would have to come up with the money to pay the entire debt. In some cases the creditor imposes a higher interest rate, in accordance with the credit agreement, on a debtor who defaults on or is late in making payments.

As well as facing additional costs from not paying the debt, the following consequences may occur:

- The debtor's credit rating and overall credit score will be negatively affected, such that it may be difficult to secure further credit, rental premises, insurance, or, in some cases, even a job.
- The debtor may have to deal with repeated calls and contact from a collection agency.
- The debtor may be sued, which will result in a judgment and possibly a writ of seizure and sale that can block the sale of the debtor's real estate or prevent the debtor from obtaining a mortgage. A judgment against the debtor can also result in a garnishment of the debtor's wages, other income, bank accounts, and investments.
- The debtor may be petitioned into bankruptcy by a creditor.
- If the debtor gave collateral to secure the loan, then the collateral may be repossessed. For example, if the loan was used to buy a car and that car was

> the collateral, the vehicle can be seized if the debtor has paid less than two-thirds of the loan. The *Consumer Protection Act, 2002*[1] provides that if a consumer has paid more than two-thirds of a consumer loan, then the collateral cannot be repossessed.

In most cases, it is to the debtor's advantage to find the funds to pay the debts owed. In some cases, preparing a debt-focused budget (see the Debtor Budget Worksheet in Figure 15.1) can help identify expenses that can be cut or opportunities to sell assets to obtain funds to pay the debts. In many cases, debt is caused by excess spending on gambling or substance abuse. If this is the case, a debtor can seek support by contacting the Ontario Problem Gambling Helpline at 1-888-230-3505 or at <http://www.opgh.on.ca> or the Drug and Alcohol Helpline at 1-800-565-8603 or at <http://www.drugandalcoholhelpline.ca>. If the debtor is able to do so, taking on a part-time, temporary, or seasonal position may help the debtor to earn funds to pay debts. There are a variety of good debt-payment and budgeting books on the market that can help debtors organize their affairs so that they can pay their debts.[2]

Consolidation of Debt Loans

It is useful for a debtor to make a list of all debts (see the Debtor Budget Worksheet in Figure 15.1) and set out the interest rate applied to each debt. In some cases, a debtor may be able to shift higher interest debt to a lower interest rate credit card or line of credit. If a debtor's credit rating is good, the debtor may be able to apply for a lower interest rate credit card or line of credit. A better interest rate can usually be obtained by requesting a credit card or line of credit from the institution the debtor most frequently uses. If the debtor's credit rating is good and there is sufficient monthly income to do so, it is usually advantageous to try to qualify for a bank consolidation-of-debt loan. Monthly credit card payments at various rates of interest, which are often high, would be replaced by one monthly payment, usually at a lower rate of interest. A better rate of interest can sometimes be obtained if the debtor has real estate or a vehicle that can be offered as collateral. The lender will usually want to see the debtor's monthly budget, list of debts, and proof of income (usually in the form of paystubs) to ensure that the debtor can make the monthly loan payments. In some cases, the lender will request that someone co-sign the loan along with the debtor as extra security for repayment of the loan.

Renegotiation of Debt

The debtor may be able to approach the creditor to discuss renegotiation of the debt. As mentioned earlier, some credit agreements provide that one payment may be

1 SO 2002, c 30, Schedule A.

2 An excellent Canadian book on debt management is Gail Vaz-Oxlade, *Debt-Free Forever* (Toronto: HarperCollins, 2009).

missed and added onto the end of the debt. When asking to change payment terms, loan balances, or interest rates, it is usually helpful if the debtor is honest with the creditor and explains what hardship has resulted from the debt. The creditor may be able to move the credit card balance over to another lower-interest card or unsecured or secured line of credit, which should result in a better rate, or the creditor may even provide a loan to replace the debt. Remember that creditors may be receptive to renegotiation of a debt, even if the creditor ends up collecting less than the full value of the outstanding debt. Creditors are not in the morality business; they recognize that "a bird in the hand is worth two in the bush"—that is, they may take less than the full amount due if they think they have little chance of recovering all of the debt, or if they have to spend more to collect the full amount than they would get if they settled with the debtor. As well, there is always the possibility that a debtor may go bankrupt, leaving the creditor with little or no repayment on the debt.

If the debt is a student loan, the debtor should contact the student loan Repayment Assistance Plan to discuss restructuring the loan payments. While the amount owing cannot be altered, monthly payments can be reduced and spread out over a longer period of time. Information on the Repayment Assistance Plan can be found at <https://www.canada.ca/en/employment-social-development/services/student-financial-aid/student-loan/student-loans/student-loans-repayment-assistance-plan.html>. A student loan cannot be included in a bankruptcy until seven years after the student has left school; however, in hardship cases, this waiting period may be reduced to five years.

If the debt is for unpaid income tax, the Canada Revenue Agency (CRA) has a department that handles requests for individuals to request payment plan arrangements to spread payments out over a longer time period. In some cases, the CRA will consider a reduction on compassionate grounds, such as the occurrence of a natural disaster or serious illness. To discuss alternative income tax payment arrangements, the debtor should call the CRA at 1-888-863-8657.

In the event that the debtor and creditor agree to a new arrangement for payment of the debt, the details should be confirmed in writing.

Responding to a Collection Agent

Once a payment on a debt is late or has been missed, the debtor may be contacted by a collection agent. Before a collection agent can contact a debtor by telephone, the agent must send the debtor a written notice that sets out the debt and confirms who the agent is and who the agent is acting for. Once the agent has provided the debtor with this notice, the debtor may be contacted by phone or email three times over the next seven days, or more often with the debtor's consent. The *Collection and Debt Settlement Services Act*,[3] as detailed in Chapter 1, restricts the times during which an agent may call.

3 RSO 1990, c C.14.

Debtors can stop a collection agent from contacting them in two ways:

- by sending a letter to the collection agency disputing the debt and suggesting that they take the matter to court, or
- by having a lawyer or paralegal send a letter to the agency confirming that they are acting for the debtor and directing that the agency deal with the legal representative.

Once the debtor has notified the collection agency that they dispute the debt or have turned the matter over to a legal representative, if a collection agent persists in contacting the debtor or calls the debtor outside of permitted hours or more often than is allowed, the debtor should request the agent's registration identification number. Complaints about collection agents should be directed to the Ministry of Government and Consumer Services' Consumer Protection Branch at 1-800-889-9768. The Ontario government also provides information about a debtor's rights when dealing with a collection agent at <https://www.ontario.ca/page/collection-agency-your-rights>.

Responding to a Superior Court Action

A creditor may commence a lawsuit in the Superior Court of Justice to obtain judgment for the debt. Claims for up to $25,000 or less are usually brought in the Small Claims Court.[4] The debtor, upon being served with such a claim, may want to ignore it; however, doing so can result in increased costs. The debtor should review the claim for accuracy and to identify possible defences concerning product quality, limitation period, **set-offs**, or other issues. Superior Court documents and procedures are fairly technical, and most people use the services of a lawyer to represent them. But in many cases a debtor cannot afford a lawyer. A debtor can obtain a free 30-minute consultation with a lawyer specializing in debtor–creditor law by contacting the Law Society of Ontario's Lawyer Referral Service at <https://lsrs.lsuc.on.ca/lsrs>. If the matter is urgent, the service can be reached by phone at 1-855-947-5255 (in Toronto 416-947-5255). Debtors experiencing severe hardship may obtain assistance through Pro Bono Ontario's legal help clinics. For more information on Pro Bono Ontario, go to their website at <https://www.probonoontario.org> or call their free legal advice hotline at 1-855-255-7256.

set-off
a legal remedy used where a creditor owes a debtor money, and the debtor seeks to have the amount owing to the creditor deducted from any money that the debtor is found to owe the creditor

For those who are not eligible for legal aid and who cannot afford the usual services offered by lawyers, there may be another solution. The Law Society of Ontario permits the use of limited retainers, also known as the "unbundling of legal services." Clients who cannot afford the full range of a lawyer's or paralegal's services may agree to have the legal representative provide some services, with the client doing the rest. A debtor who wants to make this kind of arrangement should discuss the options carefully with the legal representative, and the services to be provided should be clearly spelled out in the retainer.

---

4 As mentioned in a note in Chapter 13, the Small Claims Court monetary jurisdiction is expected to be increased to $50,000 in the near future.

Lastly, a debtor who cannot afford to defend a lawsuit may apply for a fee waiver with respect to court filing fees. A guide and accompanying forms for fee waivers can be found on the Attorney General's website at <http://www.attorneygeneral.jus.gov.on.ca/english/courts/feewaiver/guide-forms.asp>.

A debtor, served with a statement of claim, can find the contact information for the creditor's lawyer on the last page of the claim. If the debtor acknowledges the debt and would like to make payment arrangements, possibly avoiding a judgment, the debtor should call the creditor's lawyer and inquire about making an offer to settle the case. The lawyer has a duty to pass on any offers made to the creditor for its consideration. In order to save the time and expense associated with going further with the court claim, a settlement may be possible.

In some cases a debtor may be judgment proof and will at that point in time not have anything to lose by not responding to a lawsuit. If the debtor's income is from a benefits program such as welfare, CPP, or an Old Age Security pension, these funds cannot be garnished in order to pay a judgment unless the debt is for child or spousal support payments. However, if a judgment is made against the debtor and a writ put in place, if the debtor's circumstances change, perhaps as a result of an inheritance, the creditor will then be able to enforce its judgment plus accumulated costs and interest. The debtor will then end up paying more to the creditor than if the debtor had responded to the claim at the time it was served and made arrangements to pay at that time.

Responding to a Small Claims Court Claim

A debtor served with a Small Claims Court action may be able to be self-represented with the help of the guides and forms available online at <http://www.ontariocourtforms.on.ca>. Most consumer debt claims in Ontario are brought in the Small Claims Court because they are usually claims for $25,000 or less. If served with a Small Claims Court claim, the debtor may consider one of the following responses:

- Contact the plaintiff's lawyer or paralegal to discuss a possible settlement of the claim.
- File a defence form that contains a proposal to pay some or all of the debt in monthly payments. If the creditor does not respond within 20 days, the debtor should begin making the payments proposed to the creditor. If the creditor disagrees with the proposal, a court hearing may be set to determine payments. If the proposal is for partial payment, the court will schedule a settlement conference wherein the parties will be encouraged to try to resolve the entire matter by agreement. The fee to file a defence is $50. If it is a financial hardship for a defendant to pay the filing fee and the defendant has limited assets, an application may be made to the court for a Fee Waiver Assistance form that will allow the defendant to file a defence and any other court paperwork for free and to obtain an interpreter paid for by the court, should one be needed. The Pro Bono Ontario organization mentioned earlier has drop-in clinics at the Small Claims Courts in Toronto and Ottawa that can provide some assistance to qualifying parties. Parties residing outside these two locations can receive assistance from Pro Bono Ontario's helpline at 1-855-255-7256.

- File a defence and possibly a defendant's claim for any issues—for example, product quality—that the defendant may have in defence of their failure to pay. See Chapter 10 for more information on defences and defendant's claims. Once a defence is filed, the court will schedule a settlement conference for the parties to attend.
- If the debtor does not defend the claim and a judgment is made, the debtor can bring a motion to request permission to pay the judgment in installments. Once an installment order is made, the creditor cannot take any steps to enforce the judgment other than to issue and file a writ of seizure and sale of land.
- If the claim discloses no reasonable cause of action or is an abuse of process, a motion may be brought to strike the claim.
- If there is already one or more Small Claims Court judgments against the defendant, when this latest judgment is made, a motion can be brought requesting a consolidation order to bring the orders together and permit one monthly payment to be made to the court. A consolidation order prevents the creditor from taking any steps to enforce, other than to issue and file a writ of seizure and sale of land. The procedure for obtaining a consolidation order is set out in Chapter 11.

Responding to Enforcement Proceedings

Once a creditor has obtained a judgment, the creditor may try to enforce it through the use of garnishments and writs, and may schedule an examination in aid of execution of the debtor.

Examination in Aid of Execution

A judgment debtor is required to attend an examination in aid of execution up to once a year, or more often if ordered by the court. The debtor should complete the required Financial Information Form and bring it to the examination along with supporting financial documentation. A judge in Small Claims Court presides over the examination and, even at this stage, payment agreements can sometimes be reached. The debtor should be forthright and honest at all times. Failure to attend an examination or to respond to relevant questions asked can result in a contempt of court order and a possible jail sentence.

Garnishments

To pay an outstanding judgment, 20 percent of a debtor's net pay may be garnished. In some cases, this may cause financial hardship to the debtor. The debtor can bring a motion under the *Wages Act*[5] to increase the exempt portion of wages from 80 percent to a higher exempt amount, resulting in a reduction in the amount garnished.

5 RSO 1990, c W.1.

Writs of Seizure and Sale

A judgment creditor will usually issue and file a writ of seizure and sale of land, and, in some cases, of personal property, against the name of the judgment debtor. A writ filed against land prevents the debtor from selling real property or obtaining a mortgage. In order to remove the writ, the creditor will usually want full payment of the judgment and accrued interest and costs. If the property is to be sold, the creditor and the debtor's real estate lawyer can usually make arrangements to have the writ lifted, provided that the debtor's lawyer agrees to direct funds from the sale proceeds to pay the debt.

If the debtor chooses to execute the land writ and have the sheriff seize and sell the real estate, the debtor should closely monitor market conditions, the listing price, and any expenses charged to get the property ready for sale. If it appears that the sheriff is undervaluing the property or spending excessive sums of money to ready the property for sale, the debtor may bring an interpleader motion to the court for an order directing the sheriff with respect to how the enforcement process is to be carried out by the sheriff's office.

If the debtor exercises a writ of seizure and sale of personal property, the debtor is entitled to demand from the bailiff an inventory of all of the items sold. Debtors should also familiarize themselves with the provisions of the *Execution Act*[6] that stipulate property that is exempt from seizure. More information on the *Execution Act* can be found in Chapter 9.

Credit Counselling and Debt Management Plans

If a debtor is unable to qualify for a debt consolidation loan from a financial institution, the debtor may wish to consider seeking help from a debt settlement service provider, formerly known as a credit counsellor, and possibly enter into a debt management plan. Debt settlement service providers are regulated under the *Collection and Debt Settlement Services Act*. For more information on the Act, consult Chapter 1. A debt settlement service provider can be found through an online search using a site such as <http://www.yellowpages.ca> or by visiting <https://www.ontario.ca/page/collection-agency-your-rights>, where several credit counselling agencies are listed. Most debt settlement agencies are run on a not-for-profit basis and are in fact funded by commercial creditors.

If a debtor is lacking in budgeting skills, credit counselling is a good place to start. With the implementation of a careful budget, funds with which to start paying off debts can sometimes be found.

If a debtor is seeking relief from interest that is being paid, a credit counsellor can put forward a debt management plan to the debtor's creditors, which, if accepted, usually gives the debtor a reduced interest rate and a longer time period to complete

6 RSO 1990, c E.24.

payment. The principal due is usually not reduced. Unlike a consumer proposal (see below), the debt management plan does not stop creditors from taking other enforcement actions if they wish to do so. A debt management plan is usually made to run over a four- to five-year period, with the debtor making one monthly payment to the debt settlement service provider who then pays the creditors. Joining in a debt management plan is voluntary for creditors, so the debtor may be faced with making the monthly plan payment and payments to creditors who did not join the plan.

Consumer Proposals and Bankruptcy

Under the federal *Bankruptcy and Insolvency Act*,[7] a debtor may hire a trustee in bankruptcy either to make a consumer proposal to their creditors or to file for bankruptcy. As well, a creditor may petition a debtor into bankruptcy. The filing of a consumer proposal or a bankruptcy stops all enforcement action by the creditors.

Consumer Proposals

A debtor who owes $250,000 or less, exclusive of a mortgage, may make a consumer proposal to their creditors to pay a reduced amount of the debt. Generally the proposal is to pay 35 to 50 percent of the amount owed. The creditors have 45 days to vote on the proposal, which must be accepted by a 50 percent plus 1 vote from the creditors. If a proposal is not accepted, bankruptcy is not automatic. The debtor can then choose to do nothing or to go bankrupt. Once a consumer proposal is filed, all interest stops accruing on the debts. The debtor surrenders all credit cards to the trustee and makes one monthly payment to the trustee. Consumer proposals may be set up to run over a five-year period.[8] All of the creditors are bound by the proposal. The advantage of a consumer proposal is that the debtor gets to keep all of their property and pays a reduced amount over a longer time period.

If the debtor owes more than $250,000, then a Division I proposal can be made, for which there is no set monetary limit. With a Division I proposal, a higher percentage of creditors must accept the proposal in a shorter period of time (21 days). If the Division I proposal is not accepted, then the debtor is automatically put into bankruptcy.

Bankruptcy

A Canadian resident who owes at least $1,000 and cannot meet financial obligations as they come due may file for bankruptcy. With a bankruptcy, most of the debtor's property is surrendered to a trustee to sell and pay the sale proceeds to creditors. A bankruptcy clears most of the debtor's debts. A few debts, however, such as child and spousal support, court fines, judgments based on fraud, and court orders to pay damages for personal injuries or assault, survive the bankruptcy and must be paid.

---

7 RSC 1985, c B-3, as amended.

8 *Ibid*, s 66.12(5).

Compared with a consumer proposal, there is a higher fee to be paid to a trustee to go bankrupt. If the debtor, based on net income and family size, is considered to have surplus income (over $1,870 per month for a single person), the surplus monthly income must be paid to the trustee for the benefit of creditors for 21 months on a first bankruptcy. Once all of the debtor's obligations under the bankruptcy are met, the trustee applies for a discharge from the bankruptcy.

Bankruptcy and Consumer Proposal Comparison

Bankruptcy	Consumer Proposal
Must owe at least $1,000	No minimum
No maximum limit	Must be debts of $250,000 or less (though a Division I proposal can be made if debt is higher)
Debtor must surrender most property to the trustee	Debtor keeps all property
Property is liquidated and funds used to pay creditors	Payments on a reduced debt amount are made to creditors
If surplus income, monthly payments are made for 21 months on a first bankruptcy	Payments made to creditors over a 5-year time period
Credit rating drops to R9	Credit rating drops to R7
Discharged from first bankruptcy in 9 to 21 months from time of filing depending on where payments being made	Proposal is generally paid in 5 years' time
Bankruptcy remains on credit record for 6 years from discharge date	Proposal remains on credit record for 3 years after final payment has been made
Student loans can be included in bankruptcy 7 years after debtor ceases to be a student	Student loans cannot form part of the proposal
Higher fee to be paid to trustee	Lower trustee fee

Credit Reports

Anyone who has ever applied for a bank account or credit card has a credit record. There are two major credit bureaus in Canada: Equifax and TransUnion. An annual review of the debtor's credit record should be undertaken by the debtor with each of the bureaus to ensure accuracy and to flag any suspicious activity that may be a sign of identity theft. Credit reports are available to debtors by regular letter mail at no cost.

Credit bureaus obtain their information from debtors, creditors, collection agencies, and public agencies. Whenever a debtor fills out a credit, job, tenancy, or insurance application, the information on the form is provided, with their consent, to the credit bureaus. Creditors provide information to the bureaus on how much the debtor owes, what payments have been made, and how long the debtor takes to make payments. Public agencies such as the Superintendent of Bankruptcy and the courts provide information to the bureaus on proposals, bankruptcies, judgments, and executions against the debtor.

There is an example of a consumer credit report in Chapter 3. A credit report has two sets of payment data in it—the nine-point R rating scale and the overall credit score. The free report that can be obtained has a debtor's R ratings on it. R stands for revolving credit such as credit cards and reflects the debtor's payment trends on credit cards. If a debtor has an R1 rating, which is the highest, this means that all debts are paid on time. The filing of a consumer proposal drops the debtor's rating to R7, while a bankruptcy drops it to R9. However, on discharge from bankruptcy, the rating status is zero. The debtor can then work to build up a new credit rating. Some banks will give the discharged bankrupt the opportunity to have a secured credit card whereby the debtor gives the bank $1,000 to hold in exchange for a $500 secured credit card. If all payments are made in full and on time, the debtor's credit rating will slowly improve.

Credit scores range from 300 to 900 and are based on payment history, how long the debtor has been using credit, recent credit history, how many credit cards the debtor has, and how high the outstanding debt on those cards is. A high score is ideal and can result in lower insurance premiums and better credit limits on approved cards. To keep the score favourable, a debtor should not use more than 30 to 50 percent of the available credit on their cards. As well, the debtor should not make several credit card applications at the same time, because this will reduce the debtor's credit score.

Correcting Inaccuracies on Credit Reports

A debtor's credit bureau report may contain inaccuracies. When inaccuracies are discovered by the debtor, they should be put in writing and submitted to the credit bureau and to the financial institutions they relate to, and a correction should be requested. If the financial institution agrees that an error has been made, the credit bureau has 30 days to correct the report. If the correction cannot be made, the debtor can submit an entry consisting of 100 words or less to be added to the report. If there is a complaint against the financial institution or credit bureau about the debtor's report, the debtor can call the Financial Consumer Agency of Canada at 1-866-461-3222.

The best ways to build and maintain a good credit report are to:

- review credit reports annually;
- demand in writing that errors be fixed—if they cannot, add a personal statement of explanation to the report;

- accurately complete credit card applications;
- apply for a minimal number of credit cards;
- pay bills, if possible, in full by the due date—if bills cannot be paid in full, try to pay more than the minimum payment amounts;
- pay debts off as soon as possible;
- keep card balances well below the credit limit;
- open a bank savings account and make regular deposits after a consumer proposal or a bankruptcy has concluded; and
- obtain a secured credit card after a consumer proposal or bankruptcy to start rebuilding a positive credit report.

CHAPTER SUMMARY

This chapter pulled together in one place the various remedies that debtors can avail themselves of. The steps that a debtor should take to respond to a court action were reviewed. Bankruptcy and consumer proposals were compared, and information was provided on credit counselling and debt management, as well as how to obtain and repair a credit report.

KEY TERMS

acceleration clause, 458
set-off, 461

REVIEW QUESTIONS

1. Outline three possible consequences of failing to pay a debt.
2. Describe two criteria that a lender will look for before approving a debtor for a consolidation loan.
3. List three options that a debtor has to respond to a Small Claims Court debt collection claim.
4. List two ways in which a debtor can request that a collection agent stop contacting them.
5. Who should consider using credit counselling?
6. What is the difference between a debt management plan and a consumer proposal?
7. Give two advantages that a consumer proposal has over a bankruptcy.
8. Explain how student loans can be dealt with in a bankruptcy.
9. Explain the difference between a credit rating and a credit score.
10. What should a debtor do about a credit report error?

DISCUSSION QUESTION

Andrea owes $35,000 in credit card debt. Her husband left her and moved in with another woman outside the country. Before he left, he charged his trip and various purchases to their joint credit cards. Andrea has been late in making some payments and has missed other payments altogether. She now has a poor credit rating. She is a single mother with three children. She works full-time and earns $40,000 per year. She has a heavily mortgaged house and a six-year-old car that has been paid off. The interest rates on four of her credit cards with outstanding balances run from 8 to 19 percent. Explain what options Andrea has to deal with this situation.

FIGURE 15.1 Debtor Budget Worksheet

DEBTOR BUDGET WORKSHEET

DEBTS AT A GLANCE

Creditor	Amount Owing	Interest Rate	Minimum Monthly Payment

TOTAL OWED: ___________

TOTAL MONTHLY MINIMUM PAYMENTS: ___________

MAJOR ASSETS AT A GLANCE

Asset	Value	Debt on the Asset

INCOME FROM EMPLOYMENT

Full time job: ______________________ Monthly salary: ______________________

Part time jobs: ______________________ Monthly salary: ______________________

Bonuses: ______________________ Monthly amount: ______________________

Self-employment: ______________________ Monthly income: ______________________

FIGURE 15.1 Debtor Budget Worksheet (*continued*)

OTHER INCOME

Benefit payments (EI, WSIB, Disability): ____________________

Pension payments: ____________________

Old Age Security pension: ____________________

Spousal/Child support: ____________________

Child Tax Benefit: ____________________

Universal Child Tax Benefit: ____________________

HST Rebate Credit: ____________________

Investment income: ____________________

Rental Income: ____________________

Gifts: ____________________

TOTAL MONTHLY INCOME: ____________________

EXPENSES

Work-Related Expenses

Expense	Monthly Amount Spent
Income tax	
CPP	
EI	
Pension contribution	
Union dues/Prof. fees	
Health benefits plan	
Workplace life insurance	

TOTAL: ____________

Transportation Costs

Expense	Monthly Amount Spent
Gas	
Public transit/Taxis	
Car insurance	
Parking	
Car repairs, maintenance and licensing	
Car loan/lease payments	

TOTAL: ____________

FIGURE 15.1 **Debtor Budget Worksheet (*continued*)**

Housing Costs

Expense	Monthly Amount Spent
Rent or Mortgage	
Property taxes	
Condo fees	
Property insurance	
Repairs and maintenance	
Water	
Heating	
Hot Water tank rental	
Electricity	
Furniture	
Cable/Satellite TV/Radio	
Phone	
Internet	
Electricity	

TOTAL: ____________

Health Costs

Expense	Monthly Amount Spent
Dental expenses	
Medicines	
Vitamins/Supplements	
Eye care	
Hearing care	
Therapy: physio, chiropractor, massage	
Private insurance: life, disability, critical illness, health	

TOTAL: ____________

Personal Expenses

Expense	Monthly Amount Spent
Clothes	
Hair care, nails, beauty treatments	
Other	

TOTAL: ____________

FIGURE 15.1 Debtor Budget Worksheet (*continued*)

Household Expenses

Expense	Monthly Amount Spent
Groceries	
Meals out and takeout	
Pet care	
Dry cleaning	
Other	

TOTAL: ____________

Children's Expenses

Expense	Monthly Amount Spent
Daycare/Babysitters/ Summer camp	
Education-related expenses	
Gifts for birthday parties	
Lessons/Sports	
RESP contributions	
Clothing	
Child support paid	
Other	

TOTAL: ____________

Investment Expenses

Expense	Monthly Amount Spent
RRSP contributions	
Automatic deposit savings	
Banking service fees	
Safety deposit box fee	
Other	

TOTAL: ____________

FIGURE 15.1 Debtor Budget Worksheet (*continued*)

Recreational Spending

Expense	Monthly Amount Spent
Movies/Theatre	
Video and game rentals	
Lottery tickets	
Sports: golf, swimming, skating, skiing entry fees	
Books and periodicals	
Gambling: casinos and video terminals	
Alcohol	
Tobacco	
Hobbies	
Gifts	
Vacations	
Other	

TOTAL: ____________

DEBT PAYMENTS

Expense	Monthly Amount Spent
Total minimum credit card payments	
Total line of credit minimum payments	
Total loan payments	
Payments on court judgments	
Spousal support payments	
Other	

TOTAL: ____________

Total Monthly Income __________ – Total Monthly Expenses __________ = Surplus/Deficit __________

Glossary

acceleration clause provides that if the debtor misses a payment, the entire debt is accelerated and becomes immediately due and payable

affiant a person who swears to the truth of statements set out in their affidavit

affidavit a sworn or affirmed statement of facts that can be used as evidence in court proceedings in lieu of oral evidence

affidavit of documents an affidavit in which a party identifies those documents that are relevant to the issues in the proceeding and that the party has in its possession, power, and control and can produce; the party must also identify those documents that it once had in its possession, power, and control but no longer has and those that it objects to producing; privileged documents, such as solicitor–client correspondence, will fall in the latter category; the documents being produced and relied on are usually contained in a document brief that may be filed as evidence in the proceeding and may be referred to in court

assignment in bankruptcy when a debtor has insufficient income to pay debts when due, they can retain a trustee in bankruptcy and assign most of their assets to the trustee for distribution to creditors, then they emerge from bankruptcy with most of their debts wiped out; sometimes called voluntary bankruptcy, it is distinguished from a petition in bankruptcy, where a creditor forces the debtor into involuntary bankruptcy by filing a petition in bankruptcy

Bankruptcy Court in Ontario, several judges of the Superior Court, with expertise in bankruptcy law, have been assigned to sit in what is called Bankruptcy Court, which is not a formal statutory part of the Superior Court; its judges sit in Toronto, Ottawa, and London

certificate of appointment of estate trustee with a will confirmation from the court that the will is the deceased's last will and that the estate trustee named in the will is the proper estate trustee

certificate of appointment of estate trustee without a will when a person dies without a will, it is necessary for someone, usually a relative, to apply to the court for a certificate of appointment of estate trustee without a will; until the appointment is made, no one has authority to do anything with the deceased's assets; once an appointment is made, the estate trustee may deal with the estate, settling its debts and distributing remaining assets to relatives in accordance with a statutory formula that determines the shares family members get

chattel an item of tangible personal property (tangible means it is a thing, like a car); intangible personal property refers to a right to something of value—for example, a cheque, which is a right to payment

Children's Lawyer a public official whose legal staff looks after the financial and other interests of children who are involved in or have an interest in civil proceedings

collection agent a person or a corporation, licensed and governed by the Ontario government to act on behalf of creditors to collect debts

condition precedent a situation where one must do A before one is allowed to do B—A is the condition precedent to the performance of the condition B

conditional sale contract also called an executory contract or an installment contract; the vendor finances the debtor's purchase, taking security in the item sold

consumer proposal a debtor's plan submitted to their creditors, through a trustee in bankruptcy, suggesting a reduction of debt, interest, and/or a longer period to pay debt

contempt an act that demonstrates disrespect or defiance of the court and the administration of justice

counterclaim where A sues B and B defends A's claim and makes their own claim against A

Crown in right of Ontario the legal title used to refer to the government of Ontario and how the government is usually named when it is a party to a legal proceeding

debt settlement service provider a person or a corporation authorized by the Ontario government to act on behalf of debtors to negotiate debt settlements with creditors

declaratory judgment a judgment where the court declares the rights of the parties on some issue before it; also referred to as a declaration

default judgment a plaintiff obtains a default judgment when the defendant takes no action and files no defence when they are sued, meaning the defendant is deemed to have admitted the debt and the plaintiff may apply to the court clerk, who, on behalf of the court, will sign a judgment for the amount claimed

disbursements amounts paid out by the law office on its own account to third parties on behalf of a client

discovery a process where each party is asked questions under oath or affirmation about the fact allegations in their pleadings and where the strength of the evidence with respect to the facts alleged can be tested; as well, credibility of the parties can be assessed and settlement options explored

estate trustee the deceased's legal representative for estate administration purposes; the estate trustee may be named in the will or appointed by the court

estate trustee during litigation a person appointed by the court to act for the estate when there is a dispute about the validity of the will or about who should administer the estate; during litigation the estate trustee has control of estate assets but has no authority to make payouts until the court has dealt with the validity of the will or decided who should administer the estate

examination for discovery a pretrial process where lawyers get to ask the opposite party (plaintiff or defendant) questions about the allegations in the statement of claim or statement of defence

execution an act of the sheriff in enforcing a writ of seizure and sale (commonly referred to as a writ of execution), writ of delivery, or writ of sequestration; the word "execution" is also used to describe individual writs of execution on file; when lawyers "search executions" they are examining the sheriff's records to see if any writs of seizure and sale are filed with the sheriff

execution creditor a creditor who has obtained a judgment and is in the process of executing or enforcing a judgment for debt

execution debtor a debtor who is the subject of enforcement proceedings by an execution creditor

exigible a word used to describe assets that the sheriff may seize when executing a writ of seizure and sale; if an asset is exempt from seizure it is referred to as a non-exigible asset

exigible assets assets that are available to be legally seized under a writ of seizure and sale; non-exigible assets are those that are exempt from seizure under the *Execution Act* (RSO 1990, c E.24) or under the provisions of another statute

extortion The act of threatening, oppressing, or abusing authority over another person to obtain money or favours.

full legal age and capacity to sue or be sued, an individual usually has to have reached the age of majority and be mentally capable of taking part in a lawsuit; a person who is capable of participating and who is over 18 years of age is referred to as being of full age and capacity

gazetteer a directory in which the entries are arranged by geographical location—various geographical places in the province are listed with the corresponding Small Claims Court to use listed across from the geographical entry

guarantor one who is obliged to pay a creditor when the principal debtor defaults

holdback an amount of money (note that under the CLAA 2017, a letter of credit, a bond, or other security can take the place of money) kept back from the amount due to the contractor that is not paid but is held in trust by the owner until the dispute is resolved, the time for filing a lien has expired, or a registered lien has been discharged or satisfied

information a sworn written statement made before a justice of the peace that can initiate criminal proceedings against a person

interest the amount of money (usually expressed as a percentage of the amount of money borrowed or the amount financed to purchase an item) charged by the creditor to the debtor to compensate the creditor for advancing the funds or for selling the item to the debtor on a conditional sale contract.

intestate, intestacy when a person dies without having made a valid will, they are said to have died intestate; dying without a will creates an intestacy, which is a situation where the estate has to be administered without a will

issue the act whereby the court office, for a fee, assigns the action a file number, signs the claim, and affixes a court seal to it; the act of issuing stops the limitation period from running out

issued and entered a judgment or order is issued when it is signed by a judge or registrar and the court's seal is affixed to it; it is then entered (recorded) by the registrar, using a system for referencing and recording an issued judgment; an entered judgment or order will usually have a stamp on it, indicating the place of storage so that it can be found in court files

judgment creditor a creditor who has obtained a judgment for debt against a debtor

judgment debtor a debtor against whom a judgment has been obtained

judgment proof describes a debtor against whom a judgment may be obtained, but where the judgment will be unenforceable because the debtor has no assets to pay the judgment or has hidden or encumbered assets preventing easy seizure; a judgment in these circumstances is sometimes described as a "paper judgment"—that is, it is worth no more than the paper it is printed on because it cannot be enforced in any practical way

lien a claim to a right to sell or seize property, either real or personal, on the fulfillment of certain conditions

limitation period a time period in which a legal procedure must be commenced—after the time period has expired, a party is barred from commencing a proceeding.

liquidated amount a specific sum of money that can be easily and objectively calculated; if a debtor borrows $1,000 for a one-year period at 10 percent interest per year, the amount owing —$1,100—would be a liquidated amount because it is precise and specific and the total is easily calculated using an objective standard or formula

litigation guardian an individual who conducts a lawsuit and instructs counsel on behalf of a party who is under a disability or who is not of full age and capacity

Mareva injunction permits a creditor to obtain an injunction to secure the debtor's assets in a case where it is likely that the debtor will dispose of or remove all assets from the jurisdiction, before judgment, leaving no assets to satisfy the judgment debt

master a judicial officer of the Superior Court who decides procedural issues on pretrial matters and performs some other judicial functions

motion a proceeding before the court within the main proceeding to settle a legal issue that has arisen in the main proceeding—for example, a plaintiff might bring a motion to court asking that the defendant provide more detail in the statement of defence; a motion is brought by a notice of motion, which states what remedy is sought and the reasons for it; the facts in support of the motion are usually presented in an affidavit

net 30 used in contracts to indicate that the principal amount can be paid, without interest, within 30 days of the start of the billing period (which begins the date of purchase), after which interest is charged on the principal amount; this interest-free period is sometimes also described as a grace period

notice of motion a court document used to initiate a motion that states what remedy is sought and the reasons for it

Official Receiver a government official in the Office of the Superintendent of Bankruptcy who receives proposals, examines bankrupts under oath, and chairs meetings of creditors

owner's equity refers to how much of a property's value is actually that of the owner's—for example, if a house is worth $500,000 and is mortgaged for $250,000, the mortgagee is entitled to $250,000 to cover what is owing by the owner on the mortgage loan; the remaining $250,000 is free and clear of the mortgage claim and is the owner's equity in the house

partial indemnity usual order for costs, based on a cost grid that establishes hourly rates for tariff items listed in the grid; provides less than full recovery of legal fees for the client

per annum Latin for "per year"

peremptory an order that absolutely must be followed such that the person the order is peremptory against must be ready for trial on the next scheduled trial date; the court will not tolerate any further excuses from that party

perfect a lien a lien that has been preserved is perfected by commencing legal proceedings and filing a certificate of action within 90 days of preserving the lien

personal property consists of tangibles, such as consumer goods, other goods, inventory and equipment, and intangibles, including investments and securities

pleadings noted closed the act of noting pleadings closed means that no party may file any further claims, defences, or other court documents; this act brings the pretrial stage to a close—in a defended proceeding, the matter may be listed for trial; in a default proceeding, the defendant is barred from filing a statement of defence and the plaintiff is free to have judgment signed

practice directions instructions as to how court rules of procedure are supplemented by specialized procedures that apply within a judicial region, usually drafted by the Chief Justice of the Superior Court or the Regional Senior Judge; they can be found on the Superior Court of Justice website at <www.ontariocourts.ca/scj>

preserve a lien a right to lien is preserved by registering a claim for lien on title within 60 days of the last work done on the property

privity of contract a rule that only parties to a contract can enforce contract rights

Public Guardian and Trustee a government office whose staff are responsible for looking after the interests of mentally incapable persons (formerly called mentally incompetent) where no attorney under a power of attorney, guardian of the person, or guardian of property has been appointed

purchaser in good faith also called bona fide purchaser; describes an individual who has bought something in circumstances where there is nothing to tell them that the seller is trying to unload the asset quickly for cash before creditors manage to seize the asset or its proceeds; in a bad-faith sale there are usually signs that tip off a reasonable and prudent buyer—for example, a price below fair market value, secrecy in the transaction, undue haste, insistence on payment in cash—so that a purchaser would be presumed to be on notice that the seller's title is flawed or questionable and the purchaser is deemed to acquire ownership subject to the claims of creditors

receivable money owing to a creditor (also called an account receivable); because it describes a right to future payment or income, a creditor can sell or assign its receivables as a way of paying others—a creditor thereby gives the purchaser or assignee the right to be paid the amount of the receivable by the debtor

reference a judicial proceeding used where it is necessary to inquire into an issue in an action in great detail; rather than tie up the court's time in a formal proceeding, a judge may order a reference to be held before a judge or other judicial official, such as a master, with expertise or time or both to delve into the matter using a less formal process than the process used in a formal trial

relief from forfeiture a remedy granted to a debtor whose property has been seized by a creditor who has acted in an oppressive or capricious manner

retainer a document that records the contractual relationship between legal service provider and client, usually stating that the legal service provider acts for the client and stipulating generally what the legal service provider has been retained to do; also used to describe an amount of money that the client pays the legal service provider as a down payment for services to be rendered—in this case, the legal service provider is required to account for how this money is used on the client's behalf; also used to describe a situation where a client does not hire a legal service provider for anything specific, but simply wants the legal service provider to be available to them to perform legal work for a specified period—in this case, the legal service provider does not have to account for the money and may use it for their own purposes; they are deemed to be entitled to the money for making themselves available to the client, although they may charge for any services actually performed during the period of the retainer

reverse search a reverse search allows someone to submit an address, telephone number, or email address to obtain the name of a resident or subscriber

secured credit transaction a transaction where the debtor has put up some asset of value as collateral that the creditor may use as security for the unpaid debt; if the debtor defaults, the creditor can recover what is owing by seizing the collateral; the debt is secured by the creditor's rights in the collateral

set-off a legal remedy used where a creditor owes a debtor money, and the debtor seeks to have the amount owing to the creditor deducted from any money that the debtor is found to owe the creditor

specific performance a non-monetary remedy such as an order compelling a party to carry out completion of a contract

stayed a legal proceeding may be stopped from proceeding further by a judge, until one of the parties does something they are obliged to do; for example, a plaintiff who is suing using an unregistered business name may have the proceeding stayed until they prove that they have registered the name as they are legally required to do

substantial indemnity costs scale usually used as a punitive costs award that results in near indemnity for the winner on a dollar-for-dollar basis

Superintendent of Bankruptcy a government official in Ottawa who supervises and oversees the administration of the *Bankruptcy and Insolvency Act*

taking of accounts a court may order that there be a taking of accounts where an issue involving complex financial transactions needs to be examined in some detail in a less formal process than a trial; accounts may be taken before a judge or other judicial officers, usually masters of the Superior Court; the process is similar to that used in a reference

testamentary trust a trust set up in a will to preserve and administer assets for specific purposes—for example, for a child beneficiary, capital is set aside for investment by a trustee and the income is used for the child's benefit until the child reaches an age set by the trust when the capital can be paid out

testator one who makes a will to dispose of assets upon death

title the legal ownership of something; often refers to a document that indicates ownership or an ownership interest—to say someone has title to a car usually means that the car is registered with the province in the name of that person

to purge contempt when an order has been made by the court finding someone in contempt, the person may avoid punishment for contempt by doing what was required; this is referred to as purging contempt—for example, a person who refuses to answer questions on an examination may purge their contempt by re-attending and answering the questions

trial record a record filed with the court before trial; consists of pleadings, any pretrial orders, a lawyer's certificate confirming that the record is complete, and, depending on the nature of the case, other documents as well

trustee in bankruptcy an individual, usually an accountant, who is licensed to act as a trustee under the *Bankruptcy and Insolvency Act*; the trustee assists individuals and corporations making proposals or assignments into bankruptcy and creditors who want to petition a debtor into bankruptcy

unsecured credit a loan or extension of credit to a debtor where the creditor has no right to seize the debtor's property to satisfy an unpaid debt

white prints large maps of subdivisions that are kept in a file of subdivisions and that show all of the lots in the subdivision; the white print will usually show an existing street or other identifiable landmark at the edge of the subdivision that will allow one to identify and locate a particular property, identified as a lot on the plan

with prejudice a phrase used to signify that the writer is prepared to disclose the contents of the document to the court during the trial because they believe that it will enhance their case by showing them to be reasonable

without prejudice a phrase used to indicate that a document may not be disclosed to the court, even if it contains damaging statements or admissions; the use of this phrase allows for a free and frank discussion of settlement options

writ of seizure and sale also called a writ of execution; allows the sheriff to seize and sell goods or land belonging to the judgment debtor and apply the proceeds to the judgment creditor's claim

Index

Credits

Figures 3.3-3.9, 5.1- 5.5, 6.1-6.5, 7.1-7.3, 9.2, 10.7-10.19, 10.21-10.23, 11.1-11.15, 13.1-13.4: © QUEEN'S PRINTER FOR ONTARIO, 2008-2017. Used with permission. This document is subject to change without notice. The ministry of the Attorney general and the Queen's Printer for Ontario played no role in preparing *Debtor–Creditor Law and Procedure*, 5th edition.

Figures 3.10, 3.11: Copyright 2017 Equifax, Inc.

Case Study (Chapter 6, page 151): © QUEEN'S PRINTER FOR ONTARIO, 2008-2017. Used with permission. This document is subject to change without notice. The ministry of the Attorney general and the Queen's Printer for Ontario played no role in preparing *Debtor–Creditor Law and Procedure*, 5th edition.

Proposed Prompt Payment Timeline (Chapter 13, page 394): © QUEEN'S PRINTER FOR ONTARIO, 2008-2017. Used with permission. This document is subject to change without notice. The ministry of the Attorney general and the Queen's Printer for Ontario played no role in preparing *Debtor–Creditor Law and Procedure*, 5th edition.

Prompt Payment, Dispute and Adjudication Process (Chapter 13, page 395): © QUEEN'S PRINTER FOR ONTARIO, 2008-2017. Used with permission. This document is subject to change without notice. The ministry of the Attorney general and the Queen's Printer for Ontario played no role in preparing *Debtor–Creditor Law and Procedure*, 5th edition.

Figures 14.1-14.3, 14.5: Reproduced with the permission of the Minister of Industry, 2009.